CONVERSATIONAL MODERN GREEK IN 20 LESSONS

$4.00

Book Attic

Hard Cover Edition: MODERN GREEK IN 20 LESSONS

ILLUSTRATED

Intended for self-study and for use in schools

With a Simplified System of Phonetic Pronunciation

By

GEORGE C. PAPPAGEOTES, Ph.D.

LECTURER IN MODERN GREEK LANGUAGE
AND LITERATURE
DEPARTMENT OF LINGUISTICS,
COLUMBIA UNIVERSITY

and

PHILIP D. EMMANUEL

LECTURER IN MODERN GREEK HISTORY AND
CIVILIZATION, COLUMBIA UNIVERSITY
PROFESSOR AT THE TEACHERS COLLEGE
OF THE GREEK ARCHDIOCESE

An Owl Book

HENRY HOLT AND COMPANY

New York

CORTINA LEARNING INTERNATIONAL, INC.
Publishers • WESTPORT, CT 06880

Cataloging Information

Cortina Method Modern Greek in 20 Lessons, intended for self-study and for
use in schools, with a simplified system of phonetic pronunciation and a
reference grammar of both demotic and puristic (katharevousa) by
George C. Pappageotes and Philip D. Emmanuel. New York, R. D.
Cortina Co., 1977.
    288 p. illus. 22 cm.

    1. Greek language, Modern—Grammar. 2. Greek language, Modern—
Conversation and phrase books. I. Emmanuel, Philip D., joint author.
II. Title.
PA1058.P25 1977   489.328242   58-14427
ISBN 0-8327-0007-X (hardbound)
ISBN 0-8327-0014-2 (paperback)

Printed in the United States of America
HH Editions 9 8 7 6 5 4 3 2   *9405-5.0

INTRODUCTION

There are many reasons why a practical knowledge of modern Greek is both desirable and profitable for forward-looking Americans and especially for Americans of Greek descent. No matter what your reason for wanting to learn Greek, you will find the rewards enormously satisfying and helpful.

You will have the pleasure of being able to speak Greek while traveling in Greece, where land and sea live up to their legendary beauty the year 'round.

You will have the opportunity to make business contacts with Greeks either in person or by correspondence.

You will be able to read a language which gave to the world most of its scientific vocabulary and in which the New Testament was originally written.

You will have the satisfaction of exploring the cultural world of present-day Greece; its literature, theater, art, music, films, scientific and industrial progress.

If you are an American of Greek descent, you will be proud to speak, read, and write the language of your forefathers.

We believe that this book provides a sorely needed text-book and self-teacher of modern Greek. It is a practical means toward the quick mastery of the fundamentals of this language. This attainment is within the reach of everyone, regardless of his background.

Cortina's GREEK IN 20 LESSONS consists of:

1. THE GUIDE TO PRONUNCIATION, which explains the sounds of Greek in easy-to-understand terms. This section includes some interesting hints about Greek spelling—easy to grasp and easy to remember.

2. The Basic Sentence Patterns, in which the main sentence constructions and most important and common uses of the various parts of speech are illustrated in easy-to-follow, frequently-used sentences which are cross-referenced with the grammar. Thus, an acquaintance is made with the grammatical forms, the actual function of which is illustrated in the sentences. When the same forms and constructions are encountered in the conversation of the Twenty Lessons, they will provide an excellent opportunity for review.

3. The Twenty Lessons cover everyday situations in a series of interesting conversations which feature Mr. Smith, an American in Greece. These lessons are arranged so that the student can follow them easily. For each of the first sixteen lessons there is a vocabulary of two classes of words: 1. those of a general character found in the lesson, and 2. those of a specific character covering the topic of the lesson and the conversations which show how these vocabularies are used in everyday conversations. To the right of each word or sentence is given the phonetic spelling so that the student can pronounce it correctly, and in the next column is given the English translation of the Greek text.

The last four lessons differ in form. Since the student will have mastered the basic elements of modern Greek, when he has completed lesson 16, the remaining lessons 17 through 20 consist of dialogues (with footnotes) centering around topics of cultural, historical, and practical interest. All the words used are given in the Greek-English Dictionary in the back of the book.

4. A Reference Grammar for both Katharevousa (the language in which the official documents, editorials, and news reports are written) and Demotic (the standard spoken and literary language) where you can easily find all the essential points of Grammar.

5. A two-way Greek-English and English-Greek Dictionary of over 5000 words.

The authors wish to thank Mrs. Artemis P. Emmanuel, of the faculty of the Greek Archdiocese Teacher's College, for her valuable help, especially in the preparation of the manuscript of the dictionary.

G. C. P., P. D. E.

TABLE OF CONTENTS

GUIDE TO GREEK PRONUNCIATION

The pronunciation of modern Greek is not difficult for the English-speaking student as nearly all the sounds of Greek occur in English. Moreover, modern Greek is highly "phonetic" in its spelling. Letters and combinations of letters almost always represent the same sounds. When the student has become familiar with the basic sounds which the spellings stand for, he can pronounce any Greek word correctly.

Our scheme for indicating the pronunciation of Greek letters and letter combinations is not based on a special system of phonetic symbols but on common English sounds as normally represented in English spelling.

Syllable divisions are indicated by a hyphen (-) and accented syllables are printed in capitals; thus, in the word ἄνθρωπος meaning "man", the stress would fall on the first syllable, as indicated in AHN-throh-pohs.

THE VOWELS

Modern Greek has only five vowel sounds (similar to those of Spanish):

i (as in *machine*)	*u* (as in *rule*)
e (as in *met*)	*o* (as in *port*)
	a (as in *father*)

Each of these sounds is represented by one or more letters or letter combinations because Greek adheres to its historical orthography.

The sound *i* (as in *machine* or *ee* as in *see*) is represented by the letters ι, η, υ, (and ῃ) and the letter combinations ει, οι and υι.

The sound *e* (as in *met*) is represented either by the letter ε or the letter combination αι.

The sound *a* (as in *father*) is represented by α (and ᾳ).

The sound *o* (as in *port*) is represented by ο or ω (ῳ).

The sound *u* (as in *rule* or as *oo* in *fool* or *moon*) is always represented by the letter combination ου.

In our phonetic transcription these vowels are transcribed as follows: *i* by *ee*, *e* by *eh*, *a* by *ah*, *o* by *oh*, and *u* by *oo*.

The ι is transcribed by *y* when it forms a kind of diphthong with the following vowel as in πιὸ πολύ (pyoh poh-LEE) much more.

A final piece of instruction concerning the vowels: Be careful to avoid pronouncing single vowel sounds as diphthongs.

THE CONSONANTS

Most Greek consonants have equivalents in English. Double consonants are pronounced as the corresponding single consonants.

GREEK SPELLING	PHONETIC SYMBOL	DESCRIPTION	EXAMPLES
β or ϐ	v	As English v.	βάρος (VAH-rohs) weight
γ	gh or y	This sound does not occur in English. It is the voiced counterpart of Χ (see below). Before i and e, it sounds almost as y in yes and is transcribed by y. But before a, o, and u, or a consonant, it sounds like g in brag but continued.	γῆ (YEE) earth γελῶ (yeh-LOH) I laugh γάλα (GHAH-lah) milk ἀργός (ahr-GHOHS) slow
δ	th	As th in that.	δίνω (THEE-noh) I give
ζ	z	As z in zest.	ζωή (zoh-EE) life
θ	th	As th in thin.	θέλω (THEH-loh) I want
κ	k	As k in task.	κρασί (krah-SEE) wine
λ	l	Almost as l in like.	λάδι (LAH-thee) oil
μ	m	As m in man.	μάτι (MAH-tee) eye
ν	n	Almost as n in not.	νερό (neh-ROH) water
ξ	ks	As x in six.	ξύλο (KSEE-loh) wood
π	p	As p in step.	πουλί (poo-LEE) bird
ρ	r	As in British English very. It is slightly trilled.	μέρος (MEH-rohs) part; toilet
σ (-ς)	s	As s in sea. However, it is pronounced as z in zone before m or other voiced consonants.	σῶμα (SOH-mah) body κόσμος (KOH-zmohs) people, world, cosmos

τ	t	Almost as *t* in *stop*.	τυρί (tee-REE) cheese
φ	f	As *f* in *fire*.	φῶς (FOHS) light
χ	kh	No English equivalent. It resembles *h* in *hue*, but is much more strongly aspirated. It is pronounced with the back of the tongue raised against the soft palate so that it will impede the breath-stream in a way that will form some friction. It is like *ch* in Scottish *loch* (lake), German *Bach* (brook) or *g* in Spanish *gente* (people) or *gitano* (gypsy).	ὄχι (OH-khee) no χέρι (KHEH-ree) hand χαρά (khah-RAH) joy χωριό (khoh-RYOH) village χρῆμα (KHREE-mah) money
ψ	ps	As *ps* in *rhapsody*.	ψωμί (psoh-MEE) bread

LETTER COMBINATIONS

μπ	b	At the beginning of a word as *b* in *bet*.	μπάλα (BAH-lah) ball
	mb	In the middle of a word as *mb* in *timber*.	μπλέ (BLEH) blue τύμπανο (TEEM-bah-noh) drum
ντ	d	At the beginning of a word almost as *d* in *door*.	ντομάτες (doh-MAH-tehs) tomatoes
	nd	In the middle of a word as *nd* in *tender*.	γάντια (GHAHN-dyah) gloves
γκ	g	At the beginning of a word as *g* in *go*.	γκρί (GREE) gray
	ng	In the middle of a word as *ng* in *finger*.	πάγκος (PAHN-gohs) bench
γγ	ng	As *ng* in *finger*.	ἄγγελος (AHN-geh-lohs) angel
τσ	ts	Almost as *ts* in *sits*.	σάλτσα (SAHL-tsah) sauce
τζ	dz	As in *red zone* but pronounced as one unit.	τζίτζικας (DZEE-dzee-kahs) grasshopper

ευ	*ehf*	As *ef* in *chef* before voiceless consonants (π, τ, κ, φ, θ, χ, σ, ξ, ψ).	εὐχαριστῶ (ehf-khah-ree-STOH) [almost as the English name F. Harry Stow] (I) thank you
	ehv	As *ev* in *eleven* before all other (voiced) consonants and before vowels.	Εὔα (EHV-ah) Eve
αυ	*ahf*	Before voiceless consonants.	αὐτό (ahf-TOH) this *or* that
	ahv	Before voiced consonants or vowels.	αὐγό (ahv-GHOH) egg

ACCENTUATION

The accent can fall on any one of the last three syllables.

There are two types of accent with which we have to deal: the stress accent in spoken Greek which is indicated in the phonetic transcription by capitals, and the orthographical accent in written Greek which is based on historical spelling. There are three written accents; the acute ´ (ὀξεῖα), the circumflex ῀ (περισπωμένη) and the grave ` (βαρεῖα).

The acute is used on every accented short syllable*; on the accented third from the last syllable (antepenult); and on the accented second from the last syllable (penult) when both the penult and the last syllable (ultima) are long: νεότης (youth); θάλασσα (sea); πρώτη (first *fem.*).

The circumflex is used on the accented penult when the last syllable is short and the next to the last is long: πρῶτος (first *masc.*); and on the last syllable when the long vowel or diphthong of this syllable is the result of a contraction, as τιμαω → τιμῶ (I honor).

The grave is used on the last syllable. When words, written in isolation, take the acute, this acute becomes grave when these words are written in a sentence context and are not followed by a punctua-

---

* The syllables are considered short or long on the basis of the quantity of their vowels in historical orthography. Syllables with ε or ο are short; with η or ω long; and with α, ι, υ either short or long. Syllables with orthographic dipthongs are long except those with οι or αι at the absolute end of the word.

tion mark or an enclitic*, e.g. ὁ ἀδελφός (the brother); ὁ ἀδελφός τοῦ Παύλου (Paul's brother); ὁ ἀδελφός του (his brother). Most Greeks do not observe the distinction between acute and grave, and use the acute for both.

Other orthographical marks in Greek are the breathings which are placed on the initial vowel of any Greek word beginning with a vowel, or on the second vowel of a diphthong of any Greek word beginning with a diphthong. There are two breathings: the smooth breathing or spiritus lenis ' (ψιλή) and the rough breathing or spiritus asper ' (δασεῖα).

Most words beginning with a vowel take the smooth breathing. All words beginning with υ take the rough breathing. The most important words taking the rough breathing are: ἅγιος (saint), ἁγνός (pure), αἷμα (blood), ἁλάτι (salt), ἁμάξι (coach), ἁρπάζω (I grab), ἑβδομάδα (week), ἕκαστος (each), Ἑλλάδα (Greece), ἕνας (one), ἕξ (six), ἑπτά (seven), ἑκατό (hundred), ἑορτή (holiday), ἕτοιμος (ready), εὑρίσκω (I find), ἕως (till, until), ἡλικία (age), ἡμέρα (day), ἥσυχος (quiet), ἱερός (holy, sacred), ἱκανός (able), ἱστορία (history, story), ὅλος (whole), ὅμως (however), ὥρα (hour), ὡραῖος (handsome).

PUNCTUATION

The punctuation marks in Greek are:

Period . (τελεία)   Exclamation point ! (θαυμαστικό)
Comma , (κόμμα)   Semicolon · (ἄνω τελεία)
Question mark ; (ἐρωτηματικό)   Quotes « » (εἰσαγωγικά)
Note that the Greek question mark looks like the English semicolon.

CAPITALIZATION

All common nouns, adjectives, and pronouns are written with small initial letters, except when beginning a sentence. Proper names only

---

* Enclitics are primarily one-syllable words which, losing their own accent, are attached in pronunciation to a preceding word, in which a secondary accent is caused on the final syllable, if it is accented on the third from the last syllable.

are capitalized, i.e., names of individual persons (Christian names, patronymics, surnames), institutions, inhabited places (cities, towns), provinces, countries. Names of languages and adjectives of nationality are written with a small initial letter.

THE GREEK ALPHABET

The Greek alphabet has twenty-four letters:

PRINTED		NAMES OF LETTERS		PRONUNCIATION
CAPITAL	SMALL			
Α	α	Ἄλφα	Alpha	AHL-fah
Β	β	Βῆτα	Veeta	VEE-tah
Γ	γ	Γάμμα	Ghamma	GHAH-mah
Δ	δ	Δέλτα	Dhelta	THEHL-tah
Ε	ε	Ἔψιλον	Epsilon	EH-psee-lohn
Ζ	ζ	Ζῆτα	Zeeta	ZEE-tah
Η	η	Ἦτα	Eeta	EE-tah
Θ	θ	Θῆτα	Theeta	THEE-tah
Ι	ι	Ἰῶτα	Yiota	YOH-tah
Κ	κ	Κάππα	Kappa	KAH-pah
Λ	λ	Λάμβδα	Lamvdha	LAHM-thah
Μ	μ	Μῦ	Mee	MEE
Ν	ν	Νῦ	Nee	NEE
Ξ	ξ	Ξῦ	Ksee	KSEE
Ο	ο	Ὄμικρον	Omicron	OH-mee-krohn
Π	π	Πῖ	Pee	PEE
Ρ	ρ	Ρῶ	Rho	ROH
Σ	σ, ς	Σῖγμα	Seegma	SEEGH-mah
Τ	τ	Ταῦ	Taf	TAHF
Υ	υ	Ὕψιλον	Eepsilon	EE-psee-lohn
Φ	φ	Φῖ	Fee	FEE
Χ	χ	Χῖ	Hee	KHEE
Ψ	ψ	Ψῖ	Psee	PSEE
Ω	ω	Ὠμέγα	Omegha	oh-MEH-ghah

BASIC SENTENCE PATTERNS

In each language there are a few basic types of sentences which are used more often than others in everyday speech.

On the basis of such sentences, one can form many others by substituting one or two of the words of each of these basic sentences. The sentences we selected to illustrate the basic patterns are short, easy to memorize, and useful. Learning them before you enter the main section of the book (Twenty Lessons) will automatically enable you to acquire an idea of the structure of the language. You will also learn indirectly through them some of the most important grammatical categories and their function in the construction of sentences the natural way, — the way a child absorbs them as he encounters them in actual usage.

Cross references have been supplied to establish a correlation between the basic sentence patterns and the Reference Grammar in this book. This will help you to relate the grammatical knowledge you will acquire from the basic sentences to the systematic presentation of Greek grammar.

BASIC QUESTIONS AND ANSWERS
(See Grammar 5.4; 5.1; 5.3; 2.0; 2.1; 3.1; 7.3)

Πῶς εἶσθε; or (Τί κάνετε;)
POHS EE-stheh? (TEE KAH-neh-teh?)
How are you? (*lit.*, What are you doing?)

Καλά, εὐχαριστῶ. [Καὶ] σεῖς (πῶς εἶσθε);
kah-LAH, ehf-khah-ree-STOH. [keh] SEES (POHS EE-stheh)?
Fine, thank you. And you (how are you)?

Πολὺ καλά. Εὐχαριστῶ.
poh-LEE kah-LAH. ehf-khah-ree-STOH.
Very well. Thank you.

Τί εἶναι αὐτό;
TEE EE-neh ahf-TOH?
What is that?

Εἶναι ἕνα καινούριο βιβλίο.
EE-neh EH-nah keh-NOOR-yoh vee-VLEE-oh.
It is a new book.

Ποιὸς εἶναι αὐτός;
PYOHS EE-neh ahf-TOHS?
Who is he?

[Εἶναι] ὁ πατέρας μου (ὁ θεῖος μου, ὁ παππούς μου).
EE-neh oh pah-TEH-rahz-moo (oh THEE-ohz-moo, oh pah-POOZ-moo).
He is my father (uncle, grandfather).

Ποιὰ εἶναι αὐτή;
PYAH EE-neh ahf-TEE?
Who is she?

[Εἶναι] ἡ μητέρα μου (ἡ θεία μου, ἡ γιαγιά μου).
EE-neh ee mee-TEH-rah-moo (ee THEE-ah-moo, ee yah-YAH-moo).
She is my mother (aunt, grandmother).

Ποιὸ εἶναι αὐτὸ τὸ παιδί;
PYOH EE-neh ahf-TOH toh peh-THEE?
Who is that boy?

[Εἶναι] ὁ ἀδελφός μου (ὁ ἐξάδελφός μου, ὁ ἀνεψιός μου).
EE-neh oh ah-thehl-FOHZ-moo (oh eh-KSAH-thehl-FOHZ-moo, oh ah-neh-PSYOHZ-moo).
He is my brother (cousin, nephew).

Ποιὸ εἶναι τὸ ἄλλο παιδί;
PYOH EE-neh toh AH-loh peh-THEE?
Who is the other boy?

[Εἶναι] ὁ μεγαλύτερος ἀδελφός μου.
EE-neh oh meh-ghah-LEE-teh-rohs ah-thehl-FOHZ-moo.
He is my older brother.

Ποιὸ εἶναι αὐτὸ τὸ κορίτσι;
PYOH EE-neh ahf-TOH toh koh-REE-tsee?
Who is that girl?

[Εἶναι] ἡ μικρότερή μου ἀδελφή (ἐξαδέλφη, ἀνεψιά).
EE-neh ee mee-KROH-teh-REE-moo ah-thehl-FEE (eh-ksah-THEHL-fee, ah-neh-PSYAH).
She is my younger sister (cousin, niece).

Ποιοί εἶναι αὐτοί;
PYEE EE-neh ahf-TEE?
Who are they?

[Εἶναι] ὁ παππούς μου καὶ ἡ γιαγιά μου.
EE-neh oh pah-POOZ-moo keh ee yah-YAH-moo.
They are my grandparents.

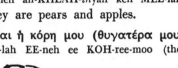

Τί εἶναι αὐτά;   Εἶναι ἀχλάδια καὶ μῆλα.
TEE EE-neh ahf-TAH?   EE-neh ah-KHLAH-thyah keh MEE-lah.
What are they?   They are pears and apples.

Αὐτὴ ἡ ψηλὴ κοπέλ(λ)α εἶναι ἡ κόρη μου (θυγατέρα μου).
ahf-TEE ee psee-LEE koh-PEH-lah EE-neh ee KOH-ree-moo (thee-ghah-TEH-rah-moo).
That tall girl is my daughter.

'Αλήθεια;
ah-LEE-thyah?
Is that so?

Ποῦ εἶναι τὸ καπέλλο μου;   'Εδῶ εἶναι.
POO EE-neh toh kah-PEH-loh-moo? eh-THOH EE-neh.
Where is my hat?   Here it is.

Ποῦ εἶναι ἡ ὀμπρέλλα σας;   Εἶναι ἐκεῖ (πέρα).
POO EE-neh ee ohm-BREH-lah-sahs? EE-neh eh-KEE (PEH-rah).
Where is your umbrella?   It's over there.

Ποῦ εἶναι ἡ τσάντα της;   Εἶναι ἐδῶ.
POO EE-neh ee TSAHN-dah-tees? EE-neh eh-THOH.
Where's her handbag?   It's over here.

Ποῦ εἶναι ἡ κουζίνα;
POO EE-neh ee koo-ZEE-nah?
Where's the kitchen?

Εἶναι [πρὸς τὰ] δεξιά (ἀριστερά).
EE-neh [prohs tah] theh-ksee-AH (ah-ree-steh-RAH).
It's on the right (on the left).

Ποῦ εἶναι τὸ δωμάτιο τοῦ Γιάννη;
POO EE-neh toh thoh-MAH-tee-oh too YAH-nee?
Where is John's room?

Εἶναι κατ' εὐθεῖαν ἐμπρός.
EE-neh kah-tehf-THEE-ahn ehm-BROHS.
It's straight ahead.

Ποῦ εἶναι τὸ δωμάτιο τῆς Μαρίας;
POO EE-neh toh *th*oh-MAH-tee-oh tees mah-REE-ahs?
Where is Mary's room?

Εἶναι στὸ (ἐ)πάνω πάτωμα.
EE-neh stoh (eh-) PAH-noh PAH-toh-mah.
It's one flight up.

SENTENCES WITH INTERROGATIVE
PRONOUNS
(See Grammar 5.4; 5.5; 10; 2)

Ποιὸς ἔχει τὰ τετράδιά μου; Ὁ Παῦλος τὰ ἔχει.
PYOHS EH-khee tah teh-TRAH-*th*ee-AH-moo? oh PAHV-lohs tah
EH-khee.
Who has my notebooks? Paul has them.

Μὲ ποιὸν μιλούσατε; Μὲ τὸ φίλο μου τὸν Πέτρο.
meh PYOHN mee-LOO-sah-teh? meh toh FEE-loh-moo toh̩n -PEH-
troh.
With whom were you talking? With my friend Peter.

Ποιοὶ εἶναι αὐτοὶ οἱ νέοι; Εἶναι φίλοι τοῦ γυιοῦ μου.
PYEE EE-neh ahf-TEE ee NEH-ee? EE-neh FEE-lee too YOO-moo.
Who are those young men? They are my son's friends.

Ποιὲς εἶναι αὐτὲς οἱ κοπέλες; Εἶναι συμμαθήτριες τῆς κόρης
μου.
PYEHS EE-neh ahf-TEHS ee koh-PEH-lehs? EE-neh see-mah-THEE-
tree-ehs tees KOH-reez-moo.
Who are those girls? They are my daughter's schoolmates.

Τί σᾶς εἶπε (αὐτή); Μᾶς εἶπε ὅτι δὲν θὰ ἔλθη.
TEE sahs EE-peh (ahf-TEE)? mahs EE-peh OH-tee *th*ehn thah EHL-
thee.
What did she tell you? She told us that she will not come.

Τί εἶναι ἡ πίστη; Εἶναι τὸ θεμέλιο τῆς ζωῆς.
TEE EE-neh ee PEE-stee? EE-neh toh theh-MEH-lee-oh tees zoh-EES.
What is faith? It's life's foundation.

Ποιὸ εἶναι τὸ ἐπάγγελμά σας; Εἶμαι ράφτης.
PYOH EE-neh toh eh-PAHN-gehl-MAH-sahs? EE-meh RAHF-tees.
What is your occupation? I am a tailor.

Ποιά ἀπ' αὐτὲς τὶς εἰκόνες σᾶς ἀρέσει περισσότερο; Αὐτὴ
ἐδῶ (τούτη).
PYAH ah-pahf-TEHS tees ee-KOH-nehs sahs ah-REH-see peh-ree-SOH-
teh-roh? ahf-TEE eh-THOH (TOO-tee).
Which one of these pictures do you like best? This one right here.

SENTENCES WITH PERSONAL OBJECT PRONOUNS

(See Grammar 5.2)

Ο Γιῶργος τοῦ τὸ ἔδωσε (σ'αὐτόν).
oh YOHR-ghohs too toh EH-thoh-seh (sahf-TOHN).
George gave it to him.

Μοῦ τὸ ἔδωσε.   Τῆς τὸ ἔδωσα.
moo toh EH-thoh-seh.   tees toh EH-thoh-sah.
He gave it to me.   I gave it to her.

(Αὐτὴ) μᾶς τὸ ἔστειλε.   Σᾶς τὸ δώσαμε.
ahf-TEE mahs toh EH-stee-leh.   sahs toh THOH-sah-meh.
She sent it to us.   We gave it to you.

Δὲν τοὺς τὸ δώσατε.
thehn toos toh THOH-sah-teh.
You did not give it to them.

Δός μου το. (Δῶστε το σὲ μᾶς).
THOHZ-moo-toh. (THOH-steh-toh seh-MAHS).
Give it to me. (Give it to us).

Μὴ τοῦ τὸ δίνετε.   Στεῖλτε το σ' αὐτή(ν).
MEE too toh THEE-neh-teh.   STEE-lteh-toh sahf-TEEN.
Don't give it to him.   Send it to her.

Ταχυδρομῆστε το σὲ μᾶς.
tah-khee-throh-MEE-steh-toh seh-MAHS.
Mail it to us.

Μὴ(ν) τοὺς τὸ στέλλετε.   Δὲν τὶς τὸ στείλατε;
MEE(N) toos toh STEH-leh-teh.   THEHN tees toh STEE-lah-teh?
Don't mail it to them.   Didn't you send it to them (fem.)?

SENTENCES ON THE USE OF THE ARTICLE

(See Grammar 1.0-1.5; 2.2; 2.3; 9.2)

'Η φιλοξενία είναι ἑλληνικὴ ἀρετή.
ee fee-loh-kseh-NEE-ah EE-neh eh-lee-nee-KEE ah-reh-TEE.
Hospitality is a Greek virtue.

'Εκτιμῶ τὴν ἀλήθεια.
eh-ktee-MOH teen ah-LEE-thyah.
I appreciate truth.

'Η ἐγκράτεια είναι πολὺ καλὴ γιὰ τοὺς νέους.
ee ehn-GRAH-tee-ah EE-neh poh-LEE kah-LEE yah toos NEH-oos.
Restraint is very good for young people.

'Ο ἑλληνικὸς οὐρανὸς είναι σχεδὸν πάντοτε γαλανός.
oh eh-lee-nee-KOHS oo-rah-NOHS EE-neh skheh-THOHN PAHN-doh-
teh ghah-lah-NOHS.
The Greek sky is nearly always blue.

'Η 'Ελλάδα είναι μία ἀπὸ τὶς πιὸ ὄμορφες χῶρες τῆς
Εὐρώπης.
ee eh-LAH-thah EE-neh MEE-ah ah-POH tees pyoh OH-mohr-fehs
KHOH-rehs tees ehv-ROH-pees.
Greece is one of the most beautiful countries in Europe.

Μένουν στὴν Τρίτη Λεωφόρο.
MEH-noon steen TREE-tee leh-oh-FOH-roh.
They live on Third Avenue.

'Η "Αννα μένει στὴν ὁδὸν Σοφοκλέους.
ee AH-nah MEH-nee steen oh-THOHN soh-foh-KLEH-oos.
Ann lives on Sophocles Street.

'Ο κύριος Μάνος δὲν μένει στὴ Νέα 'Υόρκη.
oh KEE-ree-ohs MAH-nohs thehnn MEH-nee stee NEH-ah ee-OHR-kee.
Mr. Manos does not live in New York.

Τὸ σπίτι τοῦ Νίκου είναι στὴν 'Αστόρια.
toh SPEE-tee too NEE-koo .EE-neh steen ah-STOH-ree-ah.
Nick's house is in Astoria.

'Ο Κώστας είναι μηχανικός.
oh KOH-stahs EE-neh mee-khah-nee-KOHS.
Gus (Costas) is an engineer.

Ἡ Πόπη εἶναι ἔξυπνη κοπέλα.
ee POH-pee EE-neh EH-ksee-pnee koh-PEH-lah.
Penny is an intelligent girl.

Τί ἀνόητος! (m.) Τί ἀνόητη! (f.) Τί ἀνόητο! (n.)
TEE ah-NOH-ee-tohs. TEE ah-NOH-ee-tee. TEE ah-NOH-ee-toh.
What a fool!

Τί κρῖμα!   Τί ὡραῖο αὐτοκίνητο!
TEE KREE-mah.   TEE oh-REH-oh ahf-toh-KEE-nee-toh.
What a pity!   What a beautiful car!

SENTENCES WITH INDEFINITE PRONOUNS
(See Grammar 5.6; 7.1; 2.4; 2.5)

⁺Ἦλθε κανένας; Κανένας δὲν ἦλθε.
EEL-theh kah-NEH-nahs? kah-NEH-nahs thehn EEL-theh.
Has anybody come? Nobody has come.

⁺Ἦταν κανένας ἐδῶ; Ναί, κάποιος ἦταν ἐδῶ.
EE-tahn kah-NEH-nahs eh-THOH? NEH, KAH-pyohs EE-tahn eh-THOH.
Has anybody been here?   Yes, somebody has been here.

Λάβατε (or πήρατε) κανένα γράμμα; Ναί, ἔλαβα μερικά.
    Ὄχι, δὲν ἔλαβα κανένα.
LAH-vah-teh (PEE-rah-teh) kah-NEH-nah GHRAH-mah? NEH, EH-lah-
    vah meh-ree-KAH. OH-khee, thehn EH-lah-vah kah-NEH-nah.
Have you received any letters? Yes, I received some. No, I
    have not received any.

Ἔχετε ἀμερικανικὰ περιοδικά; Ναί, ἔχω μερικά. Ὁρίστε
    ἕνα.
EH-kheh-teh   ah-meh-ree-kah-nee-KAH   peh-ree-oh-thee-KAH?   NEH,
    EH-khoh meh-ree-KAH. oh-REE-steh EH-nah.
Have you any American magazines? Yes, I have some. There
    is one.

Ἔχετε ἀγγλικὲς ἐφημερίδες; Λυποῦμαι μὰ δὲν ἔχω.
EH-kheh-teh ahn-glee-KEHS eh-fee-meh-REE-thehs? lee-POO-meh mah
    thehn EH-khoh.
Have you any English newspapers? I'm sorry, but I don't have
    any.

Ἔχετε σπίρτα; Δυστυχῶς ὄχι.
EH-kheh-teh SPEER-tah? *thees*-tee-KHOHS OH-khee.
Have you got a match? Sorry. No. (Lit. unfortunately not).

Πωλεῖτε γάλα; Μάλιστα. Σᾶς παρακαλῶ, δῶστε μου ἕνα
μπουκάλι.
poh-LEE-teh GHAH-lah? MAH-lee-stah. sahs pah-rah-kah-LOH *T*HOH-
steh-moo EH-nah boo-KAH-lee.
Do you sell milk? Yes. We do. Please give me a bottle.

Ἔχετε λεφτά (or χρήματα); Ὄχι, δὲν ἔχω (χρήματα).
EH-kheh-teh leh-FTAH (KHREE-mah -tah)? OH-khee, *th*ehn EH-khoh
KHREE-mah-tah.
Have you got any money? No, I have no money.

Τί φάγατε; Ἔφαγα σούπα, ψάρι, τυρὶ καὶ ψωμί.
TEE FAH-ghah-teh? EH-fah-ghah SOO-pah, PSAH-ree, tee-REE keh
psoh-MEE.
What did you eat? I ate soup, fish, cheese and bread.

Τί ἀγοράσατε; Ἀγόρασα μερικὰ φορέματα κι' ἕνα καπέλλο.
TEE ah-ghoh-RAH-sah-teh? ah-GHOH-rah-sah meh-ree-KAH foh-REH-
mah-tah KYEH-nah kah-PEH-loh.
What did you buy? I bought some dresses and a hat.

Τί κοιτά(ζε)τε (or κυττάτε); Κοιτάζω μερικὲς εἰκόνες.
TEE kee-TAH-teh? kee-TAH-zoh meh-ree-KEHS ee-KOH-nehs.
What are you looking at? I am looking at some pictures.

SENTENCES ON ADJECTIVES
(See Grammar 3.2-3.53; 7.2)

Ἡ Ἑλένη εἶναι ψηλότερη ἀπὸ τὴν Μαρία.
ee eh-LEH-nee EE-neh psee-LOH-teh-ree ah-POH teen mah-REE-ah.
Helen is taller than Mary.

Ἡ Ἀλίκη εἶναι λιγώτερο ἐπιμελὴς ἀπὸ τὴ Βαρβάρα.
ee ah-LEE-kee EE-neh lee-GHOH-teh-roh eh-pee-meh-LEES ah-POH
tee vahr-VAH-rah.
Alice is less diligent than Barbara.

Ἡ Κατίνα εἶναι τόσο ψηλὴ ὅσο (καὶ) ἡ Μαρία.
ee kah-TEE-nah EE-neh TOH-soh psee-LEE OH-soh (keh) ee mah-
REE-ah.
Kate is as tall as Mary.

Ἡ Ρίτά δὲν εἶναι τόσο ψηλὴ ὅσο (καὶ) ἡ Σοφία.
ee REE-tah *the*hn EE-neh TOH-soh psee-LEE OH-soh (keh) ee soh-
FEE-ah.
Rita is not so tall as Sophie.

Ἡ "Αννα εἶναι ἡ ψηλότερη ἀπὸ τὰ κορίτσια.
ee AH-nah EE-neh ee psee-LOH-teh-ree ah-POH tah koh-REE-tsyah.
Ann is the tallest of the girls.

Θὰ πάρω ἀκόμη λίγο κρέας.
thah PAH-roh ah-KOH-mee LEE-ghoh KREH-ahs.
I will take a little more meat.

Παρακαλῶ, πάρτε καὶ ἄλλο.
pah-rah-kah-LOH, PAH-rteh keh AH-loh.
Please have some more.

Δὲ θέλω ἄλλο.
*TH*EH THEH-loh AH-loh.
I don't want any more.

Δὲ θέλουν νὰ καθήσουν ἐδῶ πιά.
*TH*EH THEH-loon nah kah-THEE-soon eh-*TH*OH PYAH.
They don't want to stay here any longer.

Δὲν μπορεῖ νὰ πάη πιὰ ἐκεῖ.
*TH*EHN boh-REE nah PAH-ee PYAH eh-KEE.
He can no longer go there.

Ἡ κοπέλα μὲ τὰ μεγάλα καστανὰ μάτια ἐξελέγη βασίλισσα
τοῦ χοροῦ.
ee koh-PEH-lah meh tah meh-GHAH-lah kah-stah-NAH MAH-tyah
eh-kseh-LEH-yee vah-SEE-lee-sah too khoh-ROO.
The girl with the big brown eyes was elected the queen of the
ball.

Ὁ κουνιάδος μου ἔχει ἕνα καινούργιο φορτηγό (αὐτοκίνητο).
oh koo-NYAH-*TH*ohz-moo EH-khee EH-nah keh-NOO-ryoh fohr-tee-
GHOH (ahf-toh-KEE-nee-toh).
My brother-in-law has a new truck.

Ἡ ὄμορφη Ἑλληνίδα δὲν ἦλθε νὰ μᾶς ἰδῆ (νὰ μᾶς
ἐπισκεφθῆ).
ee OH-mohr-fee eh-lee-NEE-*th*ah *TH*EHN EEL-theh nah mahs ee-
THEE (nah mahs eh-pee-skeh-FTHEE).
The beautiful Greek girl didn't come to see us (to visit us).

BASIC TYPES OF SENTENCES
(See Grammar 10.1-10.15; 5.7; 8.1-2)

Affirmative: Αὐτὸ τὸ μάθημα εἶναι εὔκολο.
ahf-TOH toh MAH-thee-mah EE-neh EHF-koh-loh.
This lesson is easy.

Negative: Αὐτὸ τὸ μάθημα δὲν εἶναι δύσκολο.
ahf-TOH toh MAH-thee-mah *th*ehn EE-neh *TH*EES-koh-loh.
This lesson is not difficult.

Interrogative: Εἶναι αὐτὸ τὸ μάθημα εὔκολο; (or Εἶναι εὔκολο αὐτὸ τὸ μάθημα;)
EE-neh ahf-TOH toh MAH-thee-mah EHF-koh-loh?
(EE-neh EHF-koh-loh ahf-TOH toh-MAH-thee-mah?)
Is this lesson easy?

Εἶναι εὔκολο.
EE-neh EHF-koh-loh.
It's easy.

Δὲν εἶναι αὐτὸ τὸ δωμάτιο μεγάλο;
*th*ehn EE-neh ahf-TOH toh *th*oh-MAH-tee-oh meh-GHAH-loh?
Isn't this room large?

Ναί, εἶναι μεγάλο.
NEH, EE-neh meh-GHAH-loh.
Yes, it's large.

Τί μέρα εἶναι σήμερα;
TEE MEH-rah EE-neh SEE-meh-rah?
What day is today?

Σήμερα εἶναι Σάββατο.
SEE-meh-rah EE-neh SAH-vah-toh.
Today is Saturday.

Χθὲς ἦταν Παρασκευή.
KHTHEHS EE-tahn pah-rah-skehv-EE
Yesterday was Friday.

Αὔριο (θὰ) εἶναι Κυριακή.
AHV-ree-oh (thah) EE-neh kee-ryah-KEE.
Tomorrow will be Sunday.

Ἔδωσα τὸ βιβλίο στὴ Μαρία.
EH-*thoh*-sah toh vee-VLEE-oh stee mah-REE-ah.
I gave Mary the book.

Τὸ ἔδωσα στὴ Μαρία.
toh EH-*thoh*-sah stee mah-REE-ah.
I gave it to Mary.

Τοῦ (τῆς) τὸ ἔδωσα.
TOO (TEES) toh EH-*thoh*-sah.
I gave it to him (her).

(Αὐτὴ) (ἐ)πῆγε ἐκεῖ.
(ahf-TEE) (eh-) PEE-yeh eh-KEE.
She went there.

('Ε)πῆγε (αὐτὸς) ἐκεῖ;
(eh-) PEE-yeh (ahf-TOHS) eh-KEE?
Did he go there?

(Αὐτὸς) δὲν (ἐ)πῆγε ἐκεῖ.
(ahf-TOHS) *the*hn (eh-) PEE-yeh eh-KEE.
He didn't go there.

Δὲν (ἐ)πῆγαν (αὐτοὶ) ἐκεῖ;
*the*hn (eh-) PEE-ghahn (ahf-TEE) eh-KEE?
Didn't they go there?

Ναί, (ἐ)πῆγαν.
NEH, (eh-) PEE-ghahn.
Yes, they did.

Θέλω νὰ πάω στὸ σχολεῖο.
THEH-loh nah PAH-oh stoh skhoh-LEE-oh.
I want to go to school.

Δὲν θέλετε νὰ πᾶτε στὸ σχολεῖο;
*the*hn THEH-leh-teh nah PAH-teh stoh skhoh-LEE-oh?
Don't you want to go to school?

Ποιὸς θέλει νὰ πάῃ στὸ σχολεῖο;
PYOHS THEH-lee nah PAH-ee stoh skhoh-LEE-oh?
Who wants to go to school?

Θέλουν πράγματι νὰ πᾶν(ε) στὸ σχολεῖο;
THEH-loon PRAH-ghmah-tee nah PAH-n (eh) stoh skhoh-LEE-oh?
Do they really want to go to school?

Ποιὰ ἦταν ἡ κυρία μὲ τὴν ὁποία σᾶς εἶδα χθὲς τὸ βράδυ
    (or ψές);
PYAH EE-tahn ee kee-REE-ah meh teen oh-PEE ah sahs EE-*tha*h
    KHTHEHS toh VRAH-*thee* (PSEHS)?
Who was the lady with whom I saw you last night?

*Ηταν ἡ θεία μου, ποὺ μόλις ἦλθε ἀπὸ τὴν Εὐρώπη.
EE-tahn ee THEE-ah-moo poo MOH-lees EEL-theh ah-POH teen eħv-ROH-pee.
She was my aunt who just came from Europe.

Ἡ κοπέλα μὲ τὴν ὁποία μιλοῦσα εἶναι ἡ ἀρραβωνιαστικιά μου.
ee koh-PEH-lah meh teen oh-PEE-ah mee-LOO-sah EE-neh ee ah-rah-voh-nyah-stee-KYAH-moo.
The girl to whom I was speaking is my fiancee.

Τὸ ἀγόρι ποὺ ἡ μητέρα του εἶναι ἡ δασκάλα μου μένει ἐδῶ.
toh ah-GHOH-ree poo ee mee-TEH-rah-too EE-neh ee thah-SKAH-lah-moo MEH-nee eh-THOH.
The boy whose mother is my teacher lives here.

Μὴ μοῦ λέτε, ὅτι αὐτὸ τὸ γαλάζιο βιβλίο δὲν εἶναι δικό μου.
MEE moo LEH-teh OH-tee ahf-TOH toh ghah-LAH-zyoh vee-VLEE-oh thehn EE-neh thee-KOH-moo.
Don't tell me that this blue book is not mine.

῎Οταν ἡ Μαρία ἦλθε, ὁ Γιῶργος ἔφυγε.
OH-tahn ee mah-REE-ah EEL-theh, oh YOHR-ghohs EH-fee-yeh.
When Mary came, George left.

῍Αν ἔλθη ὁ Χρῖστος, θὰ τοῦ μιλήσω γιὰ (τὸ ζήτημα) αὐτό.
AHN EHL-thee oh KHREE-stohs, thah too mee-LEE-soh yah toh ZEE-tee-mah ahf-TOH.
If Chris comes, I will tell him about that.

῍Αν ἐρχόταν ὁ Χρῖστος, θὰ τοῦ ἔλεγα γι' αὐτὸ (τὸ ζήτημα).
AHN ehr-KHOH-tahn oh KHREE-stohs, thah too EH-leh-ghah yahf-TOH toh ZEE-tee-mah.
If Chris came, I would tell him about that.

Ἐὰν εἶχε ἔλθει ὁ Χρῖστος, θὰ τοῦ (τὸ) εἶχα πεῖ γι' αὐτό.
eh-AHN EE-kheh EHL-thee oh KHREE-stohs, thah too (toh) EE-khah PEE yahf-TOH.
If Chris had come, I would have told him about it.

῎Οταν ἔλθη ὁ Χρῖστος, θὰ τοῦ (τὸ) πῶ γι' αὐτό.
OH-tahn EHL-thee oh KHREE-stohs, thah too (toh) POH yahf-TOH.
When Chris comes, I will tell him about it.

῎Οταν ἦλθε ὁ Χρῖστος, τοῦ εἶπα τὰ νέα.
OH-tahn EEL-theh oh KHREE-stohs, too EE-pah tah NEH-ah.
When Chris came, I told him the news.

GREEK IN 20 LESSONS

Vocabularies
and
Conversations

The spelling of the Greek text of the Twenty Lessons is based on that used and recommended in the official *Grammar of Modern Greek* (Νεοελληνικὴ Γραμματική, Ο. Ε. Σ. Β., Athens, 1941) and in the *Etymological Dictionary of Modern Greek* by N. P. Andriotis (published by the French Institute of Athens in 1953) with a few exceptions in which the traditional spelling has been used as closer reflecting the orthographical reality of present-day Greek.

ΠΡΩΤΟ ΜΑΘΗΜΑ

First Lesson

Vocabulary for this Lesson

καλημέρα (kah-lee-MEH-rah) — good morning [*lit.* good day]
κύριος (KEE-ree-ohs) — mister; lord
[δèν] [ὁ]μιλῶ ([oh-]mee-LOH) — I [don't] speak
ἡ γλῶσσα (ee GHLOH-sah) — language; tongue

καλά (kah-LAH) well
θέλω (THEH-loh) I want

μαθαίνω (mah-THEH-noh) I learn
ἄλλος, -η, -ο (AH-lohs) other

ναί (NEH) yes
μάλιστα (MAH-lee-stah) yes [slightly more emphatic]
εἶμαι (EE-meh) I am
εἶναι (EE-neh) he, she, it is; they are

ὄχι (OH-khee) no

παντρεμένος, -η (pahn-dreh-MEH-nohs) married
ἡ οἰκογένεια (ee ee-koh-YEH-nee-ah) family
ξένος, -η, -ο (KSEH-nohs) foreign; stranger
πόσοι, -ες, -α (POH-see) how many
πολλοί, -ες, -α (poh-LEE) many
ἀρκετοί, -ες, -α (ahr-keh-TEE) enough

ἔχω (EH-khoh) I have
πολύ (poh-LEE) much; very

ἡ καταγωγή (ee kah-tah-ghoh-YEE) origin; descent
ἡ ἱστορία (ee ee-stoh-REE-ah) history; story
ταξιδεύω (tah-ksee-*THEH*-voh) I travel
τὸ μέρος (toh MEH-rohs) part; washroom
μοῦ ἀρέσει (moo ah-REH-see) I like
γνωρίζω (ghnoh-REE-zoh) I know

σχεδόν (skheh-*THOHN*) almost
τὸ ἔθνος (toh EH-thnohs) nation

ὁ ἀντιπρόσωπος (oh ahn-dee-PROH-soh-pohs) representative; delegate
ἔρχομαι (EHR-khoh-meh) I come
μπορῶ (boh-ROH)
συναντῶ (see-nahn-DOH)

πηγαίνω (pee-YEH-noh) I go
I am able; I can
I meet

26

'Η Οἰκογένεια (ee ee-koh-YEH-nee-ah) The Family

ὁ σύζυγος	(oh SEE-zee-ghohs)	husband	ἡ σύζυγος	(ee SEE-zee-ghohs)	wife
ὁ πατέρας	(oh pah-TEH-rahs)	father	ἡ μητέρα	(ee mee-TEH-rah)	mother
ὁ γυιός	(oh YOHS)	son	ἡ κόρη	(ee KOH-ree)	daughter
ὁ παππούς	(oh pah-POOS)	grandfather	ἡ γιαγιά	(ee yah-YAH)	grandmother
ὁ ἐγγονός	(oh ehn-goh-NOHS)	grandson	ἡ ἐγγονή	(ee ehn-goh-NEE)	granddaughter
ὁ ἀδελφός	(oh ah-thehl-FOHS)	brother	ἡ ἀδελφή	(ee ah-thehl-FEE)	sister
ὁ θεῖος	(oh THEE-ohs)	uncle	ἡ θεία	(ee THEE-ah)	aunt
ὁ ἀνεψιός	(oh an-neh-PSYOHS)	nephew	ἡ ἀνεψιά	(ee ah-neh-PSYAH)	niece
ὁ ἐξάδελφος	(oh eh-KSAH-thehl-fohs)	cousin (male)	ἡ ἐξαδέλφη	(ee eh-ksah-THEHL-fee)	cousin (female)
ὁ πεθερός	(oh peh-theh-ROHS)	father-in-law	ἡ πεθερά	(ee peh-theh-RAH)	mother-in-law
ὁ γαμπρός	(oh ghahm-BROHS)	son-in-law brother-in-law	ἡ νύφη	(ee NEE-fee)	daughter-in-law sister-in-law
οἱ γονεῖς	(ee ghoh-NEES)	parents	τὰ παιδιά	(tah peh-THYAH)	children
οἱ συγγενεῖς	(ee seen-gheh-NEES)	relatives	τό ἀγόρι	(toh ah-GHOH-ree)	boy
τὸ παιδί	(toh peh-THEE)	child	τὸ κορίτσι	(toh koh-REE-tsee)	girl

Χῶρες (KHOH-rehs) Countries

ἡ Ἑλλάδα (ee eh-LAH-thah)   Greece

ἡ Γαλλία (ee ghah-LEE-ah)   France

ἡ Ἀμερική (ee ah-meh-ree-KEE)   America

ἡ Ἀγγλία (ee ahn-GLEE-ah)   England

Ἐθνικότητες καὶ γλῶσσες
(eh-thnee-KOH-tee-tehs keh GHLOH-sehs)

The Nationalities and the Languages

ὁ Ἕλληνας (oh EH-lee-nahs)   the Greek

ὁ Ἀμερικανός (oh ah-meh-ree-kah-NOHS)   the American

ὁ Γάλλος (oh GHAH-lohs)   the Frenchman

ὁ Ἱσπανός (oh ee-spah-NOHS)   the Spaniard

ὁ Ἰταλός (oh ee-tah-LOHS)   the Italian

ὁ Γερμανός (oh yehr-mah-NOHS)   the German

Γλῶσσα (GHLOH-sah) Language

τὰ Ἑλληνικά (tah eh-lee-nee-KAH)   Greek

τὰ ἀγγλικά (tah ahn-glee-KAH)   English

τὰ γαλλικά (tah ghah-lee-KAH)   French

τὰ ἰσπανικά (tah ee-spah-nee-KAH)   Spanish

τὰ ἰταλικά (tah ee-tah-lee-KAH)   Italian

τὰ γερμανικά (tah yehr-mah-nee-KAH)   German

CONVERSATION

1 Καλημέρα, κύριε[1] Πετρίδη.
2 Καλημέρα, κύριε Σμίθ.
3 Μιλᾶτε[2] ἑλληνικά[3];
4 Δὲν μιλῶ καλά. Θέλω νὰ μάθω[4] ἑλληνικὰ πολὺ καλά.
5 Μιλᾶτε ἄλλες γλῶσσες;
6 Μάλιστα. Μιλῶ γαλλικά, ἰταλικὰ καὶ γερμανικά.
7 Εἶστε[5] "Αγγλος[3]; Καναδός; Αὐστραλός;
8 "Οχι. Εἶμαι 'Αμερικανός. Εἶμαι ἀπὸ τὶς Ἡνωμένες Πολιτεῖες τῆς 'Αμερικῆς.
9 Εἶστε παντρεμένος;
10 Μάλιστα, εἶμαι (παντρεμένος).

11 Ποῦ εἶναι ἡ οἰκογένειά σας[6];
12 (Ἡ οἰκογένειά μου) εἶναι στὴ Νέα Ὑόρκη.
13 "Εχετε παιδιά;
14 Μάλιστα. "Εχω ἕνα γυιὸ καὶ μία κόρη.
15 Τὰ παιδιά σας μιλοῦν ξένες γλῶσσες;

16 Μάλιστα. Ὁ γυιός μου μιλᾶ ἰσπανικά. Ἡ κόρη μου μαθαίνει γαλλικὰ καὶ ἑλληνικά.
17 "Εχετε πολλοὺς συγγενεῖς;
18 "Εχω ἀρκετούς (συγγενεῖς). "Εχω ἕνα ἀδελφό, δύο ἀδελφές, δύο ἐξαδέλφους καὶ τρεῖς ἐξαδέλφες.
19 "Εχετε συγγενεῖς στὴν Ἑλλάδα;

FOOTNOTES: *1.* Κύριε is the vocative singular of the noun κύριος which is abbreviated as κ. in all the cases in the singular. Κύριος means "mister" or "lord", but in the vocative, when used alone, it may also be considered as the equivalent of "sir" used in direct address. The abbrevation for οἱ κύριοι (plural of κύριος) is οἱ κ. κ.; for ἡ κυρία (Mrs.) ἡ κ.; for κυρίες or κυρίαι (plural of κυρία) αἱ κ. κ.; for δεσποινίς (Miss) δις; for δεσποινίδα (accusative of δεσποινίς) διδα; and for δεσποινίδες (plural of δεσποινίς) διδες.   *2.* The same form of the verb is used for both declarative and interrogative sentences. In spoken Greek the distinction between the two is indicated by modulation of the voice.   *3.* Names of languages are usually expressed by the neuter plural of the adjective of nationality. Ἡ ἑλληνική γλῶσσα

PRONUNCIATION	TRANSLATION
1 kah-lee-MEH-rah, KEE-ree-eh peh-TREE-*the*e.	Good morning, Mr. Petrides.
2 kah-lee-MEH-rah, KEE-ree-eh Smith.	Good morning, Mr. Smith.
3 mee-LAH-teh eh-lee-nee-KAH?	Do you speak Greek?
4 *THE*HN mee-LOH kah-LAH. THEH-loh nah MAH-thoh eh-lee-nee-KAH poh-LEE kah-LAH.	I don't speak it well. I want to learn (to speak) Greek very well.
5 mee-LAH-teh AH-lehs GHLOH-sehs?	Do you speak other languages?
6 MAH-lee-stah. mee-LOH ghah-lee-KAH, ee-tah-lee-KAH keh yehr-mah-nee-KAH.	Yes. I speak French, Italian, and German.
7 EE-steh AHN-glohs? kah-nah-*TH*OHS? ahf-strah-LOHS?	Are you an Englishman? ... a Canadian? ... an Australian?
8 OH-khee. EE-meh ah-meh-ree-kah-NOHS. EE-meh ah POH tees ee-noh-MEH-nehs poh-lee-TEE-ehs tees ah-meh-ree-KEES.	No. I am an American. I am from the United States of A-merica.
9 EE-steh pahn-dreh-MEH-nohs?	Are you married?
10 MAH-lee-stah, EE-meh (pahn-dreh-MEH-nohs).	Yes, I am (married).
11 POO EE-neh ee ee-koh-YEH-nee-AH sahs?	Where is your family?
12 (ee ee-koh-YEH-nee-AH-moo) EE-neh stee NEH-ah ee-OHR-kee.	My family is in New York.
13 EH-kheh-teh peh-*TH*YAH?	Do you have children?
14 MAH-lee-stah. EH-khoh EH-nah YOH keh MEE-ah KOH-ree.	Yes. I have a son and a daughter.
15 tah peh-*TH*YAH-sahs mee-LOON KSEH-nehs GHLOH-sehs?	Do your children speak (any) foreign languages?
16 MAH-lee-stah. oh YOHZ-moo mee-LAH ee-spah-nee-KAH. ee KOH-ree-moo mah-*TH*EH-nee ghah-lee-KAH keh eh-lee-nee-KAH.	Yes. My son speaks Spanish. My daughter is learning French and Greek.
17 EH-kheh-teh poh-LOOS seen-geh-NEES?	Do you have many relatives?
18 EH-khoh ahr-keh-TOOS (seen-geh-NEES). EH-khoh EH-nah ah-*the*hl-FOH, *THE*E-oh ah-*the*hl-FEHS, *THE*E-oh eh-ksah-*TH*EHL-foos keh TREES eh-ksah-*TH*EHL-fehs.	I have several (relatives). I have a brother, two sisters, two male cousins and three female cousins.
19 EH-kheh-teh seen-geh-NEES steen eh-LAH-*t*hah?	Do you have relatives in Greece?

20 Μάλιστα. Ἔχω τοὺς συγγενεῖς τῆς νύφης μου.

21 Ἡ νύφη σας, εἶναι Ἑλληνίδα[3];
22 Ὄχι. Εἶναι Ἀμερικανίδα ἑλληνικῆς καταγωγῆς.
23 Ποῦ εἶναι οἱ συγγενεῖς της;
24 Ὁ παππούς καὶ ἡ γιαγιά της εἶναι στὴ[7] Θεσσαλονίκη. Ὁ θεῖος καὶ ἡ θεία της εἶναι στὴν Κρήτη. Ὁ ἀνεψιὸς καὶ ἡ ἀνεψιά της εἶναι στὴ Νέα Ὑόρκη.
25 Σᾶς ἀρέσει ἡ Ἑλλάδα;

26 Μοῦ ἀρέσει πολὺ ἡ Ἑλλάδα. Γνωρίζω καλὰ τὴν ἑλληνικὴ ἱστορία.
27 Ταξιδέψατε[8] σὲ ἄλλες χῶρες;
28 Μάλιστα. Πῆγα στὴν Αἴγυπτο, στὴν Τουρκία, στὴ Ρουμανία, στὴν Ἰταλία, στὴ Γαλλία, στὴ Γερμανία, στὴν Ἀγγλία καὶ στὴ Ρωσία.
29 Τότε, γνωρίζετε καλὰ τὴν Εὐρώπη.
30 Μάλιστα. Γνωρίζω ὅλη σχεδὸν τὴν Εὐρώπη, ἕνα μέρος τῆς Ἀσίας καὶ ἕνα μέρος τῆς Ἀφρικῆς.

31 Αὐτοὶ οἱ κύριοι ἐκεῖ εἶναι ὅλοι Ἀμερικανοί[9];
32 Ὄχι ὅλοι. Μερικοὶ εἶναι Ἀμερικανοί καὶ οἱ ἄλλοι εἶναι Καναδοί, Ἄγγλοι, Γάλλοι, Ἰσπανοί, Γερμανοί, Ἰταλοί, Ρῶσοι.

(the Greek language) is usually expressed as ἑλληνικά. The same with all other languages. Note that both the adjectives of nationality and the names of languages are not capitalized. However, nouns indicating nationality are capitalized. The masculine form of most of them is a noun in -ος as Ἀμερικανός (an American) — an important exception is Ἕλληνας or Ἕλλην (Greek) — and the feminine form is a noun in -ιδα or -ις as Ἀμερικανίδα or Ἀμερικανίς (an American woman). Ἑλληνίδα or Ἑλληνίς (a Greek woman). *4.* The subjunctive (preceded by νά) is used in Greek when the infinitive is used in English. Among its other functions the subjunctive in modern Greek has that of replacing the infinitive. *5.* Both the Demotic form εἶστε and the Puristic εἶσθε are used in spoken Greek. *6.* The possessive pronouns and the corresponding genitive of the personal pronouns have the same form. The only difference between the two is that the possessive pro-

20 MAH-lee-stah. EH-khoh toos seen-geh-NEES tees NEE-feez-moo.
21 ee NEE-fee-sahs, EE-neh eh-lee-NEE-thah?
22 OH-khee. EE-neh ah-meh-ree-kah-NEE-thah eh-lee-nee-KEES kah-tah-ghoh-YEES.
23 POO EE-neh ee seen-geh-NEES-tees?
24 oh pah-POOS keh ee yah-YAH-tees EE-neh stee theh-sah-loh-NEE-kee. oh THEE-ohs keh ee THEE-ah-tees EE-neh steen KREE-tee. oh ah-neh-PSYOHS keh ee ah-neh-PSYAH-tees EE-neh stee NEH-ah ee-OHR-kee.
25 sahs ah-REH-see ee eh-LAH-thah?
26 moo ah-REH-see poh-LEE ee eh-LAH-thah. ghnoh-REE-zoh kah-LAH teen eh-lee-nee-KEE ee-stoh-REE-ah.
27 tah-ksee-THEH-psah-teh seh AH-lehs KHOH-rehs?
28 MAH-lee-stah. PEE-ghah steen EH-yee-ptoh, steen toor-KEE-ah, stee roo-mah-NEE-ah, steen ee-tah-LEE-ah, stee ghah-LEE-ah, stee yehr-mah-NEE-ah, steen ahn-GLEE-ah keh stee roh-SEE-ah.
29 TOH-teh, ghnoh-REE-zeh-teh kah-LAH teen eh-VROH-pee.
30 MAH-lee-stah. ghnoh-REE-zoh OH-lee skheh-THOHN teen eh-VROH-pee, EN-nah MEH-rohs tees ah-SEE-ahs keh EH-nah MEH-rohs tees ah-free-KEES.
31 ahf-TEE ee KEE-ree-ee eh-KEE EE-neh OH-lee ah-meh-ree-kah-NEE?
32 OH-khee OH-lee. meh-ree-KEE EE-neh ah-meh-ree-kah-NEE. keh ee AH-lee EE-neh kah-nah-THEE, AHN-glee, GHAH-lee, ee-spah-NEE, yehr-mah-NEE, ee tah-LEE, ROH-see.

Yes. The family of my sister-in-law lives in Greece (*lit.*, I have the relatives of the wife of my brother).
Is your sister-in-law Greek?
No. She is an American of Greek origin.
Where are her relatives?
Her grandfather and her grandmother are in Salonika. Her uncle and her aunt are in Crete. Her nephew and her niece are in New York.
Do you like Greece? (*lit.*, Does Greece please you?)
I like Greece very much. (*lit.*, To me Greece pleases much).
I know Greek history well.
Have you traveled to other countries?
Yes. I went to Egypt, to Turkey, to Rumania, to Italy, to France, to Germany, to England, and to Russia.
Then you know Europe well.
Yes. I know nearly all of Europe, part of Asia, and part of Africa.
Are all those gentlemen over there Americans? (*lit.*, Those gentlemen there, are they all Americans?)
Not all. Some are Americans and the others are Canadians, Englishmen, Frenchmen, Spaniards, Germans, Italians, and Russians.

33 Εἶναι ταξιδιῶτες;
34 "Οχι. Εἶναι ἀντιπρόσωποι στὸ Διεθνὲς Συνέδριο τῶν Ἀρχαιολόγων.
35 Πόσα ἔθνη, πόσες ἐθνικότητες, πόσες γλῶσσες! Σωστὴ Βαβυλωνία.
36 Στὴν Ἀθήνα ἔρχονται πολλοὶ ξένοι;
37 Μάλιστα, ἔρχονται ἀπὸ ὅλα τὰ μέρη τοῦ κόσμου.
38 Πολλοὶ Ἕλληνες μιλοῦν ξένες γλῶσσες.
39 Αὐτὸ εἶναι σωστό.
40 Ποῦ μάθατε[8] ἀγγλικά;

41 "Εμαθα ἀγγλικὰ στὴν Ἀγγλία.
42 Τὰ παιδιά σας μιλοῦν ἀγγλικά;
43 Μάλιστα. Ὁ γυιός μου πηγαίνει στὸ ἀγγλικὸ σχολεῖο. Ἡ κόρη μου πηγαίνει στὸ Ἀμερικανικὸ Κολλέγιο τῶν Ἀθηνῶν.
44 Μαζί σας, κύριε Πετρίδη, μπορῶ νὰ μάθω καλὰ τὰ ἑλληνικά.

45 Τότε, ἀπὸ σήμερα εἶμαι ὁ δάσκαλός σας!
46 Σᾶς εὐχαριστῶ πολύ. Θὰ σᾶς[6] συναντήσω αὔριο. Χαίρετε[10].
47 Χαίρετε καὶ καλὴ ἀντάμωση[11] αὔριο.

nouns follow the noun they modify and are enclitic (unaccented) words while the genitive of the personal pronoun precedes the verbs and is accented. Compare σας in sentences 10 and 45, where it functions as a possessive pronoun, to σᾶς in 46 where it is used as object pronoun. Σᾶς is actually an accusative, but in the plural of the personal pronouns of the first and second persons, the same form is used for both the accusative and the genitive. 7. The preposition εἰς and the accusative of the definite article are contracted into one word: εἰς + τόν = στό(ν), εἰς + τήν = στή(ν), εἰς + τό = στό, εἰς + τούς = στούς, εἰς + τάς or τίς = στίς, εἰς + τά = στά. Each of these forms may translate the English "to the", "in the", "on the" and "at the". 8. Ταξίδεψα or (ἐ)ταξίδευσα is tne aorist of ταξιδεύω; ἔμαθα is the aorist of μαθαίνω; for the formation of the aorist, see Grammar 10.12 — 10.15 and 10.3. 9. This is another case in which an interrogative sentence has the same words and the same word order as its corresponding declarative one; cf. footnote 2. 10. Χαίρετε is a little more formal than ἀντίο (σας) which in its turn is more formal than γειά σου. 11. Καλὴ ἀντάμωση literally means

33 EE-neh tah-ksee-*TH*YOH-tehs?

34 OH-khee. EE-neh ahn-dee-PROH-soh-pee stoh *th*ee-eh-THNEHS see-NEH-*th*ree-oh tohn ahr-kheh-oh-LOH-ghohn.

35 POH-sah EH-thnee, POH-sehs eh-th n ee-K O H-tee-tehs,   P O H-sehs GHLOH-sehs. soh-STEE vah-vee-loh-NEE-ah .

36 Steen ah-THEE-nah EHR-khoh-deh poh-LEE KSEH-nee?

37 MAH-lee-stah, EHR-khohn-deh ah-POH OH-lah tah MEH-ree too KOH-zmoo.

38 poh-LEE EH-lee-nehs mee-LOON KSEH-nehs GHLOH-sehs.

39 ahf-TOH EE-neh soh-STOH.

40 POO MA H-th a h-teh ahn-glee-KAH?

41 EH-mah-thah ahn glee-KAH steen ahn-GLEE-ah.

42 tah peh-*TH*YAH-sahs mee-LOON ahn-glee-KAH?

43 MAH-lee1stah. oh YOHZ-moo pee-YEH-nee stoh ahn-glee-KOH skhoh-LEE-oh. ee KOH-ree-moo pee-YEH-nee stoh ah-meh-ree-kah-nee-KOH koh-LEH-yee-oh tohn ah-thee-NOHN.

44 mah-ZEE-sahs, KEE-ree-eh peh-TREE-*th*ee, boh-ROH nah MAH-thoh kah- LAH tah eh-lee-ńee-KAH.

45 TOH-teh, ah-POH SEE-meh-rah EE-meh oh *TH*AH-skah-LOH-sahs.

46 sahs ehf-khah-ree-STOH poh-LEE. thah sahs see-nahn-DEE-soh AHV-ree-oh .

47 KHEH-reh-teh keh kah-LEE ahn-DAH-moh-see AHV-ree-oh.

Are they tourists (*lit.*, travelers)?

No. They are delegates to the International Congress of Archeologists.

So many nations, so many nationalities, so many languages — a real Babylon .

Do many foreigners come to Athens? (*lit.*, To Athens come many foreigners?)

Yes, they come from all corners of the world.

Many Greeks speak foreign languages.

That is correct.

Where did you learn English?

I learned English in England.

Do your children speak English?

Yes. My son goes to the English school. My daughter goes to the American College in Athens.

With you, Mr. Petrides, I can learn Greek well.

Then, from today on, I will be your teacher.

Thank you very much. I'll see you tomorrow. Good-bye.

Good-by, see you (*lit.*, and good meeting) tomorrow .

"good encounter" and corresponds to French *au revoir*, Italian *arrivederci*, Spanish *hasta la vista*, German *Auf Wiedersehen* and Russian *do svidanya*. In Greek, however, it is used more often when the parting is likely to be of long duration.

ΔΕΥΤΕΡΟ ΜΑΘΗΜΑ
Second Lesson

New Vocabulary for this Lesson

τρώγω* (TROH-(gh)oh) I eat
μαζί (mah-ZEE) together
παίρνω⁺ (PEHR-noh) I take
τὶ (TEE) what
ὅτι (OH-tee) that

γιά (yah) for
πλούσιος, -α, -ο (PLOO-see-ohs) rich
καλός, -η, -ο (kah-LOHS) good
κακός, -η, -ο (kah-KOHS) bad
κουζίνα (koo-ZEE-nah) kitchen

εὐχαρίστως (ehf-khah-REE-stohs) with pleasure
πολὺ πρωί (poh-LEE proh-EE) early in the morning
συνηθίζω (see-nee-THEE-zoh) I am accustomed
πιστεύω (pee-STEHV-oh) I believe
ἔρχομαι* (EHR-khoh-meh) I come

νομίζω (noh-MEE-zoh) I think
ὥρα (OH-rah) hour, time
πηγαίνω* (pee-YEH-noh) I go
διαβάζω (thyah-VAH-zoh) I read
κάτι (KAH-tee) something

ξέρω (KSEH-roh) I know
ἐργασία (ehr-ghah-SEE-ah) work
ἔτσι (EH-tsee) thus; so
πρέπει (PREH-pee) must
στομάχι (stoh-MAH-khee) stomach

εὐχαριστῶ (ehf-kha-ree-STOH) thank you
παρακαλῶ (pah-rah-kah-LOH) you're welcome; please
ἡ ἐκλογή μου (ee eh-kloh-YEE-moo) [my] choice
διακοπή (thee-ah-koh-PEE) interruption
κρατῶ (krah-TOH) I keep; I hold

μᾶλλον (MAH-lohn) rather
φέρω (FEH-roh) I bring
πίνω* (PEE-noh) I drink
κρύος, -α, -ο (KREE-ohs) cold
ὑγεία (ee-YEE-ah) health

μόνο (MOH-noh) only
τώρα (TOH-rah) now
προτιμῶ (proh-tee-MOH) I prefer
τάξις (TAH-ksees) class, order
ἀλλάζω (ah-LAH-zoh) I change

ἐλαφρός, -η, -ο (eh-lah-FROHS) light
καταλαβαίνω (kah-tah-lah-VEH-noh) I understand
πατριώτης (pah-tree-OH-tees) fellow-country man; patriot
ἀτμόσφαιρα (ah-TMOH-sfeh-rah) atmosphere
ἀναπαύομαι (ah-nah-PAHV-oh-meh) I rest

*For the forms of the various tenses of the irregular verbs marked in the vocabularies by an asterisk, see the List of Irregular Verbs.

ἀκριβῶς (ah-kree-VOHS) exactly
παράγω (pah-RAH-ghoh) I produce

Τρόφιμα καὶ Φαγητά
(TROH-fee-mah keh fah-yee-TAH)
Foods and Meals

τὸ πρόγευμα (PROH-yehv-mah) breakfast
τὸ γεῦμα (YEHV-mah) lunch or noon dinner
τὸ δεῖπνο (THEE-pnoh) dinner or supper
τὰ χορταρικά (khohr-tah-ree-KAH) vegetables
τὸ γλύκισμα (GHLEE-kee-zmah) cake

τὸ ψωμί (psoh-MEE) bread   τὸ βωδινό (voh-thee-NOH) beef
τὸ κρέας (KREH-ahs) meat   τὸ ἀρνὶ (ahr-NEE) lamb
ἡ σούπα (SOO-pah) soup   τὸ χοιρινό (khee-ree-NOH) pork
τὸ φροῦτο (FROO-toh) fruit   τὸ μοσχάρι (mohs-KHAH-ree) veal
τὸ τυρί (tee-REE) cheese   τὸ ψάρι (PSAH-ree) fish

τὸ ἐπιδόρπιο (eh-pee-THOHR-pee-oh) dessert
τὸ κοτόπουλο (koh-TOH-poo-loh) chicken
τηγανητό (tee-ghah-nee-TOH) fried

τὸ αὐγό (ahv-GHOH) egg   τὸ νερό (neh-ROH) water
βραστό (vrah-STOH) boiled   ὁ καφές (kah-FEHS) coffee
ψητό (psee-TOH) roasted   τὸ κρασί (krah-SEE) wine
ἡ πήττα (PEE-tah) pie   τὸ γάλα (GHAH-lah) milk
ὠμός, -ή -ό (oh-MOHS) raw   ἡ ζάχαρη (ZAH-khah-ree) sugar

καλὰ ψημένο (kah-LAH psee-MEH-noh) well done
τὰ παϊδάκια (pah-ee-THAH-kyah) chops
μαγειρεμένο (mah-yee-reh-MEH-noh) cooked
τὸ γλυκό (ghlee-KOH) jam
τὰ κουλουράκια (koo-loo-RAH-kyah) cookies
τὸ τραπεζομάνδηλο (trah-peh-zoh-MAHN-thee-loh) tablecloth

τὸ πιάτο (PYAH-toh) plate, dish   τὸ φλυτζάνι (fleed-ZAH-nee) cup
τὸ κουτάλι (koo-TAH-lee) spoon   τὸ πιατάκι (pyah-TAH-kee) saucer
τὸ πηρούνι (pee-ROO-nee) fork   τὸ μπουκάλι (boo-KAH-lee) bottle
τὸ μαχαίρι (mah-KHEH-ree) knife   ἡ πετσέτα (peh-TSEH-tah) napkin
τὸ ποτήρι (poh-TEE-ree) glass   τὸ κανάτι (kah-NAH-tee) pitcher

CONVERSATION

1 Σήμερα θὰ φᾶμε μαζί, κύριε Σμίθ.
2 Εὐχαρίστως.
3 Πήρατε τὸ πρόγευμά[1] σας;
4 Μάλιστα. Παίρνω τὸ πρόγευμά μου πολὺ πρωΐ.
5 Τί παίρνετε γιὰ πρόγευμα;
6 Παίρνω τσάϊ, βούτυρο, ἕνα παξιμάδι καὶ λίγο τυρὶ ἑλ-
ληνικό.
7 Στὴν Ἀμερικὴ τὸ πρόγευμα εἶναι πιὸ[2] πλούσιο.
8 Μάλιστα. Στὴν Ἀμερικὴ συνηθίζουν[3] πολὺ τὰ αὐγά, τὸ
χοιρομέρι καὶ τὰ μικρὰ λουκάνικα. Ἐπίσης, συνηθίζουν
τὸ γάλα καὶ τοὺς χυμοὺς τῶν φρούτων.
9 Τὸ μεσημέρι θὰ πάρωμε μαζὶ τὸ γεῦμα στὸ ἑστιατόριο
«Ἀβέρωφ».
10 Ἄκουσα ὅτι τὸ ἑστιατόριο αὐτὸ εἶναι τὸ πιὸ καλὸ στὴν
Ἀθήνα. Ἔχει πολὺ καλὴ ἑλληνικὴ κουζίνα.
11 Νομίζω ὅτι εἶναι ὥρα γιὰ τὸ γεῦμα. Πᾶμε...

12 Γκαρσόν!
13 Μάλιστα, κύριοι.
Τί θά πάρετε;
14 Διαβάσ(ε)τε, σᾶς
παρακαλῶ, τὸν
«κατάλογο τῶν
φαγητῶν».
15 Ἔχομε σούπα ἀ-
πὸ κοτόπουλο[4],
σούπα ἀπὸ βοδινὸ
κρέας καὶ σούπα
ἀπὸ ψάρι.

FOOTNOTES: *1*. Μπρέκφαστ is also used for "breakfast". *2*. Πιό is a
shortened form of περισσότερο (more). It is used before adjectives to form
comparatives; the comparative is also formed by the suffix -τερος. See the two
forms of the comparative of πλούσιος in sentences 7 and 27; for the formation
of the comparative and the superlative, see also Grammar 3.5. *3*. Συνηθίζουν literally means "they accustom themselves (to)". *4*. Σούπα ἀπὸ κοτόπουλο is also expressed as κοτόσουπα and σούπα ἀπὸ ψάρι as ψαρόσουπα.

PRONUNCIATION	TRANSLATION

PRONUNCIATION

1 SEE-meh-rah thah FAH-meh mah-ZEE, KEE-ree-eh Smith.
2 ehf-khah-REE-stohs.
3 PEE-rah-teh toh PROH-yehv-MAH-sahs?
4 MAH-lee-stah. PEHR-noh toh PROH-yehv-MAH-moo poh-LEE proh-EE.
5 TEE PEHR-neh-teh yah PROH-yehv-mah?
6 PEHR-noh TSAH-ee, VOO-tee-roh, EH-nah pah-ksee-MAH-thee keh LEE-ghoh tee-REE eh-lee-nee-KOH.
7 steen ah-meh-ree-KEE toh PROH-yehv-mah EE-neh pyoh PLOO-see-oh.
8 MAH-lee-stah. steen ah-meh-ree-KEE see-nee-THEE-zoon poh-LEE tah ahv-GHAH, toh khee-roh-MEH-ree keh tah mee-KRAH loo-KAH-nee-kah. eh-PEE-sees see-nee-THEE-zoon toh GHAH-lah keh toos khee-MOOS tohn FROO-tohn.
9 toh meh-see-MEH-ree thah PAH-roh-meh mah-ZEE toh YEHV-mah stoh eh-stee-ah-TOH-ree-oh ah-VEH-rohf.
10 AH-koo-sah OH-tee toh eh-stee-ah-TOH-ree-oh ahf-TOH EE-neh toh PYOH kah-LOH steen ah-THEE-nah. EH-khee poh-LEE kah-LEE eh-lee-nee-KEE koo-ZEE-nah.
11 noh-MEE-zoh OH-tee EE-neh OH-rah yah toh YEHV-mah. PAH-meh . . .
12 gahr-SOHN!
13 MAH-lee-stah, KEE-ree-ee. TEE thah PAH-reh-teh?
14 thyah-VAH-s(e)h-teh, sahs pah-rah-kah-LOH, tohn kah-TAH-loh-ghoh tohn fah-yee-TOHN.
15 EH-khoh-meh SOO-pah ah-POH koh-TOH-poo-loh, SOO-pah ah-POH voh-thee-NOH KREH-ahs keh SOO-pah ah-POH PSAH-ree.

TRANSLATION

Today we shall eat together, Mr. Smith.
With pleasure.
Have you had (lit., taken) your breakfast?
Yes. I had my breakfast early in the morning (lit., very morning).
What do you take for breakfast?
I have tea, butter, a slice of toast, and a little Greek cheese (lit., cheese Greek).
Most Americans like a heavy breakfast. (lit., In America, breakfast is richer.)
Yes. In America they usually eat eggs, ham, and small sausages. They also drink milk and fruit juices.

At noon we will have lunch together at the "Averoff" Restaurant.

I've heard that this restaurant is the best in Athens. It has a very good Greek cuisine.

I think that it is time for lunch. Let's go . . .
Waiter!
Yes, gentlemen. What will you have?
What is on the menu (lit., read the list of foods), please.
We have chicken soup (lit., soup of chicken), beef soup, and fish soup.

16 Ἔχετε ἐντράδες;
17 Μάλιστα. Ἔχομε κρέας μὲ χορταρικά (μὲ κολοκυθάκια, μὲ φασολάκια, μὲ μελιτζάνες καὶ μὲ σπανάκι).

18 Ἔχετε κάτι τοῦ φούρνου;
19 Ἔχομε ἀρνὶ μὲ κριθαράκι. Εἶναι τὸ πιάτο τῆς ἡμέρας.
20 Ἔχετε κάτι τῆς ὥρας;

21 Ἔχομε σουβλάκια, ἀρνὶ τῆς σούβλας καὶ μπριζόλες μοσχαράκι.
22 Φέρτε μας μία σαλάτα ἑλληνική, μία κοτόσουπα καὶ τὸ «πιάτο τῆς ἡμέρας».
23 Σᾶς ἀρέσει ἡ ἐκλογή μου, κύριε Σμίθ;
24 Μοῦ ἀρέσει, ἀλλὰ νομίζω ὅτι εἶναι πολλά.
25 Ξέρω ὅτι στὴν Ἀμερικὴ δὲν τρώγουν πολὺ τὸ μεσημέρι.

26 Αὐτὸ εἶναι ἀλήθεια. Ἐκεῖ δὲν ἔχομε διακοπὴ ἐργασίας τὸ μεσημέρι καὶ ἔτσι πρέπει νὰ κρατοῦμε τὸ στομάχι[5] ἐλαφρό.
27 Στὴν Ἑλλάδα, τὸ γεῦμα εἶναι πλουσιώτερο[2] ἀπὸ τὸ δεῖπνο.
28 Ναί. Τὸ γεῦμα εἶναι πιὸ πλούσιο. Τὸ δεῖπνο[6] εἶναι μᾶλλον ἐλαφρό.
29 Γκαρσόν, φέρτε μας κάτι νὰ πιοῦμε.
30 Θέλετε κοκκινέλι, μαῦρο κρασὶ ἢ ρετσίνα;

5. Νὰ κρατοῦμε τὸ στομάχι ἐλαφρό may also be expressed as νὰ μὴ βαραίνουμε τὸ στομάχι.   6. The terms δεῖπνο and γεῦμα do not absolutely coincide with the terms "dinner" and "lunch" because of the difference in eating habits between America and Greece, as pointed out in this lesson. Some tend

16 EH-kheh-teh ehn-DRAH-*th*ehs?

17 MAH-lee-stah. EH-khoh-meh KREH-ahs meh khohr-tah-ree-KAH (meh koh-loh-kee-THAH-kyah, meh fah-soh-LAH-kyah, meh mehlee-DZAH-nehs keh meh spah-NAH-kee).

18 EH-kheh-teh KAH-tee too FOOR-noo?

19 EH-khoh-meh ahr-NEE meh kreethah-RAH-kee. EE-neh toh PYAH-toh tees ee-MEH-rahs.

20 EH-kheh-teh KAH-tee tees OH-rahs?

21 EH-khoh-meh soo-VLAH-kyah,ahr-NEE tees SOO-vlahs keh bree-DZOH-lehs moh-skhah-RAH-kee.

22 FEHR-teh-mahs MEE-ah sah-LAH-tah eh-lee-nee-KEE, MEE-ah koh-TOH-soo-pah keh toh PYAH-toh tees ee-MEH-rahs.

23 sahs ah-REH-see ee eh-kloh-YEE-moo, KEE-ree-eh Smith?

24 moo ah-REH-see, ah-LAH noh-MEE-zoh oh-TEE EE-neh poh-LAH.

25 KSEH-roh OH-tee steen ah-meh-ree-KEE *th*ehn TROH-ghoon poh-LEE toh meh-see-MEH-ree.

26 ahf-TOH EE-neh ah-LEE-thyah. eh-KEE *th*ehn EH-khoh-meh *th*ee-ah-koh-PEE ehr-ghah-SEE-ahs toh meh-see-MEH-ree keh EH-tsee PREH-pee nah krah-TOO-meh toh stoh-MAH-khee eh-lah-FROH.

27 steen eh-LAH-*th*ah toh YEHV-mah EE-neh ploo-see-OH-teh-roh ah-POH TOH *TH*EE-pnoh.

28 NEH. toh YEHV-mah EE-neh pyoh PLOO-see-oh. toh *TH*EE-pnoh EE-neh MAH-lohn eh-lah-FROH.

29 gahr-SOHN, FEHR-teh-mahs KAH-tee nah PYOO-meh.

30 THEH-leh-teh koh-kee-NEH-lee, MAHV-roh krah-SEE EE reh-TSEE-nah?

Do you have any casserole dishes?

Yes. We have meat with vegetables (with squash, with beans, with eggplant, and with spinach).

Do you have anything baked?

We have lamb with vermicelli. It is today's special. (*lit.*, the dish of the day).

Do you have anything from the grill (*lit.*, of the hour)?

We have barbecued ribs, spit-roasted lamb, and veal chops.

Bring us a Greek salad, chicken soup, and today's special.

Do you like my choice, Mr. Smith?

I like it, but I think that all this is too much (*lit.*, that they are many).

I know that in America they don't eat much at noon.

That is true (*lit.*, that is truth). There is no interruption of work at noon, so we have to keep our stomach light.

In Greece, lunch is heavier (*lit.*, richer) than dinner.

Yes, lunch is heavier. Dinner is rather light.

Waiter, bring us something to drink.

Do you want red wine, black or retsina?

31 Φέρτε μας ἕνα μπουκάλι κρύα ρετσίνα.
32 Στὴν ὑγεία σας[7], κύριε Σμίθ.
33 Στὴν ὑγεία σας, κύριε Πετρίδη.
34 Τὶ θὰ πάρετε γιὰ ἐπιδόρπιο[8], κύριε Σμίθ; Θέλετε μπακλαβᾶ, γαλακτομπούρεκο, ριζόγαλο, φροῦτα;
35 Θὰ πάρω μόνο ἕνα ἑλληνικὸ καφέ.

36 Φάγατε καλά, κύριε Σμίθ;
37 Ἔφαγα καὶ πολὺ καὶ καλά.
38 Σᾶς ἀρέσει ἡ ἑλληνικὴ κουζίνα;
39 Μοῦ ἀρέσει πολύ. Τώρα καταλαβαίνω, γιατὶ οἱ πατριῶτες μου στὴν Ἀμερικὴ προτιμοῦν τὰ ἑλληνικὰ ἑστιατόρια.
40 Πῶς σᾶς φαίνεται τὸ ἑστιατόριο «Ἀβέρωφ»;

41 Εἶναι ἑστιατόριο πρώτης τάξεως. Τὰ πιάτα, τὰ μαχαίρια, τὰ κουτάλια, τὰ πηρούνια καὶ τὰ τραπεζομάντηλα λάμπουν.

42 Σᾶς ἀρέσει ἡ ἑλληνικὴ ταβέρνα;
43 Μοῦ ἀρέσει πολὺ ἡ ἀτμόσφαιρα τῆς ἑλληνικῆς ταβέρνας, τὰ τραγούδια, ἡ ρετσίνα...
44 Οἱ Ἕλληνες ἀναπαύονται μετὰ τὸ γεῦμα. Πᾶμε;
45 Σᾶς εὐχαριστῶ, κύριε Πετρίδη, γιὰ τὸ θαυμάσιο τραπέζι.

---

to translate γεῦμα as "dinner" and δεῖπνο as "supper". Σουπέ is also used for "supper"; "lunch" is also referred to as μεσημεριανὸ γεῦμα.   7. Εἰς ὑγείαν (σας) may be used interchangeably with Στὴν ὑγεία σας.   8. Ἐπιδόρπιο has the same meaning as "dessert", but it is not used as frequently. The more specific terms γλύκισμα (any sweet concoction served as dessert) and φροῦτα (fruits) are used instead.

31 FEHR-teh-mahs EH-nah boo-KAH-lee KREE-ah reh-TSEE-nah.

Bring us a bottle of chilled (*lit.*, cold) retsina.

32 steen ee-YEE-ah-sahs, KEE-ree-eh Smith.

To your health, Mr. Smith.

33 steen ee-YEE-ah-sahs, KEE-ree-eh peh-TREE-*th*ee.

To your health, Mr. Petrides.

34 TEE thah PAH-reh-teh yah eh-pee-*TH*OHR-pee-oh, KEE-ree-eh Smith? THEH-leh-teh bah-klah-VAH, ghah-lah-ktohm-BOO-reh-koh, ree-ZOH-ghah-loh, FROO-tah?

What will you have for dessert, Mr. Smith? Do you want baklavah, milk-custard pie, rice pudding, fruits?

35 thah PAH-roh MOH-noh EH-nah eh-lee-nee-KOH kah- FEH.

I'll have only Greek coffee.

36 FAH-ghah-teh kah-LAH, KEE-ree-eh Smith?

Did you eat well, Mr. Smith?

37 EH-fah-ghah keh poh-LEE keh kah-LAH.

(Yes,) I ate much and well.

38 sahs ah-REH-see ee eh-lee-nee-KEE koo-ZEE-nah?

Do you like the Greek cuisine?

39 moo ah-REH-see poh-LEE. TOH-rah kah-tah-lah-VEH-noh yah-TEE ee pah-tree-OH-tehz-moo steen ah-meh-ree-KEE proh-tee-MOON tah eh-lee-nee-KAH eh-stee-ah-TOH-ree-ah.

I like it very much. Now I understand why my countrymen in America prefer Greek restaurants.

40 pohs sahs FEH-neh-teh tohn eh-stee-ah-TOH-ree-oh ah-VEH-rohf?

How do you like (*lit.*, how does it seem to you) the Averoff Restaurant?

41 EE-neh eh-stee-ah-TOH-ree-oh PROH-tees TAH-kseh-ohs. tah PYAH-tah, tah mah-KHEH-ryah, tah koo-TAH-lyah, tah pee-ROO-nyah keh tah trah-peh-zoh-MAHN-dee-lah LAHM-boon.

It is a first class restaurant (*lit.*, of first class). The plates, the knives, the spoons, the forks, and the tablecloths sparkle.

42 sahs ah-REH-see ee eh-lee-nee-KEE tah-VEHR-nah?

Do you like Greek taverns? (*lit.*, the Greek tavern?)

43 moo ah-REH-see poh-LEE ee ah-TMOH-sfeh-rah tees eh-lee-nee-KEES tah-VEHR-nahs, tah trah-GHOO-*th*yah, ee reh-TSEE-nah.

I like the atmosphere of the Greek tavern very much, the songs, the retsina.

44 ee EH-lee-nehs ah-nah-PAH-vohn-deh meh-TAH toh YEHV-mah. PAH-meh?

The Greeks rest after lunch. Shall we go?

45 sahs ehf-khah-ree-STOH, KEE-ree-eh peh-TREE-*th*ee,yah toh thahv-MAH-see-oh trah-PEH-zee.

Thank you, Mr. Petrides, for the wonderful lunch (*lit.*, table).

TΡITO MAΘHMA
Third Lesson

New Vocabulary for this Lesson

ἀγορά (ah-ghoh-RAH) market
ἀγοράζω (ah-ghoh-RAH-zoh) I buy
λεωφορεῖο (leh-oh-foh-REE-oh) bus
βλέπω* (VLEH-poh) I see
πάτωμα (PAH-toh-mah) floor

φορῶ (foh-ROH) I wear
βάρος (VAH-rohs) weight
κάνω (KAH-noh) I do; I make
πρᾶγμα (PRAHGH-mah) thing
ὑλικό (ee-lee-KOH) material

κατάστημα (kah-TAH-stee-mah) store
ἀνδρικός, -ή, -ό (ahn-three-KOHS) men's
προθήκη (proh-THEE-kee) store window
φθάνω (FTHAH-noh) I arrive; I reach
φοβοῦμαι (foh-VOO-meh) I fear; I am afraid

βαρύς, -ιά, -ύ (vah-REES) heavy
μακρύς, -ιά, -ύ (mah-KREES) long
κοντός, -ή, -ό (kohn-DOHS) short
(ὑ)ψηλός, -ή, -ό (psee-LOHS) high
παλιός, -ά, -ό (pah-LYOHS) old
καινούργιος, -α, -ο (keh-NOOR-yohs) new
ἀκριβός, -ή, -ό (ah-kree-VOHS) expensive

ποιότης (pee-OH-tees) quality
γοῦστο (GHOO-stoh) good taste
μέτρο (MEH-troh) meter; measure
φθηνός, -ή, -ό (fthee-NOHS) cheap

διορθώνω (thee-ohr-THOH-noh) I correct; I adjust
διαμέρισμα (thee-ah-MEH-ree-zmah) department
χειμωνιάτικο (khee-moh-NYAH-tee-koh) for the winter

καλοκαιρινό (kah-loh-keh-ree-NOH) for the summer
φαρδύς, -ιά, -ύ (fahr-THEES) wide; loose
στενός, -ή, -ό (steh-NOHS) narrow; tight
χαμηλός, -ή, -ό (khah-mee-LOHS) low
μαλακός, -ή, -ό (mah-lah-KOHS) soft

σκληρός, -ή, -ό (sklee-ROHS) hard; stiff
ἄριστος, -η, -ο (AH-ree-stohs) excellent
δοκιμάζω (thoh-kee-MAH-zoh) I try [on]
ἀνησυχῶ (ah-nee-see-KHOH) I worry

42

'Ενδύματα καὶ Παπούτσια
(ehn-THEE-mah-tah keh pah-POO-tsyah)
Clothing and Footwear

τὸ κοστούμι (koh-STOO-mee) suit
τὸ σακκάκι (sah-KAH-kee) coat
τὸ παλτό (pahl-TOH) overcoat
τὸ καπέλλο (kah-PEH-loh) hat
τὸ παπούτσι (pah-POO-tsee) shoe

ἡ γραβάτα (ghrah-VAH-tah) tie
ἡ φανέλλα (fah-NEH-lah) sweater
τὸ γελέκο (yeh-LEH-koh) vest
τὸ τακούνι (tah-KOO-nee) heel
τὸ φόρεμα (FOH-reh-mah) dress

τὸ παντελόνι (pahn-deh-LOH-nee) trousers
τὸ ἀδιάβροχο (ah-thee-AH-vroh-khoh) rain coat
τὸ πουκάμισο (poo-KAH-mee-soh) shirt
ἡ κάλτσα. (KAHL-tsah) sock, stocking
οἱ παντόφλες (pahn-DOH-flehs) slippers

ἡ φούστα (FOO-stah) skirt
ἡ μπλούζα (BLOO-zah) blouse
ἡ·τσάντα (TSAHN-dah) handbag
τὰ γάντια (GHAHN-dyah) gloves
τὸ ᾿ζευγάρι (zehv-GHAH-ree) pair

τὸ μανίκι (mah-NEE-kee) sleeve
τὸ κουμπί (koom-BEE) button
ὁ γιακάς (yah-KAHS) collar
ἡ τσέπη (TSEH-pee) pocket
τὸ ὕφασμα (EE-fah-zmah) material

τὰ ἐσώρουχα (eh-SOH-roo-khah) underwear
τὸ μαντήλι (mahn-DEE-lee) handkerchief
τὸ μανικέτι (mah-nee-KEH-tee) cuff
ἡ δωδεκάδα (thoh-theh-KAH-thah) dozen
τὸ πορτοφόλι (pohr-toh-FOH-lee) wallet

μεταξωτό (meh-tah-ksoh-TOH) silk
μάλλινο · (MAH-lee-noh) wool
βαμβακερό (vahm-vah-keh- ROH) cotton

λινό (lee-NOH) linen
χρῶμα (KHROH-mah) color

ἄσπρο (AHS-proh) white
γκρί(ζο) (GREE-zoh) gray
μπλέ (BLEH) blue
πράσινο (PRAH-see-noh) green
κόκκινο (KOH-kee-noh) red

μαῦρο (MAHV-roh) black
καφέ (kah-FEH) brown
γαλάζιο (ghah-LAH-zyoh) blue
κίτρινο (KEE-tree-noh) yellow
μώβ (MOHV) purple

CONVERSATION

1 Καλησπέρα, κύριε Σμίθ.

2 Καλησπέρα, κύριε Πετρίδη.

3 Σήμερα θὰ πᾶμε στὴν ἀγορά. Θέλω νὰ ἀγοράσω μερικὰ ροῦχα καὶ ἕνα ζευγάρι παπούτσια.

4 Θέλετε νὰ πᾶμε στὰ καταστήματα τῆς ὁδοῦ[1] Σταδίου;

5 Πᾶμε. Στὴν ὁδὸ Σταδίου εἶναι τὰ μεγαλύτερα καταστήματα ἀνδρικῶν εἰδῶν.

6 Θὰ περπατήσωμε ἢ θὰ πᾶμε μὲ τὸ λεωφορεῖο;

7 Προτιμῶ νὰ περπατήσωμε, γιὰ νὰ ἰδοῦμε ὅλες τὶς προθῆκες[2] τῶν καταστημάτων.

8 Φτάσαμε. Νὰ τὸ μεγάλο κατάστημα τῶν ἀδελφῶν Πουλοπούλου.

9 Δεσποινίς, ποῦ εἶναι τὸ διαμέρισμα ἀνδρικῶν κοστουμιῶν[3];

10 Στὸ τρίτο πάτωμα, κύριε.

11 Θέλω ἕνα κοστούμι γκρί(ζο).

12 Τί ἀριθμὸ φορᾶτε, κύριε;

13 Φορῶ ἀριθμὸ σαραντατέσσερα. Πολὺ φοβοῦμαι, ὅτι ἐδῶ στὴν Ἑλλάδα πῆρα πολὺ βάρος[4].

14 Δοκιμάστε αὐτό, κύριε.

15 Τὸ σακκάκι εἶναι καλό. Τὸ γελέκο[5] εἶναι στενό. Τὸ παντελόνι εἶναι στενὸ καὶ μακρύ.

FOOTNOTES: *1.* Ὁδός is one of the very few feminine nouns of the second declension still used. It appears on street signs. A typical Greek address would read as follows: Κύριον Ἰωάννην Γνωστικόν, ὁδὸς Ὀδυσσέως 37 (Mr. John Gnosticos, 37 Ulysses Street). The common Greek word for street (not associated with any specifically named street) is δρόμος. *2.* Βιτρίνα is also used for "window display". *3.* Κουστούμι is a variant of κοστούμι. *4.* (Ἐ)πάχυνα is another expression that is used for the concept «πῆρα

PRONUNCIATION

1 kah-lee-SPEH-rah, KEE-ree-eh Smith.

2 kah-lee-SPEH-rah KEE-ree-eh peh-TREE-*thee*.

3 SEE-meh-rah thah PAH-meh steen ah-ghoh-RAH. THEH-loh nah ah-ghoh-RAH-soh meh-ree-KAH ROO-khah keh EH-nah zehv-GHAH-ree pah-POO-tsyah.

4 THEH-leh-teh nah PAH-meh stah kah-tah-STEE-mah-tah tees oh-*TH*OO stah-*TH*EE-oo?

5 PAH-meh. steen oh-*TH*OH stah-*TH*EE-oo EE-neh tah meh-ghah-LEE-teh-rah kah-tah-STEE-mah-tah ahn-*th*ree-KOHN ee-*TH*OHN.

6 *th*ah pehr-pah-TEE-soh-meh EE thah PAH-meh meh toh leh-oh-foh-REE-oh?

7 proh-tee-MOH nah pehr-pah-TEE-soh-meh yah nah ee-*TH*OO-meh OH-lehs tees proh-THEE-kehs tohn kah-tah-stee-MAH-tohn.

8 FTAH-sah-meh. NAH toh meh-GHAH-loh kah-TAH-stee-mah tohn ah-*th*ehl-FOHN poo-loh-POO-loo.

9 *th*eh-spee-NEES, POO EE-neh toh *th*ee-ah-MEH-reez-mah ahn-*th*ree-KOHN koh-stoo-MYOHN?

10 stoh TREE-toh PAH-toh-mah, KEE-ree-eh.

11 THEH-loh EH-nah koh-STOO-mee GREE (-zoh).

12 TEE ah-ree-THMOH foh-RAH-teh, KEE-ree-eh?

13 foh-ROH ah-reeth-MOH sah-rahn-dah-TEH-seh-rah. poh-LEE foh-VOO-meh, OH-tee eh-*TH*OH steen eh-LAH-*th*ah PEE-rah poh-LEE VAH-rohs.

14 *th*oh-kee-MAH-steh ahf-TOH, KEE-ree-eh.

15 toh sah-KAH-kee EE-neh kah-LOH. toh yeh-LEH-koh EE-neh steh-NOH. toh pahn-deh-LOH-nee EE-neh steh-NOH keh mah-KREE.

TRANSLATION

Good evening, Mr. Smith.

Good evening, Mr. Petrides.

Today we'll go shopping (*lit.*, to the market); I want to buy some clothes and a pair of shoes.

Would you like to go to the stores on Stadiou Street?

Let's go. On Stadiou Street are the largest men's wear stores.

Shall we walk or go by bus?

I prefer to walk in order to see all the window displays.

Here we are (*lit.*, we arrived). Here is the large store of the Poulopoulos Brothers.

Miss, where is the men's department?

On the third floor, sir.

I want a gray suit.

What size do you wear, sir?

I wear size . forty-four. I am very much afraid that here in Greece I've gained a lot of weight.

Try this, sir.

The coat is good. The vest is tight. The trousers are tight and long.

16 Μὴ[6] ἀνησυχεῖτε, κύριε. Θὰ τὸ διορθώσωμε ὅλο τὸ κοστούμι καὶ θὰ τὸ κάμωμε στὰ μέτρα σας.

17 Πόσο κοστίζει τὸ κοστούμι αὐτό;

18 Κοστίζει χίλιες πεντακόσιες δραχμές.

19 Θέλω καὶ ἕνα παλτὸ χειμωνιάτικο.

20 Ἔχομε ὁλόμαλλα καὶ στὰ μέτρα σας.

21 Εὐχαριστῶ. Ποῦ εἶναι τὸ διαμέρισμα μὲ τὰ ὑποκάμισα[7] καὶ τὰ ἐσώρρουχα;

22 Στὸ πρῶτο πάτωμα.

23 Δεσποινίς, θέλω τέσσερα πουκάμισα, μερικὰ ἐσώρρουχα, μερικὲς γραβάτες, καὶ μιὰ δωδεκάδα[8] μαντήλια.

24. Μάλιστα, κύριε. Τί ἀριθμὸ πουκάμισα φορᾶτε;

25 Τὸ κατάστημα αὐτὸ ἔχει διαμέρισμα παπουτσιῶν;

26 Μάλιστα. Κατεβῆτε στὸ ὑπόγειο.

27 Θέλω ἕνα ζευγάρι παπούτσια.

28 Ἔχομε παπούτσια ἀρίστης ποιότητος στὰ μέτρα σας. Τί χρῶμα προτιμᾶτε;

29 Δὲν θέλω μαῦρα. Προτιμῶ καφέ, δέρμα μαλακό.

30 Δοκιμάστε αὐτὰ ἐδῶ τὰ δύο ζευγάρια.

πολὺ βάρος». 5. Γιλέκο is another form of γελέκο. 6. Μή is the negative particle used before a subjunctive or an imperative. Δέν is used before an indicative. Μήν is another form of μή used in colloquial Greek before verbs beginning with a vowel or with p, t, k with which it assimilates to mb, nd, ng respectively. 7. Πουκάμισα is a colloquial form of ὑποκάμισα.

16 MEEN ah-nee-see-KHEE-teh ,KEE ree-eh. thah toh *thee*-ohr-THOH-soh-meh OH-loh toh koh-STOO-mee keh thah toh KAH-moh-meh stah MEH-trah-sahs.

17 POH-soh koh-STEE-zee toh koo-STOO-mee ahf-TOH?

18 koh-STEE-zee KHEE-lyehs pehn-dah-KOH-syehs *th*rahkh-MEHS.

19 THEH-loh keh EH-nah pahl-TOH khee-moh-NYAH-tee-koh.

20 EH-khoh-meh oh-LOH-mah-lah keh stah MEH-trah-sahs.

21 ehf-khah-ree-STOH. POO EE-neh toh *th*ee-ah-MEH-ree-zmah meh tah ee-poh-KAH-mee-sah keh tah eh-SOH-roo-khah?

22 stoh PROH-toh PAH-toh-mah.

23 *th*eh-spee-NEES, THEH-loh TEH-seh-rah poo-KAH-mee-sah, meh-ree-KAH eh-SOH-roo-khah, meh-ree-KEHS ghrah-VAH-tehs, keh myah *th*oh-*th*eh-KAH-*th*ah mahn-DEE-lyah.

24 MAH-lee-stah, KEE-ree-eh. TEE ah-reeth-MOH poo-KAH-mee-sah foh-RAH-teh?

25 toh kah-ˈTAH-stee-mah ahf-TOH EH-khee *th*ee-ah-MEH-ree-zmah pah-poo-TSYOHN?

26 MAH-lee-stah. kah-teh-VEE-teh stoh ee-POH-yee-oh.

27 THEH-loh EH-nah zehv-GHAH-ree pah-POO-tsyah.

28 EH-khoh-meh pah-POO-tsyah ah-REE-stees pee-OH-tee-tohs stah MEH-trah-sahs. TEE KHROH-mah proh-tee-MAH-teh?

29 *TH*EHN THEH-loh MAHV-rah. proh-tee-MOH kah-FEH, *TH*EHR-mah mah-lah-KOH.

30 *th*oh-kee-MAH-steh ahf-TAH eh-*TH*OH tah *TH*YOH zehv-GHAH-ryah.

Don't worry, sir. We'll alter the entire suit and make it to your size.

How much does this suit cost?

It costs fifteen hundred (*lit.*, a thousand five hundred drachmas).

I also want a winter overcoat.

We have all-wool overcoats in your size.

Thank you. Where is the shirt and underwear department?

On the first floor.

Miss, I would like four shirts, some underwear, a few ties, and a dozen handkerciefs.

Yes, sir. What size shirt do you wear?

Has this store a shoe department?

Yes. Go down to the basement.

I would like a pair of shoes.

We have shoes of excellent quality in your size. What color do you prefer.

I don't want black. I prefer brown, in soft leather.

Try these two pairs here.

31 Αὐτὸ τὸ ζευγάρι εἶναι ἀκριβῶς στὰ μέτρα μου. Τὸ ἄλλο ζευγάρι ἐκεῖ εἶναι στενό. Μὲ στενεύει στὰ δάκτυλα.

32 Θέλετε παντόφλες, παπούτσια ἀθλητικά, μπότες ψηλές;

33 "Οχι, εὐχαριστῶ.

34 Πῶς σοῦ⁸ φαίνονται τὰ ἑλληνικὰ καταστήματα, κύριε Σμίθ;

35 Εἶναι ἄριστα. "Εχουν θαυμάσια πράγματα. Τὰ κοστούμια, τὰ παλτά, τὰ ὑποκάμισα, τὰ ἐσώρρουχα, τὰ παπούτσια, οἱ γραβάτες ὅλα εἶναι καμωμένα σύμφωνα μὲ τὸ πολὺ γνωστὸ ἑλληνικὸ γοῦστο.

36 'Αλήθεια, οἱ "Ελληνες ἔχουν πολὺ γοῦστο. Τὰ ὑλικὰ ἐπίσης εἶναι ἑλληνικά. Ἡ 'Ελλάδα τὰ τελευταῖα χρόνια παράγει ὡραῖα μάλλινα, βαμβακερὰ καὶ μεταξωτὰ ὑφάσματα.

37 Μὲ τὸ νέο κοστούμι δὲν θὰ μοιάζω πιὰ σὰν 'Αμερικανός!

38 "Αν μάθης μάλιστα καὶ τὴν ἑλληνικὴ γλῶσσα λίγο καλύτερα, ὅλοι θὰ νομίζουν ὅτι εἶσαι 'Αθηναῖος.

39 Τότε πρέπει νὰ ἀλλάξω καὶ τὸ ὄνομά μου. Δὲν πρέπει νὰ ὀνομάζομαι Οὐΐλιαμ Σμίθ, ἀλλά... Βασίλης Σιδέρης¹⁰.

---

8. Ντουζίνα is used colloquially for "dozen". 9. Σοῦ is the familiar counterpart of σᾶς. 10. Βασίλης Σιδέρης is the closest Greek equivalent of William Smith, but it actually is Basil Smith instead of William, a name not used in Greek, but rendered in translations of *William* or German *Wilhelm* as Γουλιέλμος (compare Italian *Guglielmo*).

31 ahf-TOH toh zehv-GHAH-ree EE-neh ah-kree-VOHS stah MEH-trah-moo. toh AH-loh zehv-GHAH-ree eh-KEE EE-neh steh-NOH. meh steh-NEH-vee stah *TH*AH-ktee-lah.

32 T H E H-leh-teh pahn-D O H-flehs, pah-POO-tsyah ah-thlee-tee-KAH, BOH-tehs psee-LEHS?

33 OH-khee, ehf-khah-ree-STOH.

34 POHS soo FEH-nohn-deh tah eñ-lee-nee-KAH kah-tah-STEE-mah-tah, KEE-ree-eh Smith?

35 EE-neh AH-ree-stah. EH-khoon thahv-MAH-see-ah PRAHG-mah-tah. tah koh-STOO-myah, tah pahl-TAH, tah ee-poh-KAH-mee-sah, tah eh-SOH-roo-khah, tah pah-POO-tsyah, ee ghrah-VAH-tehs OH-lah EE-neh kah-moh-MEH-nah SEEM-foh-nah meh toh poh-LEE ghnoh-STOH eh-lee-nee-KOH GHOO-stoh.

36 ah-LEE-thyah, ee EH-lee-nehs EH-khoon poh-LEE GHOO-stoh. tah ee-lee-KAH eh-PEE-sees EH-neh eh-lee-nee-KAH. ee eh-LAH-*th*ah tah teh-lehf-T E H-ah K H R O H-nyah pah-RAH-yee oh-REH-ah MAH-lee-nah, vahm-vah-keh-RAH keh meh-tah-ksoh-TAH ee-FAH-zmah-tah.

37 meh toh NEH-oh koh-STOO-mee *th*ehn thah MYAH-zoh PYAH sahn ah-meh-ree-kah-NOHS.

38 AHN MAH-thees MAH-lee´ stah keh teen eh-lee-nee-KEE GHLOH-sah LEE-ghoh kah-LEE-teh-RAH, OH-lee thah noh-MEE-zoon OH-tee EE-seh ah-thee-NEH-ohs.

39 TOH-teh PREH-pee nah ah-LAH-ksoh keh toh OH-noh-MAH-moo. *TH*EHN PREH-pee nah oh-noh-MAH-zoh-meh William Smith, ah-LAH . . . vah-SEE-lees see-*TH*EH-rees.

This pair is exactly my size. The other over there is tight. It pinches (*lit.*, it is tight at the) my toes.

Would you like slippers, sport shoes, high boots?

No, thanks.

How do you like the Greek stores, Mr. Smith? (*lit.*, How do the Greek stores seem to you?)

They are excellent. They have wonderful things. The suits, the overcoats, the shirts, the underwear, the shoes, and the ties are all made according to the well known Greek taste.

Indeed, the Greeks have good taste (*lit.*, much taste). The materials are also Greek. In the last few years Greece has been producing beautiful woolen, cotton, and silk fabrics.

In my new suit I will not look like an American.

If you also learn the Greek language a little better, everybody will think that you are an Athenian.

Then I'd also have to change my name. I should not be called William Smith, but . . . Basil Sideris.

ΤΕΤΑΡΤΟ ΜΑΘΗΜΑ
Fourth Lesson

New Vocabulary for this Lesson

πότε (POH-teh) when
φεύγω* (FEHV-ghoh) I leave
ἐρωτῶ (eh-roh-TOH) I ask
γυρίζω (yee-REE-zoh) I return
σκέψη (SKEH-psee) thought

μένω* (MEH-noh) I stay; I live
ἡμέρα (ee-MEH-rah) day
καιρός (keh-ROHS) time; weather
ἀπαντῶ (ah-pahn-DOH) I answer
κοστίζει (koh-STEE-zee) it costs

λογαριάζω (loh-ghah-RYAH-zoh) I plan; I expect
ἐπιθυμῶ (eh-pee-thee-MOH) I wish; I desire
ταξιδεύω (tah-ksee-THEHV-oh) I travel
ἀποφασίζω (ah-poh-fah-SEE-zoh) I decide
διάθεση (thee-AH-theh-see) disposition; mood

δίνω (THEE-noh) I give
ἐλπίζω (ehl-PEE-zoh) I hope

ἀφήνω (ah-FEE-noh) I leave; I let
εὔχομαι (EHF-khoh-meh) I wish
πάντοτε (PAHN-doh-teh) always

ὁ φίλος, ἡ φίλη (oh FEE-lohs, ee FEE-lee) friend
πληροφορία (plee-roh-foh-REE-ah) information
θαυμάσιος, -α, -ο (thahv-MAH-see-ohs) wonderful
πιάνω (PYAH-noh) I touch; I catch
ἐξετάζω (eh-kseh-TAH-zoh) I examine; I inquire

κάθε φορά (KAH-theh foh-RAH) every time
ἀναχωρῶ (ah-nah-khoh-ROH) I leave; I depart
(ἐξ)υπηρετῶ (eh-ksee-pee-reh-TOH) I serve
πρόθυμος, -η, -ο (PROH-thee-mohs) willing; eager
σχεδιάζω (skheh-thee-AH-zoh) I plan

ὄμορφος, -η, -ο (OH-mohr-fohs) beautiful; pretty
χαίρομαι (KHEH-roh-meh) I am glad
χρησιμοποιῶ (khree-see-moh-pee-OH) I use
ὀργανώνω (ohr-ghah-NOH-noh) I organize
χάνω (KHAH-noh) I lose; I miss

διεύθυνση (thee-EHF-theen-see) address
τὸ πρωί (toh proh-EE) [in] the morning
τὸ μεσημέρι (toh meh-see-MEH-ree) at noon

τὸ ἀπόγευμα (toh ah-POH-yehv-mah) [in] the afternoon
τὸ βράδυ (toh VRAH-thee) [in] the evening
τὰ μεσάνυχτα (tah meh-SAH-nee-khtah) at midnight

Μέσα Συγκοινωνίας
(MEH-sah seen-gee-noh-NEE-ahs)
Means of Transportation

τὸ πρακτορεῖο ταξιδιῶν
(prah-ktoh-REE-oh tah-ksee-THYOHN)
travel agency

τὸ ταξίδι (tah-KSEE-thee) trip
τὸ πλοῖο (PLEE-oh) boat
ὁ σταθμός (stahth-MOHS) station
τὸ λιμάνι (lee-MAH-nee) harbor

τὸ τραῖνο (TREH-noh) railroad
τὸ μπαοῦλο (bah-OO-loh) trunk
τὸ βαγόνι (vah-GHOH-nee) car
ἡ ἄφιξη (AH-fee-ksee) arrival

ἡ διαδρομή (thee-ah-throh-MEE) journey
τὸ λεωφορεῖο (leh-oh-foh-REE-oh) bus
τὸ ἀεροπλάνο (ah-eh-roh-PLAH-noh) airplane
σιδηροδρομικῶς (see-thee-roh-throh-mee-KOHS) by railroad
ἀτμοπλοϊκῶς (ah-tmoh-ploh-ee-KOHS) by boat
ἀεροπορικῶς (ah-eh-roh-poh-ree-KOHS) by plane
ὁ πράκτορας (PRAH-ktoh-rahs) agent
τὸ εἰσιτήριο (ee-see-TEE-ree-oh) ticket
τὸ εἰσιτήριο μετ' ἐπιστροφῆς (... meht eh-pee-stroh-FEES)
round trip ticket

ἡ θυρίδα εἰσιτηρίων (thee-REE-thah ...) ticket window
ἡ βαλίτσα (vah-LEE-tsah) suitcase
οἱ ἀποσκευές (ah-poh-skehv-EHS) baggage
τὸ ἀεροδρόμιο (ah-eh-roh-THROH-mee-oh) airport
ἡ ταχεῖα (tah-KHEE-ah) the express

ἡ ἀποβάθρα (ah-poh-VAH-thrah) pier
ὁ ἀχθοφόρος, ὁ χαμάλης (akh-thoh-FOH-rohs or khah-MAH-lees) porter
τὸ διαβατήριο (thee-ah-vah-TEE-ree-oh) passport
ἡ αἴθουσα ἀναμονῆς (EH-thoo-sah ah-nah-moh-NEES) waiting room
ἡ ἀναχώρηση (ah-nah-KHOH-ree-see) departure

τὸ δρομολόγιο (throh-moh-LOH-yee-oh) time-table
ἄνετος, -η, -ο (AH-neh-tohs) comfortable

ταξιδιωτικὲς ἐπιταγές (tah-ksee-thyoh-tee-KEHS eh-pee-tah-YEHS)
traveler's checks

CONVERSATION

1 Πότε θὰ φύγετε γιὰ τὴ Θεσσαλονίκη, κύριε Σμίθ;

2 Λογαριάζω νὰ φύγω αὔριο.

3 Θὰ μείνετε ἐκεῖ πολλὲς ἡμέρες;

4 Θὰ μείνω μόνο τὸ Σαββατοκύριακο. Ἐπιθυμῶ νὰ συναντήσω ἐκεῖ τοὺς συγγενεῖς τῆς νύφης[1] μου, τῆς γυναίκας τοῦ ἀδελφοῦ μου.

5 Θὰ ταξιδέψετε μὲ τὸ τραῖνο; Μὲ τὸ λεωφορεῖο; Μὲ τὸ ἀεροπλάνο; Μὲ τὸ πλοῖο;

6 Ἀκόμη δὲν ἀποφάσισα πῶς[2] θὰ ταξιδέψω. Φυσικά, δὲν θὰ πάρω τὸ πλοῖο, γιατὶ δὲν ἔχω πολὺ καιρὸ στὴ διάθεσή μου.

7 Πᾶμε στὸ Πρακτορεῖο Ταξιδιῶν ὁ «Φάρος» νὰ ρωτήσωμε. Ὁ πράκτορας εἶναι φίλος μου.

8 Καλησπέρα, κύριε Παπαδόπουλε. Ὁ φίλος μου κύριος Σμίθ ταξιδεύει γιὰ τὴν Θεσσαλονίκη καὶ θέλει μερικὲς πληροφορίες.

9 Θὰ ταξιδέψετε σιδηροδρομικῶς ἢ ἀεροπορικῶς;

10 Προτιμῶ νὰ πάω μὲ τὸ τραῖνο καὶ νὰ γυρίσω μὲ τὸ ἀεροπλάνο. Ἔτσι, θὰ πάρω μιὰ καλύτερη ἰδέα γιὰ τὴν Βόρειο[3] Ἑλλάδα.

FOOTNOTES: *1*. Νύφη or νύμφη means "bride", "daughter-in-law and "sister-in-law", as in this lesson. *2*. Πῶς with a circumflex means "how", as in sentence 6; πώς (that) is a conjunction, the equivalent of ὅτι, as in sentence 19. *3*. Geographical terms are usually expressed in Puristic even when the rest of the text is in Demotic, because they have become quite stereotyped as official designations. Βορεινός, -ή, -ό is the Demotic counterpart of ὁ, ἡ βό-

1 POH-teh thah FEE-yeh-teh yah tee theh-sah-loh-NEE-kee, KEE-ree-eh Smith?

When will you leave for Salonika, Mr. Smith?

2 loh-ghah-RYAH-zoh nah FEE-ghoh AHV-ree-oh.

I expect to leave tomorrow.

3 thah MEE-neh-teh eh-KEE-poh-LEHS ee-MEH-rehs?

Will you stay there long (*lit.*, many days)?

4 thah MEE-noh MOH-noh toh sah-vah-toh-KEE-ryah-koh. eh-pee-thee-MOH nah see-nahn-DEE-soh eh-KEE toos seen-geh-NEES tees NEE-feez-moo, tees yee-NEH-kahs too ah-*th*ehl-FOO-moo.

I will stay only over the weekend. I want (*lit.*, I wish) to meet the relatives of my sister-in-law, my brother's wife, there.

5 thah tah-ksee-*TH*EH-pseh-teh meh toh TREH-noh? meh toh leh-oh-foh-REE-oh? meh toh ah-eh-roh-PLAH-noh? meh toh PLEE-oh?

Will you travel by (*lit.*, with) train? by bus? by plane? by ship?

6 ah-KOH-mee *th*ehn ah-poh-FAH-see-sah POHS thah tah-ksee-*TH*EH-psoh. fee-see-KAH *th*ehn thah PAH-roh toh PLEE-oh yah-TEE *th*ehn EH-khoh poh-LEE keh-ROH stee *th*ee-AH-theh-SEE-moo.

I have not decided yet how I'll travel. Naturally, I will not take the boat because I don't have much time at my disposal.

7 PAH-meh stoh prah-ktoh-REE-oh tah- ksee-*th*yohn oh FAH-rohs nah roh-TEE-soh-meh. oh PRAH-ktoh-rahs EE-neh FEE-lohz-moo.

Let's go to the "Pharos" Travel Agency and ask. The agent is a friend of mine. (*lit.*, is my friend).

8 kah-lee-SPEH-rah, KEE-ree-eh pah-pah-*TH*OH-poo-leh. oh FEE-lohz-moo KEE-ree-ohs Smith tah-ksee-*TH*EH-vee yah tee theh-sah-loh NEE-kee keh THEH-lee meh-ree-KEHS plee-roh-foh-REE-ehs.

Good evening, Mr. Papadopoulos. My friend Mr. Smith is traveling to Salonika and wants some information.

9 thah tah-ksee-*TH*EH-pseh-teh see-*th*ee-roh-*th*roh-mee-KOHS EE ah-eh-roh-poh-ree-KOHS?

Will you travel by train or by plane?

10 proh-tee-MOH nah PAH-oh meh toh TREH-noh keh nah yee-REE-soh meh toh ah-eh-roh-PLAH-noh. EH-tsee, thah PAH-roh myah kah-LEE-teh-ree eh-*TH*EH-ah yah teen VOH-ree-oh eh-LAH-*th*ah.

I prefer to go by train and return by plane. Thus, I will get a better idea of Northern Greece.

11 Ἡ σκέψη σας εἶναι θαυμάσια. Τὸ τραῖνο φεύγει ἀπὸ τὸ Σταθμὸ Λαρίσης στὶς δέκα τὸ πρωΐ, τὸ μεσημέρι, στὶς τέσσερες τὸ ἀπόγευμα καὶ στὶς δώδεκα, τὰ μεσάνυχτα.

12 Προτιμῶ νὰ πάρω τὸ τραῖνο τὸ μεσημέρι.

13 Πολὺ καλά. Τὸ τραῖνο αὐτὸ εἶναι «ἡ ταχεῖα»[4]. Δὲν κάμει[5] πολλοὺς σταθμούς.

14 Πόσο κοστίζει τὸ εἰσιτήριο;

15 Ἡ πρώτη θέση κοστίζει τριακόσιες δραχμές. Ἡ δευτέρα θέση κοστίζει διακόσιες δραχμές.

16 Δῶστε μου, σᾶς παρακαλῶ, ἕνα εἰσιτήριο πρώτης θέσεως.

17 Θέλετε νὰ κρατήσω θέση γιὰ τὴν ἐπιστροφή σας μὲ τὸ ἀεροπλάνο;

18 Μάλιστα. Σᾶς παρακαλῶ πολὺ νὰ μοῦ κρατήσετε μιὰ θέση γιὰ τὸ ἀπόγευμα τῆς Κυριακῆς.

19 Ἐλπίζω πῶς[2] ὅλες οἱ θέσεις δὲν εἶναι πιασμένες ἀκόμη. Θὰ ἐξετάσω καὶ θὰ σᾶς τηλεφωνήσω.

20 Τί ὥρα ἀναχωρεῖ τὸ πρῶτο ἀεροπλάνο ἀπὸ τὴ Θεσσαλονίκη γιὰ τὴν Ἀθήνα;

ρειος, τὸ βόρειον. *4.* Ἡ «ταχεῖα» is a substantivized adjective standing for the expression «ταχεῖα ἀμαξοστοιχία» which is the official way of referring to «ἐξπρές». *5.* The verb κάνω or κάμνω is one of the few verbs which do not have clear-cut distinct forms for the imperfect and aorist (ἔκανα can be used for both of them) and for the durative and punctual futures (θὰ κάνω can be used for both of them). In order to make the distinction, many use κάν- as the stem of the present and κάμ- as the stem of the aorist. Thus, ἔκανα (I was doing) is the imperfect, ἔκαμα (I did) the aorist, θὰ κάνω (I will be doing) the durative future and θὰ κάμω (I'll do) the

11 ee SKEH-psee-sahs EE-neh thahv-MAH-see-ah. toh TREH- noh FEHV-yee ah-POH toh stah-THMOH lah-REE-sees stees *TH*EH-kah toh proh-EE, toh meh-see-MEH-ree, stees TEH-seh-rehs toh ah-POH-yeh-mah keh stees *TH*OH-*th*eh-kah, tah meh-SAH-nee-khtah.

That's a wonderful idea (*lit.*, your thought is wonderful). The train leaves from Larisa Station at ten in the morning, at noon, at four in the afternoon, or at midnight.

12 proh-tee-MOH nah PAH-roh toh TREH-noh toh meh-see-MEH-ree.

I prefer the noon train.

13 poh-LEE kah-LAH. toh TREH-noh ahf-TOH EE-neh ee tah-KHEE-ah. *TH*EHN KAH-nee poh-LOOS stah-THMOOS.

Very well. That train is "the express". It does not make many stops.

14 POH-soh koh-STEE-zee toh ee-see-TEE-ree-oh?

How much does a ticket cost?

15 ee PROH-tee *TH*EH-see koh-STEE-zee tree-ah-KOH-syehs *th*rahkh-MEHS. ee *th*ehf-TEH-rah *TH*EH-see koh-STEE-zee *th*ee-ah-KOH-syehs *th*rahkh-MEHS.

First class costs three hundred drachmas. Second class costs two hundred drachmas.

16 *TH*OH-steh-moo, sahs pah-rah-kah-LOH, EH-nah ee-see-TEE-ree-oh PROH-tees *TH*EH-seh-ohs.

Give me a first class ticket, please.

17 *TH*EH-leh-teh nah krah-TEE-soh *TH*EH-see yah teen eh-pee-stroh-FEE-sahs meh toh ah-eh-roh-PLAH-noh?

Would you like me to reserve a seat for your return, by plane?

18 MAH-lee-stah. sahs pah-rah-kah-LOH poh-LEE nah moo krah-TEE-seh-teh myah *TH*EH-see yah toh ah-POH-yehv-mah tees kee-ryah-KEES.

Yes. Please, reserve a seat for me for Sunday afternoon (*lit.*, the afternoon of Sunday).

19 ehl-PEE-zoh OH-tee OH-lehs ee *TH*EH-sees *th*ehn EE-neh pyah-ZMEH-nehs ah-KOH-mee. thah eh-kseh-TAH-soh keh thah sahs tee-leh-foh-NEE-soh.

I hope that all the seats have not been taken yet. I will inquire and call you.

20 TEE OH-rah ah-nah-KHOH-ree toh PROH-toh ah-eh-roh-PLAH-noh ah-POH tee theh-sah-loh-NEE-kee yah teen ah-*TH*EE-nah?

What time does the first plane from Salonika to Athens leave?

21 Τὸ πρῶτο ἀεροπλάνο ἀναχωρεῖ στὶς ἑπτὰ καὶ μισὴ τὸ πρωΐ. Τὸ δεύτερο ἀναχωρεῖ τὸ ἀπόγευμα στὴ μία ἡ ὥρα. Τὸ τελευταῖο ἀναχωρεῖ στὶς πέντε καὶ τέταρτο καὶ φθάνει στὸ ἀεροδρόμιο στὶς ἕξι καὶ σαράντα.

22 Εὐχαριστῶ γιὰ τὶς πληροφορίες. Μπορῶ νὰ ἀφήσω[6] τὴ βαλίτσα μου στὸ πρακτορεῖο σας, κύριε Παπαδόπουλε;

23 Εὐχαρίστως, κύριε Σμίθ. Θέλετε τίποτε ἄλλο; Τὸ πρακτορεῖο μας[7] εἶναι πρόθυμο νὰ σᾶς ἐξυπηρετήση. Κάθε φορὰ ποὺ ταξιδεύετε, ἀπευθυνθῆτε σὲ μᾶς.

24 Εὐχαριστῶ πολύ. Σχεδιάζω νὰ ταξιδέψω σὲ ὅλη τὴν Ἑλλάδα. Θέλω νὰ γνωρίσω ἀπὸ κοντὰ ὅλες τὶς ὅμορφες γωνιὲς τῆς Ἑλλάδας. Χαίρομαι, ποὺ βλέπω, ὅτι ἡ συγκοινωνία στὴν Ἑλλάδα εἶναι τόσο καλὰ ὠργανωμένη.

25 Ἀλήθεια, κύριε Σμίθ, ἡ συγκοινωνία εἶναι θαυμάσια. Ὁ ταξιδιώτης μπορεῖ νὰ χρησιμοποιήση ὅλα τὰ μέσα μεταφορῶν καὶ ταξιδιῶν. Τὸ σιδηρόδρομο, τὸ ἀεροπλάνο, τὸ λεωφορεῖο, τὸ ἀτμόπλοιο, τὰ μικρὰ βενζινόπλοια.

---

punctual future. Κάνω means both "to make" and "to do". It is also used in many idiomatic expressions in which the verb "to be" is used in English, as for example κάνει κρύο (it is cold). 6. Ἀφήνω (to leave, to let) is one of a number of words in Greek that have two acceptable spellings. The other spelling is ἀφίνω. In cases of doublets we tried to use what we consider as the most widely used spelling, especially in current literature, and the most au-

21 toh PROH-toh ah-eh-roh-PLAH-noh ah-nah-khoh-REE stees eh-PTAH keh .mee-SEE toh proh-EE. toh *THE*HF-teh-roh ah-nah-khoh-REE toh ah-POH-yehv-mah stee MEE-ah ee OH-rah. toh teh-lehf-TEH-oh ah-nah-khoh-REE stees PEHN-deh keh TEH-tahr-toh keh FTHAH-nee stoh ah-eh-roh-*TH*ROH-mee-oh stees EH-ksee keh sah-RAHN-dah.

22 ehf-khah-ree-STOH yah tees plee-roh-foh-REE-ehs. boh-ROH nah ah-FEE-soh tee vah-LEE-tsah-moo stoh prah-ktoh-REE-oh-sahs, KEE-ree-eh pah-pah-*TH*OH-poo-leh?

23 ehf-khah-REE-stohs, KEE-ree-eh Smith. THEH-leh-teh TEE-poh-teh AH-loh? toh prah-ktoh-REE-oh-mahs EE-neh PROH-thee-moh nah sahs eh-ksee-pee-reh-TEE-see. KAH-theh foh- RAH poo tah-ksee-*TH*EH-veh-teh, ah-pehf-theen-THEE-teh seh MAHS.

24 ehf-khah-ree-STOH poh-LEE. skheh-*th*ee-ah-zoh nah tah-ksee-*TH*EH-psoh seh OH-lee teen eh-LAH-*th*ah. THEH-loh nah ghnoh-REE-soh ah-POH kohn-DAH OH-lehs tees OH-mohr-fehs ghoh-NYEHS tees eh-LAH-*th*ohs. KHEH-roh-meh poo VLEH-poh OH-tee ee seen-gee-noh-NEE-ah steen eh-LAH-*th*ah EE-neh TOH-soh kah-LAH ohr-ghah-noh-MEH-nee.

25 ah-LEE-thyah, KEE-ree-eh Smith, ee seen-gee-noh-NEE-ah EE-neh thahv- MAH-see-ah. oh tah-ksee-*TH*YOH-tees boh-REE nah khree-see-moh-pee-EE-see OH-lah tah MEH-sah meh-tah-foh-ROHN keh tah-ksee-*TH*YOHN. toh see-*th*ee-ROH-*th*roh-moh, toh ah-eh-roh-PLAH-noh, toh leh-oh-foh-REE-oh, toh ah-TMOH-plee-oh, tah mee-KRAH vehn-zee-NOH-plee-ah.

The first plane leaves at half past seven in the morning, the second at one o'clock in the afternoon, the last one leaves at quarter past five and arrives at the airport at six-forty.

Thank you for the information. May I leave my bag at your agency, Mr. Papadopoulos?

Gladly, Mr. Smith. Would you like anything else? Our agency is eager to serve you. Whenever (*lit.*, Every time that) you travel, call us.

Thank you very much. I plan to travel all over Greece. I want to become acquainted with all the beautiful spots (*lit.*, corners) of Greece. I am glad to see that transportation in Greece is so well organized.

Indeed, Mr. Smith, the transportation is marvelous. The traveler may use any (*lit.*, all the) means of transportation and travel: railroad, plane, bus, steamer, small motor boats .

26 Λοιπόν, κύριε Πετρίδη, θά σᾶς χάσω γιά δυό ἡμέρες. Πότε θά συναντηθοῦμε;

27 Θά συναντηθοῦμε τή Δευτέρα τό μεσημέρι. Ἐλᾶτε στό σπίτι μου. Ἔχετε τή διεύθυνσή μου[7];

28 Μάλιστα. Ὁδός Ὁμήρου, ἀριθμός 145.

29 Πῶς μπορῶ νά ἔλθω στό σπίτι σας[7] ἀπ' τό ἀεροδρόμιο;

30 Μπορεῖτε νά πάρετε τό λεωφορεῖο τῆς γραμμῆς ἤ ἔνα ταξί. Σᾶς εὔχομαι καλό ταξίδι καί καλή ἀντάμωση.

31 Σᾶς εὐχαριστῶ πολύ, κύριε Πετρίδη.

32 Ὅταν ταξιδεύετε, εἶναι καλό νά ἔχετε πάντοτε μαζί σας τό διαβατήριό σας, μερικά δολλάρια σέ ταξιδιωτικές ἐπιταγές καί μερικές δραχμές.

___

thoritative, used in the official grammar of the Demotic.   7. The accent of the possessive pronoun, which is an enclitic word, is lost when the preceding word is accented on the last syllable or on the syllable next to the last (as in sentences 23 and 29); it falls on the last syllable of the preceding word when the preceding word is accented on the third from the last syllable (as in sentence 27).

26 lee-POHN, KEE-ree-eh peh-TREE-*thee*, thah sahs KHAH-soh yah *THYOH* ee-MEH-rehs. POH-teh thah see-nahn-dee-THOO-meh?

Then, Mr. Petrides, I'll miss (*lit.,* lose) you for two days. When shall we meet?

27 thah see-nahn-dee-THOO-meh tee *the*hf-TEH-rah toh meh-see-MEH-ree. eh-LAH-teh stoh SPEE-tec-moo. EH-kheh-teh tee *thee*-EHF-theen-SEE-moo?

We'll meet Monday at noon. Come to my house. Do you have my address?

28 MAH-lee-stah. oh-*THO*HS oh-MEE-roo, ah-reeth-MOHS eh-kah-TOHN sah-RAHN-dah-PEHN-deh.

Yes. 145 Homer Street. (*lit.,* Street of Homer, number 145.)

29 POHS boh-ROH nah EHL-thoh stoh SPEE-tee-sahs ah-POH toh ah-eh-roh-*TH*ROH-mee-oh?

How can I get to your house from the airport?

30 boh-REE-teh nah PAH-reh-teh toh leh-oh-foh-REE-oh tees ghrah-MEES EE EH-nah tah-KSEE. sahs EHF-khoh-meh kah-LOH tah-KSEE-*thee* keh kah-LEE ahn-DAH-moh-see.

You can take the bus or a taxi. I wish you a pleasant trip, till we meet again.

31 sahs ehf-khah-ree-STOH, poh-LEE KEE-ree-eh peh-TREE-*thee*.

I thank you very much, Mr. Petrides.

32 OH-tahn tah-ksee-*TH*EHV-eh-teh, EE-neh kah-LOH nah EH-kheh-teh PAHN-doh-teh mah-ZEE-sahs toh *thee*-ah-vah-TEE-ree-OH-sahs, meh-ree-KAH *th*oh-LAH-ree-ah seh tah-ksee-*th*yoh-tee-KEHS eh-pee-tah-YEHS keh meh-ree-KEHS *th*rahkh-MEHS.

When you travel, it is always good to have your passport with you. You'll also need a few dollars in traveler's checks and a few drachmas.

ΠΕΜΠΤΟ ΜΑΘΗΜΑ
Fifth Lesson

New Vocabulary for this Lesson

κοιμίζω (kee-MEE-zoh) I put to sleep
λυποῦμαι (lee-POO-meh) I am sorry
ἐπιτρέπω (eh-pee-TREH-poh) I allow
νανουρίζω (nah-noo-REE-zoh) I lullaby
θυμοῦμαι or θυμᾶμαι (thee-MAH-meh) I remember

ξυπνῶ (ksee-PNOH) I wake up
εὔκολα (EHF-koh-lah) easily
ἔπειτα (EH-pee-tah) then
θόρυβος (THOH-ree-vohs) noise
μετρῶ (meh-TROH) I count

κοιμοῦμαι (kee-MOO-meh) I sleep
ἐπίσης (eh-PEE-sees) too, also
τραῖνο (TREH-noh) train
σταθμός (stahth-MOHS) station
καθώς (kah-THOHS) as

μηχανή (mee-khah-NEE) engine; machine
βαγόνι (vah-GHOH-nee) car; wagon
δρόμος (THROH-mohs) street; road; way
κίνηση (KEE-nee-see) motion, movement; activity
ρυθμικός, -ή, -ό (reeth-mee-KOHS) rhythmic

ἀλλά (ah-LAH) but
σχεδόν (skheh-THOHN) almost
στιγμή (steegh-MEE) moment
ὕπνος (EE-pnohs) sleep
ἀϋπνία (ah-ee-PNEE-ah) insomnia

στύλος (STEE-lohs) pole
σκεπάζω (skeh-PAH-zoh) I cover
περνῶ (pehr-NOH) I pass
ὄνομα (OH-noh-mah) name
ξένος, -η, -ο (KSEH-nohs) foreign

ξεκινῶ (kseh-kee-NOH) I start [moving]; I depart
μεταξύ (meh-tah-KSEE) between, among
πλησιάζω (plee-see-AH-zoh) I approach, I near
κατεβαίνω (kah-teh-VEH-noh) I get down
ἀνεβαίνω (ah-neh-VEH-noh) I go up
καλύπτω (kah-LEE-ptoh) I cover; I cover a distance
δυσκολία (thees-koh-LEE-ah) difficulty
ζήτημα (ZEE-tee-mah) question; matter
ζητῶ συγγνώμην (zee-TOH see-GNOH-meen)
I am sorry (*lit.*, I beg your pardon)

ΑΡΙΘΜΟΙ (ah-reeth-MEE) NUMBERS

(See also Reference Grammar pages 199-201)

CARDINAL NUMBERS

0	μηδέν (mee-THEHN)	
1	ἕνα (EH-nah)	
2	δύο (THEE-oh)	
3	τρία (TREE-ah)	
4	τέσσερα (TEH-seh-rah)	
5	πέντε (PEHN-deh)	
6	ἕξι (EH-ksee)	
7	ἑπτά or ἑφτά (eh-FTAH)	
8	ὀκτώ or ὀχτώ (oh-KHTOH)	
9	ἐννέα or ἐννιά (eh-NYAH)	
10	δέκα (THEH-kah)	
11	ἕνδεκα (EHN-deh-kah)	
12	δώδεκα (THOH-theh-kah)	
13	δεκατρία	
14	δεκατέσσερα	
15	δεκαπέντε	
20	εἴκοσι (EE-koh-see)	
21	εἴκοσι ἕνα	
22	εἴκοσι δύο	
23	εἴκοσι τρία	
25	εἰκοσιπέντε	
30	τριάντα (tree-AHN-dah)	
31	τριάντα ἕνα	
40	σαράντα (sah-RAHN-dah)	
50	πενήντα (peh-NEEN-dah)	
60	ἐξήντα (eh-KSEEN-dah)	
70	ἐβδομήντα (ehv-thoh-MEEN-dah)	
80	ὀγδόντα (ohgh-THOHN-dah)	
90	ἐνενήντα (eh-neh-NEEN-dah)	
100	ἑκατό (eh-kah-TOH)	
101	ἑκατόν ἕνα	
168	ἑκατὸν ἑξῆντα ὀχτώ	
200	διακόσια (thee-ah-KOH-syah)	
300	τριακόσια (tree-ah-KOH-syah)	
400	τετρακόσια (teh-trah-KOH-syah)	
500	πεντακόσια (pehn-dah-KOH-syah)	
1,000	χίλια (KHEE-lyah)	
2,000	δύο χιλιάδες (...khee-LYAH-thehs)	
1,000,000	ἕνα ἑκατομμύριο (eh-kah-toh-MEE-ree-oh)	
1,000,000,000	ἕνα δισεκατομμύριο (thee-seh-kah-toh-MEE-ree-oh)	

ORDINAL NUMBERS

1st	πρῶτος (PROH-tos)	
2nd	δεύτερος (THEHF-teh-rohs)	
3rd	τρίτος (TREE-tohs)	
4th	τέταρτος (TEH-tahr-tohs)	
5th	πέμπτος (PEHM-tohs)	
6th	ἕκτος (EH-ktohs)	
7th	ἕβδομος (EHV-thoh-mohs)	
8th	ὄγδοος (OHGH-thoh-ohs)	
9th	ἔνατος (EH-nah-tohs)	
10th	δέκατος (THEH-kah-tohs)	
20th	εἰκοστός (ee-koh-STOHS)	
30th	τριακοστός (tree-ah-koh-STOHS)	
40th	τεσσαρακοστός (teh-sah-rah-koh-STOHS)	
50th	πεντηκοστός (pehn-dee-koh-STOHS)	
60th	ἐξηκοστός (eh-ksee-koh-STOHS)	
70th	ἐβδομηκοστός (ehv-thoh-mee-koh-STOHS)	
80th	ὀγδοηκοστός (ohgh-thoh-ee-koh-STOHS)	
90th	ἐνενηκοστός (eh-neh-nee-koh-STOHS)	
100th	ἑκατοστός (eh-kah-toh-STOHS)	
1,000th	χιλιοστός (khee-lee-oh-STOHS)	

Κλάσματα (KLAH-zmah-tah) Fractions

ἕνα τρίτο
(EH-nah TREE-toh)
one third

τρία τέταρτα
(TREE-ah TEH-tahr-tah)
three fourths

Conversation

1 Σᾶς ζητῶ συγγνώμη, κύριε. Σᾶς ξύπνησα χωρὶς νὰ τὸ θέλω.

2 Σᾶς παρακαλῶ, κύριε. Κοιμήθηκα μία, δύο, τρεῖς ὧρες. Δὲν θυμοῦμαι ἀκριβῶς. Τὸ τραῖνο μὲ κοιμίζει εὔκολα.

3 Αὐτὸ εἶναι σωστό. Ὁ θόρυβος τῆς μηχανῆς καὶ οἱ ρυθμικὲς κινήσεις τῶν βαγονιῶν μᾶς νανουρίζουν.

4 ῞Οταν ξεκινᾶ τὸ τραῖνο, μετρῶ τὰ τελευταῖα σπίτια τῆς πόλης[1] ὕστερα τὰ δέντρα, ὕστερα τοὺς στύλους τοῦ τηλεγράφου ... ἕνα, δύο, τρία, τέσσερα, πέντε,ἕξι, ἑφτά, ὀχτώ, ἐννιά, δέκα[2]... καὶ ἔπειτα ὁ ὕπνος ἔρχεται.

5 Αὐτὸ εἶναι πολὺ καλό. Πολλοὶ μετροῦν πρόβατα, ὅταν ἔχουν ἀϋπνία. Μετροῦν δέκα, εἴκοσι, τριάντα, ἑκατό, χίλια, ὡς τὸ πρωΐ.

6 Σὲ ποιὸ σταθμὸ θὰ κατεβῆτε;

7 Θὰ κατεβῶ στὴ Θεσσαλονίκη. Πλησιάζομε;

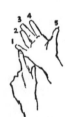

8 ῎Οχι ἀκόμη. Εἴμαστε στὸν ἕβδομο σταθμό. ῎Εχομε ἀκόμη τρεῖς σταθμούς. ᾿Αλλὰ μιὰ στιγμὴ νὰ μετρήσω. Πρῶτος, δεύτερος, τρίτος, τέταρτος, πέμπτος, ἕκτος, ἕβδομος. Μάλιστα. Μᾶς μένουν τρεῖς σταθμοί, ὁ ὄγδοος, ὁ ἔννατος καὶ ὁ δέκατος.

FOOTNOTES: *1.* The feminine nouns like πόλη , which originally were of the third declension, form the genitive in Demotic either in -ης or in -εως (as in Puristic). Those forms are used sometimes interchangeably in spoken Greek even by the same speaker. 2. Being strictly grammatical, we may say ἕνας, δύο, τρεῖς, τέσσερες, πέντε, etc. since the numbers refer to the telegraph poles which are expressed by the noun στύλοι which is a masculine noun.

1 sahs zee-TOH see-GHNOH-meen, KEE-ree-eh. sahs KSEE-pnee-sah khoh-REES nah toh THEH-loh.

2 sahs pah-rah-kah-LOH, KEE-ree-eh. kee-MEE-thee-kah MEE-ah, *THEE*-oh, *TREES* OH-rehs. *THE*HN thee-MOO-meh ah-kree-VOHS. toh TREH-noh meh kee-MEE-zee EHF-koh-lah.

3 ahf-TOH EE-neh soh-STOH. oh *THOH*-ree-vohs tees mee-kah-NEES keh ee reeth-mee-KES kee-mahs nah-noo-REE-zoon.

4 OH-tahn kseh-kee-NAH toh TREH-noh, meh-TROH tah teh-lehf-TEH-ah SPEE-tyah tees POH-lees, EE-steh-ra tah *THE*HN-drah, EE-steh-rah toos STEE-loos too tee-leh-G H R A H-foo ... E H-nah, *THE*E-oh, TREE-ah, TEH-seh-rah, PEHN-deh, EH-ksee, eh-FTAH, oh-KHTOH, eh-NYAH, *THE*H-kah ...keh EH-pee-tah oh EE-pnohs EHR-kheh-teh.

5 ahf-TOH EE-neh-poh-LEE kah-LOH. poh-LEE meh-TROON PROH-vah-tah, OH-tahn EH-khoon ah-ee-P N E E-ah. meh-TROON *THE*H-kah, EE-koh-see, tree- A H N-dah, eh-kah-TOH, KHEE-lyah, ohs toh proh-EE.

6 seh PYOH stahth-MOH thah kah-teh-VEE-teh?

7 thah kah-teh-VOH stee theh- sah-loh-NEE-kee. plee-see-AH-zoh-meh?

8 OH-khee ah-KOH-mee. EE-mah-steh stohn EHV-*th*oh-moh stahth-MOH. EH-khoh-meh ah-KOH-mee TREES stahth-MOOS. ah-LAH M Y A H steegh-M E E nah meh-TREE-soh. PROH-tohs, *THE*HF-teh-rohs, TREE-tohs, TEH-tahr-tohs, PEHM-ptohs, EH-ktohs, EHV-*th*oh-mohs. MAH-lee-stah. mahs MEH-noon TREES stahth-MEE, oh OHGH-*th*oh-ohs, oh EH-nah-tohs keh oh *THE*H-kah-tohs.

I am sorry (*lit.*, I beg your pardon), sir. I woke you up without intending to.

It is all right, sir. I slept one, two, three hours. I don't remember exactly. The train puts me to sleep easily.

That's right. The noise of the engine and the rhythmic movements of the cars make us drowsy (*lit.*, lullaby us).

When the train starts I count the last houses of the city, then the trees, then the telegraph poles ... one, two, three, four, five, six, seven, eight, nine, ten, ... and then sleep comes.

That's very. good. Many people count sheep when they suffer from insomnia. They count ten, twenty, thirty, a hundred, a thousand, until morning.

At what station will you get out? I'll get off at Salonika. Are we almost there (*lit.*, nearing)?

Not yet. We are at the seventh station. We have three more stations (to go). But just a moment, let me see (*lit.*, to count) ... first, second, third, fourth, fifth, sixth, seventh, ... Yes. There are three stations left—(*lit.*, remain to us three stations) the eighth, the ninth, and the tenth.

9 Πόση εἶναι ἡ ἀπόσταση μεταξὺ ᾿Αθηνῶν καὶ Θεσσαλονίκης;

10 Εἶναι περίπου τετρακόσια χιλιόμετρα.

11 Καλύψαμε τὰ τρία τέταρτα τοῦ δρόμου.

12 Νομίζω, ναί. Περάσαμε ἴσως τὰ τέσσερα πέμπτα.

13 Πῶς σᾶς λέγουν[3], κύριε, ἂν μοῦ ἐπιτρέπετε;

14 Μὲ λένε[3]Μιχαηλίδη. Τὸ ὄνομα μου εἶναι Σωκράτης Μιχαηλίδης. Τὸ δικό σας ὄνομα;

15 Τὸ ὄνομά μου εἶναι Οὐΐλιαμ Σμίθ. Εἶμαι ᾿Αμερικανός.

16 Κατάλαβα ὅτι εἶσθε ξένος. ᾿Αλλὰ μιλᾶτε ἀρκετὰ καλὰ τὰ ἑλληνικά.

17 ῎Οχι πολὺ καλά. Ξέρω μερικὲς ἑκατοντάδες λέξεις. Πρέπει νὰ ξέρω μερικὲς χιλιάδες, γιὰ νὰ μιλῶ καλά.

18 Νομίζω ὅτι, ὅταν ἕνας ξέρει τρεῖς—τέσσερες[2] χιλιάδες λέξεις, μπορεῖ νὰ ἐκφρασθῆ πολὺ καλά.

19 Καθὼς μοῦ μιλᾶτε, βρίσκω, ὅτι ἔχω κάποια δυσκολία στοὺς ἀριθμούς. Ἑλληνικὰ λέγουν ἕνας, μία, ἕνα, τρία, τρεῖς.

20 ῎Εχετε δίκιο. Αὐτὸ εἶναι ζήτημα (τῆς) γραμματικῆς. Λέγομε ἕνας ἄντρας, μία γυναίκα, ἕνα παιδί, τρία χιλιόμετρα, τρεῖς ὧρες, τέσσερα κορίτσια, τέσσερες στρατιῶτες. Αὐτὸ εἶναι ὅλο.

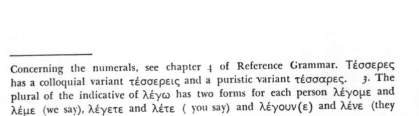

───────────
Concerning the numerals, see chapter 4 of Reference Grammar. Τέσσερες has a colloquial variant τέσσερεις and a puristic variant τέσσαρες. 3. The plural of the indicative of λέγω has two forms for each person λέγομε and λέμε (we say), λέγετε and λέτε (you say) and λέγουν(ε) and λένε (they

9 POH-see EE-neh ee ah-POH-stah-see meh-tah-KSEE ah-thee-NOHN keh theh-sah-loh-NEE-kees?

10 EE-neh peh-REE-poo teh-trah-KOH-syah khee-LYOH-meh-trah.

11 kah-LEE-psah-meh tah TREE-ah TEH-tahr-tah too *TH*ROH-moo.

12 noh-MEE-zoh NEH. peh-RAH-sah-meh EE-sohs tah TEH-seh-rah PEHM-ptah.

13 POHS sahs LEH-ghoon, KEE-ree-eh, ahn moo eh-pee-'TREH-peh-teh?

14 meh LEH-neh mee-khah-ee-LEE-*thee*. tohn oh-noh-MAH-moo EE-neh soh-KRAH-tees mee-khah-ee-LEE-*thees*. toh *th*ee-KOH-sahs OH-noh-mah?

15 toh OH-noh-MAH-moo EE-neh William Smith. EE-meh ah-meh-ree-kah-NOHS.

16 kah-TAH-lah-vah OH-tee EE-stheh KSEH-nohs. ah-LAH mee-LAH-teh ahr-keh-TAH kah-LAH tah eh-lee-nee-KAH.

17 OH-khee poh-LEE kah-LAH. KSEH-roh meh-ree-KEHS eh-kah-tohn-DAH-*th*ehs LEH-ksees. PREH-pee nah KSEH-roh meh-ree-KEHS khee-LYAH-*th*ehs yah nah mee-LOH kah-LAH.

18 noh-MEE-zoh OH-tee, OH-tahn EH-nahs KSEH-ree TREES-TEH-seh-rehs khee-LYAH-*th*ehs LEH-ksees, boh-REE nah ehk-frah-STHEE poh-LEE kah-LAH.

19 kah-THOHS moo mee-LAH-teh, VREE-skoh OH-tee EH-khoh KAH-pyah *th*ees-koh-LEE-ah stoos ah-reeth-MOOS. eh-lee-nee-KAH LEH-ghoon EH-nahs, MEE-ah, EH-nah, TREE-ah, TREES.

20 EH-kheh-teh *TH*EE-kyoh. ahf-TOH EE-neh ZEE-tee-mah (tees) ghrah-mah-tee-KEES. LEH-(ghoh-)meh EH-nahs AHN-drahs, MEE-ah yee-NEH-kah, EH-nah peh-*TH*EE, TREE-ah khee-lee-OH-meh-

What is the distance between Athens and Salonika?

It is about four hundred kilometers.

We've covered three fourths. of the way.

I think so. (*lit.*, I think, yes.) We've probably done (*lit.*, passed) four fifths.

May I ask you what your name is? (*lit.*, How do they call you, sir, if you allow me?)

I'm called Michaelides. My name is Socrates Michaelides. What is your name?

My name is William Smith. I am an American.

I see (*lit.*, understood) that you are a foreigner. But you speak Greek pretty well.

Not very well. I can speak a few hundred words. I must know a few thousand in order to speak well.

I think that when you know three, four thousand words you can express yourself very well.

As you are speaking to me I find that I have some difficulty with the numbers; in Greek they say one (masc.), one (fem.), one (neuter), three (n.), three (m. and f.)

You are right (*lit.*, you have right). That is a question of grammar. We say one (m.) man, one (f.) woman, one (n.) child, three (n.) kilometers,

21 Τώρα καταλαβαίνω. "Επειτα δὲν ἔχομε σχεδὸν καμιά διαφορά. Λέγομε πέντε ἄντρες, πέντε γυναῖκες, πέντε ἀγόρια, ἔξι στρατιῶτες, ἔξι κοπέλες, ἔξι ζῶα, ἑπτά, κ.τ.λ.

22 Οἱ ἄλλες ἀλλαγὲς εἶναι πολὺ λίγες. Λέγομε διακόσιοι ἄνδρες, διακόσιες γυναῖκες, διακόσια παιδιά.

23 Ἑλληνικὰ ἐπίσης λέγουν ὁ πρῶτος, ἡ πρώτη, τὸ πρῶτο, ὁ δεύτερος, ἡ δεύτερη, τὸ δεύτερο, ὁ δέκατος, ἡ δέκατη, τὸ δέκατο, ὁ ἑκατοστός, ἡ ἑκατοστή, τὸ ἑκατοστό.

24 Θαυμάσια. Ξέρετε ἐπίσης πῶς γράφομε ἑλληνικὰ τὰ σημεῖα στὴν πρόσθεση, τὴν ἀφαίρεση, τὸν πολλαπλασιασμὸ καὶ τὴν διαίρεση;

25 Πρόσθεση: πέντε καὶ πέντε ἴσον δέκα[4]. (5+5=10).
'Αφαίρεση: διακόσια ἔξω πενῆντα ἴσον ἑκατὸν πενῆντα. (200-50=150).
Πολλαπλασιασμός: τριάντα φορὲς δέκα ἴσον τριακόσια[5]. (30X10=300).
Διαίρεση: ἑξῆντα διὰ ἔξι ἴσον δέκα. (60:6=10).

---

say). *4.* Mathematical addition can also be expressed as πέντε καὶ πέντε κάνουν δέκα. The sign of subtraction used most frequently in schools is μεῖον or πλήν. *5.* In multiplication φορές and ἴσον may be omitted. One may say: τριάντα οἱ δέκα τριακόσια.

trah, TREES OH-rehs, TEH-seh-rah koh-REE-tsyah, TEH-seh-rehs strah-tee-OH-tehs. ahf-TOH EE-neh OH-loh.

21 TOH-rah kah-tah-lah-VEH-noh. EH-pee-tah *THE*HN EH-khoh-meh skheh-*THO*HN kah-MYAH *th*ee-ah-foh-RAH. LEH-ghoh-meh PEHN-' deh AHN-drehs, PEHN-deh yee-NEH-kehs PEHN-deh ah-GHOH-ryah, EH-ksee strah-tee-OH-tehs, EH-ksee koh-PEH-lehs. EH-ksee ZOH-ah eh-PTAH, keh-tah-lee-PAH.

22 ee AH-lehs ah-lah-YEHS EE--neh poh-LEE LEE-yehs. LEH- (ghoh-) meh *th*ee-ah-KOH-see-ee AHN-drehs, *th*ee-ah-KOH- see-ehs yee-NEH-kehs, *th*ee-ah-KOH-see-ah peh-*TH*YAH.

23 eh-lee-nee-KAH eh-PEE-sees LEH-ghoon oh PROH-tohs, ee PROH-tee, toh PROH-toh, oh THEHF-teh-rohs, ee *THE*HF-teh-ree, toh *THE*HF-teh-roh, oh *THE*H-kah-tohs, ee *THE*H-kah- tee, toh *THE*H-kah-toh, oh eh-kah-toh-STOHS, ee eh-kah-toh-STEE, toh eh-kah-toh-STOH.

24 thahv-MAH-see-ah. KSEH-reh-teh eh-PEE-sees POHS GHRAH-foh-meh eh-lee-nee-KAH tah see-MEE-ah steen PROH-stheh-see, teen ah-FEH-reh-see, tohm poh-lah-plah-see-ah-ZMOH keh teen *th*ee-EH-reh-see?

25 PROH-stheh-see: PEHN-deh keh PEHN-deh EE-sohn *THE*H-kah. ah-FEH-reh-see: *th*ee-ah-KOH-see-ah EH-ksoh peh-NEEN-dah EE-sohn eh-kah-TOHN peh-NEEN-dah.
poh-lah-plah-see-ah-ZMOHS: tree-AHN-dah foh-REHS *THE*H-kah EE-sohn tree-ah-KOH-see-ah.
*th*ee-E H-reh-see: eh-KS E EN-dah *th*ee--AH EH-ksee EE-sohn *THE*H-kah.

three (f.) hours, four (n.) girls, four (m.) soldiers. That's all.

Now I understand. Beyond that we have almost no distinction. We say five men, five women, five boys, six soldiers, six girls, six animals, seven ... etc.

The other changes are very few. We say two hundred (m.) men, two hundred (f.) women, two hundred (n.) children ...

In Greek they also say the first (m.), the first (f.), the first (n.), the second (m.), the second (f.), the second (n.), the tenth (m.), the tenth (f.), the tenth (n.), the hundredth (m.), the hundredth (f.), the hundredth (n.) ...

Wonderful! Do you also know how we write in Greek, addition, subtraction, multiplication and division signs?

Addition: five plus five equals ten.

Subtraction: two hundred minus fifty equals a hundred and fifty.

Multiplication: thirty times ten equals three hundred.

Division: sixty divided by six equals ten.

Sixth Lesson

New Vocabulary for this Lesson

χαρά (khah-RAH) joy

χρῶμα (KHROH-mah) color

οὐρανός (oo-rah-NOHS) sky

βόρειος (VOH-ree-ohs) northern

δυτικός (thee-tee-KOHS) western

γνωρίζω (ghnoh-REE-zoh) I know

ἀέρας (ah-EH-rahs) air

βουνό (voo-NOH) mountains

ἀσφαλῶς (ah-sfah-LOHS) certainly

νότιος (NOH-tee-ohs) southern

ἀνατολικός (ah-nah-toh-lee-KOHS) eastern

ἀδύνατο (ah-THEE-nah-toh) impossible

ἐργάζομαι (ehr-GHAH-zoh-meh) I work

ἐνθουσιασμένος, -η, -ο (ehn-thoo-see-ah-ZMEH-nohs) enthused, delighted

γαλανός, -η, -ο (ghah-lah-NOHS) blue

εὐχάριστος, -η, -ο (ehf-KHAH-ree-stohs) pleasant

καθαρός, -η, -ο (kah-thah-ROHS) clear, clean

ὁρίζοντας (oh-REE-zohn-dahs) horizon

ἀτμόσφαιρα (ah-TMOH-sfeh-rah) atmosphere

ἀκρογιάλι (ah-kroh-YAH-lee) seaside

γνωστός, -η, -ο (ghnoh-STOHS) well-known

ὑπέροχος, -η, -ο (ee-PEH-roh-khohs) wonderful

ἀγαπημένος, -η, -ο (ah-ghah-pee-MEH-nohs) favorite; beloved

μεγάλος, -η, -ο (meh-GHAH-lohs) great

στὴ διάθεσή μου (stee thee-AH-theh-SEE-moo) at my disposal

τὰ νέα (NEH-ah) news

προτιμῶ (proh-tee-MOH) I prefer

διάθεση (thee-AH-theh-see) mood

κλῖμα (KLEE-mah) climate

ἐστιατόριο (eh-stee-ah-TOH-ree-oh) restaurant

ἐπισκέπτομαι (eh-pee-SKEH-ptoh-meh) I visit

τακτικά (tah-ktee-KAH) regularly, often

χιλιοτραγουδισμένος, -η, -ο (khee-lyoh-trah-ghoo-thee-ZMEH-nohs) most praised

Ή (ή) μέρα   (ee MEH-rah)   The day

πρωί (proh-EE) morning
μεσημέρι (meh-see-MEH-ree) noon
ἀπόγευμα (ah-POH-yehv-mah) afternoon
βράδυ (VRAH-thee) evening
νύχτα (NEEKH-tah) night
μεσάνυχτα (meh-SAH-nee-khtah) midnight

προχθές (proh-KHTHEHS) day before yesterday
χθές (KHTHEHS) yesterday
σήμερα (SEE-meh-rah) today
αὔριο (AHV-ree-oh) tomorrow
μεθαύριο (meh-THAV-ree-oh) the day after tomorrow

μήνας (MEE-nas) month   ἑβδομάδα (ehv-thoh-MAH-thah) week
αἰώνας (eh-OH-nahs) century   ἔτος (EH-tohs) year
ἐποχή (eh-poh-KHEE) season; epoch
ἄνοιξη (AH-nee-ksee) spring
καλοκαίρι (kah-loh-KEH-ree) summer
φθινόπωρο (fthee-NOH-poh-roh) autumn
χειμώνας (khee-MOH-nahs) winter

Κυριακή (kee-ryah-KEE) Sunday   Δευτέρα (thehf-TEH-rah) Monday
Τρίτη (TREE-tee) Tuesday   Τετάρτη (teh-TAHR-tee) Wednesday
Πέμπτη (PEHM-tee) Thursday   Σάββατο (SAH-vah-toh) Saturday
Παρασκευή (pah-rah-skehv-EE) Friday

Οἱ μῆνες (ee MEE-nehs) The months
Ἰανουάριος (ee-ah-noo-AH-ree-os) January
Φεβρουάριος (feh-vroo-AH-ree-os) February
Μάρτιος (MAHR-tee-ohs) March
Ἀπρίλιος (ah-PREE-lee-ohs) April   Μάϊος (MAH-ee-ohs) May
Ἰούνιος (ee-OO-nee-ohs) June   Ἰούλιος (ee-OO-lee-ohs) July
Αὔγουστος (AHV-ghoo-stohs) August
Σεπτέμβριος (seh-PTEHM-vree-ohs) September
Ὀκτώβριος (oh-KHTOH-vree-ohs) October
Νοέμβριος (noh-EHM-vree-ohs) November
Δεκέμβριος (theh-KEHM-vree-ohs) December

CONVERSATION

1 Κύριε Σμίθ, εἶναι μεγάλη μας χαρά, ποὺ σᾶς ἔχομε μαζί μας.

2 Καὶ ἐγὼ χαίρομαι πολύ, ποὺ[1] γνωρίζω τοὺς συγγενεῖς τοῦ ἀδελφοῦ μου καὶ τῆς νύφης μου.

3 Θὰ μείνετε μαζί μας μία ἑβδομάδα, τὸ λιγώτερο.

4 Μοῦ εἶναι ἀδύνατο. Θὰ μείνω ἐδῶ τὸ Σάββατο καὶ τὴν Κυριακή. Τὴ Δευτέρα πρέπει νὰ εἶμαι στὴν Ἀθήνα. Ἡ Τρίτη, ἡ Τετάρτη, ἡ Πέμπτη καὶ ἡ Παρασκευὴ εἶναι ἡ-μέρες ποὺ πρέπει νὰ ἐργασθῶ.

5 Σᾶς ἀρέσει ἡ Ἑλλάδα, ὁ καιρός, τὸ κλῖμα;

6 Εἶμαι ἐνθουσιασμένος. Ὁ οὐρα-νὸς εἶναι γαλανός. Ἡ ἀτμόσφαι-ρα εἶναι καθαρή. Στὴν Ἀθήνα ξυπνῶ τὴν αὐγὴ καὶ χαίρομαι τὰ χρώματα στὸν ὁρίζοντα.

7 Εἶναι καλοκαίρι καὶ ὁ καιρὸς εἶναι εὐχάριστος. Ὁ Ἰούνιος, ὁ Ἰούλιος καὶ ὁ Αὔγουστος, οἱ μῆ-νες τοῦ καλοκαιριοῦ, εἶναι μῆνες ζεστοί, ἀλλὰ ἀρκετὰ εὐχάριστοι. Τὸ πρωῒ εἶναι δροσιά. Τὸ μεσημέρι εἶναι ζέ-στη. Τὸ βράδυ ὁ ἀέρας εἶναι δροσερός.

FOOTNOTES: *1.* Ποὺ is not only used as a relative pronoun (see footnote **2** of Lesson 4), but also as a conjunction in idiomatic Greek, as in this case

PRONUNCIATION	TRANSLATION

1 KEE-ree-eh Smith, EE-neh meh-GHAH-lee mahs khah- RAH, poo sahs EH-khoh-meh mah-ZEE-mahs.

2 keh eh-GHOH KHEH-roh-meh poo ghnoh-REE-zoh toos seen-geh-NEES too ah-*th*ehl-FOO-moo keh tees NEE-feez-moo.

3 thah MEE-neh-teh mah-ZEE-mahs MEE-ah ehv-*th*oh-MAH-*th*ah, toh lee-GHOH-teh-roh.

4 moo EE-neh ah-*THEE*-nah-toh. thah MEE-noh toh SAH-vah-toh keh teen-gee-ryah-KEE. tee *th*ehf-TEH-rah PREH-pee nah EE-meh steen ah-THEE-nah. ee TREE-tee, ee teh-TAHR-tee, ee PEHM-ptee keh ee pah-rah-skeh-VEE EE-neh ee-MEH-rehs poo PREH-pee nah ehr-ghah-STHOH.

5 sahs ah-REH-see ee eh-LAH-*th*ah, oh keh-ROHS, toh KLEE-mah?

6 EE-meh ehn-thoo-see-ah-ZMEH-nohs. oh oo-rah-NOHS EE-neh ghah-lah-NOHS. ee ah-TMOH-sfeh-rah EE-neh kah-thah-REE. steen ah-THEE-nah ksee-PNOH teen ahv-YEE keh KHEH-roh-meh tah KHROH-mah-tah stohn oh-REE-zohn-dah.

7 EE-neh kah-loh-KEH-ree keh oh keh-ROHS EE-neh ehf-KHAH-ree-stohs. oh ee-OO-nee-ohs, oh ee-OO-lee-ohs keh oh AHV-ghoo-stohs, ee MEE-nehs too kah-loh-keh-RYOO, EE-neh MEE-nehs zeh-STEE-ah-LAH ahr-keh-TAH ehf-KHAH-ree-stee. toh proh-EE EE-neh *th*roh-SYAH. toh meh-see-MEH-ree EE-neh ZEH-stee. toh VRAH-*th*ee oh ah-EH-rahs EE-neh *th*roh-seh-ROHS.

Mr. Smith, we are very glad (*lit.*, it is great joy to us) to have you with us.

I, also, am very glad to meet the relatives of my brother and my sister-in-law.

You will stay with us at least one week.

That's impossible. I will stay here Saturday and Sunday. On Monday I must be in Athens. Tuesday, Wednesday, Thursday and Friday are days on which I must work.

Do you like Greece, the weather, the climate?

I am delighted. The sky is blue. The atmosphere is clear. In Athens I wake at dawn and enjoy the colors on the horizon.

It is summer and the weather is pleasant. June, July and August, the summer months, are warm but quite pleasant. In the morning it is cool. At noon it is hot. In the evening the air is cool.

8 "Ολες οἱ ἐποχὲς στὴν Ἑλλάδα ἔχουν τὶς χάρες τους. Ὁ Ἀττικὸς οὐρανὸς εἶναι γνωστὸς γιὰ τὸ γαλάζιο του χρῶμα. Καὶ τὸ ὑπέροχο κλῖμα στὰ Ἑλληνικὰ βουνά, στὰ ἀκρογιάλια καὶ στὰ νησιὰ εἶναι ξακουστὸ σὲ ὅλο τὸν κόσμο.

9 Τὸ φθινόπωρο² ἐπίσης εἶναι ὡραία ἐποχή. Οἱ μῆνες τοῦ φθινοπώρου, ὁ Σεπτέμβριος, ὁ Ὀκτώβριος καὶ ὁ Νοέμβριος, μᾶς δίνουν ἡμέρες εὐχάριστες.

10 Τὸ χειμώνα³ κάνει κρύο, βρέχει πολύ, χιονίζει.

11 Στὴ βορεινὴ Ἑλλάδα ὁ χειμώνας εἶναι βαρύς. Οἱ μῆνες τοῦ χειμώνα, ὁ Δεκέμβριος, ὁ Ἰανουάριος, ὁ Φεβρουάριος⁴, εἶναι μῆνες δύσκολοι.

12 Ἡ ἄνοιξη εἶναι, ἀσφαλῶς, ἡ πιὸ καλὴ ἐποχή. "Ακουσα πολλὰ γιὰ τὴν ἄνοιξη στὴν Ἑλλάδα.

13 Ναί. Ἡ ἄνοιξη εἶναι ἡ ἀγαπημένη ἐποχή. Ὁ Μάρτιος, ὁ Ἀπρίλιος καὶ ὁ Μάϊος εἶναι μῆνες χιλιοτραγουδισμένοι.

14 Ἀλήθεια, ὅλες οἱ ἐποχὲς ἔχουν τὶς χάρες τους. Ὁ χειμώνας, τὸ καλοκαίρι, τὸ φθινόπωρο, ἡ ἄνοιξη.

where it is used as a causative conjunction. 2. Χινόπωρο is a colloquial dialectal and poetic variant of φθινόπωρο. 3. Nouns originally of the third declension as χειμών, χειμῶνος are spelled by some with a circumflex even when they are used as nouns of the first declension because the accusative χειμῶνα of the third declension takes the circumflex since the -α of the third declension is short, but in the first declension this spelling is not justified because the -α of the first declension is long. Therefore, it should be considered as such and χειμώνας should be spelled with an acute. 4. The months of the year in dialectal and poetic Greek have the following forms: Γενάρης,

8 OH-lehs ee eh-poh-KHEHS steen
eh-LAH-*th*ah EH-khoon tees
KHAH-rehs-toos. oh ah--tee-KOHS
oo-rah-NOHS EE-neh ghnoh-
STOHS yah toh ghah-LAH-zyoh-
too KHROH-mah. keh to ee-PEH-
roh-khoh KLEE-mah stah eh-lee-
nee-KAH voo-NAH, stah ah-kroh-
YAH-lyah keh stah nee-SYAH EE-
neh ksah-koo-STOH seh OH-loh
tohn-GOH-zmoh.

9 toh fthee-NOH-poh-roh eh-PEE-
sees EE-neh oh-REH-ah eh-poh-
KHEE. ee MEE-nehs too fthee-noh-
POH-roo, oh seh-PTEHM-vree-
ohs, oh oh-KTOH-vree-ohs keh oh
noh-EHM-vree-ohs mahs *TH*EE-
noon ee-MEH-rehs ehf-KHAH-ree-
stehs.

10 toh khee-MOH-nah KAH-nee
KREE-oh, VREH-khee poh-LEE,
khyoh-NEE-zee.

11 stee voh-ree-NEE eh-LAH-*th*ah oh
khee-MOH-nahs EE-neh vah-REES.
ee MEE-nehs too khee-MOH-nah
oh *th*eh-KEHM-vree-ohs, oh ee-ah-
noo-AH-ree-ohs, EE-neh MEE-nehs
*TH*EES-koh-lee.

12 ee AH-nee-ksee EE-neh ah-sfah-
LOHS ee PYOH kah-LEE eh-poh-
KHEE. AH-koo-sah poh-LAH yah
teen AH-nee-ksee steen eh-LAH-
*th*ah.

13 NEH. ee AH-nee-ksee EE-neh ee
ah-ghah-pee-MEH-nee eh-poh-
KHEE. oh MAHR-tee-ohs, oh ah-
PREE-lee-ohs keh oh MAH-ee-ohs
EE-neh MEE-nehs khee-lyoh-trah-
ghoo-*th*e-MEH-nee.

14 ah-LEE-thyah, OH-lehs ee eh-poh-
KHEHS EH-khoon tees KHAH-
rehs-toos. oh khee-MOH-nahs, toh
kah-loh-KEH-ree, toh fthee-NOH-
poh-roh, ee AH-nee-ksee.

All the seasons in Greece have their charm. The Attic sky is known for its blue color; and the excellent climate in the Greek mountains, on the shores and on the islands is famous all over the world.

Autumn is also a beautiful season. The autumn months, September, October and November give us pleasant days.

In winter it is cold (*lit.*, it does cold), it rains a great deal and it snows.
In Northern Greece the winter is severe (*lit.*, heavy). The winter months December, January, February are difficult.

Spring is certainly the best season. I've heard a great deal about spring in Greece.

Yes. Spring is the favorite season. March, April and May are the most praised (*lit.*, sung a thousand times) months.

Indeed, all the seasons have their charms. Winter, summer, autumn, spring.

15 Εἴχατε νέα ἀπὸ τὴν Ἀμερική;

16 Μάλιστα. Χθὲς πῆρα γράμμα ἀπὸ τὴν οἰκογένειά μου. Θὰ τοὺς γράψω αὔριο ἢ μεθαύριο. Σήμερα θὰ περάσωμε τὴν ἡμέρα μαζί.

17 Θέλετε νὰ ἰδοῦμε τὴν πόλη τώρα, ἢ θέλετε νὰ γευματίσωμε πρῶτα;

18 Ἔχω λίγο καιρὸ στὴ διάθεσή μου. Θὰ προτιμοῦσα νὰ ἰδῶ τὴν πόλη τώρα.

19 Πᾶμε, λοιπόν, τώρα καὶ ὕστερα παίρνομε τὸ γεῦμα μας σ' ἕνα ἑστιατόριο.

20 Πότε θὰ ἔλθη στὴν Ἑλλάδα ἡ κόρη σας καὶ τὰ παιδιά της;

21 Μᾶς γράφουν, ὅτι θὰ ἔλθουν τὸν ἄλλο χρόνο, τὸ καλοκαίρι.

22 Πέρυσι ἢ προπέρυσι ἦταν ἐδῶ ὁ ἀδελφός σας;

23 Ἦταν ἐδῶ πρὶν δυὸ χρόνια. Ἐφέτος εἶμαι ἐγώ. Ὅπως βλέπετε, ἡ οἰκογένειά μου ἐπισκέπτεται τακτικά[5] τὴν Ἑλλάδα.

Φλεβάρης, Μάρτης, Ἀπρίλης, Μάης, Ἰούνης (Θεριστής), Ἰούλης (Ἀλωνάρης), Αὔγουστος, Σεπτέμβρης, Ὀκτώβρης, Νοέμβρης and Δεκέμβρης. 5. Consonant clusters of two stops or two fricatives become clusters of fricative plus stop in colloquial speech; in other words, πτ becomes φτ (as ἑπτά⟩ ἐφτά), κτ⟩ χτ (as ὀκτώ⟩ ὀχτώ); φθ⟩ φτ (φθάνω⟩ φτάνω); χθ⟩ χτ (χθές⟩χτές), σθ⟩ στ (πιάσθηκε⟩ πιάστηκε [he was caught]), σχ⟩ σκ (ἄσχημος⟩ ἄσκημος).

15 EE-khah-teh NEH-ah ah-POH teen ah-meh-ree-KEE?

Have you had any news from America?

16 MAH-lee-stah. KHTHEHS PEE-rah GHRAH-mah ah-POH teen ee-koh-YEH-nee-AH-moo. thah toos GHRAH-psoh AHV-ree-oh EE meh-THAHV-ree-oh. SEE-meh-rah thah peh-RAH-soh-meh teen ee-MEH-rah mah-ZEE.

Yes. I had a letter from my family. I will write them tomorrow or the day after tomorrow. Today we shall spend the day together.

17 THEH-leh-teh nah ee-*TH*OO-meh teem-BOH-lee TOH-rah EE THEH-leh-teh nah yehv-mah-TEE-soh-meh PROH-tah?

Do you want to see the city now or do you want to have lunch (*lit.*, to dine) first?

18 EH-khoh LEE-ghoh keh-ROH stee *th*ee-*ah*-theh-SEE-moo. thah proh-tee-MOO-sah nah ee-*TH*OH teem-BOH-lee TOH-rah.

I have a little time (at my disposal) and I would rather see the city now.

19 PAH-meh, lee-POHN, TOH-rah keh EE-steh-rah PEHR-noh-meh toh YEHV-mah-mahs SEH-nah eh-stee-ah-TOH-ree-oh.

Let's go then, now, and we will have our lunch at a restaurant.

20 POH-teh thah EHL-thee steen eh-LAH-*th*ah ee KOH-ree-sahs keh tah peh-*TH*YAH-tees?

When will your daughter come to Greece with her children?

21 mahs GHRAH-foon OH-tee thah EHL-thoon tohn AH-loh KHROH-noh, toh kah-loh-KEH-ree.

They write us that they will come in the summer, next year.

22 PEH-ree-see EE proh-PEH-ree-see EE-tahn eh-*TH*OH oh ah-*th*ehl-FOHS-sahs?

Was your brother here last year, or the year before?

23 EE-tahn eh-*TH*OH preen *TH*YOH KHROH-nyah. eh-FEH-tohs EE-meh eh-GHOH. OH-pohs VLEH-peh-teh, ee ee-koh-YEH-nee-AH-moo eh-pee-SKEH-pteh-teh tah-ktee-KAH teen eh-LAH-*th*ah.

He was here two years ago. This year I am here. As you see, my family visits Greece regularly.

EBΔOMO MAΘHMA

Seventh Lesson

New Vocabulary for this Lesson

ξεχνῶ (ksehkh-NOH) I forget
ἀνάγκη (ah-NAHN-gee) need
περίπου (peh-REE-poo) about
ἀργά (ahr-GHAH) late, slowly
ἐννοῶ (eh-noh-OH) I mean

ἐλπίζω (ehl-PEE-zoh) I hope
φθάνω (FTHAH-noh) I arrive
ἐνωρίς (eh-noh-REES) early
κρύβω (KHREE-voh) I hide
πετῶ (peh-TOH) I fly

φιλοξενία (fee-loh-kseh-NEE-ah) hospitality
ἐνθύμιο (ehn-THEE-mee-oh) souvenir
ἀεροπλάνο (ah-eh-roh-PLAH-noh) airplane
καθυστέρηση (kah-thee-STEH-ree-see) delay
βιάζομαι (vee-AH-zoh-meh) I am in a hurry

ξυπνητήρι (ksee-pnee-TEE-ree) alarm clock

Τὸ ρολόϊ (toh roh-LOH-ee) The clock

ἐλατήριο (eh-lah-TEE-ree-oh) spring

γρήγορα (GHREE-ghoh-rah) soon, fast
χαζεύω (khah-ZHEV-oh) I loaf; I gaze; I gape
χαίρομαι (KHEH-roh-meh) I rejoice
χαίρω (KHEH-roh) I am glad

παντοῦ (pahn-DOO) everywhere   δείκτης (*TH*EE-ktees) hand (of a clock)
χρῆμα (KHREE-mah) money   γυαλί (yah-LEE) glass
λεπτό (leh-PTOH) minute   κουρδίζω (koor-*TH*EE-zoh) I wind

δευτερόλεπτο (*th*ehf-teh-ROH-leh-ptoh) second
διορθώνω (*th*ee-ohr-THOH-noh) I repair
ἀναχωρῶ (ah-nah-khoh-ROH) I depart
ἡ ὥρα (OH-rah) hour   φθάνω (FTHAH-noh) I arrive
σιγά (see-GHAH) slow   χρ(ε)ωστῶ (kh'r (eh) oh-STOH) I owe

(ὡ)ρολό(γ)ι ([oh-]roh-LOH-yee) clock, watch
τὸ ρολόϊ τοῦ χεριοῦ (...too kheh-RYOO) wrist watch
τὸ ρολόϊ τῆς τσέπης (...tees TSEH-pees) pocket watch

CONVERSATION

1 Εἶναι ἡ ὥρα νὰ ἀναχωρήσω. Σᾶς εὐχαριστῶ θερμὰ γιὰ τὴ φιλοξενία.

2 Ἐλπίζομε νὰ σᾶς ἰδοῦμε καὶ πάλι στὴ Θεσσαλονίκη.

3 Τὶ ὥρα εἶναι, ἀκριβῶς, σᾶς παρακαλῶ; Νομίζω, ὅτι τὸ ρολόϊ μου μένει πίσω.

4 Ἡ ὥρα εἶναι τρεῖς καὶ εἰκοσιδύο λεπτά, ἀκριβῶς.

 5 Τὸ ρολόϊ μου μένει πίσω δέκα λεπτά. Πρέπει νὰ τὸ δώσω στὸν ὡρολογᾶ νὰ τὸ διορθώση. Εἶναι ἀρκετὰ παλιὸ καὶ ξεχνῶ νὰ τὸ κουρδίζω τακτικά. Εἶναι (ἕνα) ἐνθύμιο.

6 Τὶ ὥρα φεύγει τὸ ἀεροπλάνο; Ποιά ὥρα πρέπει νὰ εἶσθε στὸ ἀεροδρόμιο;

7 Τὸ ἀεροπλάνο φεύγει στὶς πέντε καὶ μισή. Ἐλπίζω, ὅτι δὲν ἔχει καθυστέρηση.

8 Τότε ἔχετε ἀρκετὸ καιρό. Δὲν εἶναι ἀνάγκη νὰ βιασθοῦμε.

9 Πόση ὥρα θὰ μοῦ πάρη γιὰ νὰ φθάσω στὸ ἀεροδρόμιο;

10 Τὸ λεωφορεῖο τῆς ἑταιρίας κάμει σαράντα πέντε λεπτὰ περίπου. Φθάνει ἐκεῖ εἴκοσι ὡς εἰκοσιπέντε λεπτὰ πρὸ

PRONUNCIATION

1 EE-neh ee OH-rah nah ah-nah-khoh-REE-soh. sahs ehf-khah-ree-STOH thehr-MAH yah tee fee-loh-kseh-NEE-ah.

2 ehl-PEE-zoh-meh nah sahs ee-*TH*OO-meh keh PAH-lee stee theh-sah-loh-NEE-kee.

3 TEE OH-rah EE-neh, ah-kree-VOHS, sahs pah-rah-kah-LOH? noh-MEE-zoh OH-tee toh roh-LOH-ee-moo MEH-nee PEE-soh.

4 EE OH-rah EE-neh TREES keh ee-koh-see-*TH*EE-oh leh-PTAH, ah-kree-VOHS.

5 toh roh-LOH-ee-moo MEH-nee PEE-soh *TH*EH-kah leh-PTAH. PREH-pee nah toh THOH-soh stohn oh-roh-LOH-ghah nah toh *th*ee-ohr-THOH-see. EE-neh ahr-keh-TAH pah-LYOH keh kseh-KHNOH nah toh koor-*TH*EE-zoh tah-ktee-kah. EE-neh EH-nah ehn-*TH*EE-mee-oh.

6 TEE OH-rah FEHV-yee toh ah-eh-roh-PLAH-noh? PYAH OH-rah PREH-pee nah EE-stheh stoh ah-eh-roh-*TH*ROH-mee-oh?

7 toh ah-eh-roh-PLAH-noh FEHV-yee stees PEHN-deh keh mee-SEE. ehl-PEE-zoh OH-tee *th*ehn EH-khee kah-thee-STEH-ree-see.

8 TOH-teh EH-kheh-teh ahr-keh-TOH keh-ROH. *TH*EHN EE-neh ah-NAHN-gee nah vee-ah-STHOO-meh.

9 POH-see OH-rah thah moo PAH-ree yah nah FTHAH-soh stoh ah-eh-roh-*TH*ROH-mee-oh?

10 toh leh-oh-foh-REE-oh tees eh-teh-REE-ahs KAH-mee sah-RAHN-dah PEHN-deh leh-PTAH peh-REE-poo. FTHAH-nee eh-KEE EE-koh-

TRANSLATION

It is time to leave. Thank you very much for your hospitality.

We hope to see you again in Salonika.

What is the exact time (*lit.*, what hour is it exactly), please? I think my watch is slow (*lit.*, stays behind).

The time is exactly twenty-two minutes past three (*lit.*, three and twenty-two minutes).

My watch is ten minutes slow. I must give it to the watchmaker for repairs. It's pretty (*lit.*, sufficiently) old, and I forget to wind it regularly. It is a souvenir.

What time does the plane leave? What time do you have to be at the airport?

The plane leaves at half past five (*lit.*, five and half), I hope it is not behind schedule (*lit.*, that it does not have a delay).

Then you have enough time. There is no need to hurry.

How long (*lit.*, how much hour) will it take to get to the airport?

The airline company bus takes about forty-five minutes. It gets there from twenty to twenty-five minutes before the flight.

τῆς ἀπογειώσεως τοῦ ἀεροπλάνου. Τὸ ταξὶ φθάνει δέκα ὡς δεκαπέντε λεπτὰ πιὸ γρήγορα.

11 Θὰ πάρω ἕνα ταξί. Ἡ ὥρα εἶναι τρεῖς καὶ εἰκοσιπέντε ἀκριβῶς. Θὰ φθάσω στὸ ἀεροδρόμιο στὶς τέσσερες περίπου.

12 Λοιπόν, δὲν εἶναι νωρὶς νὰ φύγετε ἀμέσως τώρα; Ἔχετε στὴ διάθεσή σας δυὸ ὧρες περίπου.

13 Προτιμῶ νὰ φύγω. Θέλω νὰ ἔχω λίγη ὥρα στὴ διάθεσή μου, γιὰ νὰ ἰδῶ τὸ ἀεροδρόμιο. Δὲν σᾶς κρύβω, ὅτι μοῦ ἀρέσει πολὺ νὰ χαζεύω στοὺς σταθμούς, στὰ ἀεροδρόμια, στὰ λιμάνια.

14 Στὸ καλό. Καλὸ ταξίδι.
15 Σᾶς εὐχαριστῶ πολὺ καὶ σᾶς ἀφήνω ὑγεία.

16 Ταξί, ταξί! Γιὰ τὸ ἀεροδρόμιο, σᾶς παρακαλῶ. Βιάζομαι. Θὰ πάρω τὸ ἀεροπλάνο τῶν πέντε καὶ μισὴ γιὰ τὴν Ἀθήνα.

17 Μάλιστα, κύριε, ἀλλὰ ἔχομε ἀρκετὴ ὥρα. Σὲ λίγα δευτερόλεπτα θὰ εἴμαστε στὸ ἀεροδρόμιο.

18 Σὲ λίγα δευτερόλεπτα; Τὶ ἐννοεῖτε; Θὰ πετάξωμε;

see ohs ee-koh-see-PEHN-deh leh-
PTAH proh tees ah-poh-yee-OH-
seh-ohs too ah-eh-roh-PLAH-noo.
toh tah-KSEE FTHAH-nee *TH*EH-
kah ohs *th*eh-kah-PEHN-deh leh-
PTAH PYOH GHREE-ghoh-rah.

11 thah PAH-roh EH-nah tah-KSEE.
ee OH-rah EE-neh TREES keh
ee-k o h-s ee-P E H N-d e h   ah-kree-
VOHS, thah FTHAH-soh stoh ah-
eh-roh-*TH*ROH-mee-oh stees TEH-
seh-rehs peh-REE-poo.

12 lee-POHN, *TH*EHN EE-neh noh-
REES nah FEE-yeh-teh ah-MEH-
sohs TOH-rah? EH-kheh-teh stee
*th*ee-*ah*-theh-*see*-s a h s   *TH*EE-o h
OH-rehs peh-REE-poo.

13 proh-tee-MOH   nah   FEE-ghoh.
THEH-loh nah EH-khoh LEE-yee
OH-rah stee *th*ee-*ah*-theh-*see*-moo,
yah nah ee-*TH*OH toh ah-eh-roh-
*TH*ROH-mee-oh. *TH*EHN sahs
KREE-voh OH-tee moo ah-REH-
see poh-LEE nah khah-ZEH-voh
stoos stahth-MOOS, stah ah-eh-roh-
*TH*ROH-mee-ah, stah lee-MAH-
nyah.

14 stoh kah-L O H kah-L O H tah-
KSEE-*th*ee.

15 sahs ehf-khah-ree-STOH poh-LEE
keh sahs ah-FEE-noh ee-YEE-ah.

16 tah-KSEE, tah-KSEE. yah toh ah-
eh-roh-*TH*ROH-mee-oh, sahs pah-
rah-kah-LOH. VYAH-zoh-meh. thah
PAH-roh toh ah-eh-roh-PLAH-noh
tohn PEHN-deh keh mee-SEE yah
teen ah-*TH*EE-nah.

17 MAH-lee-stah, KEE-ree-eh, ah-LAH
EH-khoh-meh ahr-keh-TEE OH-
rah. seh LEE-ghah *th*ehf-teh-ROH-
leh-ptah thah EE-mah-steh stoh
ah-eh-roh-*TH*ROH-mee-oh.

18 seh LEE-ghah *th*ehf-teh-ROH-leh-
ptah? TEE eh-noh-EE-teh? thah
peh-TAH-ksoh-meh?

The taxi gets there ten or fifteen minutes faster.

I will take a taxi. The time is
now twenty-five past three exactly. I will get to the airport
at about four.

Then, is it not too early to leave
right now? You have (*lit.,* you
have at your disposal) about
two hours.

I prefer to leave. I want to have
a little time to see the airport.
I don't keep it a secret (*lit.*
hide it) that I like looking at
stations, airports, ports.

Good-bye (*lit.,* to the good). Bon
voyage.

Thank you very much and good-
bye.

Taxi, taxi! To the airport please.
I am in a hurry. I am taking
(*lit.* will take) the five thirty
plane to Athens.

Yes, sir, but we have enough
time. In a few seconds we will
be at the airport.

In a few seconds? What do you
mean? Are we going to fly?

19 Ἐννοῶ, σὲ λίγα λεπτὰ τῆς ὥρας. Σὲ δεκαπέντε ὡς εἴ- κοσι λεπτὰ τῆς ὥρας.

20 Τώρα καταλαβαίνω. Γιὰ μιὰ στιγμὴ νόμισα, ὅτι ἡ ὥρα ἐδῶ ἔχει ἑξῆντα δευτερόλεπτα.

21 Ὄχι, κύριε. Ἡ ὥρα παντοῦ εἶναι ἡ ἴδια. Ἔχει ἑξῆντα πρῶτα λεπτά. Κάθε πρῶτο λεπτὸ ἔχει ἑξῆντα δευτερό- λεπτα, ἂν δὲν κάνω λάθος.

22 Πολὺ σωστά, φίλε μου. Ἀλλὰ φοβοῦμαι, ὅτι παντοῦ, οἱ ὁδηγοὶ τῶν αὐτοκινήτων κάνουν τὰ πρῶτα λεπτὰ δευ- τερόλεπτα.

23 Ὁ χρόνος εἶναι χρῆμα.

24 Πιὸ σιγά, σᾶς παρακαλῶ, γιὰ νὰ χαροῦμε τὴν διαδρομή.

25 Τὸ ἀεροδρόμιο, κύριε. Ἡ ὥρα εἶναι τέσσερες παρὰ δέκα λεπτά. Ἡ διαδρομὴ μᾶς πῆρε εἰκοσιπέντε λεπτά.

26 Τὶ σᾶς χρωστῶ;

27 Εἴκοσι δραχμὲς καὶ πενῆντα λεπτά.

28 Καλησπέρα, δεσποινίς. Τί ὥρα ἀνα- χωρεῖ τὸ ἀεροπλάνο γιὰ τὴν Ἀθήνα;

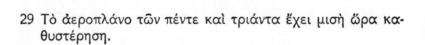

29 Τὸ ἀεροπλάνο τῶν πέντε καὶ τριάντα ἔχει μισὴ ὥρα κα- θυστέρηση.

19 eh-noh-OH, seh LEE-ghah leh-PTAH tees OH-rahs. seh *th*eh-kah-PEHN-deh ohs EE-koh-see leh-PTAH tees OH-rahs.

I mean in a few minutes (*lit.*, minutes of the hour), from fifteen to twenty minutes.

20 TOH-rah kah-tah-lah-VEH-noh. yah myah stee-GHMEE NOH-mee-sah, OH-tee ee OH-rah eh-*TH*OH EH-khee eh-KSEEN-dah *th*ehf-teh-ROH-leh-ptah.

Now I understand. For a moment I thought that the hour here has sixty seconds.

21 OH-khee, KEE-ree-eh. ee OH-rah pahn-DOO EE-neh ee EE-*th*yah. EH-khee eh-KSEEN-dah PROH-tah leh-PTAH. KAH-theh PROH-toh leh-PTOH EH-khee eh-KSEEN-dah *th*ehf-teh-ROH-leh-ptah, ahn *TH*EHN KAH-noh LAH-thohs.

No, sir. The hour is the same everywhere. It has sixty (first) minutes. In each minute, there are sixty seconds, if I am not mistaken.

22 poh-LEE soh-STAH, FEE-leh-moo. ah-LAH foh-VOO-meh OH-tee pahn-DOO ee oh-*th*ee-YEE tohn ahf-toh-kee-NEE-tohn KAH-noon tah PROH-tah leh-PTAH *th*ehf-teh-ROH-leh-ptah.

Very correct, my friend, but I am afraid that motorists, everywhere, make the minutes seconds.

23 oh KHROH-nohs EE-neh KHREE-mah.

Time is money.

24 PYOH see-GHAH, sahs pah-rah-kah-LOH, yah nah khah-ROO-meh tee *th*ee-ah-*th*roh-MEE.

Slower, please, so that we may enjoy the trip.

25 toh ah-eh-roh-*TH*ROH-mee-oh, KEE-ree-eh. ee OH-rah EE-neh TEH-seh-rehs pah-RAH *TH*EH-kah leh-PTAH. ee *th*ee-ah-*th*roh-mee mahs PEE-reh ee-koh-see-PEHN-deh leh-PTAH.

Here is the airport, sir. The time is ten minutes to four. It (*lit.*, the trip) took us about twenty-five minutes.

26 TEE shahs khroh-STOH?

What do I owe you?

27 EE-koh see *th*rahkh-MEHS keh peh-NEEN-dah leh-PTAH.

Twenty drachmas and fifty cents.

28 kah-lee-SPEH-rah, *th*eh-spee-NEES. TEE OH-rah ah-nah-khoh-REE toh ah-eh-roh-PLAH-noh yah teen ah-THEE-nah?

Good evening, miss. What time does the plane leave for Athens?

29 toh ah-eh-roh-PLAH-noh tohn PEHN-deh keh tree-AHN-dah EH-khee mee-SEE OH-rah kah-thee-STEH-ree-see.

The five-thirty plane is half an hour late (*lit.*, has a half an hour delay).

ΟΓΔΟΟ ΜΑΘΗΜΑ
Eighth Lesson

New Vocabulary for this Lesson

ἐπιτρέπω (eh-pee-TREH-poh) I allow
ὁ ἐπισκέπτης (eh-pee-SKEH-ptees) visitor
ἡ ἐπιτυχία (eh-pee-tee-KHEE-ah) success
ἡ ἐκμάθηση (ehk-MAH-thee-see) the learning of
ὑπερβάλλω (ee-pehr-VAH-loh) I exaggerate

κρίνω (KREE-noh) I judge
ἄλλωστε (AH-loh-steh) after all
ἐπιμένω (eh-pee-MEH-noh) I insist
σχέση (SKHEH-see) relation
καπνά (kah-PNAH) tobacco

ἄν (AHN) if
ἄν καὶ (AHN KEH) although
καλύπτω (kah-LEE-ptoh) I cover
σιτηρά (see-tee-RAH) cereals
ὀρυκτά (oh-ree-KTAH) minerals

ἡ κίνηση (KEE-nee-see) activity, movement
σημαντικός, -ή, -ό (see-mahn-dee-KOHS) important
λειτουργῶ (lee-toor-GHOH) I function
ἀσχολοῦμαι (ah-skhoh-LOO-meh) I deal with
διευθύνω (thee-ehf-THEE-noh) I direct, I manage

ἐνδιαφέρων, -ουσα, -ον (ehn-thee-ah-FEH-rohn) interesting
ὑποχρεωμένος, -η, -ο (ee-poh-khreh-oh-MEH-nohs) obliged
ἐκλεκτός, -ή, -ό (eh-kleh-KTOHS) excellent
κάνω λάθος (KAH-noh LAH-thohs) I am mistaken
ἐξαρτῶμαι ἀπὸ (eh-ksahr-TOH-meh) I depend upon
μεγαλώνω (meh-ghah-LOH-noh) I increase, I grow
μειώνομαι (mee-OH-noh-meh) I decrease
περιορισμένος, -η, -ο (peh-ree-oh-ree-ZMEH-nohs) limited
ἐξαρτήματα (eh-ksahr-TEE-mah-tah) accessories
προχωρῶ (proh-khoh-ROH) I continue, proceed

συγκεντρωμένος, -η, -ο
(seen-gehn-droh-MEH-nohs) concentrated, centered

84

'Εμπόριο   (ehm-BOH-ree-oh)   Trade

έμπορικός, -ή, -ό   (ehm-boh-ree-KOHS)   commercial
ύφάσματα   (ee-FAH-zmah-tah)   fabrics
μάλλινα   (MAH-lee-nah)   (of) wool
μεταξωτά   (meh-tah-ksoh-TAH)   (of) silk, silken
βαμβακερά   (vahm-vah-keh-RAH)   (of) cotton
βαμβάκι   (vahm-VAH-kee)   cotton

έξοικειωμένος, -η, -ο   (eh-ksee-kee-oh-MEH-nohs)   familiar
τὸ έθνικὸ εἰσόδημα   (eh-thnee-KOH ee-SOH-thee-mah)   national income
ὁ ἔμπορος   (EHM-boh-rohs) the merchant
ὁ ἰδιοκτήτης   (ee-thee-oh-KTEE-tees)   owner

ὁ συνέταιρος   (see-NEH-teh-rohs)   partner
τὸ συνάλλαγμα   (see-NAH-lahgh-mah)   exchange
τὰ οἰκονομικά   (ee-koh-noh-mee-KAH)   finances
ἡ βιομηχανία   (vee-oh-mee-khah-NEE-ah)   industry
ἡ γεωργία   (yeh-ohr-YEE-ah)   agriculture

μηχανή   (mee-khah-NEE)   machine   τὸ προϊόν   (proh-ee-OHN)   product
εἰσάγω   (ee-SAH-ghoh)   I import   έξάγω   (eh-KSAH-ghoh)   I export
ἀγοράζω   (ah-ghoh-RAH-zoh)   I buy   πωλῶ or πουλῶ   (poo-LOH)   I sell
ὁ οἶκος   (EE-kohs)   house   τὸ γραφεῖο   (ghrah-FEE-oh)   office

τὰ έμπορεύματα   (ehm-boh-REHV-mah-tah)   goods
τὸ έργοστάσιο   (ehr-ghoh-STAH-see-oh)   factory
παράγω   (pah-RAH-ghoh)   I produce
ἡ παραγωγή   (pah-rah-ghoh-YEE)   production
ἡ εἰσαγωγή   (ee-sah-ghoh-YEE)   import

ἡ έξαγωγή   (eh-ksah-ghoh-YEE)   export
προμηθεύω   (proh-mee-THEHV–oh)   I provide
τὸ παράρτημα   (pah-RAHR-tee-mah)   branch (of a firm)
ἡ έταιρία   (eh-teh-REE-ah)   company
ὑπογράφω   (ee-poh-GHRAH-foh)   I sign

ἡ ὑπογραφή   (ee-poh-ghrah-FEE)   signature
ἡ άλληλογραφία   (ah-lee-loh-ghrah-FEE-ah)   correspondence
ἡ δακτυλογράφος   (thah-ktee-loh-GHRAH-fohs)   typist
ἡ γραμματεύς   (ghrah-mah-TEHFS)   secretary
ὑπαγορεύω   (ee-pah-ghoh-REHV-oh)   I dictate

CONVERSATION

1 Κύριε Σμίθ, ἐπιτρέψετέ μου νὰ σᾶς συστήσω τὸ φίλο μου κύριο Οἰκονομίδη. Ὁ κύριος Εὐριπίδης Οἰκονομίδης, ἔμπορος. Ὁ κύριος Οὐΐλιαμ Σμίθ, ἀπὸ τὶς Ἡνωμένες Πολιτεῖες τῆς Ἀμερικῆς.

2 Χαίρω πολύ, κύριε Σμίθ.

3 Χαίρω πολύ, κύριε Οἰκονομίδη.

4 Ὁ φίλος μας κύριος Πετρίδης μοῦ μίλησε γιὰ σᾶς, γιὰ τὸ ταξίδι σας στὴ Θεσσαλονίκη, γιὰ τὴν ἐπιτυχία σας στὴν ἐκμάθηση τῆς ἑλληνικῆς γλώσσας.

5 Ὁ κύριος Πετρίδης εἶναι ἕνας πολὺ καλὸς φίλος. Ἔτσι, φοβοῦμαι, ὑπερβάλλει λίγο.

6 Πῶς περάσατε στὴ Θεσσαλονίκη; Σᾶς ἄρεσε ἡ πόλη;

7 Πέρασα ἐκεῖ ἕνα εὐχάριστο Σαββατοκύριακο. Ἡ Θεσσαλονίκη εἶναι ὡραία πόλη. Ἂν κρίνω ἀπὸ τὴν κίνηση στὸ σταθμὸ τοῦ σιδηροδρόμου, στὸ λιμάνι, στὴν ἀγορά, στὸ ἀεροδρόμιο, νομίζω, ὅτι ἡ πόλη αὐτὴ εἶναι ἕνα σημαντικὸ ἐμπορικὸ κέντρο.

8 Βεβαιότατα. Ἡ Θεσσαλονίκη εἶναι ἡ δεύτερη μεγάλη ἐμπορικὴ πόλη. Ἄλλωστε, αὐτὸς εἶναι ὁ λόγος ποὺ γίνεται ἐκεῖ ἡ Διεθνὴς Ἔκθεσις.

PRONUNCIATION	TRANSLATION

1 KEE-ree-eh Smith, eh-pee-TREH-ps (eh) -teh-moo nah sahs see-STEE-soh toh FEE-loh-moo KEE-ree-oh ee-koh-noh-MEE-*th*ee. oh KEE-ree-ohs ehv-ree-PEE-*th*ees ee-koh-noh-MEE-*th*ees, EHM-boh-rohs. oh KEE-ree-ohs William Smith, eh-pee-SKEH-ptees ah-POH tees ee-noh-MEH-nehs poh-lee-TEE-ehs tees ah-meh-ree-KEES.

Mr. Smith, allow me to introduce you to my friend Mr. Economides. Mr. Euripides Economides, a businessman. Mr. William Smith, from the United States of America.

2 KHEH-roh poh-LEE, KEE-ree-eh Smith.

I am very glad to meet you, (*lit.,* I am very glad,) Mr. Smith.

3 KHEH-roh poh-LEE, KEE-ree-eh ee-koh-noh-MEE-*th*ee.

I am very glad, Mr. Economides.

4 oh FEE-lohz-moo KEE-ree-ohs peh-TREE-*th*ees moo MEE-lee-seh yah sahs, yah toh tah-KSEE-*th*ee-sahs stee theh-sah-loh-NEE-kee, yah teen eh-pee-tee-KHEE-ah-sahs steen ehk-MAH-thee-see tees eh-lee-nee-KEES GHLOH-sahs.

Our friend Mr. Petrides spoke to me about you, about your trip to Salonika, about your success in learning the Greek language.

5 oh KEE-ree-ohs peh-TREE-*th*ees EE-neh EH-nahs poh-LEE kah-LOHS FEE-lohs. EH-tsee, foh-VOO-meh, ee-pehr-VAH-lee LEE-ghoh.

Mr. Petrides is a very good friend, so, I am afraid he exaggerates a little.

6 POHS peh-RAH-sah-teh stee theh-sah-loh-NEE-kee? sahs AH-reh-seh ee POH-lee?

Did you have a good time (how did you pass) in Salonika? Did you like the city?

7 PEH-rah-sah eh-KEE EH-nah ehf-KHAH-ree-stoh sah-vah-toh-KEE-ryah-koh. ee theh-sah-loh-NEE-kee EE-neh oh-REH-ah POH-lee. ahn KREE-noh ah-POH teen-GEE-nee-see stoh stahth-MOH too see-*th*ee-roh-*TH*ROH-moo, stoh lee-MAH-nee, steen ah-ghoh-RAH, stoh ah-eh-roh-*TH*ROH-mee-oh, noh-MEE-zoh OH-tee ee POH-lee ahf-TEE EE-nah see-mahn-dee-KOH ehm-boh-ree-KOH KEHN-droh.

I spent a pleasant week-end there. Salonika is a beautiful city. Judging by the activity at the railroad station, in the harbor, at the market, and the airport, I would say that this city is an important commercial center.

8 veh-veh-OH-tah-tah. ee theh-sah-loh-NEE-kee EE-neh ee *TH*EHF-teh-ree meh-GHAH-lee ehm-boh-ree-KEE POH-lee. AH-loh-steh, ahf-

Of course. Salonika is the second largest commercial city in Greece. After all, that is the

9 Τὶ παράγει κυρίως ἡ Μακεδονία;

10 Παράγει σιτηρὰ καὶ κυρίως καπνά. Ἡ Θεσσαλονίκη εἶναι ἕνα μεγάλο κέντρο ἐξαγωγῆς καπνοῦ. Εἶναι, ἐπίσης, τὸ μεγαλύτερο κέντρο εἰσαγωγῆς τῆς Βορείου Ἑλλάδος.

11 Ἡ βιομηχανία τῆς Βορείου Ἑλλάδος εἶναι συγκεντρωμένη στὴ Θεσσαλονίκη;

12 Μάλιστα. Στὴν πόλη αὐτὴ λειτουργοῦν πολλὰ ἐργοστάσια. Ἡ βιομηχανία ὅμως τῶν μαλλίνων, τῶν βαμβακερῶν καὶ τῶν μεταξωτῶν ὑφασμάτων εἶναι συγκεντρωμένη στὶς γειτονικὲς πόλεις.

13 Σεῖς, κύριε Οἰκονομίδη, μὲ ποιὸ ἐμπορικὸ κλάδο ἀσχολεῖσθε;

14 Διευθύνω τὴν ἑταιρία εἰσαγωγῶν καὶ ἐξαγωγῶν «Ἑρμῆς».

15 Εἶναι πολὺ ἐνδιαφέρον. "Αν καὶ δὲν εἶμαι ἔμπορος, μπορῶ ἀσφαλῶς νὰ μάθω μερικὰ ἐνδιαφέροντα πράγματα γιὰ τὴν οἰκονομικὴ ζωὴ τῆς χώρας σας.

16 Εὐχαρίστως. Εἶμαι ἔτοιμος νὰ σᾶς ἀπαντήσω, ἂν δὲν

TOHS EE-neh oh LOH-ghohs poo YEE-neh-teh eh-KEE ee *th*ee-eth-NEES EHK-theh-sees.

9 TEE pah-RAH-yee kee-REE-ohs ee mah-keh-*th*oh-NEE-ah?

10 pah-RAH-yee see-tee-RAH keh kee-REE-ohs kah-PNAH. ee theh-sah-loh-NEE-kee EE-neh EH-nah meh-GHAH-loh KEHN-droh eh-ksah-ghoh-YEES kah-PNOO. EE-neh, eh-PEE-sees, toh meh-ghah-LEE-teh-roh KEHN-droh ee-sah-ghoh-YEES tees voh-REE-oo eh-LAH-*th*ohs.

11 ee vee-oh-mee-khah-NEE-ah tees voh-REE-oo eh-LAH-*th*ohs EE-neh seen-gehn-droh-MEH-nee stee theh-sah-loh-NEE-kee?

12 mah-LEE-stah. steem POH-lee ahf-TEE lee-toor-GHOON poh-LAH ehr-ghoh-STAH-see-ah. ee vee-oh-mee-khah-NEE-ah OH-mohs tohn mah-LEE-nohn, tohn vahm-vah-keh-ROHN keh tohn meh-tah-ksoh-TOHN ee-fah-ZMAH-tohn EE-neh seen-gehn-droh-MEH-nee stees yee-toh-nee-KEHS POH-lees.

13 SEES, KEE-ree-eh ee-koh-noh-MEE-*th*ee, meh PYOH ehm-boh-ree-KOH KLAH-*th*oh ah-skhoh-LEE-stheh?

14 *th*ee-ehf-THEE-noh teen eh-teh-REE-ah ee-sah-ghoh-GHOHN keh eh-ksah-ghoh-GHOHN ehr-MEES.

15 EE-neh poh-LEE ehn-*th*ee-ah-FEH-rohn. ahn keh *THE*HN EE-meh EHM-boh-rohs, boh-ROH ah-sfah-LOHS nah MAH-thoh meh-ree-KAH ehn-*th*ee-ah-FEH-rohn-dah PRAHGH-mah-tah yah teen ee-koh-noh-mee-KEE zoh-EE tees KHOH-rah-sahs.

16 ehf-khah-REE-stohs. EE-meh EH-tee-mohs nah sahs ah-pahn-dee-soh, ahn *THE*HN eh-pee-MEH-

reason that the International Fair takes place (*lit.*, is made) there.

What does Macedonia produce? It produces cereals and primarily tobacco. Salonika is the great center of tobacco export. It is also the greatest import center in Northern Greece.

Is the industry of Northern Greece concentrated in Salonika?

Yes. In this city there are (*lit.*, function) many factories. However, the industry of wool, cotton and silk fabrics is concentrated in the neighboring cities.

What is your business, Mr. Economides?

I am the manager of (*lit.*, I manage) the import and export company "Hermes".

That is very interesting. Even though I am not a businessman, I can certainly learn a few interesting things about the business (*lit.*, economic) life of your country.

With pleasure. I am ready to answer you if you don't insist

ἐπιμένετε σὲ ἀπολύτως ἀκριβεῖς ἀριθμούς, μὲ τοὺς ὁ-
ποίους σεῖς οἱ ᾿Αμερικανοὶ εἶσθε τόσο ἐξοικειωμένοι.

17 Ἡ γεωργικὴ παραγωγὴ
καλύπτει ὅλες τὶς ἀνά-
γκες τῆς χώρας;

18 Δυστυχῶς, ὄχι. Εἴμαστε
ὑποχρεωμένοι νὰ εἰσάγω-
με ἀρκετὲς ποσότητες σιτηρῶν. Πάντως, παράγομε τώρα ἀρκετὰ σιτηρὰ καθὼς καὶ μερικὰ βιομηχανικὰ φυτά,
ὅπως τὸ βαμβάκι.

19 Ὁ ὀρυκτὸς πλοῦτος τῆς χώρας εἶναι μᾶλλον περιωρισμένος. ᾿Εννοῶ, σὲ πρῶτες ὕλες.

20 Αὐτὸ εἶναι σωστό. ῞Οπως ἴσως ξέρετε, τὰ προϊόντα ποὺ
παράγει ὁ τόπος εἶναι τὸ λάδι, ἡ σταφίδα, τὰ σύκα, τὰ
πορτοκάλια καὶ ὁ καπνός.

21 Μάλιστα. Τὰ προϊόντα αὐτὰ εἶναι γνωστὰ σὲ ὅλο τὸν
κόσμο γιὰ τὴν ἐκλεκτὴ τους ποιότητα. Παράγει, ἐπίσης,
ἂν δὲν κάνω λάθος, κρασιὰ ἐκλεκτὰ καὶ ἄλλα ὡραῖα
ποτά. ῞Ενας φίλος μου μιλᾶ γιὰ τὸ κονιὰκ «Μεταξᾶ»
καὶ κολλᾶ ἡ γλῶσσα του στὸν οὐρανίσκο.

22 Αὐτὸ εἶναι ἀλήθεια. Ἡ ἑταιρία μας ἐξάγει ποτὰ στὴν
᾿Αμερική, στὸν Καναδᾶ, στὴν ᾿Αγγλία, σὲ ὅλη τὴν Εὐρώπη.

neh-teh seh ah-poh-LEE-tohs ah-kree-VEES ah-reeth-MOOS, meh toos oh-PEE-oos SEES ee ah-meh-ree-kah-NEE EE-stheh TOH-soh eh-ksee-kee-oh-MEH-nee.

17 ee yeh-ohr-yee-KEE pah-rah-ghoh-YEE kah-LEE-ptee OH-lehs tees ah-NAHN-gehs tees KHOH-rahs?

18 thees-tee-KHOHS, OH-khee. EE-mah-steh ee-poh-khreh-oh-MEH-nee nah ee-SAH-ghoh-meh ahr-keh-TEHS poh-SOH-tee-tehs see-tee-ROHN. PAHN-dohs, pah-RAH-ghoh-meh TOH-rah ahr-keh-TAH see-tee-RAH kah-THOHS keh meh-ree-KAH vee-oh-mee-khah-nee-KAH fee-TAH, OH-pohs toh vahm-VAH-kee.

19 oh oh-ree-KTOHS PLOO-tohs tees KHOH-rahs EE-neh MAH-lohn peh-ree-oh-ree-ZMEH-nohs. eh-noh-OH seh PROH-tehs EE-lehs.

20 ahf-TOH EE-neh soh-STOH. OH-pohs EE-sohs KSEH-reh-teh, tah proh-ee-OHN-dah poo pah-RAH-yee oh TOH-pohs EE-neh toh LAH-thee, ee stah-FEE-thah, tah SEE-kah, tah pohr-toh-KAH-lyah keh oh kah-PNOHS.

21 MAH-lee-stah. tah proh-ee-OHN-dah ahf-TAH EE-neh ghnoh-STAH seh OH-loh tohn KOH-zmoh yah teen eh-kleh-KTEE-toos pee-OH-tee-tah. pah-RAH-yee eh-PEE-sees ahn THEHN KAH-noh LAH-thohs, krah-SYAH eh-kleh-KTAH keh AH-lah oh-REH-ah poh-TAH. EH-nahs FEE-lohz-moo mee-LAH yah toh koh-NYAHK meh-tah-KSAH keh koh-LAH ee GHLOH-sah-too stohn oo-rah-NEE-skoh.

22 ahf-TOH EE-neh ah-LEE-thyah. ee eh-teh-REE-ah-mahs eh-KSAH-yee poh-TAH steen ah-meh-ree-KEE, stohn kah-nah-THAH, steen ahn-GLEE-ah, seh OH-lee teen ehv-ROH-pee.

on absolutely exact figures with which you Americans are so familiar.

Does the agricultural production cover all the needs of the country?

Unfortunately, no. We are obliged to import considerable quantities of cereals. However, we produce enough cereals now, and some other plants such as cotton for industrial use (*lit.*, industrial plants).

The mineral wealth of the country is rather limited. I mean in raw materials.

That is right. As you perhaps know, the products that our land produces are oil, raisins, figs, oranges and tobacco.

Yes. These products are known all over the world (*lit.*, to all the world) for their excellent quality. It also produces, if I am not mistaken, excellent wines and other good drinks. A friend of mine talks about the Metaxas cognac and licks his lips.

That is true. Our company exports alcoholic drinks to America, to Canada, to England, to all of Europe.

23 Ἐργάζεσθε μὲ ἐμπορικοὺς οἴκους τῆς Ἀμερικῆς, κύριε Οἰκονομίδη;

24 Βέβαια. "Εχομε δικό μας Γραφεῖο στὴ Νέα Ὑόρκη. Μᾶς προμηθεύει διάφορες μηχανὲς καὶ ἐξαρτήματα μηχανῶν.

25 Γενικά, πῶς πηγαίνουν τὰ οἰκονομικὰ τῆς χώρας;

26 "Οπως ξέρετε, ἡ οἰκονομικὴ ζωὴ τῆς χώρας ἐξαρτᾶται ἀπὸ τὴν παραγωγή. Ἡ παραγωγὴ διαρκῶς μεγαλώνει.

27 Μὲ ἄλλα λόγια, τὸ ἐθνικὸ εἰσόδημα τῆς χώρας διαρκῶς μεγαλώνει.

28 Βέβαια. Σύμφωνα μὲ μιὰ τελευταία ἔκθεση τῆς «Τραπέζης τῆς Ἑλλάδος», τὸ ἐθνικὸ χρέος μειώνεται. Οἱ καταθέσεις στὶς τράπεζες μεγαλώνουν. Ὁ τόκος εἶναι λογικός. Ἡ τοποθέτηση κεφαλαίων εἶναι ἐπικερδής.

29 "Ας μὴ προχωρήσωμε περισσότερο γιατί, ὅπως σᾶς εἶπα, δὲν ἔχω μεγάλη σχέση μὲ τὰ οἰκονομικὰ θέματα, μὲ τὸ ἐμπόριο, μὲ τὰ κεφάλαια, μὲ τοὺς τόκους, μὲ τὴν ἐξαγωγὴ καὶ μὲ τὴν εἰσαγωγή.

23 ehr-GHAH-zeh-stheh meh ehm-boh-ree-KOOS EE-koos tees ah-meh-ree-KEES, KEE-ree-eh ee-koh-noh-MEE-*th*ee?

24 VEH-veh-ah. EH-khoh-meh *th*ee-KOH-mahs ghrah-FEE-oh stee NEH-ah ee-OHR-kee. mahs proh-mee-THEHV-ee *th*ee-AH-foh-rehs mee-khah-NEHS keh eh-ksahr-TEE-mah-tah mee-khah-NOHN.

25 yeh-nee-KAH, POHS pee-YEH-noon tah ee-koh-noh-mee-KAH tees KHOH-rahs?

26 OH-pohs KSEH-reh-teh, ee ee-koh-noh-mee-KEE zoh-EE tees KHOH-rahs eh-ksahr-TAH-teh ah-POH teen pah-rah-ghoh-YEE. ee pah-rah-ghoh-YEE *th*ee-ahr-KOHS meh-ghah-LOH-nee.

27 meh AH-lah LOH-yah, toh eh-thnee-KOH ee-SOH-*th*ee-mah tees KHOH-rahs *th*ee-ahr-KOHS meh-ghah-LOH-nee.

28 VEH-veh-ah. SEEM-foh-nah meh myah teh-lehf-TEH-ah EHK-theh-see tees trah-PEH-zees tees eh-LAH-*th*ohs, toh eh-thnee-KOH KHREH-ohs mee-OH-neh-teh. ee kah-tah-THEH-sees stees TRAH-peh-zehs meh-ghah-LOH-noon. oh TOH-kohs EE-neh loh-yee-KOHS. ee toh-poh-THEH-tee-see keh-fah-LEH-ohn EE-neh eh-pee-kehr-*TH*EES.

29 ahs MEE proh-khoh-REE-soh-meh peh-ree-SOH-teh-roh yah-TEE, OH-pohs sahs EE-pah, *TH*EHN EH-khoh meh-GHAH-lee SKHEH-see meh tah ee-koh-noh-mee-KAH THEH-mah-tah, meh toh ehm-BOH-ree-oh, meh tah keh-FAH-leh-ah, meh toos TOH-koos, meh teen eh-ksah-ghoh-YEE keh meh teen ee-sah-ghoh-YEE.

Do you work with trade houses in America, Mr. Economides?

Certainly. We have an office in New York. It provides us with various machines and machine accessories.

In general, how is the economy of your country?

As you know, the economic life of our country depends on production. Production increases constantly.

In other words, the national income of the country increases constantly.

Of course. According to a recent report of the "Bank of Greece", the national debt is decreasing. The deposits in the banks increase. The interest is reasonable. The investments are profitable.

Let's not continue any further because, as I told you, I am not very familiar with economic problems, (with) commerce, (with) capital and interest, (with) export and import.

ΕΝΑΤΟ ΜΑΘΗΜΑ
Ninth Lesson

New Vocabulary for this Lesson

πρέπει νά... (PREH-pee-nah) I must
θὰ ἔπρεπε νά... (thah EH-preh-peh nah...) I should
ἐργάζομαι (ehr-GHAH-zoh-meh) I work
καλύτερος (kah-LEE-teh-rohs) better
μεγαλύτερος (meh-ghah-LEE-teh-rohs) larger, bigger

ἱκανοποιητικός (ee-kah-noh-pee-ee-tee-KOHS) satisfactory
σταθεροποιῶ (stah-theh-roh-pee-OH) I stabilize
ἀριστερά (ah-ree-steh-RAH) on the left
ἐμπρός (ehm-BROHS) forward, in front
πληροφορία (plee-roh-foh-REE-ah) information

ἀνοίγω (ah-NEE-ghoh) I open
γωνία (ghoh-NEE-ah) corner
εὔκολο (EHF-koh-loh) easy
ἄλλωστε (AH-lohs-teh) besides
δανείζω (thah-NEE-zoh) I lend

δεξιά (theh-ksee-AH) on the right
δίπλα (THEE-plah) near by
δύσκολο (THEES-koh-loh) difficult
σωστά (soh-STAH) right
ἡ τράπεζα (TRAH-peh-zah) bank

δανείζομαι
(thah-NEE-zoh-meh) I borrow

σύμφωνα μέ... (SEEM-foh-nah meh...) in accordance with...
ὁ λογαριασμός (loh-ghah-ryah-ZMOHS) account
τὸ ἐπιτόκιο (eh-pee-TOH-kee-oh) rate
τοῖς ἑκατό (tees eh-kah-TOH) per cent

ἡ ἐπιταγή (eh-pee-tah-YEE) check ὁ τόκος (TOH-kohs) interest
τὸ ποσό (poh-SOH) amount τὰ ψιλά (psee-LAH) small change
ἡ δραχμή (thrahkh-MEE) drachma γράφω (GHRAH-foh) I write
τὸ δέμα (THEH-mah) parcel

Στὴν τράπεζα. Στὸ ταχυδρομεῖο.
(steen TRA-peh-zah. stoh tah-khee-*th*roh-MEE-oh)
In the Bank. In the Post Office.

οἱ καταθέσεις (kah-tah-THEH-sees) deposits
καταθέτω (kah-tah-THEH-toh) I deposit
ἀποσύρω (ah-poh-SEE-roh) I withdraw
τοῖς μετρητοῖς (tees meh-tree-TEES) in cash
ἐπὶ πιστώσει (eh-pee pee-STOH-see) on credit

τὰ χρήματα (KHREE-mah-tah) money
τὸ χαρτινόμισμα (khahr-toh-NOH-mee-zmah) bill
τὸ ταμιευτήριο (tah-mee-ehf-TEE-ree-oh) savings bank
τὸ ταχυδρομεῖο (tah-khee-*th*roh-MEE-oh) post office
ταχυδρομῶ (tah-khee-*th*roh-MOH) I mail

τὸ τηλεγραφεῖο (tee-leh-ghrah-FEE-oh) telegraph office
τηλεγραφῶ (tee-leh-ghrah-FOH) I telegraph
τὸ τηλεγράφημα (tee-leh-ghrah-FEE-mah) telegram
τὸ γράμμα or ἡ ἐπιστολή (GHRAH-mah, eh-pee-stoh-LEE) letter
τὸ φάκελλο, ὁ φάκελλος (FAH-keh-lohs) envelope

ἡ διεύθυνση (*th*ee-EHF-theen-see) address
τὸ γραμματόσημο (ghrah-mah-TOH-see-moh) stamp
ἀεροπορικῶς (ah-eh-roh-poh-ree-KOHS) by air mail
συστημένο (see-stee-MEH-noh) registered
τὸ γραμματοκιβώτιο (ghrah-mah-toh-kee-VOH-tee-oh) mail box

CONVERSATION

1 Καθὼς μιλοῦμε γιὰ ἐμπορικὰ καὶ οἰκονομικὰ ζητήματα, θυμήθηκα, ὅτι πρέπει νὰ περάσω ἀπὸ τὴν τράπεζα.

2 Μὲ ποιὰ τράπεζα ἐργάζεσθε; Μὲ τὴν Τράπεζα ᾿Αθηνῶν;
Μὲ τὴν ᾿Εμπορικὴ Τράπεζα; Μὲ τὴν Τράπεζα τῆς ῾Ελ-
λάδος;

3 ῎Εχω ἕνα μικρὸ λογαριασμὸ στὴν Τράπεζα ᾿Αθηνῶν.

4 ῾Η Τράπεζα ᾿Αθηνῶν εἶναι μιὰ ἀπὸ τὶς καλύτερες τράπεζες τῆς χώρας. Κάνει ὅλες τὶς τραπεζιτικὲς ἐργασίες.
Δέχεται καταθέσεις μὲ ἱκανοποιητικὸ τόκο. Δανείζει
χρήματα μὲ λογικὸ τόκο. ᾿Εξαργυρώνει ξένες ἐπιταγές.

5 Θέλετε νὰ ἔλθετε μαζί μου;

6 Εὐχαρίστως.

 7 Καλημέρα σας. Θὰ ἤθελα νὰ καταθέσω
δύο χιλιάδες δραχμὲς στὸ λογαριασμό
μου.

8 Εὐχαρίστως, κύριε Σμίθ. Δῶστε μου,
σᾶς παρακαλῶ, τὸ βιβλιάριο τῆς τραπέζης.

9 Θὰ ἤθελα ἐπίσης νὰ ἀνοίξω ἕνα τρεχούμενο λογαριασμό.

10 Αὐτὸ εἶναι πολὺ εὔκολο. Πόσα χρήματα θέλετε νὰ καταθέσετε στὸν λογαριασμό σας;

PRONUNCIATION

1 kah-THOHS mee-LOO-meh yah ehm-boh-ree-KAH keh ee-koh-noh-mee-KAH zee-TEE-mah-tah, thee-MEE-thee-kah, OH-tee PREH-pee nah peh-RAH-soh ah-POH teen TRAH-peh-zah.

2 meh PYAH TRAH-peh-zah ehr-G H A H-z e h-s t h e h? ... meh teen TRAH-peh-zah tees eh-LAH-*th*ohs?

3 EH-khoh EH-nah mee-KROH loh-ghah-ryah-ZMOH steen TRAH-peh-zah ah-thee-NOHN.

4 ee TRAH-peh-zah ah-thee-NOHN EE-neh myah ah-POH tees kah-LEE-teh-rehs TRAH-peh-zehs tees KHOH-rahs. KAH-nee OH-lehs tees trah-peh-zee-tee-KEHS ehr-ghah-SEE-ehs. *THEH*-kheh-teh kah-tah-THEH-sees meh ee-kah-noh-pee-ee-tee-KOH TOH-koh. *th*ah-NEE-zee KHREE-mah-tah meh loh-yee-KOH TOH-koh. eh-ksahr-yee ROH-nee KSEH-nehs eh-pee-tah-YEHS.

5 THEH-leh-teh nah EHL-theh-teh mah-ZEE-moo?

6 ehf-khah-REE-stohs.

7 kah-lee-MEH-rah-sahs. thah EE-theh-lah nah kah-tah-THEH-soh *T H E E*-oh khee-lee-A H-*th*ehs *th*rahkh-MEHS stoh loh-ghah-ryah-ZMOH-moo.

8 ehf-khah-REE-stohs, KEE-ree-eh Smith. *TH*OH-steh-moo, sahs pah-rah-kah-LOH, toh vee-vlee-AH-ree-oh tees trah-PEH-zees.

9 thah EE-theh-lah eh-PEE-sees nah ah-NEE-ksoh EH-nah treh-KHOO-meh-noh loh-ghah-ryah-ZMOH.

10 ahf-TOH EE-neh poh-LEE EHF-koh-loh. POH-sah KHREE-mah-tah THEH-leh-teh nah kah-tah-THEH-seh-teh stohn loh-ghah-ryah-ZMOH-sahs?

TRANSLATION

Talking about commercial and economic problems reminds me (*lit.*, I remembered) that I have to go (*lit.*, to pass from) to the bank.

With what bank are you doing business (*lit.*, do you work)? With the Bank of Athens, with the Commercial Bank or with the Bank of Greece?

I have a small account with the Bank of Athens.

The Bank of Athens is one of the best banks in our country. It transacts all kinds of business. It accepts deposits with satisfactory interest. It lends money at a reasonable interest. It cashes foreign drafts.

Would you like to come with me?

With great pleasure.

Good morning, I would like to deposit two thousand drachmas to my account.

With pleasure, Mr. Smith. Give me your bank book, please.

I would also like to open a checking (*lit.*, current) account.

That's very easy. How much would you like to deposit to your account?

11 Ἔχω ἐδῶ ἑκατὸ δολλάρια. Δηλαδή, τρεῖς χιλιάδες δραχμές.

12 Σωστά. Ἡ ἐπίσημη τιμὴ τοῦ δολλαρίου εἶναι τριάντα δραχμές.

13 Μοῦ δίνετε, σᾶς παρακαλῶ, ἕνα βιβλίο ἐπιταγῶν;

14 Μάλιστα. Ὑπογράψετε ἐδῶ. Σύμφωνα μὲ τοὺς κανόνας τῆς τραπέζης πρέπει νὰ ἔχωμε δεῖγμα τῆς ὑπογραφῆς σας.

15 Μήπως θέλετε καὶ μάρτυρα; Εἶναι μαζί μου ὁ κύριος Οἰκονομίδης καὶ ὁ κύριος Πετρίδης.

16 Ὁ κύριος Οἰκονομίδης εἶναι φίλος μου. Πῶς εἶσθε, κύριε Οἰκονομίδη; Πῶς πηγαίνουν οἱ δουλειές;

17 Ἀρκετὰ καλά, κύριε Ἀργυρόπουλε. Ἀπὸ τὸν καιρὸ ποὺ ἡ τιμὴ τῆς χρυσῆς λίρας ἔχει σταθεροποιηθῆ, ἔχουν σταθεροποιηθῆ καὶ οἱ τιμὲς τῶν ἐμπορευμάτων.

18 Ποιὸς εἶναι ὁ τόκος στὶς καταθέσεις;

19 Εἶναι πέντε τοῖς ἑκατό.

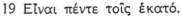

20 Θὰ θέλατε νὰ ἔλθετε στὸ Ταχυδρομεῖο; Θέλω νὰ ἀγοράσω μερικὰ γραμματόσημα καὶ νὰ ταχυδρομήσω δύο γράμματα.

11 EH-khoh eh-*TH*OH eh-kah-TOH *th*oh-LAH-ree-ah. *th*ee-lah-*TH*EE, TREES khee-LYAH-*th*ehs *th*rahkh-MEHS.

Here is a hundred dollars. That is, three thousand drachmas.

12 soh-STAH. ee eh-PEE-see-mee tee-MEE too *th*oh-lah-REE-oo EE-neh tree-AHN-dah *th*rahkh-MEHS.

Right. The official price of the dollar is thirty drachmas.

13 moo *TH*EE-neh-teh, 'sahs pah-rah-kah-LOH, EH-nah vee-VLEE-oh eh-pee-tah-GHOHN?

Will you give me a check book, please?

14 MAH-lee-stah. ee-poh-G H R A H-psah-teh eh-*TH*OH. SEEM-foh-nah meh toos kah-NOH-nehs tees trah-PEH-zees PREH-pee nah EH-khoh-meh *TH*EEGH-mah tees ee-poh-ghrah-FEE-sahs.

Yes. Sign here. According to the regulations of the bank we must have a sample of your signature.

15 MEE-pohs THEH-leh-teh keh MAHR-tee-rah? EE-neh mah-ZEE-moo oh KEE-ree-ohs ee-koh-noh-MEE-*th*ees keh oh KEE-ree-ohs peh-TREE-*th*ees.

Do you perhaps want a witness? Mr. Economides and Mr. Petrides are with me.

16 oh KEE-ree-ohs ee-koh-noh-MEE-*th*ees EE-neh FEE-lohz-moo. POHS EE-stheh, KEE-ree-eh ee-koh-noh-MEE-*th*ee? POHS pee-YEH-noon ee *th*oo-LYEHS?

Mr. Economides is a friend of mine (*lit.*, is my friend). How are you, Mr. Economides? How is business? (*lit.*, how does it go?)

17 ahr-keh-TAH kah-LAH, KEE-ree-eh ahr-yee-ROH-poo-leh. ah-POH tohn keh-ROH poo ee tee-MEE tees khree-SEES LEE-rahs EH-khee stah-theh-roh-pee-ee-*TH*EE, EH-khoon stah-theh-roh-pee-ee-*TH*EE keh ee tee-MEHS tohn ehm-boh-rehv-MAH-tohn.

Pretty good, Mr. Argyropoulos. Since the time the price of the golden pound has been stabilized, the prices of goods have also been stabilized.

18 PYOHS EE-neh oh TOH-kohs stees kah-tah-*TH*EH-sees?

What is the interest on the deposits?

19 EE-neh PEHN-deh tees eh-kah-TOH.

It is five per cent.

20 thah *TH*EH-lah-teh nah EHL-theh-teh stoh tah-khee-*th*roh-MEE-oh? *TH*EH-loh nah ah-ghoh-RAH-soh meh-ree-KAH ghrah-mah-TOH-see-mah keh nah tah-khee-*th*roh-MEE-soh *TH*EE-oh GHRAH-mah-tah.

Would you like to come to the Post Office? I would like to buy some stamps and mail two letters.

21 Εὐχαρίστως. "Αλλωστε τὸ κεντρικὸ ταχυδρομεῖο εἶναι στὸν ἴδιο δρόμο. Ἐδῶ δίπλα εἶναι ἐπίσης τὸ τηλεγραφεῖο.

22 Δεσποινίς, δῶστε μου, σᾶς παρακαλῶ, δέκα γραμματόσημα τῶν δύο δραχμῶν, δέκα τῶν πέντε καὶ εἴκοσι ἀεροπορικὰ τῶν δέκα.

23 Μάλιστα, κύριε. "Ολα μαζὶ κοστίζουν διακόσιες ἑβδομῆντα δραχμές. Θέλετε κάτι ἄλλο;

24 Μπορῶ νὰ ἔχω δεκαπέντε ταχυδρομικὰ δελτάρια;

25 Εὐχαρίστως.

26 Ποῦ εἶναι τὸ γραμματοκιβώτιο;

27 Γιὰ τὰ γράμματα τοῦ ἐσωτερικοῦ εἶναι ἐκεῖ στὴ γωνία. Γιὰ τὰ γράμματα τοῦ ἐξωτερικοῦ εἶναι δίπλα, ἐδῶ. Γιὰ τὰ ἀεροπορικὰ εἶναι ἐκεῖ ἐμπρός. Ταχυδρομικὰ δέματα δεξιὰ στὸ διάδρομο.

28 Μία ἀκόμη πληροφορία, δεσποινίς. Ποιὸς εἶναι ὁ τόκος τῶν ταχυδρομικῶν καταθέσεων;

29 Ὀκτὼ τοῖς ἑκατό, κύριε.

30 Κύριε Οἰκονομίδη, ὁ τόκος τῶν ταχυδρομικῶν καταθέσεων εἶναι μεγαλύτερος ἀπὸ τὸν τόκο τῶν τραπεζιτικῶν καταθέσων. "Ετσι θὰ ἔπρεπε νὰ . . .

21 ehf-khah-REE-stohs. AH-loh-steh toh kehn-dree-KOH tah-khee-*th*roh-MEE-oh EE-neh stohn EE-*th*yoh *TH*ROH-moh. eh-*TH*OH *TH*EE-plah EE-neh eh-PEE-sees toh tee-leh-ghrah-FEE-oh.

With pleasure. Besides, the Central Post Office is on the same street. The Telegraph Office is also nearby.

22 *th*ehs-pee-NEES, *TH*OH-steh-moo, sahs pah-rah-kah-LOH, *TH*EH-kah ghrah-mah-TOH-see-mah tohn *TH*EE-oh *th*rahkh-MOHN, *TH*EH-kah tohn PEHN-deh keh EE-koh-see ah-eh-roh-poh-ree-KAH tohn *TH*EH-kah.

Miss, give me, please, ten stamps of two drachmas, ten of five and twenty air-mail of ten.

23 MAH-lee-stah, KEE-ree-eh. OH-lah mah-ZEE koh-STEE-zoon *th*ee-ah-KOH-see-ehs ehv-*th*oh-MEEN-dah *th*rahkh-MEHS. *TH*EH-leh-teh KAH-tee AH-loh?

Yes, sir. They cost two hundred seventy drachmas all together. Would you like anything else?

24 boh-ROH nah EH-khoh *th*eh-kah-PEHN-deh ta h-khee-*th*roh-mee-KAH *th*ehl-TAH-ree-ah?

May I have fifteen post cards?

25 ehf-khah-REE-stohs.

With pleasure.

26 POO EE-neh toh ghrah-mah-toh-kee-VOH-tee-oh?

Where is the letter-box?

27 yah tah GHRAH-mah-tah too eh-soh-teh-ree-KOO EE-neh eh-KEE stee ghoh-NEE-ah. yah tah GHRAH-mah-tah too eh-ksoh-teh-ree-KOO EE-neh *TH*EE-plah eh-*TH*OH. yah tah ah-eh-roh-poh-ree-KAH EE-neh EH-kee ehm-BROHS. tah-khee-*th*roh-mee-KAH *TH*EH-mah-tah *th*eh-ksee-AH stoh *th*ee-AH-*th*roh-moh.

For ordinary letters it is there in the corner. For foreign letters it is nearby, here. For air mail it is over there. For parcel-post, it is on the right, in the corridor.

28 MEE-ah ah-KOH-mee plee-roh-foh-R EE-ah, *th*ehs-pee-N EES. PYOHS EE-neh oh TOH-kohs tohn tah-khee-*th*roh-mee-KOHN kah-tah-THEH-seh-ohn?

One more question (*lit.*, information), Miss. What is the interest on deposits in the postal savings bank?

29 oh-KTOH tees eh-kah-TOH, KEE-ree-eh.

Eight per cent, sir.

30 KEE-ree-eh ee-koh-noh-MEE-*th*ee, oh TOH-kohs tohn tah-khee-*th*roh-mee-KOHN kah-tah-T HEH-seh-ohn EE-neh meh-ghah-LEE-teh-

Mr. Economides, the interest of the postal savings bank is larger than that of the banks. Therefore, I should have...

31 Θὰ ἔπρεπε νὰ καταθέσετε τὰ χρήματά σας στὸ ταχυδρομικὸ ταμιευτήριο. 'Αλλά, ὅπως εἴπατε, δὲν εἴσθε
καλὸς στὰ οἰκονομικὰ ζητήματα.

SAMPLES OF GREEK HANDWRITING

Θὰ ἔπρεπε νὰ καταθέσετε τὰ
χρήματά σας στὸ ταχυδρομικὸ
ταμιευτήριο.'Αλλά, ὅπως εἴπατε,
δὲν εἴσθε καλὸς στὰ οἰκονομικὰ ζητήματα.

Θά ἔπρεπε νά καταθέσετε
τὰ χρήματά σῃ τό ταχυδρομι-
κό ταμιευτήριο. Ἀλλά, ὅπω
εἴπατε, δὲ εἴσθε καλὸς τὰ
οἰκονομικά ζητήματα.

rohs ah-POH tohn TOH-koh tohn
trah-peh-zee-tee-KOHN   kah-tah-
THEH-seh-ohn. EH-tsee thah EH-
preh-peh NAH...

31 thah EH-preh-peh nah kah-tah-
THEH-seh-teh tah KHREE-mah-
TAH-sahs stoh tah-khee-*THROH*-
mee-koh   tah-mee-ehf-TEE-ree-oh.
ah-LAH,   OH-pohs   EE-pah-teh,
*THE*HN EE-stheh kah-LOHS stah
ee-koh-noh-mee-KAH zee-TEE-mah-
tah.

You should have deposited your
money in the postal savings
bank. But, as you said, you are
not very good in business mat-
ters.

Θὰ ἔπρεπε νὰ καταθέσετε
τὰ χρήματά σας σὶ ταχυδρο
μικὸ ταμιευτήριο. Ἀλλά, ὅπως
εἴπατε, δὲν εἶστε καλός στὰ
οἰκονομικὰ ζητήματα.

Εἶναι παρὰ σου μεγάλος ὁ προορισμός τῆς μελρός. Ἀπὸ αὐτήν
ἐξαρτῶνται τὰ πάντα. Καὶ ὁ χαρα-
κτήρ μας καὶ ἡ ἁρμονία τῆς οἴκω
γενείας καὶ ἡ εὐημερία τῆς κοινω-
νίας καὶ ἡ ἀκμὴ τῆς χώρας.

ΔΕΚΑΤΟ ΜΑΘΗΜΑ
Tenth Lesson

New Vocabulary for this Lesson

ἐμπρός (ehm-BROHS) hello
τὸ κρεβάτι (kreh-VAH-tee) bed
τὸ μπάνιο (BAH-nyoh) bath (room)
ὁ ὁδηγός (oh-thee-GHOHS) guide
ἡ πόρτα (POHR-tah) door

τὸ πάτωμα (PAH-toh-mah) floor
ἡ βαλίτσα (vah-LEE-tsah) suitcase
ἡ ντουλάπα (doo-LAH-pah) closet
τηλεφωνῶ (tee-leh-foh-NOH) I call
ὁ χάρτης (KHAHR-tees) map

ἑτοιμάζομαι (eh-tee-MAH-zoh-meh) I am getting ready
ἡ σκέψη (SKEH-psee) thought, idea
ἀναχωρῶ (ah-nah-khoh-ROH) I leave
ἐπάνοδος (eh-PAH-noh-thohs) return
τὸ δωμάτιο (thoh-MAH-tee-oh) room

τὸ γραφεῖο (ghrah-FEE-oh) writing desk, office
πρόθυμος, -η, -ο (PROH-thee-mohs) prompt
πρόχειρος, -η, -ο (PROH-khee-rohs) handy
τὸ παράθυρο (pah-RAH-thee-roh) window
περιπλανῶμαι (peh-ree-plah-NOH-neh) I wander

ὁ κόλπος (KOHL-pohs) gulf, bay
ἡ πόλη (POH-lee) town
ἡ πλατεῖα (plah-TEE-ah) square
τὸ πλοῖο (PLEE-oh) boat, ship
ἡ ἀγορά (ah-ghoh-RAH) market

ἡ ταράτσα (tah-RAH-tsah) roof
χάνομαι (KHAH-noh-meh) I get lost
τὸ κτίριο (KTEE-ree-oh) building
τὸ λιμάνι (lee-MAH-nee) harbor
τὸ σχολεῖο (skhoh-LEE-oh) school

Στὴν πόλη (steem- POH-lee) In the City

ὁ δρόμος or ἡ ὁδός (THROH-mohs, oh-THOHS) street
τὸ πεζοδρόμιο (peh-zoh-THROH-mee-oh) pavement
ἡ λεωφόρος (leh-oh-FOH-rohs) avenue
ἡ ρυμοτομία (ree-moh-toh-MEE-ah) street plan
ἡ παραλία (pah-rah-LEE-ah) seashore

ὁ ναός or ἡ ἐκκλησία (nah-OHS, eh-klee-SEE-ah) church
τὸ νοσοκομείο (noh-soh-koh-MEE-oh) hospital
τὸ φρούριο (FROO-ree-oh) fort, castle
τὸ κατάστημα (kah-TAH-stee-mah) store
τὸ καφενείο (kah-feh-NEE-oh) coffee house

ὁ κάτοικος (KAH-tee-kohs) inhabitant
τὸ δημαρχείο (thee-mahr-KHEE-oh) town hall
ἡ νομαρχία (noh-mahr-KHEE-ah) prefecture
ὁ ἀστυνόμος (ah-stee-NOH-mohs) officer, sheriff
ὁ ἀστυφύλακας (ah-stee-FEE-lah-kahs) policeman*

τὸ δικαστήριο (thee-kah-STEE-ree-oh) court house
ἡ συνοικία (see-nee-KEE-ah) section of the city
τὰ περίχωρα (peh-REE-khoh-rah) suburbs
τὰ προάστεια (proh-AH-stee-ah) suburbs (within the city limits)
τὸ λεωφορείο (leh-oh-foh-REE-oh) bus

ὁ κινηματογράφος (kee-nee-mah-toh-GHRAH-fohs) cinema
τὸ ραδιόφωνο (rah-thee-OH-foh-noh) radio set
τὸ τράμ (TRAHM) street car   τὸ θέατρο (THEH-ah-troh) theater

* In small cities and towns the policeman is called χωροφύλακας.

CONVERSATION

1 Ἐμπρός, ἐμπρός. Ὁ κύριος Πετρίδης, παρακαλῶ;

2 Ὁ ἴδιος. Σεῖς, κύριε Σμίθ; Πῶς εἴσθε; Θὰ χαρῶ πολὺ ἂν ἔλθετε τὸ ἀπόγευμα στὸ σπίτι νὰ πάρωμε μαζὶ ἕνα καφέ, ἕνα τσάϊ...

3 Εὐχαρίστως, θὰ ἐρχόμουν, ἀλλὰ ἑτοιμάζομαι νὰ φύγω γιὰ τὴν Πάτρα. Θὰ ἤθελα νὰ περάσω ἐκεῖ τὸ Σαββατοκύριακο.

4 Ἡ σκέψη σας εἴναι πολὺ καλή. Ἡ Πάτρα εἴναι μία ὡραία παραλιακὴ πόλη.

5 Μήπως ξέρετε κανένα καλὸ ξενοδοχεῖο στὴν πόλη;

6 Τὸ ξενοδοχεῖο «Πανελλήνιον» εἴναι, νομίζω, τὸ καλύτερο. Καλὸ εἴναι νὰ τηλεγραφήσετε γιὰ νὰ σᾶς κρατήσουν δωμάτιο. Πότε ἀναχωρεῖτε;

7 Ἀναχωρῶ στὶς τέσσερες τὸ ἀπόγευμα, μὲ τὸ σιδηρόδρομο, ἀπὸ τὸ σταθμὸ Πελοποννήσου.

8 Καλὸ ταξίδι καὶ καλὴ ἐπάνοδο.

9 Εὐχαριστῶ πολύ. Καλὴ ἀντάμωση.

10 Κύριε, γνωρίζετε ποῦ εἴναι τὸ ξενοδοχεῖο «Πανελλήνιον»;

PRONUNCIATION	TRANSLATION

1 ehm-BROHS, ehm-BROHS. oh KEE-ree-ohs peh-TREE-*th*ees, pah-rah-kah-LOH.

Hello, hello. Mr. Petrides, please?

2 oh EE-*th*ee-ohs. SEES, KEE-ree-eh Smith? POHS EE-stheh? thah khah-ROH poh-LEE ahn EHL-theh teh toh ah-POH-yehv-mah stoh SPEE-tee nah PAH-roh-meh mah-ZEE EH-nah kah-FEH, EH-nah TSAH-ee...

Speaking (*lit.*, himself). Is that you Mr. Smith? How are you? I shall be very glad if you will come to my house this after-noon and have a cup of coffee or tea with me.

3 ehf-khah-REE-stohs, thah ehr-KHOH-moon, ah-LAH eh-tee-MAH-zoh-meh nah FEE-ghoh yah teem PAH-trah. thah EE-*th*eh-lah nah peh-RAH-soh eh-KEE tohn sah-vah-toh-KEE-ryah-koh.

I would come with pleasure, but I am getting ready to leave for Patra. I would like to spend the weekend there.

4 ee SKEH-psee-sahs EE-neh poh-LEE kah-LEE. ee PAH-trah EE-neh MEE-ah oh-REH-ah pah-rah-lee-ah-KEE poh-LEE.

That is a very good idea (*lit.*, Your thought is very good). Patra is a beautiful seaport.

5 MEE-pohs KSEH-reh-teh kah-NEH-nah kah-LOH kseh-noh-*th*oh-khee-OH steem POH-lee?

Do you know of any good hotel in that city?

6 toh kseh-noh-*th*oh-KHEE-oh pah-neh-LEE-nee-ohn EE-neh, noh-MEE-zoh, toh kah-LEE-teh-roh. kah-LOH EE-neh nah tee-leh-ghrah-FEE-seh-teh yah nah sahs krah-TEE-soon *th*oh-MAH-tee-oh. POH-teh ah-nah-khoh-REE-teh?

The hotel "Panhellenion", I think, is the best. You ought (*lit.*, good it is) to wire them to reserve a room for you. When do you leave?

7 ah-nah-khoh-ROH stees TEH-seh-rehs toh ah-POH-yehv-mah meh toh see-*th*ee-ROH-*th*roh-moh, ah-POH toh stath-MOH peh-loh-poh-NEE-soo.

I leave at four o'clock in the afternoon, by train from the Peloponnesus Station.

8 kah-LOH tah-KSEE-*th*ee keh kah-LEE eh-PAH-noh-*th*oh.

Bon voyage and good return.

9 ehf-khah-ree-STOH poh-LEE. kah-LEE ahn-DAH-moh-see.

Thank you and au revoir.

10 KEE-ree-eh, ghnoh-REE-zeh-teh POO EE-neh toh kseh-noh-*th*oh-KHEE-oh pah-neh-LEE-nee-ohn?

Sir, do you know where the "Pan-hellenion" hotel is?

11 Εἶναι ἐκεῖ κάτω στὸν παραλιακὸ δρόμο. Προχωρήσετε καὶ θὰ ἰδῆτε τὴ φωτεινὴ ταμπέλα.

12 Καλησπέρα, κυρία. Ὀνομάζομαι Σμίθ. Σᾶς τηλεγράφησα ἀπὸ τὴν Ἀθήνα γιὰ νὰ μοῦ κρατήσετε ἕνα δωμάτιο.

13 Μάλιστα, κύριε. Τὸ δωμάτιό σας εἶναι στὸ τρίτο πάτωμα, ἀριθμὸς τριάντα ὀκτώ. Ὁ ὑπάλληλος θὰ σᾶς ὁδηγήση.

14 Περάσετε, κύριε. Δῶστε μου, σᾶς παρακαλῶ, τὴ βαλίτσα σας.

15 Τρίτο πάτωμα, δεξιά, ἀριθμὸς τριάντα ὀκτώ.

16 Μάλιστα. Τὸ δωμάτιό σας. Τὸ κρεββάτι σας εἶναι διπλό. Ἐδῶ εἶναι ἡ ντουλάπα. Ἐδῶ εἶναι τὸ μπάνιο. Τὸ γραφεῖο σας εἶναι ἐκεῖ. "Αν χρειασθῆτε κάτι, τηλεφωνήσετε. Ἡ ὑπηρεσία εἶναι πρόθυμη.

17 "Εχετε κανένα πρόχειρο ὁδηγό, ἢ χάρτη τῆς πόλης;

18 Μπορεῖτε νὰ ζητήσετε ἕνα χάρτη ἀπὸ τὸ Γραφεῖο. Ἡ πόλη δὲν εἶναι πολὺ μεγάλη. Ἀπὸ τὸ παράθυρο μπορεῖτε νὰ ἰδῆτε τὴν παραλία, τὸ λιμάνι, τὶς κινήσεις τῶν πλοίων.

11 EE-neh eh-KEE KAH-toh stohm
pah-rah-lee-ah-KOH *TH*ROH-moh.
proh-khoh-REE-seh-teh   keh-thah
ee-*TH*EE-teh   tee   foh-tee-NEE
tahm-BEH-lah.

12 kah-lee-SPEH-rah, kee-REE-ah. oh-
noh-MAH-zoh-meh Smith. sahs tee-
leh-GHRAH-fee-sah ah-POH teen
ah-THEE-nah yah nah moo krah-
TEE-seh-teh   EH-nah   *th*oh-MAH-
tee-oh.

13 MAH-lee-stah, KEE-ree-eh. toh
*th*oh-MAH-tee-OH-sahs EE-neh
stoh TREE-toh PAH-toh-mah, ah-
reeth-MOHS   tree-AHN-dah   oh-
KTOH. oh ee-PAH-lee-lohs thah
sahs oh-*th*ee-YEE-see.

14 peh-RAH-s(eh)-teh,   KEE-ree-eh.
*TH*OH-steh-moo, sahs pah-rah-
kah-LOH, tee vah-LEE-tsah sahs.

15 TREE-toh   PAH-toh-mah,   *th*eh-
ksee-AH,   ah-reeth-MOHS   tree-
AHN-dah   OH-ktoh.

16 MAH-lee-stah. toh *th*oh-MAH-tee-
OH-sahs. toh kreh-VAH-tee-sahs
EE-neh *th*ee-PLOH. eh-*TH*OH EE-
neh ee doo-LAH-pah. eh-*TH*OH
EE-neh toh BAH-nyoh. toh ghrah-
FEE-oh-sahs EE-neh eh-KEE. ahn
khree-ah-STHEE-teh KAH-tee, tee-
leh-foh-NEE-s(eh)-teh. ee ee-pee-
reh-SEE-ah   EE-neh   PROH-thee-
mee.

17 EH-kheh-teh kah-NEH-nah PROH-
khee-roh   oh-*th*ee-GHOH   ee
KHAHR-tee tees POH-lees?

18 boh-REE-teh nah zee-TEE-seh-teh
EH-nah KHAHR-tee ah-POH toh
ghrah-FEE-oh. eePOH-lee *TH*EHN
EE-neh poh-LEE meh-GHAH-lee.
ah-POH toh pah-RAH-thee-roh
boh-REE-teh nah ee-*TH*EE-teh
teem pah-rah-LEE-ah, toh lee-
MAH-nee, tees kee-NEE-sees tohn
PLEE-ohn.

It is down there on Littoral Street.
Go straight on and you will
see the neon sign.

Good evening, madam. My name
is Smith. I wired from Athens
to reserve a room for myself.

Yes, sir. Your room is on the
third floor, room 38. The clerk
will show you there.

This way (*lit.*, pass), sir. Give
me your bag, please.

Third floor, to the right, room 38.

Yes. This is your room. You have
a double bed (*lit.*, your bed is
double). Here is the closet.
Here is the bathroom. Your
desk is there. If you need something, call. Service is prompt.

Do you have a handy guide or
map of the city?

You can ask for a map at the
office. The city is not very
large. From the window you
can see the seaboard, the waterfront, the ships coming and
going (*lit.*, the movements of
the ships).

19 Ποιά εἶναι τά ἀξιοθέατα μέρη τῆς πόλης;

20 Μπορεῖτε νά ἐπισκεφθῆτε τό φρούριο τῆς 'Ακροπόλεως Πατρῶν, τήν Πλατεῖα τῶν Ὑψηλῶν 'Αλωνιῶν, τήν πλατεῖα Γεωργίου τοῦ Α΄, τό ναό τοῦ Παντοκράτορος.

21 Ποῦ εἶναι τό κέντρο τῆς πόλεως;

22 Τά μεγαλύτερα καφενεῖα καί ξενοδοχεῖα εἶναι στόν παραλιακό δρόμο. Ἡ ἀγορά εἶναι στό ἀνατολικό τμῆμα. Τά μεγάλα καταστήματα εἶναι λίγο πιό πέρα.

23 'Από ποῦ μπορῶ νά ἔχω μιά γενική εἰκόνα τῆς πόλης;

24 'Ανεβῆτε στήν ταράτσα τοῦ ξενοδοχείου. "Αν θέλετε νά ἰδῆτε τήν πόλη, τά περίχωρα, τό λιμάνι, τόν Κορινθιακό κόλπο, ἀνεβῆτε στήν πλατεῖα Ὑψηλά 'Αλώνια.

25 Εὐχαριστῶ πολύ. Θά περιπλανηθῶ μόνος μου ἐδῶ καί ἐκεῖ. Αὐτός εἶναι ὁ καλύτερος τρόπος νά πάρη κανείς μιά ἰδέα τῆς πόλης.

26 Ποῦ εἶναι τό δημαρχεῖο, κύριε;

19 PEE-ah EE-neh tah ah-ksee-oh-THEH-ah-tah MEH-ree tees POH-lees?

What are the sights in the city?

20 boh-REE-teh nah eh-pee-skehf-THEE-teh toh FROO-ree-oh tees ah-kroh-POH-leh-ohs pah-TROHN, teem plah-TEE-ah tohn ee-psee-LOHN ah-loh-NYOHN, teem plah-TEE-ah yeh-ohr-YEE-oo too PROH-too, toh nah-OH too pahn-doh-KRAH-toh-rohs.

You can visit the fortress on the Acropolis of Patra, the "High Plains" Square, George I Square, the Pantocrator Church.

21 POO EE-neh toh KEHN-droh tees POH-leh-ohs?

Where is the center of the city?

22 tah meh-ghah-LEE-teh-rah kah-feh-NEE-ah keh kseh-noh-*th*oh-KHEE-ah EE-neh stohm pah-rah-lee-ah-KOH *TH*ROH-moh. ee ah-ghoh-RAH EE-neh stoh ah-nah-toh-lee-KOH TMEE-mah. tah meh-GHAH-lah kah-tah-STEE-mah-tah EE-neh LEE-ghoh PYOH PEH-rah.

The largest coffee-shops and hotels are on the seaboard. The market is in the eastern section. The large stores are a little farther.

23 ah-POH POO boh-ROH nah EH-khoh myah yeh-nee-KEE ee-KOH-nah tees POH-lees?

Where can I get a general view of the city?

24 ah-neh-VEE-teh steen tah-RAH-tsah too kseh-noh-*th*oh-KHEE-oo. ahn THEH-leh-teh nah ee-*TH*EE-teh teem-BOH-lee, tah peh-REE-khoh-rah, toh lee-MAH-nee, tohn koh-reen-thee-ah-KOH KOHL-poh, ah-neh-VEE-teh steem plah-TEE-ah "ee-psee-LAH ah-LOH-nyah".

Go up to the roof of our hotel. If you want to see the city, the suburbs, the waterfront, the Corinthian Gulf, go to the "High Plains" Square.

25 ehf-khah-ree-STOH poh-LEE. thah peh-ree-plah-n e e-*TH*OH MOH-nohz-moo eh-*TH*OH keh eh-KEE. ahf-TOHS EE-neh oh kah-LEEteh-rohs TROH-pohs nah PAH-ree kah-NEES myah ee-*TH*EH-ah tees POH-lees.

Thank you very much. I will wander about by myself here and there. That's the best way one can get an idea of the city.

26 POO EE-neh toh *th*ee-mahr-KHEE-oh, KEE-ree-eh?

Where is the City Hall, sir?

27 Προχωρήσετε. Πάρετε αὐτὸ τὸ δρόμο. Ἐκεῖ στὸ βάθος εἶναι τὸ Ταχυδρομεῖο, ἡ Νομαρχία, τὸ Δημαρχεῖο, τὸ Δικαστήριο καὶ πολλὰ ἄλλα δημόσια κτίρια.

28 Εὐχαριστῶ πολύ. Νομίζω, ὅτι δὲν θὰ χαθῶ. Ἡ ρυμοτο-μία τῆς πόλης εἶναι θαυμάσια.

SAMPLES OF GREEK HANDWRITING

27 proh-khoh-R E E-s (eh) -teh. P A H-r (eh)-teh ahf-TOH toh *THROH*-moh. eh-KEE stoh VAH-thohs EE-neh toh tah-khee-*throh*-MEE-oh, ee noh-mahr-KHEE-ah, toh *thee*-mahr-K H E E-o h, toh *thee*-kah-STEE-ree-oh keh poh-LAH AH-lah *thee*-MOH-see-ah KTEE-ree-ah.

Go straight on. Take that street. There at the end (*lit.*, at the depth) are the Post Office, the Prefecture, the City Hall, the Court and many other public buildings.

28 ehf-khah-ree-STOH po-LEE. noh-MEE-zoh OH-tee *THEHN* thah khah-THOH. ee ree-moh-toh-MEE-ah tees POH-lees EE-neh thahv-MAH-see-ah.

Thank you very much. I don't think I'll get lost (*lit.*, I think that I will not be lost). The street plan of the city is wonderful.

Εὐχαριστῶ πολύ. Νομίζω ὅτι δὲν θὰ χαθῶ. Ἡ ρυμοτομία τῆς πόλης εἶναι θαυμασία.

Εὐχαριστῶ πολύ. Νομίζω ὅτι δὲν θὰ χαθῶ. Ἡ ρυμοτομία τῆς πόλης εἶναι θαυμάσια.

Εὐχαριστῶ πολύ. Νομίζω ὅτι δὲν θὰ χαθῶ. Ἡ ρυμοτομία τῆς πόλης εἶναι θαυμασία.

Eleventh Lesson

New Vocabulary for this Lesson

μοιάζω (MYAH-zoh) I resemble, I look like
ἐμπορικός, -ή, -ό (ehm-boh-ree-KOHS) commercial
ἀρκετά (ahr-keh-TAH) long enough (time)
περιμένω (peh-reé-MEH-noh) I am expecting
ἡ καταγωγή (kah-tah-ghoh-YEE) origin, descent

οἱ πρόγονοι (PROH-ghoh-nee) ancestors
φιλικός, -ή, -ό (fee-lee-KOHS) of friends, friendly
ἡ φωτογραφία (foh-toh-ghrah-FEE-ah) photograph
ἀνατολικό (ah-nah-toh-lee-KOH) eastern, looks to the east
δυτικό (thee-tee-KOH) western, looks to the west

ἡ προσφορά (prohs-foh-RAH) offer
περιλαμβάνομαι (peh-ree-lahm-VAH-noh-meh) I am included
δυστυχῶς (thees-tee-KHOHS) unfortunately
ξεχωριστά (kseh-khoh-ree-STAH) separately
ἡ θέρμανση (THEHR-mahn-see) heat

τὸ τηλέφωνο (tee-LEH-foh-noh) telephone
τὸ διαμέρισμα (thee-ah-MEH-ree-zmah) apartment
ἡ πολυκατοικία (poh-lee-kah-tee-KEE-ah) apartment house
ὁ κτηματομεσίτης (ktee-mah-toh-meh-SEE-tees) real estate broker
τὸ ἀσανσέρ (ah-sahn-SEHR) elevator
κοιτάζω, κυττάζω (kee-TAH-zoh) I look at

τὸ σχέδιο (SKHEH-thee-oh) plan
ἡ θέα (THE-ah) view
τὸ φῶς (FOHS) the light
ὁ φωτισμός (foh-tee-ZMOHS) light
τὸ ἐνοίκιο (eh-NEE-kee-oh) rent

τὸ ζεῦγος (ZEHV-ghohs) couple
τὸ ὕψωμα (EE-psoh-mah) hill
τὰ ἔξοδα (EH-ksoh-thah) expenses
τὸ νερό (neh-ROH) water
ἡ σκάλα (SKAH-lah) stairway

114

Τὸ σπίτι. Ἡ ἐπίπλωση.
(toh SPEE-tee. ee eh-PEE-ploh-see)
The house. The furniture

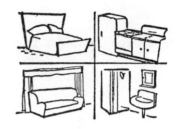

τὰ ἔπιπλα   (EH-pee-plah) furniture
ἐπιπλώνω   (eh-pee-PLOH-noh) I furnish
ἡ τραπεζαρία   (trah-peh-zah-REE-ah) dining-room
τὸ σαλόνι   (sah-LOH-nee) living-room
ἡ κρεβατοκάμαρα   (kreh-vah-toh-KAH-mah-rah) bedroom

τὸ μπαλκόνι   (bahl-KOH-nee) balcony
ἡ πολυθρόνα   (poh-lee-THROH-nah) armchair
τὸ στρῶμα   (STROH-mah) mattress
τὸ μαξιλάρι   (mah-ksee-LAH-ree) pillow
ἡ κουβέρτα   (koo-VEHR-tah) blanket

ἡ κουζίνα   (koo-ZEE-nah) kitchen
τὸ χαλί   (khah-LEE) rug
ἡ καρέκλα   (kah-REH-klah) chair
ἡ λάμπα   (LAHM-bah) lamp
ὁ καναπές   (kah-nah-PEHS) sofa

τὸ μπάνιο   (BAH-nyoh) bathroom
τὸ τραπέζι   (trah-PEH-zee) table
ἡ κουρτίνα   (koor-TEE-nah) curtain
τὸ σιντόνι   (seen-DOH-nee) sheet
τὰ πιάτα   (PYAH-tah) plates, dishes

τὸ συρτάρι   (seer-TAH-ree) drawer
ἡ βιβλιοθήκη   (vee-vlee-oh-THEE-kee) library, bookcase
τὸ ψυγεῖο   (psee-YEE-oh) refrigerator
ἡ παγωνιέρα   (pah-ghoh-NYEH-rah) ice-box
τὸ τηλέφωνο   (tee-LEH-foh-noh) telephone
τὸ τζάκι   (DZAH-kee) fireplace

CONVERSATION

1 Ἡ Πάτρα, ἀγαπητέ μου κύριε Πετρίδη, εἶναι θαυμάσια πόλη. Μοιάζει πολὺ μὲ τὴ Θεσσαλονίκη. Καὶ οἱ δυὸ εἶναι ἐμπορικὲς παραλιακὲς πόλεις.

2 Χαίρομαι νὰ βλέπω, ὅτι ἡ Ἑλλάδα σοῦ ἀρέσει τόσο πολύ. Εἶμαι βέβαιος, ὅτι θὰ μείνετε ἀρκετὰ μαζί μας καὶ ὅτι θὰ γνωρίσετε τὴν Ἤπειρο, τὴ Μακεδονία, τὴ Θράκη καὶ τὰ νησιά.

3 Αὐτὸ εἶναι τὸ σχέδιό μου. Περιμένω ἕνα φίλο μου ἀπὸ τὴν Ἀμερική. Εἶναι Ἀμερικανὸς πολίτης ἑλληνικῆς καταγωγῆς. Ἔρχεται μὲ τὴ γυναίκα του καὶ μοῦ γράφει νὰ τοῦ ἐνοικιάσω ἕνα σπίτι.

4 Θέλετε διαμέρισμα σὲ πολυκατοικία ἢ προτιμᾶτε σπίτι σὲ προάστειο τῆς Ἀθήνας;

5 Νομίζω ὅτι καλύτερα εἶναι νὰ μείνουν μέσα στὴν πόλη.

6 Τότε μποροῦμε νὰ πᾶμε μαζὶ σὲ ἕνα φίλο μου κτηματομεσίτη.

7 «Ἄμ' ἔπος ἄμ' ἔργον»[1] ἔλεγον οἱ πρόγονοί μας. Δηλαδὴ ἀπὸ τὸ λόγο στὴν πράξη. Πᾶμε.

8 Καλημέρα, κύριε Κτηματίδη[2]. Ὁ φίλος μου κύριος Σμὶθ

FOOTNOTES: 1. A more free translation of this classical Greek saying is "No sooner said than done".   2. Κτηματίδης which is a derivative of κτῆμα

PRONUNCIATION

1 ee PAH-trah, ah-ghah-pee-TEH-moo K E E-ree-eh peh-TREE-*th*ee, EE-neh thahv-MAH-see-ah POH-lee. MYAH-zee poh-LEE meh tee theh-sah-loh-NEE-kee. keh ee *TH*YOH EE-neh ehm-boh-ree-KEHS pah-rah-lee-ah-KEHS POH-lees.

2 KHEH-roh-meh nah VLEH-poh OH-tee ee eh-LAH-*th*ah soo ah-REH-see TOH-soh poh-LEE. EE-meh VEH-veh-ohs OH-tee thah MEE-neh-teh ahr-keh-TAH mah-ZEE-mahs keh OH-tee thah ghnoh-REE-seh-teh teen EE-pee-roh, tee m a h-k e h-*t h* o h-N E E-a h, tee THRAH-kee keh tah nee-SYAH.

3 ahf-TOH EE-neh toh SKHEH-*th*ee-OH-moo. peh-ree-MEH-noh EH-nah FEE-loh-moo ah-POH teen ah-meh-ree-KEE. EE-neh ah-meh-ree-kah-NOHS poh-LEE-tees eh-lee-nee-KEES kah-tah-ghoh-YEES. EHR-kheh-teh meh tee yee-NEH-kah-too keh moo GHRAH-fee nah too eh-nee-kee-A H-soh E H-nah SPEE-tee.

4 THEH-leh-teh *th*ee-ah-MEH-ree-zmah seh poh-lee-kah-tee-KEE-ah EE proh-tee-MAH-teh SPEE-tee seh proh-AH-stee-oh TEES ah-THEE-nahs?

5 noh-MEE-zoh OH-tee kah-LEE-teh-rah EE-neh nah MEE-noon MEH-sah steem-BOH-lee.

6 TOH-teh boh-ROO-meh nah PAH-meh mah-ZEE seh EH-nah FEE-loh-moo ktee-mah-toh-meh-SEE-tee.

7 "AHM-EH-pohs AHM-EHR-ghohn" EH-leh-ghahn ee PROH-ghoh-NEE-mahs. *th*ee-lah-*TH*EE ah-POH toh LOH-ghoh steem PRAH-ksee. PAH-meh.

8 kah-lee-MEH-rah, KEE-ree-eh ktee-mah-TEE-*th*ee. oh FEE-lohz-moo

TRANSLATION

Patra, my dear Mr. Petrides, is a wonderful city. It looks very much like Salonika. Both are commercial ports.

I am glad to see that you like Greece so much. I am sure you will stay with us long enough to become acquainted with Epiros, Macedonia, Thrace, and the islands.

That is my plan. I am expecting a friend of mine from America. He is an American citizen of Greek descent. He is coming with his wife and he wrote to me to rent a house for him.

Would you like an apartment in a large apartment house or do you prefer a house in the suburbs of Athens?

I think it will be better to stay in the center of the city.

Then we can go together to a real estate broker who is a friend of mine.

"With the saying, the doing," as our forefathers used to say. That is, from the word to the act, let's go .

Good morning, Mr. Ctematides.

θέλει νὰ (ἐ)νοικιάση[3] ἕνα διαμέρισμα σὲ μιὰ πολυκατοικία.

9 Εἶσθε, κύριε Σμίθ, Ἀμερικανὸς ἢ Ἄγγλος;

10 Εἶμαι Ἀμερικανός. Θέλω τὸ διαμέρισμα αὐτὸ γιὰ ἕνα φιλικὸ ζεῦγος. Ἔρχεται σὲ λίγες ἡμέρες ἀπὸ τὴν Ἀμερική.

11 Ἔχω πολλὰ διαμερίσματα γιὰ ἐνοικίαση. Κυττάξετε τὸ χάρτη τῆς Ἀθήνας. Ποιὰ συνοικία προτιμᾶτε;

12 Προτιμῶ τὸ Κολωνάκι. Εἶναι σὲ ὕψωμα καὶ ἡ θέα ἀπὸ τὰ σπίτια εἶναι ὡραία.

13 Κυττάξετε αὐτὴν τὴ φωτογραφία. Ἡ πολυκατοικία αὐτὴ εἶναι στὴν πλατεῖα Δεξαμενῆς. Ἐκεῖ ἔχει ἕνα μεγάλο διαμέρισμα.

14 Μὲ πόσα δωμάτια;

15 Τὸ διαμέρισμα αὐτὸ ἔχει ἕνα σαλόνι, δύο κρεβατοκάμαρες, ἕνα δωμάτιο γιὰ τὴν ὑπηρεσία, τραπεζαρία, κουζίνα καὶ δύο μπάνια[4].

16 Νομίζω ὅτι τὸ διαμέρισμα αὐτὸ εἶναι πολὺ μεγάλο.

17 Τότε νὰ σᾶς δώσω ἕνα μικρὸ διαμέρισμα μὲ μιὰ κρεβατοκάμαρα, ἕνα μικρὸ σαλόνι, τραπεζαρία, κουζίνα καὶ μπάνιο.

(property, estate) implies one who deals with property. 3. Ἐνοικιάζω is a Puristic and formal variant of νοικιάζω. 4. Μπάνιο is the colloquial equivalent of λουτρό(ν) which was also the classical Greek word for "bath".

KEE-ree-ohs Smith THEH-lee nah (eh) -nee-KYAH-see EH-nah *th*ee-ah-MEH-ree-zmah seh MYAH poh-lee-kah-tee-KEE-ah.

My friend Mr. Smith wants to rent an apartment in a large apartment house.

9 EE-stheh, KEE-ree-eh Smith, ah-meh-ree-kah-NOHS EE AHN-glohs?

Are you an American or an Englishman, Mr. Smith?

10 EE-meh ah-meh-ree-kah-NOHS. THEH-loh toh *th*ee-ah-MEH-ree-zmah ahf-TOH yah EH-nah fee-lee-KOH ZEHV-ghohs. EHR-kheh-teh seh LEE-yehs ee-MEH-rehs ah-POH teen ah-meh-ree-KEE.

I am an American. I want this apartment for a couple who are friends of mine. They are coming from America in a few days.

11 EH-khoh poh-LAH *th*ee-ah-meh-REE-zmah-tah yah eh-nee-KEE-ah-see. kee-TAH-ks (eh) -teh toh KHAHR-tee tees ah-THEE-nahs. PYAH see-nee-KEE-ah proh-tee-MAH-teh?

I have many apartments for rent. Look at the map of Athens. Which section do you prefer?

12 proh-tee-MOH toh koh-loh-NAH-kee. EE-neh seh EE-psoh-mah keh ee THEH-ah ah-POH tah SPEE-tyah EE-neh oh-REH-ah.

I prefer Kolonaki. It is high, and the view from the house is beautiful.

13 kee-TAH-ks (eh) -teh ahf-TEE tee foh-toh-ghrah-FEE-ah. ee poh-lee-kah-tee-KEE-ah ahf-TEE EE-neh steem plah-TEE-ah *th*eh-ksah-meh-NEES. eh-KEE EH-khee EH-nah meh-GHAH-loh *th*ee-ah-meh-ree-zmah.

Look at this picture. This large apartment house is on Dexamene Square. There is a large apartment vacant.

14 meh POH-sah *th*oh-MAH-tee-ah?

Of how many rooms?

15 toh *th*ee-ah-MEH-ree-zmah ahf-TOH EH-khee EH-nah sah-LOH-nee, *TH*EE-oh kreh-vah-toh-KAH-mah-rehs, EH-nah *th*oh-MAH-tee-oh yah teen ee-pee-reh-SEE-ah, trah-peh-zah-REE-ah, koo-ZEE-nah keh *TH*EE-oh BAH-nyah.

This apartment has a living room, two bedrooms, a room for the maid, a dining room, a kitchen and two bathrooms.

16 noh-MEE-zoh OH-tee toh *th*ee-ah-MEH-ree-zmah ahf-TOH EE-neh poh-LEE meh-GHAH-loh.

I think this apartment is too large.

17 TOH-teh nah sahs *TH*OH-soh EH-nah mee-KROH *th*ee-ah-MEH-ree-zmah meh MYAH kreh-vah-toh-KAH-mah-rah, EH-nah mee-KROH sah-LOH-nee, trah-peh-zah-REE-ah, koo-ZEE-nah keh BAH-nyoh.

Then I will give you a small apartment of one bedroom, a small living room, a dining room, a kitchen, and a bathroom.

18 Είναι ἀνατολικὸ ἢ δυτικό; "Εχει καλὴ θέα;

19 Είναι μᾶλλον δυτικό. Ἡ θέα του εἶναι θαυμάσια. ᾿Απὸ τὸ μπαλκόνι βλέπεις τὴν ᾿Ακρόπολη, τὸν ᾿Εθνικὸ Κῆπο, τὰ ᾿Ανάκτορα.

20 Είναι ἐπιπλωμένο;

21 Μάλιστα. Τὰ ἔπιπλα εἶναι καινούργια καὶ σὲ πολὺ καλὴ κατάσταση. Κρεβάτια[5], ντουλάπες, καθίσματα, ἔπιπλα τραπεζαρίας, χαλιά, σκεύη κουζίνας, ὅλα γενικῶς τὰ χρειαζόμενα γιὰ μιὰ μικρὴ οἰκογένεια.

22 Ἡ προσφορά σας εἶναι ἐνδιαφέρουσα. ᾿Αλλὰ πόσο εἶναι τὸ ἐνοίκιο;

23 Τὸ ἐνοίκιο εἶναι χίλιες ὀκτακόσιες δραχμὲς τὸ μῆνα.

24 Στὸ ἐνοίκιο αὐτὸ περιλαμβάνονται τὰ ἔξοδα φωτισμοῦ καὶ θερμάνσεως;

25 Δυστυχῶς ὄχι. Τὸ τηλέφωνο, τὸ ἠλεκτρικὸ φῶς, ἡ θέρμανση καὶ τὸ νερὸ λογαριάζονται ξεχωριστά.

26 Θὰ χαρῶ πολύ, ἂν μπορέσωμε αὔριο νὰ ἐπισκεφθοῦμε τὸ διαμέρισμα αὐτό.

27 Εὐχαρίστως. Αὔριο τὸ ἀπόγευμα, στὶς τέσσερες καὶ μισή.

_____

5. Κρεβάτι is an othographical variant of κρεββάτι and according to the best authorities, it is not only simpler, but even etymologically better justified.

18 EE-neh ah-nah-toh-lee-KOH EE *th*ee-tee-KOH? EH-khee kah-LEE THEH-ah?

19 EE-neh MAH-lohn *th*ee-tee-KOH. ee THEH-ah-too EE-neh thahv-MAH-see-ah. ah-POH toh bahl-KOH-nee VLEH-pees teen ah-KROH-poh-lee, tohn eh-thnee-KOH KEE-poh, tah ah-NAH-ktoh-rah.

20 EE-neh eh-pee-ploh-MEH-noh?

21 MAH-lee-stah. tah EH-pee-plah EE-neh keh-NOOR-yah keh seh poh-LEE kah-LEE kah-TAH-stah-see. kreh-VAH-tyah, doo-LAH-pehs, kah-THEE-zmah-tah, EH-pee-plah trah-peh-zah-REE-ahs, khah LYAH, SKEH-vee koo-ZEE-nahs, OH-lah yeh-nee-KOHS tah khree-ah-ZOO-meh-nah yah MYAH mee-KREE ee-koh-YEH-nee-ah.

22 ee prohs-foh-RAH-sahs EE-neh ehn-*th*ee-ah-FEH-roo-sah. ah-LAH POH-soh EE-neh toh eh-NEE-kee-oh?

23 toh eh-NEE-kee-oh EE-neh KHEE-lyehs oh-ktah-KOH-syehs *th*rahkh-MEHS toh MEE-nah.

24 stoh eh-NEE-kee-oh ahf-TOH peh-ree-lahm-VAH-nohn-deh tah EH-ksoh-*th*ah foh-tee-ZMOO keh thehr-MAHN-seh-ohs?

25 *th*ees-tee-KHOHS OH-khee. toh tee-LEH-foh-noh, toh ee-leh-ktree-KOH FOHS, ee THEHR-mahn-see keh toh neh-ROH loh-ghah-RYAH-zohn-deh kseh-khoh-ree-STAH.

26 thah khah-ROH poh-LEE,ahn boh-REH-soh-meh AHV-ree-oh nah eh-pee-skeh-FTHOO-meh toh *th*ee-ah-MEH-ree-zmah ahf-TOH.

27 ehf-khah-REE-stohs. AHV-ree-oh toh ah-poh-yehv-mah, stees TEH-seh-rehs keh mee-SEE.

Does it look to the east or to the west (*lit.*, Is it eastern or western)? Does it have a beautiful view?

It faces (rather) the west. Its view is wonderful. From the balcony you see the Acropolis, the National Garden, the Palace.

Is it furnished?

Yes. The furniture is modern and in very good condition. Beds, closets, chairs, a living room set, rugs, kitchen utensils, everything that is needed for a small family.

Your offer is interesting. But how much is the rent?

The rent is one thousand eight hundred drachmas per month.

Are light and heat included in the rent?

Unfortunately not. The telephone, the electric light, the heat and the water are charged separately.

I shall be very glad if we can visit this apartment tomorrow.

With pleasure. Tomorrow afternoon at half past four.

Twelfth Lesson

New Vocabulary for this Lesson

υπογράφω   (ee-poh-GHRAH-foh) I sign
η προκαταβολή   (proh-kah-tah-voh-LEE) advance
μηνιαῖος, -α, -ο   (mee-nee-EH-ohs) monthly
προχωρῶ   (proh-khoh-ROH) I go on
ἐπόμενος, -η, -ο   (eh-POH-meh-nohs) next

τὸ τετράγωνο   (teh-TRAH-ghoh-noh) block, square (in geometry)
λογοτεχνικός, -ή, -ό   (loh-ghoh-tehkh-nee-KOHS) literary
ἐπιστημονικός, -ή, -ό   (eh-pee-stee-moh-nee-KOHS) scientific
φοβοῦμαι   (foh-VOO-meh) I am afraid
ὁ λογαριασμός   (loh-ghah-ryah-ZMOHS) bill

ὁ στυλογράφος   (stee-loh-GHRAH-fohs) fountain pen
τὰ φάκελλα   (FAH-keh-lah) envelopes
ἡ γραφομηχανή   (ghrah-foh-mee-khah-NEE) typewriter
τὰ λαστιχάκια   (lah-stee-KHAH-kyah) rubber bands

Χαρτοπωλεῖο. Βιβλιοπωλεῖο.
(khahr-toh-poh-LEE-oh. vee-vlee-oh-poh-LEE-oh)
Stationery store. Bookstore

ἡ ἐφημερίδα (eh-fee-meh-REE-thah) newspaper
τὸ περιοδικό (peh-ree-oh-thee-KOH) magazine
καθημερινός, -ή, -ό (kah-thee-meh-ree-NOHS) daily
ἀλληλογραφία (ah-lee-loh-ghrah-FEE-ah) correspondence
ὁ χαρτοφύλακας (khahr-toh-FEE-lah-kahs) brief case
δερμάτινος (thehr-MAH-tee-nohs) of leather

τὸ μολύβι (moh-LEE-vee) pencil
ἡ κόλλα (KOH-lah) glue
τὸ γραφεῖο (ghrah-FEE-oh) office
τὸ κουτί (koo-TEE) box

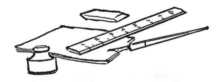

τὸ μελάνι (meh-LAH-nee) ink
τὸ χαρτί (khahr-TEE) paper
ἡ κάρτα (KAHR-tah) card
τὸ βιβλίο (vee-VLEE-oh) book

τὰ εἴδη (EE-thee) items
τὸ τμῆμα (TMEE-mah) section
ἐπίσης (eh-PEE-sees) also
ἀμελῶ (ah-meh-LOH) I neglect
ταμεῖο (tah-MEE-oh) the cashier's

τὰ χαρτιά (khahr-TYAH) papers
παλιός, -α, -ο (pah-LYOHS) old
κάτι (KAH-tee) something
πληρώνω (plee-ROH-noh) I pay
ἡ πέννα (PEH-nah) pen

Conversation

1 Κύριε Κτηματίδη, τὸ διαμέρισμα εἶναι θαυμάσιο. Εἶμαι ἔτοιμος νὰ ὑπογράψω τὸ συμβόλαιο. Θέλετε προκαταβολή;

2 Τὰ χαρτιὰ εἶναι ἔτοιμα. Ὑπογράψατε, σᾶς παρακαλῶ. Ἡ προκαταβολὴ εἶναι δύο μηνιαῖα ἐνοίκια.

3 Νὰ ἡ ἐπιταγή. Τρεῖς χιλιάδες ἑξακόσιες δραχμές.

4 Σᾶς εὐχαριστῶ πολύ.

5 Εἶναι ἐδῶ κάτω κανένα χαρτοπωλεῖο;

6 Μάλιστα. Προχωρήσετε στὴν ὁδὸ Σταδίου. Ἐκεῖ εἶναι τὸ μεγάλο βιβλιοπωλεῖο καὶ χαρτοπωλεῖο ὁ «Ἥλιος».

7 Κύριε ἀστυφύλακα, ποῦ εἶναι τὸ βιβλιοπωλεῖο ὁ «Ἥλιος»;

8 Στὸ ἐπόμενο τετράγωνο, κύριε.

9 Χαίρετε, δεσποινίς. Θὰ ἤθελα μερικὰ φάκελλα.

10 Περάστε, σᾶς παρακαλῶ στὸ τμῆμα χαρτοπωλείου. Ἐκεῖ θὰ βρῆτε χαρτί, φάκελλα, πέννες, μελάνη, μολύβια, κάρτες, γραφομηχανές, ὅλα τὰ εἴδη ἀλληλογραφίας καὶ ὅλα τὰ εἴδη γραφείου.

11 Ἔχετε τμῆμα ξένων βιβλίων;

12 Μάλιστα. Ἔχομε πολλὰ λογοτεχνικὰ καὶ ἐπιστημονικὰ βιβλία στὴν ἀγγλικὴ καὶ γαλλικὴ γλῶσσα.

1 KEE-ree-eh ktee-mah-TEE-*thee*, toh *thee*-ah-MEH-ree-zmah EE-neh thahv-MAH-see-oh. EE-meh EH-tee-mohs nah ee-poh-GHRAH-psoh toh seem-VOH-leh-oh. THEH-leh-teh proh-kah-tah-voh-LEE?

2 tah khahr-TYAH EE-neh EH-tee-mah. ee-poh-GHRAH-psah-teh sahs pah-rah-kah-LOH. ee proh-kah-tah-voh-LEE EE-neh *THEE*-oh mee-nee-EH-ah eh-NEE-kee-ah.

3 NAH ee eh-pee-tah-YEE. TREES khee-LYAH-*thehs* eh-ksah-KOH-syehs *th*rahkh-MEHS.

4 sahs ehf-khah-ree-STOH poh-LEE.

5 EE-neh eh-*THOH* KAH-toh kah-NEH-nah khahr-toh-poh-LEE-oh?

6 MAH-lee-stah. proh-*kh*oh-REE-s(eh)-teh steen oh-*THOH* stah-*THEE*-oo. eh-KEE EE-neh toh meh-GHAH-loh vee-vlee-oh-poh-LEE-oh keh khahr-toh-poh-LEE-oh oh EE-lee-ohs.

7 KEE-ree-eh ah-stee-FEE-lah-kah, POO EE-neh toh vee-vlee-oh-poh-LEE-oh oh EE-lee-ohs?

8 stoh eh-POH-meh-noh teh-TRAH-ghoh-noh, KEE-ree-eh.

9 KHEH-reh-teh, *th*ehs-pee-NEES. thah EE-theh-lah meh-ree-KAH FAH-keh-lah.

10 peh-RAH-steh sahs pah-rah-kah-LOH stoh TMEE-mah khah-rtoh-poh-LEE-oo. eh-KEE thah VREE-teh khahr-TEE, FAH-keh-lah, PEH-nehs, meh-LAH-nee, moh-LEE-vyah, KAHR-tehs, ghrah-foh-mee-khah-NEHS, OH-lah tah EE-*thee* ah-lee-loh-ghrah-FEE-ahs keh OH-lah tah EE-*thee* ghrah-FEE-oo.

11 EH-kheh-teh TMEE-mah KSEH-nohn vee-VLEE-ohn?

12 MAH-lee-stah. EH-khoh-meh poh-LAH loh-ghoh-teh-khnee-KAH keh eh-pee-stee-moh-KAH vee-VLEE-ah

Mr. Ctematides, the apartment is wonderful. I am ready to sign the contract. Would you like an advance?

The papers are ready. Sign, please. The advance is two months' rent.

Here is the check. Three thousand six hundred drachmas.

Thank you very much.

Is there any stationery store down here?

Yes. Go on to Stadiou Street. There is the large book and stationery store "Helios".

Officer (*lit.*, Mr. Policeman), where is the "Helios" book-store?

On the next block, sir.

Hello, miss. I would like some envelopes .

Go to the stationery section, please. There you will find writing paper, envelopes, pens, ink, pencils, cards, typewriters, and all correspondence and desk items.

Is there a foreign book section?

Yes. We have many literary and scientific books in English and French.

13 Ἔχετε ἐφημερίδες καὶ περιοδικά.

14 Μάλιστα. Πωλοῦμε ὅλες τὶς καθημερινὲς ἑλληνικὲς ἐ-
φημερίδες καὶ ὅλα τὰ περιοδικά. Πωλοῦμε ἐπίσης ἀμε-
ρικάνικες, ἀγγλικὲς καὶ γαλλικὲς ἐφημερίδες καὶ περιοδικά. Θέλετε κάτι;

15 Ὄχι, εὐχαριστῶ. Θὰ περάσω πρῶτα ἀπὸ τὸ χαρτοπωλεῖο.

16 Τὶ θέλετε, κύριε; Μπορῶ νὰ σᾶς βοηθήσω;

17 Θὰ ἤθελα ἀρκετὰ πράγματα. Φοβοῦμαι, ὅτι ἔχω ἀμε-
λήσει τὴν ἀλληλογραφία μου.

18 Ὅπως βλέπετε, ἔχομε ὅλα τὰ εἴδη τῆς ἀλληλογραφίας.

19 Δῶστε μου, σᾶς παρακαλῶ, μία πέννα, ἕνα μολύβι, μελάνη, ἕνα κουτὶ χαρτοφάκελλα καλῆς ποιότητος καὶ μερικὲς κάρτες.

20 Ὁρίστε, κύριε. Μήπως θέλετε καμία ἑλληνικὴ γραφομηχανή, κανένα δερμάτινο χαρτοφύλακα, κάτι ἄλλο;

21 Ὄχι. Δῶστε μου τὸ λογαριασμό, σᾶς παρακαλῶ.

22 Ὁ λογαριασμὸς εἶναι διακόσιες δραχμές. Πληρώσετε
στὸ ταμεῖο, παρακαλῶ.

steen ahn-glee-KEE keh ghah-lee-KEE GHLOH-sah.

13 EH-kheh-teh eh-fee-meh-REE-*t*hehs keh peh-ree-oh-*t*hee-KAH?

Do you also have newspapers and magazines?

14 MAH-lee-stah. poh-LOO-meh OH-lehs tees kah-thee-meh-ree-NEHS eh-lee-nee-KEHS eh-fee-meh-REE-*t*hehs keh OH-lah tah peh-ree-oh-*t*hee-KAH. poh-LOO-meh eh-PEE-sees ah-meh-ree-kah-nee-KEHS, ahn-glee-KEHS keh ghah-lee-KEHS eh-fee-meh-REE-*t*hehs keh peh-ree-oh-*t*hee-KAH. THEH-leh-teh KAH-tee?

Yes. We sell all the Greek newspapers and all the magazines. We also sell American, English and French newspapers and magazines. Do you want something?

15 OH-khee, ehf-khah-ree-STOH. thah peh-RAH-soh PROH-tah ah-POH toh khahr-toh-poh-LEE-oh.

No, thank you. I will go first to the stationery section.

16 TEE THEH-leh-teh, KEE-ree-eh? boh-ROH nah sahs voh-ee-THEE-soh?

What would you like (*lit.,* What do you want), sir? Can l help you?

17 thah EE-theh-lah ahr-keh-TAH PRAHGH-mah-tah. foh-VOO-meh OH-tee EH-khoh ah-meh-LEE-see teen ah-lee-loh-ghrah-FEE-ah-moo.

I would like a few things. I am afraid I have neglected my correspondence...

18 OH-pohs VLEH-peh-teh, EH-khoh-meh OH-lah tah EE-*t*hee tees ah-lee-loh-ghrah-FEE-ahs.

As you see, we have all the correspondence items.

19 *T*HOH-steh-moo, sahs pah-rah-kah-LOH, MEE-ah PEH-nah, EH-nah moh-LEE-vee, meh-LAH-nee, EH-nah koo-TEE khahr-toh-FAH-keh-LAH kah-LEES pee-OH-tee-tohs keh meh-ree-KEHS KAHR-tehs.

Please, give me a pen, a pencil, a box of letter- paper and envelopes of a good quality and a few cards.

20 oh-REE-steh, KEE-ree-eh. MEE-pohs THEH-leh-teh kah-MEE-ah eh-lee-nee-KEE ghrah-foh-mee-khah-NEE, kah-NEH-nah *t*hehr-MAH-tee-noh khahr-toh-FEE-lah-kah, KAH-tee AH-loh?

Here you are, sir. Would you like a Greek typewriter perhaps, a leather briefcase, anything else?

21 OH-khee. *T*HOH-steh-moo toh loh-ghah-ryah-ZMOH, sahs pah-rah-kah-LOH.

No. Give me the bill, please.

22 oh loh-ghah-ryah-ZMOHS EE-neh *t*hee-ah-KOH-see-ehs *t*hrahkh-MEHS. plee-ROH-s(eh)-teh stoh tah-MEE-oh, pah-rah-kah-LOH.

The bill is two hundred drachmas. Pay the cashier, please.

ΔΕΚΑΤΟ ΤΡΙΤΟ ΜΑΘΗΜΑ
Thirteenth Lesson

New Vocabulary for this Lesson

αἰσθάνομαι (eh-STAH-noh-meh) I feel
δυνατός, -ή. -ό (thee-nah-TOHS) strong
ἀνυπόφορος (ah-nee-POH-foh-rohs) unbearable
περαστικά σας (peh-rah-stee-KAH-sahs) speedy recovery
συνεργάζομαι (seen-ehr-GHAH-zoh-meh) I work with

ὁ εἰδικός, -ή, -ό (ee-thee-KOHS) specialist
ἀμέσως (ah-MEH-sohs) immediately
προσπαθῶ (proh-spah-THOH) I try
δέχομαι (THEH-khoh-meh) I accept
οἱ ὁδηγίες (oh-thee-YEE-ehs) instructions

σοβαρός, -ή, -ό (soh-vah-ROHS) serious
τὸ γκαρσόν(ι) (gahr-SOH-nee) waiter
ἀναθέτω (ah-nah-THEH-toh) I assign
κατάγομαι (kah-TAH-ghoh-meh) I am from
ὁ παθολόγος (pah-thoh-LOH-ghohs) general practitioner

ὁ χειροῦργος (khee-ROOR-ghohs) surgeon
ὁ ὀδοντογιατρός (oh-thohn-doh-gah-TROHS) dentist
τὸ σύμπτωμα (SEEM-ptoh-mah) symptom
ὁ πονοκέφαλος (poh-noh-KEH-fah-lohs) headache
τὸ συνάχι (see-NAH-khee) head cold

εἰδοποιῶ (ee-thoh-pee-OH) I inform   καλύτερα (kah-LEE-teh-rah) better
ἐλπίζω (ehl-PEE-zoh) I hope   σύντομα (SEEN-doh-mah) soon
καλῶ (kah-LOH) I call   ἄσχημα (AH-skhee-mah) badly
ὅμως (OH-mohs) but, though   ἡσυχία (ee-see-KHEE-ah) quiet
σωστός, -ή, -ό (soh-STOHS) right   στέλλω (STEH-loh) I send

128

Ὁ Γιατρός (yah-TROHS) Doctor
πονῶ (poh-NOH) I ache
ὁ πόνος (POH-nohs) pain
ἡ ζάλη (ZAH-lee) dizziness
ὁ σφυγμός (sfeegh-MOHS) pulse

ὁ βήχας (VEE-khahs) cough
ἡ κλινική (klee-nee-KEE) clinic
ἡ ἀμοιβή (ah-mee-VEE) fee

ἡ γνώμη (GHNOH-mee) opinion
ὁ χυμός (khee-MOHS) juice
ἄρρωστος, -η (AH-roh-stohs) sick
ὑποφέρω (ee-poh-FEH-roh) I suffer
ἡ γρίππη (GHREE-pee) influenza

ἡ θεραπεία (theh-rah-PEE-ah) cure
τὸ χάπι (KHAH-pee) pill
τὸ νησί (nee-see) island

ἡ θερμοκρασία (thehr-moh-krah-SEE-ah) temperature
ἐξετάζω (eh-kseh-TAH-zoh) I examine
ἡ διάγνωση (thee-AH-ghnoh-see) diagnosis
τὸ φαρμακεῖο (fahr-mah-KEE-oh) drugstore
τὸ φάρμακο (FAHR-mah-koh) medicine

ἡ συνταγή (seen-dah-YEE) prescription
ἡ ἀσπιρίνη (ah-spee-REE-nee) aspirin
τὸ οἰνόπνευμα (ee-NOH-pnehv-mah) alcohol
τὸ δάκτυλο (THAH-ktee-loh) finger
τὸ στομάχι (stoh-MAH-khee) stomach

Τὸ Σῶμα (SOH-mah) The Body
τὸ κεφάλι (keh-FAH-lee) head

τὸ πόδι (POH-thee) foot
τὸ νύχι (NEE-khee) nail
ἡ καρδιά (kahr-THYAH) heart
τὸ μάτι (MAH-tee) eye
ἡ γλῶσσα (GHLOH-sah) tongue

ἡ μύτη (MEE-tee) nose
τὰ μαλλιά (mah-LYAH) hair

ἡ ὑγεία (ee-YEE-ah) health
ὁ λαιμός (leh-MOHS) neck

τὸ χέρι (KHEH-ree) hand
τὸ στῆθος (STEE-thohs) chest
ἡ πλάτη (PLAH-tee) back
τὸ πρόσωπο (PROH-soh-poh) face
τὸ στόμα (STOH-mah) mouth

τὸ δόντι (THOHN-dee) tooth
τὸ αὐτί (ahf-TEE) ear

CONVERSATION

1 Ἐμπρός. Ξενοδοχεῖο Ἀθηνῶν; Μπορῶ νὰ μιλήσω στὸν κύριο Σμίθ;

2 Εὐχαρίστως, δωμάτιο διακόσια δώδεκα. Ὁμιλῆστε.

3 Σεῖς, κύριε Πετρίδη; Λυποῦμαι νὰ σᾶς πῶ ὅτι εἶμαι ἄρρωστος. Δὲν αἰσθάνομαι καλά.

4 Λυποῦμαι πολύ. Εἶσθε στὸ κρεββάτι;

5 Μάλιστα. Νομίζω, ὅτι ἔχω πυρετό.

6 Ἔχετε πονοκέφαλο; Ποῦ πονεῖτε;

7 Ἔχω δυνατὸ πονοκέφαλο καὶ μιὰ μυαλγία ἀνυπόφορη.

8 Φαίνεται, ὅτι κρυώσατε. Πρέπει νὰ πάρετε ὅλες τὶς προφυλάξεις. Εἶναι ἀνάγκη νὰ σᾶς ἰδῆ κάποιος γιατρός, ἕνας καλὸς γιατρός.

9 Ξέρετε κανένα;

10 Καλύτερα νὰ εἰδοποιήσετε τὸν γιατρὸ τοῦ ξενοδοχείου. Τηλεφωνήσετε στὴν ὑπηρεσία. Λοιπόν, περαστικά σας. Θὰ σᾶς ἐπισκεφθῶ αὔριο τὸ πρωί. Ἐλπίζω, ὅτι θὰ γίνετε καλὰ σύντομα.

11 Δεσποινίς, μπορεῖτε νὰ μοῦ πῆτε ποιός εἶναι ὁ γιατρὸς τοῦ ξενοδοχείου;

12 Τὸ ξενοδοχεῖο συνεργάζεται μὲ ἀρκετοὺς εἰδικοὺς γιατρούς. Μὲ ἕνα παθολόγο, μὲ ἕνα χειροῦργο, μὲ ἕνα παιδίατρο. Νὰ καλέσωμε τὸν κύριο Ἰατρίδη, τὸν παθολόγο;

1 ehm-BROHS. kseh-noh-*t*hoh-KHEE-oh ah-thee-NOHN? boh-ROH na̋h mee-LEE-soh stohn KEE-ree-oh Smith?

Hello. Hotel "Athens"? May I speak to Mr. Smith?

2 ehf-khah-REE-stohs, *t*hoh-MAH-tee-oh *t*hee-ah-KOH-see-ah *T*HOH-theh-kah. oh-mee-LEE-steh.

With pleasure. Room two hundred twelve. Go ahead (*lit.*, Speak).

3 SEES, KEE-ree-eh peh-TREE-*t*hee? lee-POO-meh nah sahs POH OH-tee EE-meh AH-roh-stohs. *T*HEHN ehs-THAH-noh-meh kah-LAH.

Is that you Mr. Petrides? I am sorry to tell you that I am sick. I don't feel very well.

4 lee-POO-meh poh-LEE. EE-stheh stoh kreh-VAH-tee?

I am very sorry. Are you in bed?

5 MAH-lee-stah. noh-MEE-zoh OH-tee EH-khoh pee-reh-TOH.

Yes. I think I have a fever.

6 EH-kheh-teh po h-noh-KEH-fah-loh? POO poh-NEE-teh?

Do you have a headache? Where does it hurt?

7 EH-khoh *t*hee-nah-TOH poh-noh-KEH-fah-loh keh MEE-ah mee-ahl-YEE-ah ah-nee-POH-foh-ree.

I have a bad (*lit.*, strong) headache and an unbearable muscular pain.

8 FEH-neh-teh OH-tee kree-OH-sah-teh. PREH-pee nah PAH-reh-teh OH-lehs tees proh-fee-LAH-ksees. EE-neh ah-NAHN-gee nah sahs ee-*T*HEE KAH-pyohs yah-THROHS, EH-nahs kah-LOHS yah-TROHS.

It seems that you have caught a cold. You must take good care of yourself (*lit.*, all the precautions). You should see a doctor, (*lit.*, It is need some doctor to see you) a good doctor. Do you know of one?

9 KSEH-reh-teh kah-NEH-nah?

10 kah-LEE-teh-rah nah ee-*t*hoh-pee-EE-see-teh tohn yah-TROH too kseh-noh-*t*hoh-KHEE-oo. tee-leh-foh-NEE-s(eh)-teh steen ee-pee-REH-see-ah. lee-POHN, peh-rah-stee-KAH-sahs. thah sahs eh-pee-skehf-THOH AHV-ree-oh toh proh-EE. ehl-PEE-zoh OH-tee thah YEE-neh-teh kah-LAH SEEN-doh-mah.

Better call the hotel doctor. Call the service for this. Well, speedy recovery. I will visit you tomorrow morning. I hope you will get well soon.

11 *t*hehs-pee-NEES, boh-REE-teh nah moo PEE-teh PYOHS EE-neh oh yah-TROHS too kseh-noh-*t*hoh-KHEE-oo?

Miss, can you tell me who the hotel doctor is?

12 toh kseh-noh-*t*hoh-KHEE-oh see-nehr-GHAH-zeh-teh meh ahr-keh-TOOS ee-*t*hee-KOOS yah-TROOS. meh EH-nah pah-thoh-LOH-ghoh, meh EH-nah khee-ROOR-ghoh,

The hotel works (*lit.*, cooperates) with a number of specialists, a general practitioner, a surgeon,

13 Μάλιστα. Αἰσθάνομαι πολύ ἄσχημα καὶ τὸν παρακαλῶ νὰ ἔλθη ἀμέσως, ἂν εἶναι δυνατόν.

14 Θὰ προσπαθήσω. Νομίζω ὅμως, ὅτι τὴν ὥρα αὐτὴ δέχεται στὸ ἰατρεῖο του καὶ ὅτι ἐπισκέπτεται ἐξωτερικοὺς ἀσθενεῖς μετὰ τὶς ἕξι. —᾿Εκτὸς ἂν εἶναι ἐπείγουσα ἀνάγκη.

15 Θὰ ἤθελα νὰ ἔχω τὴ γνώμη τοῦ γιατροῦ, ὅσο τὸ δυνατὸ πιὸ γρήγορα.

16 Σὲ λίγη ὥρα θὰ εἶναι κοντά σας.

17 Καλησπέρα, κύριε Σμίθ. Τὶ πάθατε; Μιὰ στιγμὴ νὰ σᾶς πάρω τὴ θερμοκρασία καὶ νὰ σᾶς ἀκροασθῶ;

18 Γιατρέ, ὑποφέρω ἀρκετά. Νοιώθω ζάλη καὶ πόνους δυνατοὺς στὸ κεφάλι, στὸ σῶμα, παντοῦ.

19 ῎Εχετε πυρετό. Εἶναι γρίππη. ῞Οπως ἴσως ξέρετε, ἔχομε ἐπιδημία γρίππης. Σᾶς παρακαλῶ νὰ.ἀκολουθήσετε αὐτὲς τὶς ὁδηγίες. Νὰ μὴ ἀμελήσετε. Πάντως, δὲν εἶναι κάτι σοβαρό.

meh EH-nah peh-*THEE*-ah-troh.
nah kah-LEH-soh-meh tohn KEE-
ree-oh ee-ah-TREE-*thee*, tohn pah-
thoh-LOH-ghoh?

13 MAH-lee-stah. ehs-THAH-noh-meh
poh-LEE AHS-khee-mah keh tohn
pah-rah-kah-LOH nah EHL-thee
ah-MEH-sohs, ahn EE-neh *thee*-
nah-TOHN.

14 thah prohs-pah-THEE-soh. noh-
MEE-zoh OH-mohs, OH-tee teen
OH-rah ahf-TEE *T*HEH-kheh-teh
stoh ee-ah-TREE-oh-too keh OH-
tee eh-pee-SKEH-pteh-teh eh-ksoh-
teh-ree-KOOS ahs-theh-NEES meh-
TAH tees EH-ksee. eh-KTOHS
AHN EE-neh eh-PEE-ghoo-sah ah-
NAHN-gee.

15 thah EE-theh-lah nah EH-khoh
tee GHNOH-mee too yah-TROO,
OH-soh toh *t*hee-nah-TOH PYOH
GHREE-ghoh-rah.

16 seh LEE-yee OH-rah thah EE-neh
kohn-DAH-sahs.

17 kah-lee-S*P*E*H-r*ah, K E E-r e e-eh
Smith. TEE PAH-thah-teh? MYAH
stee-GHMEE nah sahs PAH-roh
tee theh-rmoh-krah-SEE-ah keh
nah sahs ah-kroh-ah-STHOH.

18 yah-TREH, ee-poh-FEH-roh ahr-
keh-TAH. NYOH-thoh ZAH-lee
keh POH-noos *t*hee-nah-TOOS stoh
keh-FAH-lee, stoh SOH-mah pahn-
DOO.

19 EH-kheh-teh pee-reh-TOH. EE-neh
GHREE-pee. OH-pohs EE-sohs
KSEH-reh-teh, EH-khoh-meh eh-
pee-*T*HEE-mee-ah GHREE-pees.
sahs pah-rah-kah-LOH nah ah-
koh-loo-THEE-seh-teh ahf-TEHS
tees oh-*t*hee-YEE-ehs. nah MEE
ah-meh-LEE-seh-teh. PAHN-dohs.
*T*HEHN EE-neh KAH-tee soh-
vah-ROH.

a pediatrician. Shall we call
Mr. Iatrides, the general practitioner?

Yes. I feel very bad and I beg
him to come immediately, if
possible.

I will try. I think though, that
at this time he has office hours
(*lit.*, he receives patients at his
clinic), he visits patients after
six ... unless it is very urgent.

I would like to have a doctor's
opinion, as soon as possible .

He will be with you soon.

Good evening, Mr. Smith. What
is the matter with you? Just a
moment to take your temperature and listen to your heart.

Doctor, I feel quite bad (*lit.*,
I suffer a lot). I feel dizzy and
I have a terrible headache and
pains in the body.

You have a fever. It is the flu.
As you probably know, there
is a flu epidemic. Please follow
these instructions. Do not neglect them. It is nothing serious.

20 Δεσποινίς, μοῦ στέλλετε, σᾶς παρακαλῶ τὸ γκαρσόνι;
Θὰ ἤθελα νὰ ἔχω μερικὰ φάρμακα ἀπὸ τὸ φαρμακεῖο.

21 Μιχάλη, πήγαινε στὸ φαρμακεῖο καὶ φέρε μου ἀσπιρίνη,
οἰνόπνευμα γιὰ ἐντριβὴ καὶ λίγο βαμπάκι.

22 Μάλιστα, κύριε. Θέλετε τίποτε ἄλλο;

23 Ὁ γιατρὸς ἔκαμε τὴ διάγνωση. Σὲ μένα ἀνέθεσε τὴ θεραπεία.

24 Μπορῶ νὰ σᾶς βοηθήσω;

25 Νὰ μοῦ φέρετε ἐπίσης χυμὸ πορτοκαλιοῦ.

26 Μὴ φοβᾶσθε, κύριε. Δὲν ξέρω τὶ σᾶς εἶπε ὁ γιατρός.
Ἐγὼ νομίζω ὅτι εἶναι γρίππη. Εἶναι ζήτημα κρεββατιοῦ
καὶ ἡσυχίας.

27 Μιλᾶς σὰν σωστὸς γιατρός. Μήπως εἶσαι ἀπὸ τὸ νησὶ
τοῦ Ἱπποκράτη;

28 Δὲν εἶμαι ἀπὸ τὴν Κῶ. Κατάγομαι ἀπὸ ἕνα γειτονικὸ
νησί.

20 *THE*HS-pee-nees, moo STEH-leh-teh sahs pah-rah-kah-LOH toh ghahr-SOH-nee? thah EE-theh-lah nah EH-khoh meh-ree-KAH FAHR-mah-kah ah-POH toh fahr-mah-KEE-oh.

Miss, will you please send me the boy? I would like to have some medicines from the drug store.

21 mee-KHAH-lee, PEE-yeh-neh stoh fahr-mah-KEE-oh keh FEH-reh-moo ah-spee-REE-nee, ee-NOH-pnehv-mah yah ehn-dree-VEE keh LEE-ghoh vahm-BAH-kee.

Mike, go to the drug store and bring me some aspirin, rubbing alcohol, and a little cotton.

22 MAH-lee-stah, KEE-ree-eh. THEH-leh-teh TEE-poh-teh AH-loh?

Yes, sir. Do you want anything else?

23 oh yah-TROHS EH-kah-neh tee *thee*-AH-ghnoh-see. seh MEH-nah ah-NEH-theh-seh tee theh-rah-PEE-ah.

The doctor made his diagnosis. To me, he assigned the cure.

24 boh-ROH nah sahs voh-ee-THEE-soh?

Can I help you?

25 nah moo FEH-rteh eh-PEE-sees khee-MOH pohr-toh-kah-LYOO.

Bring me some orange juice, too.

26 MEE foh-VAH-stheh, KEE-ree-eh. *THE*HN KSEH-roh TEE sahs EE-peh oh yah-TROHS. eh-GHOH noh-MEE-zoh OH-tee EE-neh GHREE-pee. EE-neh ZEE-tee-mah kreh-vah-TYOO keh ee-see-KHEE-ahs.

Don't worry, sir. I don't know what the doctor told you. I think it is the flu. It is a question of staying in bed and resting.

27 mee-LAHS sahn soh-STOHS yah-TROHS. MEE-pohs EE-seh ah-POH toh nee-SEE too ee-poh-KRAH-tee?

You speak like a real doctor. Are you from the island of Hippocrates?

28 *THE*HN EE-meh ah-POH teen KOH. kah-TAH-ghoh-meh ah-POH EH-nah yee-toh-nee-KOH nee-SEE.

No. I am not from Kos, but (I am) from a neighboring island.

ΔΕΚΑΤΟ ΤΕΤΑΡΤΟ ΜΑΘΗΜΑ

Fourteenth Lesson

New Vocabulary for this Lesson

περιμένω (peh-ree-MEH-noh) I wait
περνῶ (pehr-NOH) I spend (time)
εὐτυχῶς (ehf-tee-KHOHS) fortunately
εὐχάριστος, -η, -ο (ehf-KHAH-ree-stohs) nice, pleasant
προφυλάγομαι (proh-fee-LAH-ghoh-meh) I protect myself

σηκώνομαι (see-KOH-noh-meh) I rise; I get up
συμβουλεύω (seem-voo-LEHV-oh) I advise
ἀνυπόμονος, -η, -ο (ah-nee-POH-moh-nohs) impatient
συνεχίζω (see-neh-KHEE-zoh) I continue; I carry on
ἡ παράδοση (pah-RAH-thoh-see) tradition

ὁ πυρετός (pee-reh-TOHS) fever (ἐ)ρωτῶ (eh-roh-TOH) I ask
ἡ ὅρεξη (OH-reh-ksee) appetite ἀπαντῶ (ah-pahn-DOH) I answer
κουράζω (koo-RAH-zoh) I tire φέρ(ν)ω (FEH-r[n]oh) I bring
ἐπείγων (eh-PEE-ghohn) urgent σύντομα (SEEN-doh-mah) soon

τὸ ἐπάγγελμα (eh-PAHN-gehl-mah) profession
τὸ ἀνέκδοτο (ah-NEHK-thoh-toh) anecdote
σιωπῶ (see-oh-POH) I remain silent
μονοπωλῶ (moh-noh-poh-LOH) I monopolize
χαρακτηριστικός, -ή, -ό (khah-rah-ktee-ree-stee-KOHS) typical (adj.)

ἀπατῶμαι (ah-pah-TOH-meh) I am mistaken, I am deceived
ἡ διαταγή (thee-ah-tah-YEE) order
ἐλεύθερος, -α, -ο (eh-LEHF-theh-rohs) free
τὰ σύνεργα (SEEN-ehr-ghah) the tools
ὁ γαμπρός (ghahm-BROHS) bridegroom

136

Τὸ κουρεῖο   (koo-REE-oh)
Barber shop

Τὸ κομωτήριο   (koh-moh-TEE-ree-oh)
Beauty parlor

ἡ ὀμορφιά   (oh-mohr-FYAH)   beauty
πανηγυρίζω   (pah-nee-yee-REE-zoh)   I celebrate
πληροφορημένος, -η, -ο   (plee-roh-foh-ree-MEH-nohs)   informed
ἡ ἀνάρρωση   (ah-NAH-roh-see)   recovery
συζητῶ   (see-zee-TOH)   I talk; I discuss

ἐκλογές   (eh-kloh-YES)   elections
ξυρίζω   (ksee-REE-zoh)   I shave
τὸ ξυράφι   (ksee-RAH-fee)   razor

κτενίζω   (kteh-NEE-zoh)   I comb
τὸ ἄρωμα   (AH-roh-mah)   perfume
τὸ σαπούνι   (sah-POO-nee)   soap

τὸ κραγιόν   (krah-YOHN)   lipstick
ἡ πούδρα   (POO-thrah)   powder
ἡ κρέμα   (KREH-mah)   cream
ἡ βούρτσα   (VOOR-tsah)   brush

ἡ χωρίστρα   (khoh-REE-strah)   parting (of hair)
ὁ κρόταφος   (KROH-tah-fohs)   temple
ξυρίζομαι   (ksee-REE-zoh-meh)   I shave myself
τὸ ξύρισμα   (KSEE-ree-zmah)   shaving
ἡ λεπίδα   (leh-PEE-thah)   razor blade

βουρτσίζω   (voor-TSEE-zoh)   I brush
τὸ ψαλίδι   (psah-LEE-thee)   scissors
ἡ τσατσάρα   (tsah-TSAH-rah)   comb
ἡ κολώνια   (koh-LOH-nyah)   cologne
τὸ σφουγγάρι   (sfoon-GAH-ree)   sponge

CONVERSATION

1 Κύριε Σμίθ, ὁ φίλος σας κύριος Πετρίδης εἶναι στὴν αἴθουσα ὑποδοχῆς. Ἐπιθυμεῖ νὰ σᾶς ἰδῆ.

2 Μάλιστα, δεσποινίς, τὸν περιμένω.

3 Πῶς εἶσθε σήμερα; Πῶς περάσατε τὴ νύχτα; Αἰσθάνεσθε καλύτερα;

4 Εὐτυχῶς, καλά. Ὁ πυρετὸς ἔπεσε καὶ ἔχω ὄρεξη τρομερή.

5 Αὐτὸ εἶναι πολὺ εὐχάριστο, ἀλλὰ πρέπει νὰ προφυλαχθῆτε. Σᾶς συμβουλεύω νὰ μείνετε καὶ σήμερα στὸ κρεβάτι.

6 Ἀδύνατο. Προτιμῶ νὰ σηκωθῶ. Τὸ κρεβάτι μὲ κουράζει πολύ.

7 Ἔχετε καμιὰ ἐπείγουσα ἐργασία; Γιατὶ εἶσθε τόσο ἀνυπόμονος;

8 Πρέπει νὰ σηκωθῶ νὰ κόψω τὰ μαλλιά μου καὶ νὰ ξυρισθῶ. Ξέρετε κανένα καλὸ κουρεῖο;

9 Ξέρω ἕνα πολὺ καλὸ κουρέα. Ἡ γλῶσσα του τρέχει πιὸ γρήγορα ἀπὸ τὸ ψαλίδι του.

10 Εἶναι συγγενὴς τοῦ κουρέα τῆς Σεβίλλης[1],[2] ἢ ἁπλῶς συνεχίζει τὴν παράδοση τοῦ ἐπαγγέλματός του;

FOOTNOTES: *1*. A humorous reference to the hero of the well-known comic opera of Rossini "The Barber of Seville".   2. The comma before ἤ as well as before ὅτι is not absolutely necessary. The tendency in Greek punctuation is towards a more liberal attitude as far as the separation of main from subordi-

PRONUNCIATION	TRANSLATION

1 KEE-ree-eh Smith, oh FEE-loh-sahs KEE-ree-ohs peh-TREE-*thee*s EE-neh steen EH-thoo-sah ee-poh-*th*oh-KHEES. eh-pee-thee-MEE nah sahs ee-*TH*EE.

Mr. Smith, your friend Mr. Petrides is downstairs in the lobby. He wishes to see you.

2 MAH-lee-stah, *th*ehs-pee-NEES, tohm peh-ree-MEH-noh.

Yes, miss. I am waiting for him.

3 POHS EE-stheh SEE-meh-rah? POHS peh-RAH-sah-téh tee NEE-khtah? eh-STHAH-neh-stheh kah-LEE-teh-rah?

How are you today? How did you spend the night? Do you feel better?

4 ehf-tee-KHOHS, kah-LAH. oh pee-reh-TOHS EH-peh-seh keh EH-khoh OH-reh-ksee troh-meh-REE.

Fortunately, I am well. The fever dropped and I have a tremendous appetite.

5 ahf-TOH EE-neh poh-LEE ehf-KHAH-ree-stoh, ah-LAH PREH-pee nah proh-fee-lahkh-THEE-teh. sahs seem-voo-LEHV-oh nah MEE-neh-teh keh SEE-meh-rah stoh kreh-VAH-tee.

That is very nice, but you must take care of yourself. I advise you to stay in bed today, too.

6 ah-*TH*EE-nah-tóh. proh-tee-MOH nah see-koh-THOH. toh kreh-VAH-tee meh koo-RAH-zee poh-LEE.

Impossible. I prefer to get up. The bed tires me a great deal.

7 EH-kheh-teh KAH-myah eh-PEE-ghoo-sah ehr-ghah-SEE-ah? yah-TEE EE-stheh TOH-soh ah-nee-POH-moh-nohs?

Do you have some urgent work to do? Why are you so impatient?

8 PREH-pee nah see-koh-THOH nah KOH-psoh tah mah-LYAH-moo keh nah ksee-ree-STHOH. KSEH-reh-teh kah-NEH-nah kah-LOH koo-REE-oh?

I must get up and have a haircut and a shave (*lit.*, to cut my hair and to shave). Do you know a good barbershop?

9 kseh-ROH EH-nah poh-LEE kah-LOH koo-REH-ah. EE GHLOH-sah-too TREH-khee PYOH GHREE-ghoh-rah ah-POH toh psah-LEE-*thee*-too.

I know a very good barber. His tongue runs faster than his scissors.

10 EE-neh seen-geh-NEES too koo-REH-ah tees seh-VEE-lees, EE ah-PLOHS see-neh-KHEE-zee teem pah-RAH-*th*oh-see too eh-pahn-GEHL-mah-TOHS-too?

Is he a relative of the barber of Seville or does he simply carry on the tradition of his profession?

11 Νομίζω, ὅτι εἶναι συγγενὴς τοῦ κουρέα τοῦ Σωκράτη. Θυμᾶσθε τὸ ἀνέκδοτο;

12 Ὄχι, θὰ χαρῶ νὰ τὸ ἀκούσω.

13 Μιὰ φορὰ ὁ κουρέας ρώτησε τὸ Σωκράτη. Πῶς θέλεις νὰ σοῦ κόψω τὰ μαλλιά; Ὁ γέρο—φιλόσοφος ἀπάντησε: Σιωπώντας, φίλε μου, σιωπώντας.

14 Εἶναι πολὺ χαρακτηριστικὸ ἀνέκδοτο. Ἀλλὰ φοβοῦμαι, ὅτι ὁ Σωκράτης ἤθελε νὰ μονοπωλῇ τὸ λόγο.

15 Μήπως θέλετε νὰ καλέσω τὸ φίλο μου νὰ ἔλθη ἐδῶ; Θὰ χαρῶ πολύ.

16 Αὐτὸ θὰ εἶναι τὸ καλύτερο. Τηλεφωνῆστε του, σᾶς παρακαλῶ.

17 Δεσποινίς, μπορῶ σᾶς παρακαλῶ νὰ ἔχω τὸ Κουρεῖο «Τὸ Κάλλος»; Εἶναι ὁδὸς Περικλέους, ἀριθμὸς ἑκατὸν τέσσερα, ἂν δὲν ἀπατῶμαι.

18 Ἐμπρός, ἐμπρός. Σεῖς κύριε Ψαλίδα₃; Εἶμαι ὁ κύριος Πετρίδης.

19 Στὶς διαταγές σας, κύριε Πετρίδη. Τὶ μπορῶ νὰ κάνω γιὰ σᾶς;

20 Εἶσθε ἐλεύθερος τὴν ὥρα αὐτή; Ἐλᾶτε στὸ Ξενοδοχεῖο

---

nate clauses is concerned. The contemporary Greek punctuation is not basically different from the English punctuation.   3. Ψαλίδας is an agent-noun derived from ψαλίδα "large scissors".

11 noh-MEE-zoh OH-tee EE-neh seen-geh-NEES too koo-REH-ah too soh-KRAH-tee. thee-MAH-stheh toh ah-NEHK-*th*oh-toh?

I think that he is a relative of the barber of Socrates. Do you remember the anecdote?

12 OH-khee, thah khah-ROH nah toh ah-KOO-soh.

No. I shall be glad to hear it.

13 MYAH foh-RAH oh koo-REH-ahs ROH-tee-seh toh soh-KRAH-tee. POHS THEH-lees nah soo KOH-psoh tah mah-LYAH? oh YEH-roh-fee-LOH-soh-fohs ah-PAHN-dee-seh: see-oh-POHN-dahs, FEE-leh-moo, see-oh-POHN-dahs.

Once the barber asked Socrates: "How do you want me to cut your hair?" and the old philosopher answered: "Silently, my friend, silently ... "

14 EE-neh poh-LEE khah-rah-ktee-ree-stee-KOH ah-NEHK-*th*oh-toh. ah-LAH foh-VOO-meh, OH-tee oh soh-KRAH-tees EE-theh-leh nah moh-noh-poh-LEE toh LOH-ghoh.

It is a very typical anecdote. But I am afraid that Socrates liked to monopolize the talking himself.

15 MEE-pohs THEH-leh-teh nah kah-LEH-soh toh FEE-loh-moo nah EHL-thee eh-*TH*OH? thah khah-ROH poh-LEE.

Would you perhaps like me to call my friend to come here? I shall be very glad to.

16 ahf-TOH thah EE-neh toh kah-LEE-teh-roh. tee-leh-foh-NEE-steh-too, sahs pah-rah-kah-LOH.

That will be best. Call him, please.

17 *th*ehs-pee-NEES, boh-ROH sahs pah-rah-kah-LOH nah EH-khoh toh koo-REE-oh "toh KAH-lohs"? EE-neh oh-*TH*OHS peh-ree-KLEH-oos, ah-reeth-MOHS eh-kah-TOHN TEH-seh-rah, ahn *TH*EHN ah-pah-TOH-meh.

Miss, may I have the barber shop "The Beauty"? It is on Pericles Street, number one hundred and four, if I am not mistaken.

18 ehm-BROHS, ehm-BROHS. SEES, KEE-ree-eh psah-LEE-*th*ah? EE-meh oh KEE-ree-ohs peh-TREE-*th*ees.

Hello, hello. Is that you, Mr. Psallidas? This is Mr. Petrides.

19 stees *th*ee-ah-tah-YEHS-sahs, KEE-ree-eh peh-TREE-*th*ee. TEE boh-ROH nah KAH-noh yah SAHS?

At your service, Mr. Petrides. What can I do for you?

20 EE-stheh eh-LEHF-theh-rohs teen OH-rah ahf-TEE- eh-LAH-teh stoh kseh-noh-*th*oh-KHEE-oh ah-*TH*EE-neh. zee-TEE-steh toh *th*oh-MAH-tee-oh too kee-REE-oo Smith. FEHR-teh mah-ZEE-sahs koh-LOH-

Are you free at this time? Come over to the Hotel "Athens". Ask for Mr. Smith's room.

«'Αθῆναι». Ζητῆστε τὸ δωμάτιο τοῦ κυρίου Σμίθ. Φέρτε μαζί σας κολώνια, μηχανές, ξυράφι, κρέμα.

21 Μήπως ὁ κύριος Σμὶθ ἑτοιμάζεται γιὰ γαμπρός;

22 Ὄχι ἀκριβῶς, ἀλλὰ εἶναι δυὸ μέρες ἄρρωστος καὶ θέλει νὰ πανηγυρίση τὴν ἀνάρρωσή του.

23 Σὲ λίγα λεπτὰ τῆς ὥρας θὰ εἶμαι κοντά σας.

24 Ἐμπρός. Σεῖς, κύριε Ψαλίδα;

25 Ὁ κύριος Ψαλίδας, ὁ καλύτερος κουρέας τῆς Ἀθήνας!

26 Χαίρω πολύ. Σὲ παρακαλῶ νὰ μοῦ κόψης τὰ μαλλιὰ καὶ νὰ μὲ ξυρίσης.

27 Ἕτοιμος, κύριε; Πῶς θέλετε νὰ σᾶς κουρέψω. Ἑλληνικὰ ἢ ἀμερικανικά;

28 Ἑλληνοαμερικανικὰ καὶ συζητώντας!

29 Αὐτὸς εἶναι ὁ καλύτερος τρόπος.
Πῶς πᾶτε στὴν Ἀμερική; Θέλετε κολώνια;

30 Δὲν θέλω οὔτε κολώνια, οὔτε πούδρα. Πῶς πᾶνε τὰ πράγματα στὴν Ἑλλάδα; Εἶμαι βέβαιος ὅτι εἶσαι ὁ πιὸ πληροφορημένος Ἕλληνας.

31 Σὰν καλύτερα, μοῦ φαίνεται. Νομίζω ὅτι σύντομα θὰ ἔχωμε νέες ἐκλογές.

nyah, mee-khah-NEHS, ksee-RAH-fee, KREH-mah.

21 MEE-pohs oh KEE-ree-ohs Smith eh-tee-MAH-zeh-teh yah ghahm-BROHS?

22 OH-khee ah-kree-VOHS, ah-LAH EE-neh *TH*YOH MEH-rehs AH-roh-stohs keh THEH-lee nah pah-nee-yee-REE-see teen ah-NAH-roh-SEE-too.

23 seh LEE-ghah leh-PTAH tees OH-rahs thah EE-meh kohn-DAH-sahs.

24 ehm-BROHS. SEES, KEE-ree-eh psah-LEE-*th*ah?

25 oh KEE-ree-ohs psah-LEE-*th*ahs. oh kah-LEE-teh-rohs koo-REH-ahs tees ah-THEE-nahs.

26 KHEH-roh poh-LEE. seh pah-rah-kah-LOH nah moo KOH-psees tah mah-LYAH keh nah meh ksee-REE-sees.

27 EH-tee-mohs, KEE-ree-eh? POHS THEH-leh-teh nah sahs koo-REH-psoh. eh-lee-nee-KAH EE ah-meh-ree-kah-nee-KAH?

28 eh-lee-noh-ah-meh-ree-k a h-nee-KAH keh see-zee-TOHN-dahs.

29 ahf-TOHS EE-neh oh kah-LEE-teh-rohs TROH-pohs. POHS PAH-teh steen ah-meh-ree-KEE? THEH-leh-teh koh-LOH-nyah?

30 *TH*EHN THEH-loh OO-teh koh-LOH-nyah OO-teh POO-*th*rah. POHS PAH-neh tah PRAHGH-mah-tah steen eh-LAH-*th*ah? EE-meh VEH-veh-ohs OH-tee EE-seh oh PYOH plee-roh-foh-ree-MEH-nohs EH-lee-nahs.

31 sahn kah-LEE-teh-rah, moo FEH-neh-teh. noh-MEE-zoh OH-tee SEEN-doh-mah thah EH-khoh-meh NEH-ehs eh-kloh-YEHS.

Bring with you cologne, clippers, a razor, cream.

Is Mr. Smith perhaps getting ready to be a bridegroom?

Not exactly, but he has been sick for two days and he wants to celebrate his recovery.

I will be with you in a few minutes.

Hello. Is that you, Mr. Psalidas?

This is Mr. Psalidas, the best barber of Athens.

I am very glad. I would like a haircut and a shave. (*lit.*, I beg you to cut my hair and to shave me).

Ready, sir? In what way do you want your hair cut? In the Greek or the American way?

In the Greek-American, accompanied by talking.

That's the best way. How are you getting along in America? Would you like cologne?

I don't want either cologne or powder. How are things going in Greece? I am sure you are the most informed Greek.

Somewhat better, it seems to me. I think we are going to have new elections soon.

ΔΕΚΑΤΟ ΠΕΜΠΤΟ ΜΑΘΗΜΑ

Fifteenth Lesson

New Vocabulary for this Lesson

φυσικά   (fee-see-KAH) naturally
ἀπόψε   (ah-POH-pseh) tonight
τὸ πνεῦμα   (PNEHV-mah) spirit, intellect, wit
γελῶ   (yeh-LOH) I laugh
τὸ ἔργο   (EHR-ghoh) play; film

ὁ συγγραφεύς   (seen-grah-FEHFS) author
ἀσύγκριτος, -η, -ο   (ah-SEEN-gree-tohs) incomparable
σύγχρονος, -η, -ο   (SEEN-khroh-nohs) modern, contemporary
ἡ πολιτικὴ σάτιρα   (poh-lee-tee-KEE SAH-tee-rah) political satire
διηγοῦμαι   (thee-ee-GHOO-meh) I tell, I narrate

ἡ ἀκμή   (ah-KMEE) highest point (of development)
ἡ ἐποχή   (eh-poh-KHEE) time
ἡ δύναμη   (THEE-nah-mee) strength, power, vigor
ἔτσι   (EH-tsee) thus
τὸ θέατρο   (THEH-ah-troh) theater

ὁ κινηματογράφος
(kee-nee-mah-toh-GHRAH-fohs)
motion picture house

τὸ ἀττικὸν ἅλας
(ah-tee-KOHN AH-lahs)
Attic salt (Athenian humor)

144

Τὰ Θεάματα (theh-AH-mah-tah) Shows
ὁ ἠθοποιός (ee-thoh-pee-OHS) actor
ἡ παράσταση (pah-RAH-stah-see) performance, show
ἡ κωμωδία (koh-moh-THEE-ah) comedy
ἡ ἐπιθεώρηση (eh-pee-theh-OH-ree-see) revue

τὸ μελόδραμα (meh-LOH-thrah-mah) opera
δραματικός, -ή, -ό (thrah-mah-tee-KOHS) dramatic
ἡ ταινία (teh-NEE-ah) motion picture; film
γυρίζεται (yee-REE-zeh-teh) is filmed
ἡ πλατεῖα (plah-TEE-ah) orchestra

τὸ θεωρεῖο (theh-oh-REE-oh) loge
ὁ ταξιθέτης (tah-ksee-THEH-tees) usher

ἡ ὑπόθεση (ee-POH-theh-see) plot   ὁ θίασος (THEE-ah-sohs) company
ἡ τέχνη (TEHKH-nee) art   τὸ δρᾶμα (THRAH-mah) drama
τὸ κέντρο (KEHN-droh) center   οἱ θέσεις (THEH-sees) seats
ὁ ἐξώστης (eh-KSOH-stees) balcony   τὰ πλάγια (PLAH-yah) sides

CONVERSATION

1 Τί ἔργο παίζεται ἀπόψε στὸν κινηματογράφο «'Αθήναιον»;

2 Δὲν ξέρω. Στὸν κινηματογράφο «Ἑρμῆς» παίζεται «ὁ 'Αγαπητικὸς τῆς Βοσκοπούλας».

3 Εἶναι ἑλληνικὴ ταινία;

4 Ναί. Τὸ ἔργο ἔχει ἑλληνικὴ ὑπόθεση καὶ γυρίσθηκε στὴν Ἑλλάδα.

5 Προτιμῶ νὰ ἰδῶ ἕνα ἑλληνικὸ θεατρικὸ ἔργο. Δὲν νομίζω, ὅτι ὁ κινηματογράφος δίνει τὴν καλύτερη ἰδέα γιὰ τὴν ἑλληνικὴ θεατρικὴ τέχνη.

6 ῎Εχετε δίκιο. Τὸ θέατρο εἶναι πολὺ πιὸ κοντὰ στὴν ἑλληνικὴ παράδοση.

7 Φυσικά, ποιὸς δὲν ξέρει, ὅτι στὴν Ἑλλάδα τὸ θέατρο ἔφθασε στὸ ἀνώτατο σημεῖο τῆς ἀκμῆς του.

8 Σωστά. Οἱ δραματικοὶ συγγραφεῖς τῆς ἀρχαίας Ἑλλάδας εἶναι ἀσύγκριτοι.

9 Θέλετε νὰ ἰδῆτε τὴν «'Αντιγόνη» τοῦ Σοφοκλῆ στὸ 'Εθνικὸ Θέατρο ἢ προτιμᾶτε ἕνα σύγχρονο ἔργο;

PRONUNCIATION	TRANSLATION
1 TEE EHR-ghoh PEH-zeh-teh ah-POH-pseh stohn kee-nee-mah-toh-GHRAH-foh ah-thee-NEH-ohn?	What movie is playing at the "Atheneon" cinema tonight?
2 *TH*EHN KSEH-roh. stohn kee-nee-mah-toh-GHRAH-foh ehr-MEES PEH-zeh-teh oh ah-ghah-pee-tee-KOHS tees voh-skoh-POO-lahs.	I don't know. At the "Hermes" cinema, "The Shepherdess' Lover" is being shown.
3 EE-neh eh-lee-nee-KEE teh-NEE-ah?	Is it a Greek film?
4 NEH. toh EHR-ghoh EH-khee eh-lee-nee-KEE ee-POH-theh-see keh yee-REE-sthee-keh steen eh-LAH-*th*ah.	Yes. This movie has a Greek plot and it was filmed (*lit.*, turned) in Greece.
5 proh-tee-MOH nah ee-*TH*OH EH-nah eh-lee-nee-KOH theh-ah-tree-KOH EHR-ghoh. *TH*EHN noh-MEE-zoh OH-tee oh kee-nee-mah-toh-GHRAH-fohs *TH*EE-nee teen kah-LEE-teh-ree ee-*TH*EH-ah yah teen eh-lee-nee-KEE theh-ah-tree-KEE TEKH-nee.	I prefer to see a Greek play. I don't think that the movies give the best idea about the Greek theatrical art.
6 EH-kheh-teh *TH*EE-keh-oh. toh *TH*EH-ah-troh EE-neh poh-LEE PYOH kohn-dah steen eh-lee-nee-KEE pah-RAH-*th*oh-see.	You are right (*lit.*, You have right). The theater is much nearer to the Greek tradition.
7 fee-see-KAH, PYOHS *TH*EHN KSEH-ree OH-tee steen eh-LAH-*th*ah toh *TH*EH-ah-troh EHF-thah-seh sto*h* ah-NOH-tah-toh see-MEE-ohn tees ahk-MEES-too.	Naturally, who doesn't know that in Greece, the theater reached its highest point of development.
8 SOH-stah. ee *th*rah-mah-tee-KEE seen-ghrah-FEES tees ahr-KHEH-ahs eh-LAH-*th*ahs EE-neh ah-SEEN-gree-tee.	Right. The dramatic authors of ancient Greece are incomparable.
9 *TH*EH-leh-teh nah ee-*TH*EE-teh teen ahn-dee-GHOH-nee too soh-foh-KLEE stoh eh-thnee-KOH *TH*EH-ah-troh EE proh-tee-MAH-teh EH-nah SEEGH-khroh-noh EHR-ghoh?	Do you want to see Sophocles' "Antigone" in the National Theater or do you prefer a modern play?

10 Δὲν ἔχω τὴ διάθεση νὰ ἰδῶ δράμα ἢ ἔργο δύσκολο. Προτιμῶ νὰ ἰδοῦμε μαζὶ ἀπόψε μιὰ ἑλληνικὴ ἐπιθεώρηση. Εἶσθε ἐλεύθερος;

11 Μάλιστα. Θὰ χαρῶ πολὺ νὰ πᾶμε στὸ «'Αθηναϊκό». Ὁ θίασος Μαρίκας Κωστῆ ἔχει καλοὺς ἠθοποιούς.

12 Τί παίζεται ἀπόψε στὸ «'Αθηναϊκό»;

13 Παίζεται ὁ «Καραγκιόζης Πολιτικός». Εἶναι, ὅπως φαίνεται, πολιτικὴ σάτιρα[1].

14 'Αλήθεια, συνεχίζεται στὴν 'Αθήνα ἡ παράδοση. Θυμοῦμαι τὸν 'Αριστοφάνη. Δὲν ἄφηνε οὔτε στιγμὴ ἥσυχους τοὺς δημόσιους ἄντρες τῆς ἐποχῆς του.

15 Δὲν νομίζω, ὅτι ὁ «Καραγκιόζης Πολιτικός» ἔχει τὸ πνεῦμα καὶ τὴ δύναμη τῶν κωμωδιῶν τοῦ 'Αριστοφάνη. 'Αλλὰ ἂς πᾶμε. Θὰ γελάσωμε. Τὸ «ἀττικὸν ἅλας»[2] δὲν λείπει ἀπὸ τὶς σύγχρονες ἑλληνικὲς ἐπιθεωρήσεις[3].

16 Ταξί, ταξί. Στὸ θέατρο «'Αθηναϊκό», παρακαλῶ.

17 Φθάσαμε στὴν ὥρα. Ἡ παράσταση ἀρχίζει στὶς ὀκτὼ ἀκριβῶς.

FOOTNOTES: *1*. Political satire is a special theatrical genre cultivated in Athens today. It is light comedy satirizing thinly veiled contemporary political personalities. «Καραγκιόζης Πολιτικός» is the "Karaguez as a Politician". Karaguez (*lit.*, black-eyed) is a character of the theater of shadows. *2*. "Attic salt" refers to the wit of the theatrical plays written by Athenians who are famous, at least in Greece. for their subtle wit. *3*. A special kind of revue

10 THEHN EH-khoh tee thee-AH-theh-see nah ee-THOH THRAH-mah EE EHR-ghoh THEES-koh-loh. proh-tee-MOH nah ee-THOO-meh mah-ZEE ah-POH-pseh MYAH eh-lee-nee-KEE eh-pee-theh-OH-ree-see. EE-stheh eh-LEHF-theh-rohs?

I am not in the mood for seeing a drama or a difficult play. I prefer, to go and see a Greek revue, with you tonight. Are you free?

11 MAH-lee-stah. thah khah-ROH poh-LEE nah PAH-meh stoh ah-thee-nah-ee-KOH. oh THEE-ah-sohs mah-REE-kahs koh-STEE EH-khee kah-LOOS ee-thoh-pee-OOS.

Yes. I'll be very glad to go the "Athenaikon". The Marika Kosti company has good actors.

12 TEE PEH-zeh-teh ah-POH-pseh stoh ah-thee-nah-ee-KOH?

13 PEH-zeh-teh oh kah-rahn-GYOH-zees poh-lee-tee-KOHS. EE-neh, OH-pohs FEH-neh-teh, poh-lee-tee-KEE SAH-tee-rah.

What play is on (lit., is played) at the "Athenaikon", tonight. They are showing the play "Karaguez as a Politician". It sounds like (lit., it is, as it seems) a political satire.

14 ah-LEE-thyah, see-neh-KHEE-zeh-teh steen ah-THEE-nah ee pah-RAH-thoh-see. thee-MOO-meh tohn ah-ree-stoh-FAH-nee. THEHN AH-fee-neh OO-teh steegh-MEE EE-see-khoos toos thee-MOH-see-oos AHN-drehs tees eh-poh-KHEES-too.

True, the tradition is carried on in Athens. I remember Aristophanes. He would not leave the politicians of his time alone one moment.

15 THEHN noh-MEE-zoh OH-tee oh kah-rahn-GYOH-zees poh-lee-tee-KOHS EH-khee toh PNEHV-mah keh tee THEE-nah-mee tohn koh-moh-thee-OHN too ah-ree-stoh-FAH-nee. ah-LAH ahs PAH-meh. thah gheh-LAH-soh-meh. toh ah-tee-KOHN AH-lahs THEHN LEE-pee ah-POH tees SEEN-khroh-nehs eh-lee-nee-KEHS eh-pee-theh-oh-REE-sees.

I dont think that "Karaguez as a Politician" has the wit and vigor of Aristophanes' come-dies. But let's go. We shall laugh. The Attic humor (lit., salt) is not lacking in the con-temporary Greek revues.

16 tah-KSEE, tah-KSEE! stoh THEH-ah-troh ah-thee-nah-ee-KOH, pah-rah-kah-LOH.

Taxi, taxi! To the "Athenaikon" theater, please.

17 FTHAH-sah-meh steen OH-rah. ee pah-RAH-stah-see ahr-KHEE-zee stees oh-KTOH ah-kree-VOHS.

We are on time. The performance starts at eight o'clock.

18 Δεσποινίς, δυὸ εἰσιτήρια, παρακαλῶ.

19 Θέλετε εἰσιτήρια πρώτης θέσεως; Μήπως προτιμᾶτε πλατεῖα ἢ θεωρεῖο[4];

20 Δῶστε μου, σᾶς παρακαλῶ, δυὸ εἰσιτήρια πρώτης θέσεως.

21 Μάλιστα, κύριε. Δραχμὲς σαράντα.

22 Εἶναι ἡ πρώτη φορὰ ποὺ θὰ ἰδῶ ἑλληνικὴ ἐπιθεώρηση. Ἔτσι θὰ ἔχω πολλὰ νὰ διηγοῦμαι στὸ φίλο μου κύριο Πάππα καὶ στὴ γυναίκα του.

which is the most popular genre of the Greek theater. *4.* It refers primarily to "loge" or "a box at a theater", but it is sometimes mistakenly used to refer to "balcony". However, the terms ἐξώστης and μπαλκόνι are normally used for the latter.

18 *th*ehs-pee-NEES, *THY*OH ee-see-TEE-ree-ah, pah-rah-kah-LOH.

Miss, two tickets, please.

19 THEH-leh-teh ee-see-TEE-ree-ah PROH-tees THEH-seh-ohs? MEE-pohs proh-tee-MAH-teh plah-TEE-ah EE theh-oh-REE-oh?

Do you want first or second class tickets? Do you prefer orchestra or loge?

20 *THO*H-steh-moo, sahs pah-rah-kah-LOH *THY*OH ee-see-TEE-ree-ah PROH-tees THEH-seh-ohs.

Give me two first class tickets, please.

21 MAH-lee-stah, KEE-ree-eh. *th*rahkh-MEHS sah-RAHN-dah.

Yes, sir. Forty drachmas.

22 EE-neh ee PROH-tee foh-RAH poo thah ee-*THO*H eh-lee-nee-KEE eh-pee-theh-O H-ree-see.   EH-tsee thah EH-khoh poh-LAH nah *th*ee-ee-GHOO-meh stoh FEE-loh-moo KEE-ree-oh PAH-pah keh stee yee-NEH-kah-too.

This is the first time I am seeing (*lit.*, will see) a Greek revue, thus I will have a great deal to tell my friend Mr. Pappas and his wife.

ΔΕΚΑΤΟ ΕΚΤΟ ΜΑΘΗΜΑ
Sixteenth Lesson

New Vocabulary for this Lesson

ὑποδέχομαι (ee-poh-*THEH*-khoh-meh) I meet: I receive
μαθαίνω (mah-THEH-noh) I learn; I hear from
ξεμπερδεύω (ksehm-behr-*THEH*V-oh) I get through; finish with
ξεμπλέκω (ksehm-BLEH-koh) I disentangle; finish with
ἐπισκέπτομαι (eh-pee-SKEH-ptoh-meh) I visit

χρήσιμος (KHREE-see-mohs) useful
ἀκριβής. (ah-kree-VEES) exact
ἄφιξη (AH-fee-ksee) arrival
μόλις (MOH-lees) just
δῶρα (*TH*OH-rah) presents

ὅπως (OH-pohs) as
βοηθῶ (voh-ee-THOH) I help
ἄχρηστος (AH-khree-stohs) useless
στέλλω (STEH-loh) I send
βάσανα (VAH-sah-nah) torments

προσεγγίζω (proh-sehn-GEE-zoh) I dock
φόρος, δασμός (FOH-rohs, *th*ah-ZMOHS) duty
ἐκτελωνιστής (ehk,teh-loh-nee-STEES) customs officer
τελωνεῖο (teh-loh-NEE-oh) customs house
δηλώνω (*th*ee-LOH-noh) I declare

ἔλεγχος (EH-lehgh-khos) inspection
ἐν τάξει (ehn-DAH-ksee) all right
ἐλεγκτής (eh-lehng-TEES) inspector
ξεκλειδώνω (kseh-klee-*TH*OH-noh) unlock
γνωριμία (ghnoh-ree-MEE-ah) acquaintance

σιγαρέττα (see-ghah-REH-tah) cigarettes
τὸ πρακτορεῖο (prah-ktoh-REE-oh) travel agency
διευθυντής (*th*ee-ehf-theen-DEES) manager
ἐπιφυλάσσω (eh-pee-fee-LAH-soh) I reserve
ταξιδεύω (tah-ksee-*THEH*V-oh) I travel; I sail

ἀποσκευές   (ah-poh-skehv-EHS) baggage
διατυπώσεις   (thee-ah-tee-POH-sees) formalities
διαβατήριο   (thee-ah-vah-TEE-ree-oh) passport

TOURIST MAP
OF
GREECE

(Scale in Kilometres)
Railways
Roads
Ancient Sites
Loutraki   Mineral Hot Springs
(underlined)

CONVERSATION

1 Ἀγαπητέ μου φίλε κύριε Πετρίδη, ἀναχωρῶ γιά τόν Πειραιᾶ[1]. Πηγαίνω νά ὑποδεχθῶ τό ζεῦγος Πάππα[2].

2 Πότε φθάνουν στόν Πειραιᾶ;

3 Φθάνουν τό ἀπόγευμα στίς τέσσερες.

4 Μὲ ποιό πλοῖο ταξιδεύουν;

5 Ταξιδεύουν μὲ τό ὑπερωκεάνειο «Ὀλυμπία».

6 Ἔχετε ἀκριβεῖς πληροφορίες ἀπό τό πρακτορεῖο;

7 Μάλιστα. Τηλεφώνησα μόλις καί ἔμαθα ὅτι τό «Ὀλυμπία» προσεγγίζει στό λιμάνι στίς τρεῖς καί μισή.

8 Μήπως θέλετε νά σᾶς βοηθήσω σέ κάτι;

9 Θά ἤθελα νά βοηθήσωμε τούς φίλους μου νά ξεμπερδέψουν[3] γρήγορα μὲ τίς διατυπώσεις τοῦ τελωνείου.

10 Φέρνουν μαζί τους πολλὲς ἀποσκευές[4];

11 Νομίζω. Πρόκειται, ὅπως σᾶς εἶπα, νά μείνουν γιά ἕνα μεγάλο διάστημα στήν Ἑλλάδα.

12 Ὅταν φθάσετε στόν Πειραιᾶ, ἐπισκεφθῆτε τό Ἐκτελωνιστικό Γραφεῖο τοῦ κυρίου Φορτικοῦ[5]. Εἶναι φίλος μου. Θά σᾶς φανῆ χρήσιμος.

FOOTNOTES: *1.* Πειραιεύς (Piraeus, the port of Athens) is an irregular noun of the third declension. Its genitive is Πειραιῶς. A Demotic variant of Πειραιεύς is Πειραιάς.   *2.* Πάππας is the Greek version of the last name of many Greek-Americans who have shortened names usually starting with Παπα- as Παπαδόπουλος, Παπακωνσταντίνου, Παπαδάκης, etc. The Greek equivalent of Πάππας is Παπᾶς.   *3.* Μπερδεύω means "entangle" and ξεμπερδεύω "disentangle".   *4.* Ἀποσκευές or its Puristic variant ἀποσκευαί is used in the plural and means baggage or luggage.   *5.* Φορτικός is a derivative of φορτίο (load; burden). Φορτικός is used as an adjective mean-

PRONUNCIATION	TRANSLATION
1 ah-ghah-pee-T E H-moo FEE-leh KEE-ree-eh peh-TREE-*thee*, ah-nah-khoh-ROH yah tohm pee-reh-AH. pee-YEH-noh nah ee-poh-*the*hkh-THOH toh ZEHV-ghohs PAH-pah.	My dear friend Mr. Petrides, I am leaving for Pireus. I am going to meet (*lit.*, welcome) the Pappas couple.
2 POH-teh FTHAH-noon stohm pee-reh-AH?	When do they arrive at Piraeus?
3 FTHAH-noon toh ah-POH-yehv-mah stees TEH-seh-rehs.	They arrive at four o'clock.
4 meh PYOH PLEE-oh tah-ksee-*TH*EHV-oon?	On board what ship are they sailing?
5 tah-ksee-*TH*EHV-oon meh toh ee-peh-roh-keh-AH-nee-oh oh-l e e m-BEE-ah.	They are sailing on the liner "Olympia".
6 EH-kheh-teh ah-kree-VEES plee-roh-foh-REE-ehs ah-POH toh prah-ktoh-REE-oh?	Do you have exact information from the agency?
7 MAH-lee-stah. tee-leh-FOH-nee-sah MOH-lees keh EH-mah-thah OH-tee toh oh-leem-BEE-ah proh-sehn-GEE-zee stoh lee-MAH-nee stees TREES keh mee-SEE.	Yes. I have just called and learned that the "Olympia" will dock at half past three.
8 MEE-pohs THEH-leh-teh. nah sahs voh-ee-THEE-soh seh KAH-tee?	Perhaps you would like me to help you with something?
9 thah EE-theh-lah nah voh-ee-THEE-soh-meh toos FEE-looz nah ksehm-behr-*TH*EH-psoon GHREE-ghoh-rah meh tees *the*e-ah-tee-POH-sees too teh-loh-NEE-oo.	I would like to help my friends finish with the customs formalities.
10 FEHR-noon mah-ZEE-toos POH-lehs ah-poh-skehv-EHS?	Do they carry much baggage with them?
11 noh-MEE-zoh. PROH-kee-teh, OH-pohs sahs EE-pah, nah MEE-noon yah EH-nah meh-GHAH-loh *the*e-AH-stee-mah steen eh-LAH-*th*ah.	I think so. As I have told you, they are going to stay in Greece for a long time.
12 OH-tahn FTHAH-seh-teh stohm pee-reh-AH, eh-pee-skeh-FTHEE-teh toh ehk-teh-loh-nee-stee-KOH ghrah-FEE-oh too kee-REE-oo fohr-tee-KOO. EE-neh FEE-lohz-moo. thah sahs fah-NEE KHREE-see-mohs.	When you arrive in Piraeus, visit the "Atlas Customs Clearing Office" of Mr. Forticos. He is a friend of mine. He will help you (*lit.*, He will seem useful to you).

13 Σᾶς εὐχαριστῶ πολύ. 'Αναχωρῶ. Βιάζομαι νὰ ἰδῶ τοὺς καλούς μου φίλους. Λογαριάζω πολὺ στὴ συντροφιά τους.

14 Καλησπέρα σας. Εἶσθε ὁ κύριος Φορτικός, ὁ διευθυντὴς τοῦ 'Εκτελωνιστικοῦ Γραφείου «"Ατλας»;

15 Μάλιστα. Μπορῶ νὰ σᾶς βοηθήσω σὲ κάτι;

16 Μ' ἔστειλε ὁ φίλος κύριος Πετρίδης. Θέλω νὰ βοηθήσετε δυὸ φίλους μου νὰ ἐκτελωνίσουν τὶς ἀποσκευές τους. "Ερχονται ἀπὸ τὴν 'Αμερικὴ μὲ τὸ «'Ολυμπία».

17 Πολὺ εὐχαρίστως. Τὸ πλοῖο εἶναι στὸ λιμάνι. Εἶμαι βέβαιος ὅτι οἱ φίλοι σας εἶναι στὸ Τελωνεῖο.

18 "Ας βιασθοῦμε. Νὰ οἱ φίλοι μου! Καλῶς ὡρίσατε.

19 Τί χαρὰ νὰ συναντηθοῦμε στὴν 'Ελλάδα! 'Αλλά, ἃς ξεμπλέξωμε πρῶτα μὲ τὸ Τελωνεῖο.

20 "Εχετε κάτι νὰ δηλώσετε; 'Ανοῖξτε, σᾶς παρακαλῶ τὶς βαλίτσες σας.

21 Εὐχαρίστως. Δὲν ἔχομε τίποτε νὰ δηλώσωμε. Τὰ πράγματά μας ὅλα εἶναι γιὰ προσωπικὴ χρήση.

22 Αὐτὰ ἐδῶ τὶ εἶναι, σᾶς παρακαλῶ;

---

ing "burdensome". *6.* Τό is used before the names of steamers and especially of transoceanic steamers regardless of whether their names are masculine or feminine because it stands for τὸ ἀτμόπλοιο (steamer) or τὸ ὑπερωκεάνειο (transoceanic) which is understood.

13 sahs ehf-khah-ree-STOH poh-LEE. ah-nah-khoh-ROH. vee-AH-zoh-meh nah ee-THOH toos kah-LOOS-moo FEE-loos. loh-ghah-RYAH-zoh poh-LEE stee seen-droh-FYAH-toos.

Thank you very much. I am leaving. I am in a hurry to see my good friends. I count a great deal on their company.

14 kah-lee-SPEH-rah-sahs. EE-stheh oh KEE-ree-ohs fohr-tee-KOHS, oh *thee*-ehf-theen-DEES too eh-kteh-loh-nee-stee-KOO ghrah-FEE-oo AH-tlahs?

Good evening. Are you Mr. Forticos, the director of the "Atlas Customs Clearing Office"?

15 MAH-lee-stah. boh-ROH nah sahs voh-ee-THEE-soh seh KAH-tee?

Yes. Can I do anything for you?

16 MEH-stee-leh oh FEE-lohs KEE-ree-ohs peh-TREE-*thees*. THEH-loh nah voh-ee-THEE-see-teh *TH*YOH FEE-looz-moo nah ehk-teh-loh-NEE-soon tees ah-poh-skehv-EHS-toos. EHR-khohn-deh ah-POH teen ah-meh-ree-KEE meh toh oh-leem-Bee-ah.

My friend Mr. Petrides sent me to you. I would like you to help my two friends to have their baggage cleared through the customs. They are coming from America on the "Olympia".

17 poh-LEE ehf-khah-REE-stohs. toh PLEE-oh EE-neh stoh lee-MAH-nee. EE-meh VEH-veh-ohs OH-tee ee FEE-lee-sahs EE-neh stoh teh-loh-NEE-oh.

With great pleasure. The ship is at the harbor. I am sure that your friends are at the custom house.

18 ahs vee-ah-STOO-meh. NAH ee FEE-lee-moo. kah-LOHS oh-REE-sah-teh.

Let's hurry. Here are my friends. Welcome.

19 TEE khah-RAH nah see-nahn-dee-THOO-meh steen eh-LAH-*th*ah. ah-LAH, ahs ksehm-BLEH-ksoh-meh PROH-tah meh toh teh-loh-NEE-oh.

What a pleasure to meet in Greece. But let's get through the customs first.

20 EH-kheh-teh KAH-tee nah *thee*-LOH-seh-teh? ah-NEE-ksteh, sahs pah-rah-kah-LOH tees vah-LEE-tsehs-sahs.

Do you have anything to declare? Open your bags, please.

21 ehf-khah-REE-stohs. *TH*EHN EH-khoh-meh TEE-poh-teh nah *thee*-LOH-soh-meh. tah PRAHGH-mah-TAH-mahs OH-lah EE-neh yah proh-soh-pee-KEE KHREE-see.

We have nothing to declare. All our things are for personal use.

22 ahf-TAH eh-*TH*OH TEE EE-neh, sahs pah-rah-kah-LOH?

What are these things here, please?

23. Εἶναι μερικὰ δῶρα γιὰ τοὺς συγγενεῖς καὶ τοὺς φίλους μας.

24 Ὁ φόρος εἶναι πολὺ μικρός. Θὰ πληρώσετε ἑκατὸ δραχμές, σύμφωνα μὲ τὸ νόμο.

25 Τελείωσε ὁ ἔλεγχος;

26 Μάλιστα. Περάστε στὸν ἐλεγκτὴ νὰ σᾶς ὑπογράψη αὐτὴ τὴν ἀπόδειξη.

28 ῎Εμενα πάντα μὲ τὸ φόβο, ὅτι τὸ Τελωνεῖο εἶναι ὁ τόπος τῶν βασάνων καὶ ἡ πρώτη κακὴ γνωριμία μὲ μιὰ χώρα.

28 Ἀλλὰ μὴ ξεχνᾶτε, ὅτι εἶσθε ἐπισκέπτες σὲ μιὰ χώρα, ποὺ γιὰ τοὺς ξένους ἐπιφυλάσσει πάντα τὴν μεγαλύτερη φιλοξενία.

23 EE-neh meh-ree-KAH *TH*OH-rah
yah toos seen-geh-NEES keh toos
FEE-looz-mahs.

They are gifts for relatives and
friends of ours.

24 oh FOH-rohs EE-neh poh-LEE
mee-KROHS. thah plee-ROH-seh-
teh eh-kah-'TOH *th*rahkh-MEHS,
SEEM-foh-nah meh toh NOH-moh.

The duty is very little. You will
pay a hundred drachmas, according to law.

25 teh-LEE-oh-seh oh EH-legh-khohs?

Is the inspection finished?

26 MAH-lee-stah. peh-RAH-steh stohn
eh-lehn-GTEE nah sahs ee-poh-
GHRAH-psee ahf-TEE teen ah-
POH-*thee*-ksee.

Yes. Go to the inspector to get
this receipt signed.

27 EH-meh-nah PAHN-dah meh toh
FOH-voh, OH-tee toh teh-loh-NEE-
oh EE-neh oh TOH-pohs tohn
vah-SAH-nohn keh ee PROH-tee
kah-KEE ghnoh-ree-MEE-ah meh
MYAH KHOH-rah.

I was always afraid that the
custom house would be a place
of torment and the first bad
acquaintance with a country.

28 ah-LAH MEE kseh-KHNAH-teh
EE-stheh eh-pee-SKEH-ptehs seh
MYAH KHOH-rah, poo yah toos
KSEH-noos eh-pee-fee-LA H-see
PAHN-dah teen meh-ghah-LEE-
teh-ree fee-loh-kseh-NEE-ah.

But don't forget that you are
visitors in a country that always
reserves the greatest hospitality
for strangers.

ΔΕΚΑΤΟ ΕΒΔΟΜΟ ΜΑΘΗΜΑ

Seventeenth
Lesson

Ο ΔΡΟΜΟΣ ΠΡΟΣ ΤΗΝ ΑΘΗΝΑ

(Gus and Helen Pappas, and their American friend William Smith, whom they call Βασίλη, *go to Athens by taxi. This lesson is the story of their taxi trip from Piraeus to Athens.)*

ΕΛΕΝΗ: Εἴμαστε ἕτοιμοι. Οἱ διατυπώσεις[1] μὲ τὸ Τελωνεῖο, νομίζω, ἐτελείωσαν.

ΚΩΣΤΑΣ: Καὶ τώρα ἐμπρὸς γιὰ τὴν ᾿Αθήνα, γιὰ τὴν πόλη τῶν ὀνείρων μας. ᾿Αθήνα, ᾿Αθήνα, πολυύμνητη πόλη!

ΣΜΙΘ: Φίλοι μου, νὰ μὴν εἶστε τόσο βιαστικοί. Θὰ ἰδοῦμε πρῶτα τὸν Πειραιᾶ. Εἶναι πόλη μεγάλη. ῎Εχει γωνιὲς ὄμορφες. ᾿Απὸ τὰ ὑψώματά του θὰ χαροῦμε τὴ δύση τοῦ ἥλιου στὰ γαλανὰ νερὰ τοῦ Σαρωνικοῦ[2]. Θὰ ρίξωμε μιὰ ματιὰ στὴν Αἴγινα[3], στὴν ἱστορικὴ Σαλαμίνα[4]. Τὸ βράδυ θὰ πᾶμε στὴν ταβέρνα τοῦ Βαγγέλη τοῦ Μερακλῆ[5], θὰ πιοῦμε ξανθὴ ρετσίνα[6], θὰ φᾶμε μπαρμπούνι[7] φρέσκο καὶ θ' ἀκούσωμε τὰ μπουζούκια[8] ἢ τὴ λατέρνα[9].

FOOTNOTES: *1. The formalities. 2. From its heights we'll enjoy the sunset in the blue waters of the Saronic Gulf.* The Saronic Gulf is an inlet of the Aegean Sea. It is bounded by Attica, the Isthmus of Corinth, and the Argolis Peninsula. Piraeus is the main port on the Saronic Gulf, which also contains many islands. *3.* Aegina is one of the islands in the Saronic Gulf. *4.* Salamis is another island in the Saronic Gulf. Off its shore the Greek fleet defeated the Persians in 480 B. C. *5. In the evening we'll go to the tavern of Vaggelis the Meraclis.* Μερακλής is a word of Turkish origin. In Turkish it means curious, but in Greek it designates a man who looks for and appreciates fine things. *6.* Retsina is a popular Greek light wine containing some resin as a preservative. *7.* Red mullet. *8.* Mandolin-like instruments used to accompany or play certain types of oriental songs which are very popular in con-

160

ΕΛΕΝΗ: Ἀγαπητὲ Bill — ἀγαπητὲ Βασίλη, θέλω νὰ πῶ — εἶσαι πιὰ σωστὸς "Ελληνας. Σὲ καμαρώνω. Ἀλλὰ προτι- μῶ νὰ πᾶμε κατ' εὐθεῖαν στὴν Ἀθήνα. Βιάζομαι νὰ ἰδῶ τὸ «κλεινὸν ἄστυ»[10].

ΣΜΙΘ: Νοιώθω καλὰ τὰ αἰσθήματά σας. Ἡ βιασύνη[11] σας εἶναι δικαιολογημένη. Θὰ ἐπισκεφθοῦμε τὸν Πειραιᾶ μιὰν ἄλλη μέρα. (Φωνάζει ἔνα ταξί.) Ταξί, ταξί, γιὰ τὴν Ἀθήνα παρακαλῶ. Δὲ θὰ πάρης τὴν ὁδὸν Πειραιῶς. Θὰ πᾶμε ἀπὸ τὸ Φάληρο[12].

ΚΩΣΤΑΣ: Μεγάλωσα μὲ τὴ σκέψη νὰ ἐπισκεφθῶ μιὰ μέρα τὴν Ἑλλάδα. Ἦταν τὸ ὄνειρό μου ἀπὸ τὰ παιδικά μου χρόνια. Ὁ πατέρας μου μιλοῦσε μὲ πάθος γιὰ τὴν Ἑλλάδα. Ἡ μητέρα μου ζοῦσε μὲ τὴ νοσταλγία στὴν καρ- διά. Στὰ φοιτητικά μου χρόνια τὸ ὄνειρο αὐτὸ μεγάλωσε, ἔγινε πιὸ ἐπίμονο[13]. Ὅταν γνώρισα καλύτερα τὸν τόπο τῶν προγόνων μου ἀπὸ τὰ βιβλία, ἀπὸ τὴν τέχνη, ἀπὸ τὶς σπου- δές μου στὸ Κολλέγιο, εἶπα μέσα μου ὅτι εἶναι καιρὸς νὰ κάμω τὸ προσκύνημα[14] αὐτό.

ΕΛΕΝΗ: Δὲν κατάγομαι ἀπὸ Ἕλληνες γονεῖς, μὰ τὸ ἴδιο ὄνειρο εἶχα πάντοτε κι' ἐγώ. Ὅταν μάλιστα παντρεύ- τηκα μὲ τὸν Κώστα ἡ ἐλπίδα ὅτι θὰ ἐπισκεφθῶ μαζί του τὴν Ἑλλάδα μεγάλωσε.

ΣΜΙΘ: Φίλοι μου, τὸ ὄνειρό σας πραγματοποιεῖται[15] σή- μερα. Νοιώθω τόσο πολὺ τὴ χαρά σας. Ὅπως ξέρετε, στὶς φλέβες μου τρέχει αἶμα καθαρὰ ἀμερικανικό. Σᾶς διαβε- βαιώνω ὅμως, ὅτι, ὅσο εὐρύνεται[16] ἡ γνώση μου, ὅσο ὁ ὁ- ρίζοντας τῆς ἐμπειρίας μου ἀπλώνεται καὶ ξανοίγει[17], τόσο περισσότερο καταλαβαίνω τὴν Ἑλλάδα. Ποιὸς εἶναι ὁ ποι- ητὴς ποὺ εἶπε, ὅτι ὅλοι οἱ σκεπτόμενοι ἄνθρωποι εἶναι, ἀπὸ πολλὲς ἀπόψεις, Ἕλληνες;

temporary Greece.   9. A special kind of large hand organ.   10. A stereotyped classical Greek expression referring to Athens as the "famous city".   11. *Your haste is justified.* Βία is another word for "haste", but it also has other mean- ings such as "force", "compulsion", "violence".   12. Phaleron is one of the favorite beaches within easy reach of Athens. It was the port of ancient Athens. The Bay of Phaleron is an inlet of the Saronic Gulf.   13. *In my student years that dream grew, it became more insistent.*   14. Pilgrimage. 15. *Your dream is materialized.*   16. *As my knowledge is broadened.*   17. *The*

ΚΩΣΤΑΣ: Γειά σου, συμπατριώτη. "Εγινες ἕνας πραγματικὸς φιλέλληνας, ἕνας ἑλληνολάτρης.

ΣΜΙΘ: Νὰ τὸ Φάληρο. Πόσο ὄμορφη ἀκρογιαλιά, Πόσο δροσερὸς εἶναι ὁ ἀέρας. Ὁ Σαρωνικὸς εἶναι στὶς χαρές του. Τὰ νερά του εἶναι καθαρὰ καὶ καταγάλανα. "Εκανα πολλὲς φορὲς μπάνιο στὶς ἀκρογιαλιὲς ἐκεῖνες ἐκεῖ κάτω.

ΚΩΣΤΑΣ: Αὐτὴ εἶναι ἡ λεωφόρος ποὺ ὁδηγεῖ στὴν Ἀθήνα;

ΟΔΗΓΟΣ: Μάλιστα, κύριε. Εἶναι ἡ λεωφόρος Συγγροῦ.

ΕΛΕΝΗ: Ἀγαπητέ μου σύζυγε, εἶναι ὁ δρόμος ποὺ ἔπαιρναν μὲ τὰ πόδια οἱ πρόγονοί σου καὶ συζητοῦσαν τὰ μεγάλα προβλήματα. Μὲ τὴ φαντασία σου μπορεῖς κιόλας νὰ ἰδῆς τὴ στιγμὴ τούτη τὸ Σωκράτη νὰ διαλέγεται, νὰ ἐρωτᾶ, νὰ εἰρωνεύεται[18] ...

ΚΩΣΤΑΣ: Ἀγαπητὴ Ἑλένη, τὰ μάτια μου τὴ στιγμὴ αὐτὴ εἶναι γυρισμένα στὸ παρόν. Τὶ φῶς! Τὶ ὄμορφα σπιτάκια! Κοίταξε τὶς ροδοδάφνες[19], τὰ παιδιὰ ἐκεῖ κάτω. (Γυρίζοντας στὸν ὁδηγό.) Πιὸ σιγά, παιδί μου. Μὴ βιάζεσαι. "Αφησέ μας νὰ χαροῦμε τὴ διαδρομὴ[20] μὲ ὅλη μας τὴν καρδιά.

ΟΔΗΓΟΣ: Εὐχαρίστως, κύριε. Ἐδῶ εἶναι τὸ ἱπποδρόμιο[21]. "Εχω κακὲς ἀναμνήσεις. Μπαίνεις μὲ λεπτά, βγαίνεις τσίτσιδος[22], ὅπως λέμε στὴ γλώσσα μας. Ἐδῶ εἶναι ἕνας ὡραῖος νέος συνοικισμός[23]. Τὰ ἐνοίκια ὅμως εἶναι ψηλότερα ἀπὸ τὰ σπίτια[24]. Νὰ τὸ ἄγαλμα τοῦ Λόρδου Βύρωνος[25]. Ἐδῶ εἶναι ἡ πύλη τοῦ Ἀδριανοῦ[26], οἱ στῆλες τοῦ Ὀλυμπίου Διός[27]. "Ολος ὁ τόπος εἶναι γεμάτος ἀπὸ ἀρχαῖα μνημεῖα. Ὁ δάσκαλός μου μοῦ ἔλεγε, ὅτι ἐμεῖς οἱ νεοέλληνες ζοῦμε μόνο μὲ τὰ περασμένα μεγαλεῖα.

---

horizon of my experience spreads and opens up. *18.* With your imagination you can see even at this very moment Socrates discussing, asking questions, speaking ironically... *19.* Oleanders (evergreen shrubs with white, pink, or red flowers). *20.* Let's enjoy the trip to the utmost (lit., with all our heart). *21.* Here are the race-tracks. *22.* Slang for "naked", here it is used in the sense of "broke". *23.* Here is a beautiful new community (lit., settlement). *24.* The rents are higher than the houses. *25.* Here is the statue of Lord Byron. (This great friend of Greece died in Mesologgi, Greece, in 1824.) *26.* Here is the Arch of Hadrian. (Hadrian or Adrian (76-138 A.D.) was a Roman emperor from 117 to 138 A.D.) *27.* The columns of Olympian Zeus. *28. You re-*

ΕΛΕΝΗ: Αὐτὸ δὲν εἶναι σωστό. Καὶ ἡ νεώτερη Ἑλλάδα ἔκανε καὶ κάνει ἔργα μεγάλα.

ΟΔΗΓΟΣ: "Εχετε δίκιο, κυρία. Τὰ κατορθώματα τῶν Ἑλλήνων στὸν τελευταῖο πόλεμο ἦσαν τὸ ἴδιο μεγάλα ὅπως οἱ νίκες στὸ Μαραθῶνα, στὴ Σαλαμίνα...

ΣΜΙΘ: Αὐτὸ τὸ γνωρίζει ὁ κόσμος ὅλος. Θυμᾶσαι τὶ εἶπε τότε ἕνας μεγάλος ἄγγλος πολιτικός[28]. Ἀπὸ τώρα καὶ στὸ ἑξῆς δὲ θὰ λέγουν, ὅτι οἱ "Ελληνες πολεμοῦν σὰν ἥρωες. Θὰ λέγουν, ὅτι οἱ ἥρωες πολεμοῦν σὰν "Ελληνες.

ΟΔΗΓΟΣ: Σὲ ποιὸ ξενοδοχεῖο θὰ μείνετε;

ΕΛΕΝΗ: Νοικιάσαμε σπίτι στὸ Κολωνάκι[29]. Νὰ ἡ διεύθυνση. Πλατεῖα Δεξαμενῆς.

ΚΩΣΤΑΣ: (Μιλώντας στὸν ὁδηγό.) Πῶς σὲ λένε;

ΟΔΗΓΟΣ: Ὀνομάζομαι Σοφοκλῆς Θηβαῖος[30]. Εἶμαι ἀπὸ τὴ Θήβα.

ΚΩΣΤΑΣ: Ἀπὸ τὴ Θήβα; Ἡ πόλη αὐτὴ εἶναι μιὰ ἀπὸ τὶς πιὸ ἱστορικὲς πόλεις τῆς Ἑλλάδος.

ΕΛΕΝΗ: Ἀγαπητὲ Κώστα, εἴπαμε, ὅτι τὴν ὥρα αὐτὴ δὲ θὰ μιλήσωμε γιὰ τὸ παρελθόν, γιὰ τὴν ἱστορία. (Γυρίζοντας στὸν ὁδηγό.) Σοφοκλῆ, τὶ εἶναι ἐδῶ δεξιά;

ΟΔΗΓΟΣ: Εἶναι τὸ Ζάππειον[31]. Δίπλα εἶναι ὁ Ἐθνικὸς Κῆπος. Στὸ Ζάππειο γίνονται διάφορες ἐκθέσεις. Τὶς ἡμέρες αὐτὲς εἶναι μία ἔκθεση ζωγραφικῆς. Στὸν κῆπο τοῦ Ζαππείου μαζεύονται τὸ βράδυ ὅλοι οἱ Ἀθηναῖοι. Ἐδῶ γίνονται οἱ συναντήσεις τῶν νέων, τὰ ραντεβουδάκια. Γνωρίζετε τὸ τραγούδι «Στὸ Ζάππειο μιὰ μέρα περιπατοῦσα, συνάντησα μιὰ νέα ξανθομαλλοῦσα...»;

ΣΜΙΘ: Κάτω ἀπὸ ἕνα τέτοιο οὐρανὸ τὰ αἰσθήματα φουντώνουν εὔκολα.

ΟΔΗΓΟΣ: Νὰ ἡ Πλατεῖα Συντάγματος[32].

---

member what a great English statesman said then. "From now on they will not say the Greeks fight like heroes, but that heroes fight like Greeks." 29. Kolonaki is an exclusive district of Athens, at the foot of Lycabettus. 30. Sophocles Thebaios. His last name implies that he is from Thebes. 31. Zappion is a building where exhibitions take place. 32. Here is (the) Constitution Square. Νά is a particle which does not have a corresponding form in English.

164   THE CORTINA METHOD

ΣΜΙΘ:Εἶναι ἡ καρδιὰ τῆς Ἀθήνας. Θὰ ἔλθωμε ἐδῶ νὰ ρουφήξωμε ἀνατολίτικα[33] τὸν καφέ μας. Στὸ καφενεῖο ἐκεῖ κάτω στὴ γωνία μαζεύονται ὅλοι οἱ τύποι, συζητοῦν, νοσταλγοῦν τὴν παλιὰ Ἀθήνα.

ΕΛΕΝΗ: Ἡ Ἀκρόπολη, ἡ Ἀκρόπολη, ὁ θεῖος βράχος πάνω στὸν ὁποῖον ὁ μεγάλος Περικλῆς[34] ἔκτισε τὸν Παρθενώνα.

ΟΔΗΓΟΣ: Ἀπέναντι εἶναι ὁ Λυκαβητός[35]. Στὴν κορυφὴ εἶναι τὸ ξωκκλήσι τοῦ Ἁγίου Γεωργίου.

ΚΩΣΤΑΣ: Ἀθήνα, πόλη τῶν ὀνείρων μας. (Γυρίζοντας στὸ Βασίλη.) Θυμᾶμαι τὴ στιγμὴ τούτη τὰ λόγια τοῦ Nicholas Murray Butler[36], τοῦ Columbia University: «Τὸ ὄνομα τῆς Ἀθήνας στέκει στὴν πρώτη γραμμὴ στὸν κατάλογο τῶν πόλεων ποὺ ἐπλούτισαν τὴν πολιτιστικὴ ζωὴ τοῦ κόσμου. Ἂν ἡ ἑλληνικὴ φιλοσοφία ἡ ρητορική, ἡ ποίηση, τὸ δρᾶμα, ἦσαν ἄγνωστα σὲ μᾶς, ἡ κατανόηση τοῦ σημερινοῦ πολιτισμοῦ θὰ ἦταν πολὺ περιωρισμένη...»

ΕΛΕΝΗ: Ἀγαπητὲ σύζυγε, ἐπῆρες τὸν ἀνήφορο. Καβάλησες τὸν Πήγασο[37] καὶ πετᾶς στὰ σύννεφα.

ΣΜΙΘ: Φθάσαμε. Νὰ ἡ Δεξαμενή! Νὰ τὸ σπίτι σας! Ἐλπίζω ὅτι θὰ σᾶς ἀρέση. (Γυρίζοντας στὸν ὁδηγό.) Πόσα σᾶς χρωστᾶμε;

ΟΔΗΓΟΣ: Ἑβδομῆντα δραχμές.

ΚΩΣΤΑΣ: Πάρε ἑκατό. Σοῦ ἀξίζουν. Εἶσαι ὁ πρῶτος πατριώτης ποὺ ἀνταμώσαμε στὴν Ἀθήνα.

ΟΔΗΓΟΣ: Εὐχαριστῶ πολύ. Ἂν θέλετε νὰ γνωρίσετε καλὰ τὴν Ἀθήνα, φωνάξτε με. Ζητῆστε τὸ Σοφοκλῆ Θηβαῖο, τὸν ὁδηγὸ τοῦ ταξὶ ἀριθμὸς 123.

It is the equivalent of French "voila" or Italian "ecco".   *33. We'll come here to sip our coffee in oriental fashion* (in other words, in a very relaxing manner, as the Orientals do). *34. Acropolis, Acropolis, the divine rock on which the great Pericles built Parthenon.* Pericles (495-429 B.C.) was an Athenian statesman who wanted to make Athens a center of culture as well as a political power. Under his leadership Athens lived the best period of its history known as its "Golden Age" («ὁ χρυσοῦς αἰών» [*lit.*, "the golden century"]). *35.* Lycabettus is a picturesque hill facing Acropolis. *36.* Nicholas Murray Butler (1862-1947) was president of Columbia University from 1902 to 1945. He is world-known for his efforts in behalf of international peace. *37.* Pegasus is the immortal winged horse of the Greek legends.

ΔΕΚΑΤΟ ΟΓΔΟΟ ΜΑΘΗΜΑ

Eighteenth
Lesson

ΣΤΟ ΣΠΙΤΙ ΤΟΥ κ. ΠΕΤΡΙΔΗ

(Gus, Helen, Mr. Smith and Mr. Petrides have a very interesting discussion about ancient and present-day Athens at Mr. Petrides' home.)

ΠΕΤΡΙΔΗΣ: Ὁ φίλος μου κύριος Σμὶθ μᾶς μιλοῦσε πολὺ συχνὰ γιὰ σᾶς.

ΚΩΣΤΑΣ: Ὁ κύριος Σμὶθ εἶναι οἰκογενειακός μας φίλος. Γνωριζόμαστε ἀπὸ τὰ παιδικά μας χρόνια. Ὁ πατέρας μου Peter the Greek, ὁ Πέτρος ὁ Ἕλληνας, ἔτσι τὸν ἔλεγαν στὴ γειτονιά, ἀγαποῦσε τὸν Bill σὰν παιδί του.

ΠΕΤΡΙΔΗΣ: Ἔτσι ἴσως ἐξηγεῖται ἡ ἀγάπη τοῦ κυρίου Σμὶθ γιὰ τοὺς Ἕλληνες καὶ γιὰ τὴν Ἑλλάδα.

ΕΛΕΝΗ: Ὁ κύριος Σμὶθ εἶναι πιὰ ἕνας σωστὸς Ἕλληνας. Στὰ γράμματά του μᾶς μιλοῦσε μὲ ἐνθουσιασμὸ γιὰ σᾶς, γιὰ τὴν Ἀθήνα, γιὰ τὴ ζωή του ἐδῶ. Ὁ Κώστας μάλιστα χάρηκε ἐξαιρετικὰ ὅταν πῆρε τὸ πρῶτο γράμμα ἀπὸ τὸν κύριο Σμὶθ γραμμένο στὰ ἑλληνικά.

ΚΩΣΤΑΣ: Ὁ Bill, ὁ Βασίλης θέλω νὰ πῶ, εἶναι ὁ ξεναγός[1] μας. Ἀλήθεια, τὸν ζηλεύω γιὰ τὶς γνώσεις του γύρω ἀπὸ τοὺς τόπους, τὰ πράγματα, τὴ ζωὴ τῆς Ἀθήνας.

ΠΕΤΡΙΔΗΣ: Πῶς σᾶς φαίνεται ἡ Ἀθήνα; Ποιὲς εἶναι οἱ ἐντυπώσεις σας ἀπὸ τὴν πόλη μας;

ΚΩΣΤΑΣ: Εἶμαι ἐνθουσιασμένος. Γνώριζα τὴν Ἀθήνα ἀπὸ τὶς διηγήσεις τῶν οἰκείων[2] καὶ τῶν φίλων μου, ἀπὸ τὶς μελέτες στὸ Γυμνάσιο καὶ στὸ Κολλέγιο. Μὲ τὴ φαντασία μου εἶχα πλάσει τὴν εἰκόνα της ὡραία, ἐπιβλητική[3].

FOOTNOTES: *1. Bill,—Basil I mean to say—is our guide. 2. I knew Athens from the stories told by my folks. 3. With my imagination I had formed its picture, beautiful, impressive (lit., imposing). 4. It's no secret that my hus-*

165

ΕΛΕΝΗ: Δὲν σᾶς κρύβω, ὅτι ὁ σύζυγός μου διακρίνεται γιὰ τὴ φαντασία του⁴. Στὸ Κολλέγιο οἱ συμφοιτητές⁵ μας τὸν φώναζαν πειρακτικὰ⁶ "Ομηρο.

ΠΕΤΡΙΔΗΣ: Μὴ ξεχνᾶτε, κυρία Πάππα, ὅτι ἡ φαντασία εἶναι ἡ προγονική μας ἀρετή⁷. (Γυρίζοντας στὸν Κώστα.) Ἀσφαλῶς, ἡ πραγματικὴ εἰκόνα τῆς Ἀθήνας εἶναι πιὸ φτωχὴ ἀπὸ τὴν εἰκόνα ποὺ πλάσατε μὲ τὴ φαντασία σας. ΚΩΣΤΑΣ: "Οχι, τὸ ἀντίθετο⁸. Ὁμολογῶ ὅτι ἡ Ἀθήνα, ἔτσι ὅπως τὴ βλέπω μὲ τὰ μάτια μου καὶ ὅπως τὴ ζῶ ἀπὸ προχθὲς μὲ ὅλες μου τὶς αἰσθήσεις, ἔχει χάρη, ὀμορφιὰ καὶ μιὰ μοναδικὴ λεπτότητα καὶ εὐγένεια ποὺ παρὰ τὴν ποιητική μου διάθεση, γιὰ τὴν ὁποία μὲ πειράζει ἡ γυναίκα μου, ἡ εἰκόνα ποὺ εἶχα σχηματίσει γιὰ τὸ «ἰοστεφὲς ἄστυ»⁹ δὲν εἶναι τόσο πλούσια ὅσο ἡ πραγματικὴ Ἀθήνα.

ΠΕΤΡΙΔΗΣ: Χαίρομαι πολὺ ποὺ σᾶς ἀκούω νὰ μιλᾶτε ἔτσι γιὰ τὴν Ἀθήνα. Ἀλήθεια, εἶναι θαυμάσια πόλη. Ὁ ἐνθουσιασμός σας εἶναι εὐεξήγητος. Μοῦ ἐπιτρέπετε ὅμως μιὰ παρατήρηση¹⁰; Πολὺ φοβοῦμαι ὅτι κάθε φορὰ ποὺ μιλοῦμε γιὰ τὴν πόλη τούτη δὲν ξεκινοῦμε ἀπὸ τὴν ἄμεση παρατήρηση. Μιλοῦμε πάντα μὲ τὴ φαντασία, μὲ τὸ συναίσθημα. Τὸ ὑπέροχο παρελθόν της μᾶς κάμει νὰ ἐξιδανικεύωμε καὶ τὸ παρόν της¹¹.

ΕΛΕΝΗ: Καταλαβαίνω καλὰ τὴν ἄποψή σας. Εἶναι πολὺ φυσικὸ νὰ κρίνωμε, νὰ ἐκτιμοῦμε καὶ νὰ λατρεύωμε τὴν Ἀθήνα, διότι ὁμιλεῖ μέσα μας τὸ παρελθόν, ὁ θρύλος. Δὲν λησμονοῦμε ὅτι στὸ χῶρο τοῦτο δημιουργήθηκε ὁ μεγαλύτερος πολιτισμός. Ἐδῶ γεννήθηκε τὸ «ἑλληνικὸ θαῦμα». Ἀλλὰ πιστέψετέ με, τὸ παρὸν δὲν ἀδικεῖ τὸ παρελθόν¹². "Εχω μάλιστα τὴ γνώμη ὅτι τὸ παρὸν ἐξηγεῖ καὶ διαφωτίζει τὶς κρίσεις μας γιὰ τὸ ἔνδοξο παρελθόν¹³.

band has a vivid imagination (lit., I don't hide that my husband is distinguished for his imagination). 5. Our fellow students. 6. Teasingly. 7. Our ancestral virtue. 8. The opposite. 9. "Violet-crowned city." As poet Palamas says: "Athens bleeds with violet abundant/each time the Afternoon's arrows pour on her." 10. Would you allow me (to make) a remark. 11. Its superb past makes us idealize its present. 12. But believe me, the present does not do injustice to the past. 13. I even have the opinion that the present explains and enlightens our views (lit., judgment) about the glorious past. 14. The

ΣΜΙΘ: Συμφωνῶ ἀπόλυτα μὲ τὴν Ἑλένη. Κοιτάξετε τὴν ἀτμόσφαιρα. Ὁ οὐρανὸς εἶναι καταγάλανος[14]. Ὁ ἀέρας εἶναι δροσερός, καθαρός, λεπτός. Ἡ διαύγεια, ἡ ὁρατότητα εἶναι μοναδική[15]. Ἡ Ἀττική, καθὼς ξαπλώνεται ἀπὸ τὰ πόδια τοῦ Ὑμηττοῦ[16] ὡς κάτω στὴ θάλασσα, εἶναι πάντοτε ἡ ἴδια. Ἡ Ἀκρόπολη μένει στὴ θέση της ὄχι μόνο γιὰ νὰ μᾶς θυμίζη τὸ παρελθόν, ἀλλὰ καὶ γιὰ νὰ κρατᾶ ζωντανή, αἰώνια τὴν ὀμορφιὰ τοῦ ἱεροῦ αὐτοῦ χώρου. Κάτω ἀπὸ ἕνα τέτοιο οὐρανό, μέσα σ᾽ ἕνα τέτοιο χῶρο, μόνο μεγάλα καὶ ὡραῖα πράγματα μποροῦσαν νὰ γεννηθοῦν.

ΠΕΤΡΙΔΗΣ: Εἴμαστε σύμφωνοι. Ἄν οἱ πρόγονοί μας εὐχαριστοῦσαν τὸ Δία[17] καὶ τοὺς ἄλλους θεοὺς τοῦ Ὀλύμπου γιὰ τὴν ὀμορφιὰ καὶ τὴ δόξα τῆς Ἀθήνας, ἐμεῖς, οἱ νεώτεροι Ἀθηναῖοι, κάνομε τὸ ἴδιο. Δοξάζομε τὸ Θεὸ γιατὶ γεννηθήκαμε καὶ γιατὶ μεγαλώσαμε στὸν ἱστορικὸ τοῦτο τόπο. Τὸ μόνο παράπονό μας εἶναι ὅτι σήμερα δὲν κυκλοφοροῦν πιὰ ἀνάμεσά μας ὁ Σωκράτης[18], ὁ Πλάτων[19] καὶ οἱ μεγάλοι τραγικοί[20]. Στὴ Βουλή[20] μας δὲν ρητορεύουν ὁ Δημοσθένης[21] καὶ ὁ Αἰσχίνης[22].

---

sky is intense blue. *15. The clearness, the visibility is unique.* *16.* Hymettos is a mountain group in Attica, famous for its honey since antiquity. *17.* Zeus, the name of the first among the Olympian gods, is an irregular noun of the third declension, declined as follows: ὁ Ζεύς, τοῦ Διός, τὸν Δία, ὦ Ζεῦ. In Demotic by analogical extension of its accusative form, it becomes a regular noun of first declension: ὁ Δίας, τοῦ Δία, τὸν Δία, ὦ Δία. *18.* Socrates (469-399 B. C.) an Athenian philosopher generally regarded as one of the wisest men of all time. His dialectic method consisted of a series of questions that made an interlocutor or a pupil think and an opponent contradict himself by skillfully showing him the inadequacy of his answers by further questions guiding to sounder answers. He was condemned to death for corrupting the youth and introducing strange divinities. He wrote nothing. He is known through the writings of Plato and Xenophon. *19.* Plato (427-347 B. C.) is famous for his philosophical dialogues in which Socrates appears as one of the characters. His idealistic philosophy stresses the permanence and reality of the ideal form behind all appearances. One of these dialogues is "Symposium". Its best edition is that of the Academy of Athens (1934, 1950). *20.* The great tragedians are: Aeschylus (525-456 B. C.), Sophocles (496-406 B. C.) and Euripides (480-406 B. C.). *21.* Demosthenes (384-322 B. C.), an Athenian orator distinguished for his orations against Philip II of Macedonia. He is considered as one of the greatest orators of all time. *22.* Aeschines

ΚΩΣΤΑΣ: 'Αγαπητέ μου κύριε Πετρίδη, τὸ παρελθὸν ζῆ μέσα στὸ παρόν. "Ισως νὰ εἶμαι κάπως ἀπόλυτος στὶς κρίσεις μου. Πιστεύω ὅτι οἱ βασικὲς ἀρετὲς ποὺ καλλιέργησαν οἱ πρόγονοί μας δὲν χάθηκαν. Ἡ λατρεία στὴ ζωὴ καὶ στὴ φύση, ἡ ἀγάπη στὴν ὀμορφιά, ἡ πίστη στὴν ἐλευθερία εἶναι ἔκδηλες ἀρετὲς τοῦ Νεοέλληνα.

ΣΜΙΘ: Κώστα, ξέχασες νὰ μιλήσης γιὰ τὴ φιλοξενία, γιὰ τὴν ἀγάπη στὴ συζήτηση καὶ στὴν κριτική, γιὰ τὴ λατρεία στὴν ἑλληνικὴ γῆ, γιὰ τὴ νοσταλγία τῶν ξενητεμένων Ἑλλήνων[23]. Θυμᾶμαι τὸν μακαρίτη τὸν πατέρα σου. Σωστὸς 'Οδυσσέας. Μιλοῦσε γιὰ τὸ χωριό του μὲ τὴν ἴδια ἀγάπη ποὺ μιλοῦσε ὁ «πολυμήχανος»[24] βασιλιὰς γιὰ τὴν 'Ιθάκη.

ΕΛΕΝΗ: Σὲ ὅλα αὐτὰ μπορῶ νὰ προσθέσω καὶ κάτι ἄλλο: "Εχω τὴ γνώμη, ὅτι πολλὰ ἀπὸ τὰ κατορθώματα τῶν ἀρχαίων Ἑλλήνων ἐπανελήφθησαν[25] πολλὲς φορὲς στὴ ζωὴ τῆς νεώτερης Ἑλλάδος. Δὲν θὰ ξεχάσω ποτὲ τὰ σχόλια τῶν ἐφημερίδων στὰ χρόνια τοῦ τελευταίου πολέμου. "Οταν οἱ ἄνδρες καὶ οἱ γυναῖκες τῆς Ἑλλάδος πολεμοῦσαν στὰ βουνὰ καὶ στὰ στενὰ γιὰ νὰ φράξουν τὸ δρόμο τῶν εἰσβολέων[26], ὅλοι θυμήθηκαν τὸ Μαραθώνα καὶ τὶς Θερμοπύλες[27].

ΠΕΤΡΙΔΗΣ: "Αν θυμοῦμαι καλὰ οἱ «εὐκλεεῖς ἡμῶν πρόγονοι»[28] ἔπιναν κάτι ὅταν συζητοῦσαν. Τὶ θέλετε νὰ πιῆτε; Θέλετε οὖζο[29], κρασὶ σαμιώτικο[30], ρετσίνα;

ΣΜΙΘ: Θὰ πάρω ἕνα οὖζο μὲ πάγο. Εἶναι τὸ καλύτερο ὀρεκτικό.

ΚΩΣΤΑΣ: Προτιμῶ λίγη ρετσίνα. Δῶστε μου, σᾶς παρακαλῶ, ἕνα ποτήρι ρετσίνα.

ΠΕΤΡΙΔΗΣ: Πίνω στὴν ὑγεία σας.

(389-314 B. C.), an Athenian orator, rival of Demosthenes. 23. *The nostalgia of the Greeks living abroad.* 24. "Resourceful" or "artful" (*lit.*, many-machined) refers to Odysseus (Ulysses). 25. 'Επανελήφθησαν (they were repeated) is the passive aorist of ἐπαναλαμβάνω. 26. *Of the invaders.* 27. Marathon is the place NE of Athens where the Athenians defeated the Persians in 490 B. C. Thermopylae is the pass in Central Greece where in 480 B. C. Leonidas and his Spartans and their allies fought against the Persians to the last man. 28. "Our illustrious ancestors" in classical Greek. 29. Ouzo is anise-flavored hard liquor which is the favorite aperitif in Greece. 30. Wine

ΣΜΙΘ: Εἰς ὑγείαν σας.

ΚΩΣΤΑΣ (Πίνει ρετσίνα καὶ σιγοτραγουδᾶ.):
«Λόντρα, Παρίσι, Νιοὺ Γιόρκ, Βουδαπέστη, Βιέννη,
μπρὸς στὴν Ἀθήνα καμιά, μὰ καμιά σας δὲ βγαίνει...»[31].

ΚΥΡΙΑ ΠΕΤΡΙΔΗ: Ἀγαπητοί μας φίλοι, τὸ τραπέζι
εἶναι ἕτοιμο. Λυποῦμαι ποὺ σᾶς διακόπτω. Ἐλᾶτε καὶ συ-
νεχίζομε τὴ συζήτηση στὸ τραπέζι. Δὲ φημίζομαι γιὰ τὴν
ἀρχαιομάθειά[32] μου, μὰ νομίζω ὅτι οἱ προγονοί μας μιλοῦσαν γιὰ τὰ ὡραιότερα πράγματα τῆς ζωῆς γύρω ἀπὸ τὸ
τραπέζι.

ΚΩΣΤΑΣ: Αὐτὸ εἶναι σωστό. Μοῦ θυμίζετε τὴ στιγμὴ
αὐτὴ τὸ περίφημο «Συμπόσ.ο»[19] τοῦ Πλάτωνος.

(Ὅλοι κάθονται γύρω στὸ τραπέζι.)

ΠΕΤΡΙΔΗΣ: Πίνω καὶ πάλι στὴν ὑγεία σας. Σᾶς εὔχομαι καλὴ διαμονὴ στὴν Ἑλλάδα.

ΣΜΙΘ: Πίνω στὴν ὑγεία τῆς ἀγαπητῆς κυρίας Πετρίδη,
ποὺ ἑτοίμασε τὸ πλούσιο τοῦτο τραπέζι. Δὲν ξέρω καλὰ
τί ἔτρωγαν οἱ Ἀθηναῖοι. Ξέρω ὅμως ὅτι ἡ «ἀμβροσία»[33]
ποὺ ἔτρωγαν οἱ Ὀλύμπιοι θεοὶ δὲν ἦταν νοστιμώτερη ἀπὸ
τοῦτο τὸ στιφάδο[34].

ΚΩΣΤΑΣ: Προσθέτω ὅτι καὶ τὸ «νέκταρ»[33] ποὺ ἔπιναν
ὁ Δίας καὶ οἱ ἄλλοι θεοὶ δὲν ἦταν καλύτερο ἀπὸ τὴ ρετσίνα
τούτη.

ΚΥΡΙΑ ΠΕΤΡΙΔΗ: Ἡ ὄρεξη κάνει ὅλα τὰ φαγητὰ νό-
στιμα.

ΠΕΤΡΙΔΗΣ: Ἀνεβήκατε στὴν Ἀκρόπολη;

ΕΛΕΝΗ: Κάναμε τὸ πρῶτο προσκύνημά μας στὸ «θεῖο
βράχο» προχθὲς τὸ πρωΐ. Ὁ ἥλιος ἔλαμπε. Ὁ Παρθενώνας
πρόβαλλε σὲ ὅλη του τὴ μεγαλοπρέπεια. Στὸ «Μουσεῖο»
θαυμάσαμε καὶ καμαρώσαμε μὲ ὅλη τὴ δύναμη τῆς ψυχῆς
μας τὰ δείγματα τῆς ἑλληνικῆς τέχνης.

ΚΩΣΤΑΣ: Μὲ τὸ ἀνέβασμά μου στὴν Ἀκρόπολη πραγμα-
τοποίησα ἕνα ἀπὸ τὰ μεγαλύτερα ὄνειρα τῆς ζωῆς μου.

---

from the island of Samos.   *31.* "London, Paris, New York, Budapest, Vienna,
none of you can be compared to Athens". These are the first two verses of a
successful popular song of the forties and fifties exalting the beauties of Athens.
The lyrics are by M. Traiforos, the husband of Sophia Vembo, who first sang
the song.   *32. I am not famous for my knowledge of the ancients.   33.* "Am-
brosia" is the food eaten by the Olympian Gods and "nectar" is the drink

ΕΛΕΝΗ: Περιττό νὰ σᾶς εἰπῶ ὅτι ἡ φαντασία τοῦ συζύγου μου ὠργίασε³⁵ κυριολεκτικά. Μίλησε μὲ τὸ Φειδία³⁶. Χαμογέλασε στὶς Καρυάτιδες³⁷. Χειροκρότησε τὸν Περικλῆ³⁸. ῍Ελαβε μέρος στὴν ἑορτὴ τῶν Παναθηναίων³⁹ καὶ εἶδε τίς ᾿Αθηναῖες κόρες νὰ μεταφέρουν τὸν πέπλο γιὰ τὸ ἄγαλμα τῆς ᾿Αθηνᾶς ...

ΣΜΙΘ: Εἶναι ἡ πέμπτη φορὰ ποὺ ἀνέβηκα στὴν ᾿Ακρόπολη. Κάθε φορὰ ποὺ στέκω κάτω ἀπὸ τὸν Παρθενῶνα, ὁ νοῦς μου καὶ ἡ καρδιά μου ἀγωνίζονται νὰ συλλάβουν τὸ θαῦμα αὐτὸ τῆς ἀρχιτεκτονικῆς καὶ τῆς ὀμορφιᾶς.

ΠΕΤΡΙΔΗΣ: Εἶσθε ὅλοι σας φανατικοὶ ἀρχαιολάτρες, ἀγαπητοί μου φίλοι. Νοιώθω καλὰ τὶς σκέψεις σας καὶ τὰ αἰσθήματά σας. Πάντως, σᾶς θυμίζω ὅτι ἀπὸ τὸν καιρὸ ποὺ ὁ «Χρυσοῦς Αἰὼν» πέρασε στὴν ἱστορία, ἡ ᾿Αθήνα εἶδε καὶ ἄλλους λαούς. Τὰ ἴχνη των εἶναι φανερά. Εἶναι οἱ Βυζαντινοὶ ναοί, τὰ Φράγκικα μοναστήρια, τὰ τζαμιά⁴⁰. ῍Εχουν ὅλα αὐτὰ κάποιο ἐνδιαφέρον γιὰ σᾶς;

ΚΩΣΤΑΣ: Ἡ καρδιά μας χτυπᾶ γιὰ τὴν Ἑλλάδα τοῦ Περικλῆ καὶ γιὰ τὴ Νέα Ἑλλάδα.

ΕΛΕΝΗ: ῍Εχω τὴ γνώμη ὅτι ἡ ἱστορία τῆς Ἑλλάδος εἶναι ἀδιάσπαστη. ᾿Εξηγοῦμαι. ῍Ενα μεγάλο μέρος ἀπὸ τὸν ἀρχαῖο ἑλληνικὸ κόσμο ἐπιζεῖ στὴ ζωὴ τῆς ἑλληνικῆς Βυζαντινῆς Αὐτοκρατορίας. ῍Εχω ἐπίσης τὴ γνώμη ὅτι στὴ ζωὴ τῆς νεώτερης Ἑλλάδος ἐπιζεῖ καὶ ὁ ἀρχαῖος ἑλληνικὸς καὶ ὁ βυζαντινὸς πολιτισμός.

ΠΕΤΡΙΔΗΣ: Αὐτὸ εἶναι ἀπολύτως σωστό.

ΣΜΙΘ: Διατηρῶ ζωηρὲς τὶς ἐντυπώσεις μου ἀπὸ τὴ χθεσινή μας ἐπίσκεψη στὸ Δαφνί⁴¹, τὸ μεσαιωνικὸ μοναστήρι. Στὸ μοναστήρι αὐτὸ συναντῶνται τόσο ἡ ἀρχαία ἑλληνικὴ παράδοση ὅσο καὶ ἡ βυζαντινὴ φιλοσοφία καὶ τεχνοτροπία.

---

drunk by them. *34.* Στιφάδο is a special type of stew made with meat and whole onions cooked in vinegar or wine. *35.* It's unnecessary to tell you that my husband's imagination really went on a spree (*lit.*, gave - itself - up - to - orgies). *36.* Phidias or Pheidias (500-432 B.C.), the greatest sculptor of ancient Athens, is said to have supervised the creation of the great works on the Acropolis. *37.* The Caryatids are six draped female figures which support the entablature of the south portico of Erechtheum, one of the great architectural works on the Acropolis. *38.* See footnote 34 of Lesson 17. *39.* Panathenaea, a festival in honor of goddess Athena (the Greek counterpart of Minerva). *40.* There are the Byzantine churches, the Frankish monasteries, the mosques. *41.* Daphni is a church near Athens decorated with magnificent

ΚΩΣΤΑΣ: Ἡ παρατήρησή σου εἶναι σωστή. Βρῆκα τὸ μοναστήρι αὐτὸ πολὺ ἐνδιαφέρον. Καθὼς περνούσαμε ἀπὸ τὸν αἰωνόβιο ἐλαιώνα, σταθήκαμε μπροστὰ στὴν κουφάλα μιᾶς γέρικης ἐλιᾶς. Εἶναι ἡ ἐλιὰ τοῦ Πλάτωνος. Ἐκεῖ στὴ ρίζα της ὁ μεγάλος φιλόσοφος συνήθιζε νὰ ἀναπαύεται, νὰ διανοεῖται καὶ νὰ γράφῃ. Πιὸ πέρα εἶναι ἕνας θαυμάσιος πευκώνας. Ὁ ἀέρας εὐωδιάζει ἀπὸ τὸ ρετσίνι καὶ ἀπὸ τὴ θαλασσινὴ αὔρα ποὺ φθάνει ἀπὸ τὸν κόλπο τῆς Ἐλευσίνος.

ΕΛΕΝΗ: Καθὼς μπαίναμε στὸ Δαφνί, ἔμενα μὲ τὴν ἐντύπωση ὅτι ἀφήσαμε τὸ παρὸν καὶ ὅτι βρεθήκαμε γιὰ μιὰ στιγμὴ στὴν ἐποχὴ τῆς Βυζαντινῆς Αὐτοκρατορίας. Δὲν εἶμαι εἰδικὴ στὸ θέμα, μὰ νομίζω ὅτι κανένας ἄλλος ρυθμὸς ναοῦ δὲν ἐκφράζει τόσο ὡραία καὶ τόσο πιστὰ τὸ περιεχόμενο καὶ τὴ μορφὴ τῆς χριστιανικῆς λατρείας.

ΚΩΣΤΑΣ: Οἱ τοῖχοι εἶναι σκεπασμένοι ἀπὸ τὸ πάτωμα ὡς τὸ θόλο ἀπὸ ὑπέροχα, πολύτιμα καὶ πολύχρωμα μωσαϊκά. Ψηλὰ στὸ κέντρο εἶναι ὁ Παντοκράτωρ[42]. Ἡ θέα του προκαλεῖ δέος καὶ ξεσηκώνει μέσα σου τὰ λεπτότερα θρησκευτικὰ συναισθήματα.

ΣΜΙΘ: Στοὺς τοίχους ἀπεικονίζονται τὰ πάθη τοῦ Χριστοῦ σὲ μωσαϊκὲς εἰκόνες. Κάθε σκηνὴ ἔχει ἀφάνταστη δύναμη καὶ χάρη.

ΕΛΕΝΗ: Ἂν δὲν ἔβλεπα στὸ μοναστήρι αὐτὸ τὴ δύναμη τῆς βυζαντινῆς ἁγιογραφίας[43], θὰ ἦταν ἀδύνατο νὰ νοιώσω γιατὶ ἡ βυζαντινὴ τέχνη ξαναζεῖ σήμερα σὲ ὅλη της τὴν ὀμορφιὰ καὶ τὴ μεγαλοπρέπεια.

ΠΕΤΡΙΔΗΣ: Χαίρομαι νὰ βλέπω ὅτι τὸ Βυζάντιο δὲν σᾶς ἀφίνει ἀδιάφορους. Ἔχω πάντα τὴ γνώμη ὅτι τὸ μέρος αὐτὸ τῆς ἑλληνικῆς ἱστορίας — ἡ βυζαντινὴ ἱστορία καὶ ὁ βυζαντινὸς πολιτισμὸς — ἢ εἶναι ἄγνωστο στοὺς πολλοὺς ἢ παρεξηγημένο.

ΚΥΡΙΑ ΠΕΤΡΙΔΗ (Ἀστειευόμενη[44]): Διαμαρτύρομαι[45], ἀγαπητοὶ φίλοι. Πολὺ φοβοῦμαι ὅτι, μιλώντας γιὰ τὰ 'περασμένα, δὲν βρήκατε καιρὸ νὰ ἐκτιμήσετε ἀρκετὰ τὰ παρόντα. (Δείχνει τὰ γλυκίσματα, τὰ φροῦτα καὶ τὴ ρετσίνα.)

Byzantine mosaics. 42. Pantocrator (omnipotent) means the All-Ruler, especially as applied to God. 43. Hagiography in Greek does not mean the biography of saints, but the paintings of saints' icons. 44. Joking. 45. I protest.

ΔΕΚΑΤΟ ΕΝΑΤΟ ΜΑΘΗΜΑ

Nineteenth Lesson

ΣΤΗΝ ΠΛΑΤΕΙΑ ΣΥΝΤΑΓΜΑΤΟΣ

(Gus, Helen, Mr. Smith and Mr. and Mrs. Petrides sitting in a side-walk cafe at Constitution Square, discuss modern Greece and especially its political life and the continuity of Greek culture from classical times to the present day.)

ΠΕΤΡΙΔΗΣ: Ἐδῶ εἶναι ἡ περίφημη Πλατεῖα Συντάγματος, τὸ κέντρο τῆς ζωῆς τῆς νέας Ἀθήνας. Ἡ πλατεῖα αὐτὴ εἶναι στενὰ δεμένη μὲ τὴ νεώτερη ἱστορία μας, μὲ τὴν πολιτική μας ζωή. Ἀπὸ ἐκείνους ἐκεῖ τοὺς ἐξῶστες οἱ πολιτικοί μας ἄνδρες δημηγοροῦν, κατακεραυνώνουν τοὺς ἀντιπάλους των, ὑπόσχονται νὰ κάμουν τὴ δόξα τὴν παλιὰ νὰ ξαναζήση πάλι.[1]

ΣΜΙΘ: Ἔχω ἀκούσει ὅτι ἡ Πλατεῖα Συντάγματος, ἡ Πλατεῖα Ὁμονοίας καὶ τὸ Ζάππειο εἶναι γιὰ τοὺς νέους Ἀθηναίους ὅ,τι ἦταν ἡ «Ἀγορὰ»[2] γιὰ τοὺς προγόνους των.

ΚΥΡΙΑ ΠΕΤΡΙΔΗ: Ἀγαπητοί μου φίλοι, ἔχετε τὴν εὐκαιρία νὰ ἰδῆτε μιὰ ἀπὸ τὶς πιὸ χαρακτηριστικὲς εἰκόνες τῆς ζωῆς τῆς νεώτερης Ἀθήνας. Σὲ λίγο οἱ δημόσιες ὑπηρεσίες, οἱ τράπεζες, τὰ καταστήματα κλείνουν. Οἱ ἀμέτρητες αὐτὲς καρέκλες θὰ γεμίσουν ἀπὸ πολιτευομένους, ἀπὸ δικηγόρους, ἀπὸ ὀνειροπόλους νέους, ἀπὸ γέρους ποὺ νοσταλγοῦν τὰ περασμένα, ἀπὸ ποιητάς, λογοτέχνας καὶ διανοουμένους καὶ ἀπὸ διάφορους ἄλλους τύπους.[3]

FOOTNOTES: *1. From those balconies over there our political figures deliver speeches, they hurl thunder at their enemies, they promise to make the old glory live again. 2. The market place. 3. These innumerable chairs will be filled by politicians, lawyers, dreamy youths, old men full of nostalgia, poets,*

172

ΠΕΤΡΙΔΗΣ: Ἡ συζήτηση ἀρχίζει μὲ τὴν πρώτη ρουφιξιὰ τοῦ καφέ[4]. Συζήτηση γύρω ἀπὸ ὅλα τὰ τοπικὰ καὶ τὰ διεθνῆ θέματα τῆς ἡμέρας. Ὁ τόνος τῆς φωνῆς, τὸ ρητορικὸ ὕφος, τὰ ἐπιχειρήματα[5], οἱ χειρονομίες[6] θυμίζουν τοὺς σοφιστάς, ποὺ τόσο σκληρὰ πολέμησε ὁ γέρο — Σωκράτης.

ΚΩΣΤΑΣ: Εἶμαι στὰ κέφια μου[7]. Νοιώθω τὴ στιγμὴ αὐτὴ σὰν τὸν πιὸ καθαρόαιμο ἀπόγονο[8] τῶν ἀρχαίων ἐκείνων Ἑλλήνων, ποὺ κάθονταν στὶς στοὲς[9] τῆς «Ἀγορᾶς», χάζευαν[10], συζητοῦσαν, μιλοῦσαν, ἔκριναν καὶ κατέκριναν ὅλους καὶ ὅλα.

ΠΕΤΡΙΔΗΣ: Καθῆστε, σᾶς παρακαλῶ. Ἂν μάλιστα θέλετε νὰ ἑλληνοποιηθῆτε ἑκατὸ τοῖς ἑκατό, πάρετε ἀπὸ τέσσερες καρέκλες ὁ καθένας. Ὁ σωστὸς «Ρωμιὸς» στὴ μιὰ καρέκλα κάθεται, στὴ δευτέρη βάζει τὸ καπέλλο του, στὴν τρίτη ἀπλώνει τὰ πόδια του καὶ στὴν τέταρτη ἀκουμπᾶ τὰ χέρια του.

ΣΜΙΘ: Ἐκτιμῶ πολὺ τὴ συνήθεια αὐτή. Ἡ καλὴ συζήτηση προϋποθέτει ἄνεση[11]. Ὁ νοῦς δὲν δουλεύει καλὰ ἂν τὸ σῶμα ὑποφέρει.

ΚΩΣΤΑΣ (Μιλώντας στὸ γκαρσόνι.): Γκαρσόν, ἐλᾶτε σᾶς παρακαλῶ. Φέρτε μας μερικὲς καρέκλες.

ΓΚΑΡΣΟΝ: Εὐχαρίστως, κύριε. Τὶ θὰ πάρετε, παρακαλῶ;

ΠΕΤΡΙΔΗΣ: Θὰ πάρωμε ὅλοι καφὲ μέτριο, μὲ ὀλίγη ζάχαρη. Κάμε τὸ καλύτερο ποὺ μπορεῖς, γιατὶ θέλω νὰ μάθουν αὐτοὶ ἐδῶ οἱ φίλοι μου, ὅτι ὁ ἀμερικάνικος καφὲς δὲν ἀξίζει πεντάρα[12] μπροστὰ στὸν ἑλληνικὸ καφέ. Πρόσεξε τὸ καϊμάκι[13]. Καφὲς μέτριος σὲ χοντρὸ φλιτζάνι.

ΚΥΡΙΑ ΠΕΤΡΙΔΗ: Φέρετε, σᾶς παρακαλῶ, τρία ποτήρια κρύο νερὸ γιὰ τὸν καθένα μας. Ἐπιθυμοῦμε νὰ συμπληρωθῆ ἡ εἰκόνα τοῦ «ρωμιοῦ».

ΕΛΕΝΗ: Καμαρώνω τὶς Ἀθηναῖες. Εἶναι χαριτωμένες. Ἔχουν γοῦστο στὸ ντύσιμό τους. Τὸ περπάτημά τους εἶναι

---

writers, intellectuals and by various other types of people. 4. Conversation starts with the first sip of coffee. 5. Reasoning. 6. Gestures. 7. I am in the right mood. 8. Full-blooded descendant. 9. In the porticos. 10. They gaped dully. 11. Good conversation presupposes comfort. 12. It is not worth a nickel. 13. It is a Turkish word referring to the thick top of Turkish

ὡραῖο, περήφανο. Κοιτάξτε ἐκεῖ τὶς δυὸ αὐτὲς νέες. Εἶναι χαριτωμένες. Τὸ πρόσωπο, τὸ χτένισμα, τὸ κεφάλι μοῦ θυμίζουν τίς «Ταναγραῖες κόρες»[14].

ΚΥΡΙΑ ΠΕΤΡΙΔΗ: Συμφωνῶ μαζί σας. Οἱ Ἀθηναῖες — ἡ ὁμιλοῦσα ἐξαιρεῖται — ἔχουν χάρη. Ἡ ἔκφρασή τους εἶναι ὡραία. Τὸ ἔμφυτο γοῦστο τῆς Ἀθηναίας καλλιεργεῖται τώρα συστηματικὰ στὰ σχολεῖα, στὰ γυμναστήρια. Χαίρομαι μάλιστα πολὺ διότι τὰ τελευταῖα χρόνια ἡ νέα Ἀθηναία δὲν μιμεῖται πολὺ τὸ ξένο ντύσιμο, τὰ ξένα φερσίματα. Στὸν τόπο μας σημειώνεται ἡ ὡραία τάση νὰ κρατήσωμε τὸ ντύσιμο, τὸ χτένισμα, τὴν ἔκφραση πιὸ κοντὰ στὴν ἑλληνικὴ παράδοση.

ΕΛΕΝΗ: Ἡ τάση αὐτὴ δείχνει ὅτι ὁ τόπος ἔχει συνείδηση τῆς μεγάλης του κληρονομιᾶς. Εἶχα τὴν εὐκαιρία νὰ διαβάσω ἕνα ἐνδιαφέρον ἄρθρο γιὰ τὴν ἑλληνικὴ μόδα. Ἐπισκέφθηκα ἐπίσης στὴ Νέα Ὑόρκη μιὰ διεθνὴ ἔκθεση μόδας. Χάρηκα ἐξαιρετικὰ ὅταν εἶδα μὲ πόση τέχνη οἱ ἑλληνικοὶ οἶκοι μιμοῦνται τὴν κλασσικὴ γραμμή.

ΚΩΣΤΑΣ: Δὲν ἐνδιαφέρομαι γιὰ τὴ γυναικεία μόδα. (Γυρίζοντας στὸν κύριο Πετρίδη.) Τὴ στιγμὴ αὐτή, φίλε κύριε Πετρίδη, ἐνδιαφέρομαι γιὰ τὸ λουστράκο[15] ἐκεῖνον ἐκεῖ, γιὰ τὸν ἐφημεριδοπώλη, γιὰ τοὺς κομψοὺς ἐκείνους νέους, γιὰ τὸν ἀσπρομάλλη αὐτὸ γέροντα, γιὰ τοὺς πολιτευομένους καὶ γιὰ τοὺς δικηγόρους, γιὰ τὰ θέματα ποὺ ὅλοι αὐτοὶ συζητοῦν τόσο ζωηρά. Ἐνδιαφέρομαι γιὰ τὴ Νέα Ἑλλάδα.

ΠΕΤΡΙΔΗΣ: Εἶμαι ἕτοιμος νὰ σᾶς δώσω κάθε πληροφορία. Καθόμαστε στὴν Πλατεῖα Συνταγμάτος καὶ πίνομε τὸν καφέ μας. Οὔτε ὁ τόπος, οὔτε ἡ ὥρα μᾶς ἐπιτρέπουν νὰ σιωποῦμε ἢ νὰ μιλοῦμε γιὰ τὰ περασμένα. Ἀπὸ ποῦ θέλεις ν' ἀρχίσωμε;

ΣΜΙΘ: Ἀπὸ πότε ἀρχίζει ἡ ἱστορία τῆς νέας Ἑλλάδας; Γνωρίζω ἀρκετὰ πράγματα γιὰ τὴν ἀρχαία Ἑλλάδα καὶ γιὰ τὴ Βυζαντινὴ Αὐτοκρατορία. Οἱ γνώσεις μας γιὰ τὴν ἱστορία τῆς νέας Ἑλλάδας εἶναι περιωρισμένες.

---

coffee.   _14. The Tanagra figurines (lit., girls) are delicate statuettes made in Tanagra (an ancient town in East Boeotia, Greece) in the Hellenistic period._

ΚΩΣΤΑΣ: Δὲν γνωρίζω καλὰ τὴν ἱστορία τῆς Βυζαντινῆς Αὐτοκρατορίας. Γνωρίζω ὅμως καλὰ τὴ νεώτερη ἱστορία. Ἡ ἱστορία τῆς νέας Ἑλλάδος ἀρχίζει ἀπὸ τὴν·ἡμέρα
ποὺ οἱ Τοῦρκοι κυρίευσαν τὴν Κωνσταντινούπολη στὰ 1453.
Πολλοὶ τοποθετοῦν τὴν ἀρχὴ τῆς ζωῆς τῆς νέας Ἑλλάδος
στὸ 1821, στὸ χρόνο δηλαδὴ ποὺ ἄρχισε ὁ Ἀγώνας τῆς Ἀ-
νεξαρτησίας. Δὲν συμφωνῶ ὅμως μαζί τους. "Εχω τὴ γνώμη
ὅτι τὰ χρόνια τῆς Τουρκοκρατίας[16], τὸ ξάπλωμα τοῦ Ἑλ-
ληνισμοῦ στὶς χῶρες τοῦ Δούναβη[17], ἡ ἑτοιμασία τῆς ἐπα-
ναστάσεως τοῦ εἰκοσιένα εἶναι ἕνα κομμάτι ἀναπόσπαστο
ἀπὸ τὴ νεώτερη ἱστορία τῆς Ἑλλάδας.
ΕΛΕΝΗ: Ἡ ἑλληνικὴ ἐπανάσταση τοῦ 1821 εἶναι ἕνα
ἀκόμη ἀπὸ τὰ θαύματα τῶν Ἑλλήνων. Εἶχα τὴν καλὴ τύχη
νὰ μελετήσω τὸ θέμα. Δὲν θὰ ξεχάσω ποτὲ τὸ ἐνδιαφέρον
ποὺ ξεσήκωσε ἡ ἐπανάσταση αὐτὴ σὲ ὅλο τὸν κόσμο. Ὁ
«φιλελληνισμὸς»[18] εἶναι ἕνα ἀπὸ τὰ πιὸ ὡραῖα καὶ πιὸ εὐ-
γενικὰ κινήματα τοῦ δεκάτου ὀγδόου καὶ τοῦ δεκάτου
ἐνάτου αἰώνα.
ΣΜΙΘ: Οἱ Ἀγγλοσάξωνες, ἂν θυμᾶμαι καλά, ἔκαμαν
τότε τὸ καθῆκον τους μὲ τὸ παραπάνω. Στὶς Ἡνωμένες
Πολιτεῖες τῆς Ἀμερικῆς οἱ φιλελληνικὲς ἐκδηλώσεις τῆς
ἐποχῆς ἐκείνης εἶναι ἀπὸ τὶς πιὸ ὡραῖες σελίδες τῆς ἱστορίας τῆς πατρίδας μου.
ΚΩΣΤΑΣ: Ποιὰ εἶναι, κατὰ τὴ γνώμη σας, κύριε Πετρίδη, τὰ μεγάλα προβλήματα ποὺ εἶχε νὰ λύση ἡ Ἑλλάδα,
ὕστερα ἀπὸ τὴν ἀπελευθέρωσή της;
ΠΕΤΡΙΔΗΣ: Τὸ μεγάλο της πρόβλημα ἦταν τὸ ἐθνικὸ
πρόβλημα. "Οπως θυμᾶστε, στὶς ἀρχὲς ἀπελευθερώθηκε
μόνον ἕνα μέρος τῆς Ἑλλάδος. Οἱ λίγοι ἐλεύθεροι Ἕλληνες εἶχαν ἀναλάβει τὴν ὑποχρέωση νὰ ἐλευθερώσουν τοὺς
«δούλους ἀδελφούς». "Ετσι ἡ ἐπανάσταση τοῦ 1821 συνε-
χίσθηκε καὶ συνεχίζεται σχεδὸν ὡς σήμερα. Οἱ Ἕλληνες
πολεμοῦν διαρκῶς γιὰ τὴν ἐθνική τους ἀποκατάσταση.

---

15. *Little bootblack.* 16. The period (*lit.*, years) of Turkish occupation
(15th ce. — 19th ce.). 17. *The spreading of the Greeks in the countries around
the Danube.* It refers to the establishment of the Greeks in Rumania in the 17th
and 18th centuries. 18. Philhellenism, a movement to help the cause of
Greece, especially during the War of Independence (1821-1828). 19. *My*

"Υστερα ἀπὸ τὴν ἀπελευθέρωση τῆς Νοτίου Ἑλλάδος, ἔπρεπε νὰ ἐλευθερωθῇ ἡ Βόρειος Ἑλλάς, τὰ Νησιά ...Ὁ χαρακτήρας τοῦ νέου Ἕλληνα διαμορφώθηκε ὡς ἕνα μεγάλο σημεῖο μέσα στοὺς εὐγενικοὺς ἀγῶνες γιὰ τὴν ἐλευθερία τῆς πατρικῆς του γῆς.

ΚΥΡΙΑ ΠΕΤΡΙΔΗ: Ὁ σύζυγός μου, ἀγαπητοὶ φίλοι, γκρινιάζει[19], ἀστειεύεται, κρύβει τὰ αἰσθήματα του, ὅταν γίνεται συζήτηση γιὰ τὶς ἀρετὲς τοῦ Ἕλληνα. Ὅταν ὅμως γίνεται λόγος γιὰ τὸν πόλεμο, γιὰ τὴν ἐλευθερία, θεριεύει. Βράζει μέσα του τὸ μακεδονικὸ αἷμα...

ΠΕΤΡΙΔΗΣ: Γυναίκα, δὲν εἶμαι ἥρωας. Δὲν ἔχω οὔτε πληγές, οὔτε παράσημα στὸ στῆθος. Ἂν μάλιστα ὁ παππούς μου δὲν ἦταν «μακεδονομάχος»[20], ἡ οἰκογένειά μου δὲν θὰ εἶχε νὰ δείξη σχεδὸν τίποτε στὸν τομέα τοῦ ἑλληνικοῦ ἡρωϊσμοῦ. (Φωνάζοντας τὸ γκαρσόνι.) Γκαρσόν, φέρε μας μερικὰ ποτήρια κρύο νερό.

ΚΩΣΤΑΣ: Ἂν εἶμαι καλὰ πληροφορημένος, ὁ νεοελληνικὸς πολιτισμὸς ἀρχίζει κυρίως μὲ τὴν πτώση τῆς Πόλης. Φυσικά, ὁ πολιτισμὸς αὐτὸς δὲν εἶναι κάτι νέο. Εἶναι ἐπηρεασμένος βαθύτατα καὶ ἀπὸ τὴν ἀρχαία ἑλληνικὴ παράδοση καὶ ἀπὸ τὴ βυζαντινὴ παράδοση.

ΠΕΤΡΙΔΗΣ: Αὐτὸ εἶναι ἀπόλυτα σωστό. Ὅσοι μελετοῦν σωστά, ἀντικειμενικά, τὴν ἑλληνικὴ ἱστορία ἀπὸ τὰ πιὸ παλαιὰ χρόνια ὡς σήμερα, διαπιστώνουν[21] εὔκολα τὴν ἑνότητα, τὴ συνέχεια. Ἀλλὰ τὸ θέμα αὐτὸ εἶναι μεγάλο.

ΚΩΣΤΑΣ: Συμφωνῶ μαζί σας, μὰ θὰ προσθέσω ἐδῶ κάτι. Πρὸ καιροῦ διάβασα μιὰ πολὺ ἐνδιαφέρουσα συγκριτικὴ μελέτη[22] γύρω ἀπὸ τὸ ζήτημα αὐτό. Δὲν θὰ ξεχάσω ποτὲ μὲ πόση τέχνη ὁ συγγραφέας συνέκρινε τὴ δημοτικὴ ποίηση μὲ τὸ ὁμηρικὸ ἔπος, τὴν πλαστικότητα[23] τῆς νέας ἑλληνικῆς γλώσσας — ποὺ τόσο ἐπιδέξια τὴ χειρίσθηκαν[24]

---

husband, dear friends, grumbles.   20. A fighter for the liberation of Macedonia.   21. All those who study Greek history correctly and objectively from the earliest years to the present may easily see its unity and continuity.   22. A while ago I read a very interesting comparative study on this question.   23. Flexibility.   24. They handled it effectively (lit., dexterously).   25. Di-

συγγραφεῖς μὲ τόσο διαφορετικὲς τάσεις ὅπως ὁ Σολω-
μός²⁵, ὁ Παλαμᾶς²⁶, ὁ Καβάφης²⁷, ὁ Σικελιανός²⁸, ὁ Κα-
ζαντζάκης²⁹ καὶ οἱ σύγχρονοι πεζογράφοι μας³⁰ — μὲ τὴν
Ἀττικὴ τῆς κλασσικῆς ἐποχῆς.

ΣΜΙΘ: Κανένας δὲν ἀρνεῖται τὴν ἑνότητα, τὴ συνέχεια
τοῦ ἑλληνικοῦ πολιτισμοῦ σὲ ὅλες του τὶς ἐκδηλώσεις, στὶς
προτιμήσεις τοῦ Ἕλληνα, στὴν τέχνη, στὴν ἀρχιτεκτονική,
στὴ μουσική, στὸ χορό, στὴν ποίηση.

ΠΕΤΡΙΔΗΣ: (Φωνάζοντας τὸν ἐφημεριδοπώλη ποὺ διαλα-
λεῖ τὶς ἀπογευματινὲς ἐφημερίδες.) Παιδί, δῶσε μου, σὲ
παρακαλῶ, μία «Ἀπογευματινή», μία «Ἑσπερινή» καὶ μία
«Βραδυνή»³¹.

ΕΛΕΝΗ: Διαβάζετε κάθε μέρα καὶ τὶς τρεῖς αὐτὲς ἐφημερίδες;

ΚΥΡΙΑ ΠΕΤΡΙΔΗ: Ὁ σύζυγός μου διαβάζει τέσσερες
πρωϊνὲς καὶ τρεῖς ἀπογευματινὲς ἐφημερίδες. Μόλις ξυ-
πνήση, θὰ πιῆ τὸν καφὲ κι' ἀμέσως ἔπειτα θὰ καρφώση
τὰ μάτια του καὶ τὴ μύτη του στὴν ἐφημερίδα.

ΠΕΤΡΙΔΗΣ: Ἡ γυναίκα μου εἶναι πάντοτε ὑπερβολικὴ
ὅταν πρόκειται νὰ ἐξάρη τὶς «ρωμαίικες» ἀρετές μου. Φυσικά, δὲν κρύβω τὴν ἀδυναμία μου. Διαβάζω ὅλες σχεδὸν
τὶς ἐφημερίδες ἀνεξάρτητα ἀπὸ τὶς πολιτικὲς ἰδέες ποὺ
ὑποστηρίζουν. Βέβαια, ἔχω τὶς προτιμήσεις μου, τὶς πολι-
τικές μου ἀρχές. Μοῦ ἀρέσει ὅμως νὰ βλέπω ὅλες τὶς ἀ-
πόψεις.

_____

onysios Solomos (1798-1857), the national poet of Greece.   26. Costes Palamas
(1859-1943) expressed the feelings, hopes and aspirations of the Greek nation
in his numerous poems. His best works are The Dodecalogue of the Gypsy, The
King's Flute, Life Immovable.   27. Constantine Cavafes or Cavafy (1868 or
1863-1933), an Alexandrian poet translated into many European languages.
28. Angelos Sicelianos (1884-1951) tried to revive the Delphic festivals with
the aid of American Eva Palmer (his first wife). He wrote long poems and
tragedies in verse. His best work is "Lyricos Vios" (3 vols.).   29. Nikos Ka-
zantzakis (1885-1957) is the best-known contemporary Greek author. His works
have been translated into many languages. He wrote essays, plays, novels,
articles and philosophical works. He is the author of Zorba the Greek, The
Greek Passion, Freedom or Death and Odyssey (a modern sequel of Homer's
Odyssey consisting of 33,333 verses), published in their English translation by
Simon and Schuster in America.   30. The most important contemporary

ΣΜΙΘ: Κάθε φορά πού οἱ ἀνταποκριτὲς τῶν ξένων ἐφημερίδων γράφουν γιὰ τὴ ζωὴ στὴν Ἑλλάδα, δὲν χάνουν εὐκαιρία νὰ ἐξάρουν τὴν πολιτικομανία³² τοῦ νεοέλληνα.

ΚΩΣΤΑΣ: Εἶναι κι' αὐτὸ ἕνα ἀκόμη δεῖγμα τῶν προγονικῶν μας ἀρετῶν. Τίποτε ἄλλο δὲν συγκινοῦσε τόσο τὸν Ἀθηναῖο ὅσο τὰ δημόσια πράγματα καὶ τὰ πολιτικὰ πρόσωπα, ἡ πολιτικὴ καὶ οἱ ἐκλογές.

ΠΕΤΡΙΔΗΣ: Τί λέτε; Πᾶμε;

ΚΥΡΙΑ ΠΕΤΡΙΔΗ: Καιρὸς νὰ πᾶμε. Ὅλοι αὐτοὶ πού γυρίζουν στοὺς διαδρόμους, ψάχνουν γιὰ καρέκλες. Θὰ μᾶς εἶναι εὐγνώμονες, ἂν φύγωμε. Βιάζονται νὰ καθίσουν, νὰ πάρουν τὸν καφὲ καὶ νὰ στρωθοῦν στὴ συζήτηση ὡς τὰ μεσάνυχτα.

ΣΜΙΘ: Φυσικά, δὲν θὰ πᾶμε γιὰ ὕπνο. Εἶναι ἀκόμη ἐνωρίς. (Μιλώντας στὸν Κώστα.) Στὴν Ἀθήνα ἡ ζωὴ ἀρχίζει στὶς ὀκτὼ τὸ πρωΐ. Σταματᾶ στὴ μία τὸ μεσημέρι. Ξαναρχίζει στὶς τέσσερες τὸ ἀπόγευμα καὶ συνεχίζεται ἔπειτα στὰ καφενεῖα, στοὺς κήπους, στὶς ταράτσες, στὰ πάρκα καὶ στὶς ταβέρνες ὡς τὶς «μικρὲς ὧρες».

Greek prose writers may be mentioned here. Strates Myriveles (b. 1892), member of the Academy of Athens, wrote novels, short stories, articles and columns. His best known work is his war novel «Ἡ ζωὴ ἐν τάφῳ». Elias Venezis (b. 1904), member of the Academy of Athens, wrote short stories and novels, the best-known of which are Beyond the Aegean (Αἰολικὴ Γῆ), Serenity (Γαλήνη) and No. 31,328. Spyros Melas (b. 1884), president of the Academy of Athens, wrote many plays, biographies, articles, columns, reports and novels. Petros Chares (b. 1902), publisher and editor of the foremost Greek literary magazine «Νέα Ἑστία», wrote novels, short stories and essays. M. Karagatsis (b. 1908), wrote short stories and novels among which the best known are «Γιούγκερμαν» and «Ὁ Κίτρινος Φάκελλος». George Theotokas (b. 1905), wrote novels, short stories, essays and articles. I. M. Panayotopoulos (b. 1901), wrote novels, short stories, essays, poems and works of literary criticism. There are many other brilliant Greek writers as Angelos Terzakis, Thrasos Kastanakis, Thanasis Petsalis, K. Polites, Pant. Prevelakis, Lilika Nakou, P. Paleologos, the satirist D. Psathas and others. 31. There is a play on words in the titles of the newspapers which literally mean "Afternoon", "Evening" and "Evening" newspapers. 32. Every time the foreign correspondents write about life in Greece, they don't miss the opportunity to stress the modern Greek's mania for politics.

Twentieth
Lesson

ΕΝΤΥΠΩΣΕΙΣ ΑΠΟ ΤΑΞΙΔΙΑ ΣΤΗΝ ΕΛΛΑΔΑ

(Gus, Helen and Mr. Smith tell the Petrides their impressions of their trip to Delphi, Corinth and Olympia and discuss their plans for future trips to other parts of Greece. They also listen to Mrs. Petrides' recommendations to visit the Greek islands.)

ΠΕΤΡΙΔΗΣ: Πέρασε σχεδὸν ἕνας μήνας ἀπὸ τὴν ἡμέρα ποὺ ἀφήσατε τὴν ᾿Αθήνα. Εἶμαι βέβαιος ὅτι τὰ ταξίδια σας στὰ διάφορα μέρη τῆς ῾Ελλάδος ἦσαν εὐχάριστα. Θὰ χαρῶ πολὺ νὰ ἀκούσω τὶς ἐντυπώσεις σας.

ΣΜΙΘ: Σᾶς ἔστειλα ἀρκετὲς κάρτες ἀπὸ τὰ μέρη ποὺ ἐπισκεφθήκαμε. Τὶς πήρατε;

ΠΕΤΡΙΔΗΣ: Βέβαια τὶς ἐπῆρα. Σᾶς εὐχαριστῶ θερμά. Στὰ γραφόμενά σας ὅμως λακωνίζετε[1]. ᾿Επιθυμῶ νὰ ἀκούσω ὅλες τὶς ἐντυπώσεις σας προφορικὰ καὶ μὲ κάθε δυνατὴ λεπτομέρεια.

ΣΜΙΘ: Νὰ σᾶς διηγηθοῦμε τὶς ἐντυπώσεις μας λεπτομερειακά; Αὐτὸ εἶναι ἀδύνατο. Εἶναι τόσο πολλὲς καὶ τόσο ζωηρὲς ποὺ μποροῦμε νὰ μιλοῦμε γιὰ ὦρες καὶ ὦρες.

ΚΩΣΤΑΣ: ῞Οταν γυρίσαμε στὸ σπίτι ὕστερα ἀπὸ τὴ συνάντησή μας στὴν Πλατεῖα Συντάγματος — πέρασε ἕνας μήνας ἀπὸ τότε — καταστρώσαμε[2] τὸ πρόγραμμα τῶν ταξιδιῶν μας. ῞Οπως εἶναι φυσικό, στὸ πρῶτο μέρος τοῦ προγράμματος βάλαμε τὶς ἐπισκέψεις μας στοὺς ἀρχαιολογικοὺς τόπους — ἐννοῶ τοὺς πιὸ σπουδαίους ἀρχαιολογικοὺς τόπους, διότι ὅλη ἡ χώρα εἶναι σκεπασμένη ἀπὸ μνημεῖα σπουδαῖα καὶ ἀπὸ ἐνδιαφέρουσες ἱστορικὲς γωνιές.

FOOTNOTES: *1. In your letters (lit., writings), however, you are laconic. 2. We drew up the plan (lit., program) of our trips. 3. Finally we gave in*

ΕΛΕΝΗ: Θυμοῦμαι τὴν προετοιμασία τοῦ πρώτου γύρου τῶν ταξιδιῶν μας καὶ γελῶ ἀκόμη. Ὁ καθένας μας ἐπέμενε ν' ἀρχίσωμε τὶς ἐπισκέψεις καὶ τὰ ταξίδια μας ἀπὸ τὰ μέρη ποὺ εἶναι πιὸ κοντὰ στὰ ἐνδιαφέροντά του. Τελικὰ ὑποκύψαμε στὴν ἐπιμονὴ τοῦ συζύγου μου[3].

ΚΩΣΤΑΣ: Δὲν νομίζω ὅτι ἀδικηθήκατε. Νομίζω ὅτι ἔχετε κάθε λόγο νὰ μοῦ εἶσθε εὐγνώμονες.

ΣΜΙΘ: Αὐτὸ εἶναι σωστό. Πάντως εἶναι πιὰ ἡ σειρά σου νὰ πειθαρχήσῃς στὶς δικές μας προτιμήσεις[4]. Τὴ Δευτέρα ἀρχίζομε τὰ ταξίδια μας στὰ νησιὰ τοῦ Αἰγαίου. Ἔχω ἀκούσει ὅτι τὸ ταξίδι στὰ νησιὰ αὐτὰ εἶναι μιὰ ἀπὸ τὶς καλύτερες χαρὲς ποὺ μπορεῖ νὰ δοκιμάσῃ ὁ ἄνθρωπος.

ΚΥΡΙΑ ΠΕΤΡΙΔΗ: Αὐτὸ εἶναι σωστό. Ἡ κάθε γωνιὰ τῆς Ἑλλάδας ἔχει τὴ δική της ὀμορφιά. Τὶς χάρες ὅμως ποὺ ἔχουν τὰ νησιὰ τοῦ Αἰγαίου δὲν τὶς βρίσκεις πουθενά. Καθὼς πηγαίνεις ἀπὸ νησὶ σὲ νησί, ἡ καρδιά σου γεμίζει ἀπὸ τὴν εὐλογία τῆς γαλήνης, τῆς ἁπλότητας, τῆς καλωσύνης. Κάθε νησὶ ἔχει τὴ δική του χάρη, μὰ ὅλα μαζὶ ἔχουν μιὰ ξεχωριστὴ λεπτότητα. Ἡ θάλασσα, τὰ ἀκρογιάλια, τὰ βουνά, οἱ ἄνθρωποι ἔχουν μιὰ ἀπερίγραπτη εὐγένεια, ποὺ κερδίζει ἀμέσως τὴν ψυχὴ τοῦ ἐπισκέπτη. Κάθε οἰκογένεια ἔχει τὸ ἀμπέλι της, λίγα χωράφια, μερικὰ ἐλαιόδεντρα, λίγες συκιές, ἕνα λαχανόκηπο κι' ἕνα ὁλοκάθαρο ὁλόλευκο σπιτάκι[5]. Οἱ νησιῶτες δὲν εἶναι οὔτε πλούσιοι οὔτε φτωχοί. Ἔχουν ὅσα τοὺς χρειάζονται γιὰ τὶς περιωρισμένες τους ἀνάγκες καὶ τίποτε περισσότερο. Πέρασα πολλὰ καλοκαίρια στὰ νησιὰ τοῦ Αἰγαίου. Λειτουργήθηκα[6] στὶς ἐκκλησίες τους, καμάρωσα τὶς ὄμορφες κοπέλες, τὶς τοπικὲς ἐνδυμασίες[7], τοὺς χοροὺς καὶ τὰ γλέντια τους. Σᾶς συνιστῶ μὲ ὅλη μου τὴν καρδιὰ νὰ ἐπισκεφθῆτε τὰ νησιὰ αὐτά.

ΕΛΕΝΗ: Φυσικά, τὰ ταξίδια αὐτὰ εἶναι μέσα στὸ πρόγραμμά μας. Θὰ ἐπισκεφθοῦμε ἐπίσης τὴν Κρήτη. Ἔχω διαβάσει πολλὰ γιὰ τὸ μεγάλο αὐτὸ νησί. Ἔτσι, εἶμαι

---

to the insistence of my husband.   4. However, it is your turn to obey our preferences.   5. Every family has its vineyard, a few acres of farm, a few olive trees, a few fig trees, a garden and a clean white little house.   6. I attended services (lit., liturgy) in their churches.   7. Native costumes.   8. Ca-

ἀνυπόμονη νὰ βρεθῶ στὰ Χανιά[8], στὸ Ἡράκλειο[9], στὴν Κνωσσό[10], νὰ ἀνεβῶ στὰ βουνά, νὰ γνωρίσω ἀπὸ κοντὰ τοὺς κατοίκους τῆς ἡρωϊκῆς αὐτῆς μεγαλονήσου. Ἀλήθεια, ἡ ἱστορία τῆς Κρήτης εἶναι ἕνας σωστὸς θρύλος. Εἶναι τὸ νησὶ ποὺ ἀνέθρεψε τὸν Δία. Τὸ νησὶ ὅπου ἀναπτύχθηκε ὁ μεγάλος μινωϊκὸς πολιτισμός[11].

ΠΕΤΡΙΔΗΣ: Προσθέτω ἐδῶ ὅτι ἡ Κρήτη εἶναι τὸ νησὶ ποὺ μᾶς ἔδωσε ἕνα μεγάλο πολιτικὸ — τὸν Βενιζέλο[12] — καὶ χιλιάδες παλληκάρια[13].

ΚΥΡΙΑ ΠΕΤΡΙΔΗ: Μιὰ ποὺ μιλᾶμε γιὰ τὰ νησιὰ τῆς Ἑλλάδας σᾶς συνιστῶ ἐπίσης νὰ ἐπισκεφθῆτε τὴν Ἑπτάνησο[14].

ΚΩΣΤΑΣ: Θὰ ἐπισκεφθοῦμε ὁπωσδήποτε τὰ νησιὰ αὐτά. Ἡ Ἰθάκη, ἡ πατρίδα τοῦ Ὀδυσσέα, ξεσηκώνει πάντα τὴ φαντασία μου καὶ τὸ ἐνδιαφέρον μου. Ἔχω τὴ γνώμη ὅτι ὁ Ὀδυσσέας ζεῖ πάντα μέσα μας. Εἶναι ὁ καλύτερος ἀπὸ τοὺς προγόνους μας.

ΠΕΤΡΙΔΗΣ: Ἀγαπητοί μου φίλοι, ἀντὶ νὰ ἀκούσω τὶς ἐντυπώσεις σας ἀπὸ τὶς ἐπισκέψεις σας στοὺς ἀρχαιολογικοὺς τόπους, ἄκουσα τὴ γυναίκα μου νὰ μιλᾶ γιὰ τὰ νησιὰ τοῦ Αἰγαίου. Ἡ ἀγάπη της γιὰ τὴ θάλασσα, γιὰ τὰ νησιὰ καὶ γιὰ τοὺς νησιῶτες τὴν κάνει πάντα φλύαρη[15]. Ἔτσι φύγαμε ἀπὸ τὴ συζήτησή μας. Περιμένω νὰ ἀκούσω τὶς ἐντυπώσεις σας ἀπὸ τοὺς ἱστορικοὺς τόπους ποὺ ἐπισκεφθήκατε.

---

nea is the capital of Crete, the native city of Venizelos. *9.* Heraklion or Candia is the largest city of Crete. *10.* Knossos or Cnossus is an ancient city near the north coast of Crete. It flourished in the third and second millennia B. C. It was the home of Minos. *11.* The Minoan civilization, named after the mythical king of Crete, Minos, was one of the world's oldest. It reached its height around 1600 B. C., then ended suddenly and mysteriously. *12.* Eleutherios Venizelos (1864-1936), leader of the Liberal Party, served as premier of Greece six times (1910- 15, 1915, 1917-20,1924, 1928-32, 1933). He secured union of Crete with Greece and governed Greece through the Balkan Wars (1912-13). He set up a provisional government at Salonica (1915) and led Greece into World War I on the side of the Allies after the abdication of King Konstantine (1917). *13.* Valiant-young-men. *14.* Heptanesos (*lit.*, seven islands) or Ionian Islands is a chain of islands off West Greece. They include Corfu, Leukas, Ithaca, Cephalonia, Zante, Paxi and Cythera. These islands have been under

ΚΥΡΙΑ ΠΕΤΡΙΔΗ: Ὁ ἄντρας μου εἶναι στεριανός[16]. "Οταν μιλοῦμε γιὰ θάλασσα καὶ γιὰ θαλασσινὰ ταξίδια, τὸ στομάχι του — δὲν σᾶς τὸ κρύβω — διαμαρτύρεται.

ΚΩΣΤΑΣ: Ὁμολογῶ ὅτι ὁ νοῦς μας εἶναι φορτωμένος ἀπὸ τὶς ἐντυπώσεις μας γύρω ἀπ' ὅσα εἴδαμε ὡς τώρα, ἀλλὰ κι' ἀπὸ τὴν ἐπιθυμία μας καὶ τὴν ἀνυπομονησία μας νὰ ἰδοῦμε τὸ κάθε τί ποὺ ἔκανε καὶ κάνει τὴν Ἑλλάδα τὸν πιὸ ἀγαπητὸ τόπο καὶ στοὺς θεοὺς καὶ στοὺς ἀνθρώπους. "Ετσι ἐξηγεῖται, νομίζω, τὸ ἀνακάτεμα[17] στὴ συζήτησή μας. Πάντως εἶμαι ἕτοιμος νὰ σᾶς γνωρίσω τὶς ἐντυπώσεις μας. Παρακαλοῦνται ἡ γυναίκα μου κι' ὁ Βασίλης νὰ μὲ συμπληρώνουν.

ΕΛΕΝΗ: "Αρχισε. Ἡ εἰσαγωγὴ δὲν εἶναι πάντοτε ἀναγκαία.

ΚΩΣΤΑΣ: Ἡ ἐπίσκεψή μας στοὺς Δελφοὺς ἦταν ἡ πρώτη στὸ πρόγραμμά μας. Ἀφήσαμε τὴν Ἀθήνα πολὺ πρωΐ. Διασχίσαμε τὴν Ἀττική. Μπήκαμε στὴ Βοιωτία. Περάσαμε τὰ ξακουστὰ βουνά, τὸν Κιθαιρῶνα καὶ τὸν Ἑλικῶνα — τὰ βουνὰ τῶν Μουσῶν — καὶ φθάσαμε στὸν Παρνασσό[18]. Ἡ Ρούμελη[19] εἶναι μπροστά μας, μὲ τοὺς βοσκούς της, μὲ τὰ πρόβατα, μὲ τὶς πέτρες καὶ μὲ τὶς μυτερὲς κορυφὲς τῶν βουνῶν της. Χαιρετήσαμε μὲ σεβασμὸ τὸν τόπο ποὺ ἔδωσε τόσους ἥρωες στὴν ἐπανάσταση τοῦ εἰκοσιένα.

ΠΕΤΡΙΔΗΣ: Μὴ ξεχνᾶς τοὺς εὐζώνους[20]. Εἶναι ὅλοι παιδιὰ τῆς Ρούμελης.

ΣΜΙΘ: Καθὼς προχωρούσαμε ἀκούσαμε μιὰ φωνὴ ἀπὸ τὴν κορυφὴ ἑνὸς λόφου: «"Ε, πατριῶτες, ἐλᾶτε νὰ πάρετε λίγο γάλα καὶ ἕνα κομμάτι τυρί». Ποτὲ δὲν θὰ ξεχάσω τὴ φωνὴ αὐτή. Εἶναι ἡ φωνὴ τῆς φιλοξενίας ποὺ τὴν θεωρῶ πάντα σὰν μία ἀπὸ τὶς ὡραιότερες ἀρετὲς τῶν Ἑλλήνων.

Venetian rule from the 14th century to 1797 and under the British from 1815 to 1863. 15. *Her love for the sea, the islands and the islanders makes her talkative.* 16. *My husband is a mainlander.* 17. *This, I think, explains the confusion* (lit., *mixing-up*) *in our discussion.* 18. Parnassus is a mountain more than 8,000 feet high in Central Greece, sacred to Apollo, Dionysus, and the Muses. 19. Rumele is another name of Sterea Hellas (Central Greece). 20. *Don't forget the evzones.* The evzones are a select corps in the Greek army. Most of them are from the mountainous regions. They wear a fustanella (a

ΚΩΣΤΑΣ: Μὴ μὲ διακόπτετε, παρακαλῶ. Ύστερα ἀπὸ μιὰ τόσο εὐχάριστη διαδρομή, φθάσαμε στὸ Μαντεῖο τῶν Δελφῶν²¹. Ήπιαμε νερὸ ἀπὸ τὴν πηγὴ τῆς Κασταλίας²². Τὸ σῶμα μας δροσίσθηκε καὶ ἡ ψυχή μας ἀγαλλίασε²³. Όπως γνωρίζετε, ἡ πηγὴ αὐτὴ δίνει τὸ ἀθάνατο νερὸ τῆς ποίησης. Ἀπὸ τὰ ψηλώματα κοιτάξαμε κάτω στὸν κάμπο τὸ ποτάμι ποὺ περνᾶ σὰν φίδι ἀνάμεσα ἀπὸ μεγάλους ἐλαιῶνες²⁴.

ΕΛΕΝΗ: Σύμφωνα μὲ τὸ μύθο, τὸ ποτάμι αὐτὸ ἦταν ἕνα πελώριο φίδι. Ὁ τοξότης Ἀπόλλων²⁵ πάλαιψε μὲ τὸ φίδι αὐτὸ καὶ τὸ σκότωσε. Οἱ Έλληνες μιλοῦσαν μὲ σεβασμὸ γιὰ τὴν πάλη αὐτὴ τοὺς ἀρχαίους χρόνους.

ΣΜΙΘ: Στὸ ἴδιο αὐτὸ μέρος ἔγινε — μιλῶ μεταφορικά — μιὰ ἄλλη πάλη. Ἀντίπαλοι ἦσαν ὁ Ἀπόλλων, ὁ θεὸς τοῦ φωτός, τῆς λογικῆς καὶ τῆς ἁρμονίας, καὶ ὁ Διόνυσος, ὁ θεὸς τοῦ πάθους, τοῦ κρασιοῦ καὶ τοῦ ὀργιαστικοῦ γλεντιοῦ²⁶. Ὁ Ἀπόλλων νίκησε.

ΕΛΕΝΗ: Ἡ νίκη αὐτὴ τοῦ Ἀπόλλωνα ἔδωσε τὸ περιεχόμενο στὸν ἑλληνικὸ πολιτισμό.

ΚΩΣΤΑΣ: Αὐτὸ εἶναι σωστό. Προσθέτω ἐδῶ ὅτι ὅποιος ἔχει τὴν τύχη νὰ ἐπισκεφθῆ τὸν ἱερὸ χῶρο καὶ ὅποιος νοιώθει ὅλα ὅσα ὁ χῶρος αὐτὸς συμβολίζει, ἔχει τὸ κλειδὶ τοῦ ἑλληνικοῦ πολιτισμοῦ.

ΕΛΕΝΗ: Τὴν ἄλλη μέρα κατεβήκαμε στὸν Πειραῖα, μπήκαμε σ' ἕνα καΐκι²⁷ καὶ πλεύσαμε πρὸς τὸν Κορινθιακὸ κόλπο. Σκοπός μας ἦταν νὰ γνωρίσωμε τὴν Πελοπόννησο.

ΣΜΙΘ: Ὁ τόπος στὴν Πελοπόννησο εἶναι ἐντελῶς διαφορετικὸς ἀπὸ τὴ Ρούμελη. Ἡ βλάστηση²⁸ εἶναι πλούσια. Τὰ ἀμπέλια καλύπτουν μεγάλες ἐκτάσεις.

---

short full skirt of stiffened white linen or cotton). *21.* Delphi is the seat of the Delphic oracle. It is near the foot of Mount Parnassus. *22.* The Castalian fountain was on the slopes of Parnassus. Here the Pythian games were held. *23. Our body was cooled and our soul was elated.* *24. Olive-tree orchards.* *25. The archer Apollo,* god of light, music, poetry, prophecy and pastoral pursuits. *26. The antagonists were Apollo,* god of light, logic and harmony, *and Dionysus,* god of passion, wine and orgiastic feasts. *27.* Small sailing-ship. *28. The flora is rich.* *29.* "Not everyone can go (*lit.,* sail) to Corinth."

ΚΥΡΙΑ ΠΕΤΡΙΔΗ: Τὰ ἀμπέλια αὐτὰ εἶναι φημισμένα. Μᾶς δίνουν τὰ καλύτερα σταφύλια καὶ τὴν ξακουστὴ σταφίδα τῆς Κορίνθου.

ΚΩΣΤΑΣ: Ἡ πρώτη πόλη ποὺ ἐπισκεφθήκαμε ἦταν ἡ Κόρινθος. Εἶναι μικρή, μὰ ὡραία πόλη. Δὲν διατηρεῖ τίποτε ἀπὸ τὸν ἀρχαῖο πλοῦτο καὶ τὸ μεγαλεῖο της. Ἀσφαλῶς θυμᾶστε τὸ γνωστὸ ρητό: «οὐ παντὸς πλεῖν εἰς Κόρινθον»[29]. Ἀνεβήκαμε στὴν Ἀκροκόρινθο[30] καὶ μὲ τὴ φαντασία μας ξαναστήσαμε τὸν ναὸ τῆς Ἀφροδίτης μὲ τὶς χιλιάδες ἱέρειες. Ἀλλὰ μὲ τὴ φαντασία μας εἴδαμε ἐπίσης τὸν Ἀπόστολο Παῦλο καὶ ἀκούσαμε τὰ σοφά του λόγια πρὸς τοὺς Κορινθίους.

ΣΜΙΘ: Μετὰ τὴν Κόρινθο πήγαμε στὸ Ναύπλιο, τὴν πρώτη πρωτεύουσα τοῦ ἐλευθέρου ἑλληνικοῦ κράτους, καὶ ἀπὸ ἐκεῖ στὶς ξακουστὲς Μυκῆνες[31], στὸ βασίλειο τοῦ Ἀγαμέμνονος.

ΕΛΕΝΗ: Ὁ σύζυγός μου ἦταν πάλι στὸ στοιχεῖο του[32]. Μᾶς μίλησε γιὰ τὰ μεγάλα χρόνια τῶν Μυκηνῶν, γιὰ τὸ ἄφθονο χρυσάφι, γιὰ τὴ λεπτὴ τέχνη, γιὰ τὴ ζωὴ τοῦ παλατιοῦ, γιὰ τὸ οἰκογενειακὸ δράμα τοῦ βασιλιᾶ, γιὰ τοὺς τραγικοὺς ποὺ ἀποθανάτησαν[33] στὰ ἔργα τους τὸν Ἀγαμέμνονα, τὸ τραγικὸ τέλος τῆς Κληταιμνήστρας, τὴν Ἰφιγένεια, τὸν Ὀρέστη.

ΣΜΙΘ: Ἀλήθεια, δοκιμάζει κανένας ἕνα δέος ὅταν περνᾶ ἀπὸ τὶς γιγαντιαῖες πέτρινες εἰσόδους, ἀπὸ τὴν πύλη τῶν λεόντων, ἀπὸ τοὺς τάφους τῶν βασιλέων.

ΚΩΣΤΑΣ: Προσθέτω ἐδῶ ὅτι εἶναι ἀδύνατο νὰ νοιώση κανένας τὸν περίφημο πολιτισμὸ τῶν Μυκηνῶν, ἂν δὲν περιπλανηθῆ στὰ ἐρείπια αὐτὰ καὶ ἂν δὲν σταθῆ μὲ προσοχὴ μπροστὰ στὰ ἔργα τῆς τέχνης ποὺ μὲ τόσο σεβασμὸ φυλάσσονται στὰ μουσεῖα.

---

30. Acrocorinthus is the site of the Acropolis of Old Corinth. On the summit of this rock stood a temple of Aphrodite.　31. Mycenae in Argolis was the center of Mycenaean civilization which reached the height of its greatness around 1600 B.C. After the 14th century B.C., invasion of the Doric tribes from the North led to the decline and end of civilization by 900 B.C.　32. My husband was again in his element.　33. They immortalized.　34. Olympia

ΕΛΕΝΗ: Βιάζομαι νά σᾶς μιλήσω γιά τήν Ὀλυμπία[34].
Δέν νομίζω ὅτι ἡ ἀρχαιομάθεια καί ἡ ἑλληνολατρεία εἶναι
προνόμιο μόνο τοῦ συζύγου μου.

ΚΩΣΤΑΣ: Ἐμπρός, λοιπόν, ἀγαπητή μου. Δεῖξε στούς
ἀγαπητούς μας κύριο καί κυρία Πετρίδη πόση ἐπίδραση
εἶχε σέ σένα ὁ σύζυγός σου.

ΕΛΕΝΗ: Δέν θά ξεχάσω ποτέ τόν ἱερό χῶρο τῆς Ὀ-
λυμπίας. Περνώντας τόπους ἥμερους καί καλλιεργημένους,
φθάσαμε στήν Ὀλυμπία τήν ὥρα ἀκριβῶς πού βασίλευε ὁ
ἥλιος καί ὁ ὁρίζοντας εἶχε ἐπιχρυσωθεῖ ἀπό τή μιά ὥς τήν
ἄλλη ἄκρη. Τά μάτια μας ἔπεσαν μέ σεβασμό πάνω στήν
ἀρχαία παλαίστρα καί στίς μισογκρεμισμένες κολόνες καί
οἰκοδομές. Ἀσφαλῶς, ὅταν οἱ ἀρχαῖοι Ἕλληνες διάλεγαν
τό εὐγενικό αὐτό τοπίο γιά τά εἰρηνικά τους ἀγωνίσματα,
ἤξεραν καλά τί ἔκαναν. Δέν ἔχω ἰδεῖ κανένα ἄλλο τόπο
πού νά εἰρηνεύη τόν νοῦ καί τήν καρδιά τοῦ ἀνθρώπου καί
νά ἐπιβάλη τήν ἁρμονία ὅπως εἶναι ὁ τόπος αὐτός, ἡ Ὀ-
λυμπία. Ὅπως εἶναι γνωστό, ἡ Σπάρτη πολεμοῦσε ἐναντίον
τῶν Ἀθηνῶν. Ἡ Θήβα ἐναντίον τῆς Σπάρτης. Ἡ Κόρινθος
ἐναντίον τῆς Κερκύρας. Ἐκεῖ, στήν Ὀλυμπία, ξεχνοῦσαν
τήν ἐχθρότητα, ἀναγνώριζαν ὅτι ὅλοι εἶναι ἀδελφοί Ἕλληνες καί ἀποζητοῦσαν τή νίκη σέ ἀναίμακτους[35] ἀγῶνες,
στήν πάλη, στό δρόμο, στό δίσκο...

ΚΥΡΙΑ ΠΕΤΡΙΔΗ: Χαίρομαι νά σ᾽ ἀκούω. Μόνο γυναῖκες μποροῦν νά μιλοῦν μέ τόσο ἐνθουσιασμό γιά τήν Ὀ-
λυμπία, γιά ἔργα εἰρηνικά.

ΣΜΙΘ: Στό περίφημο μουσεῖο τῆς Ὀλυμπίας εἴδαμε
δείγματα ἀπό τά ἀθάνατα ἔργα τέχνης πού στόλιζαν τόν
Ναό τοῦ Ὀλυμπίου Διός.

ΕΛΕΝΗ: Κάποιος νεοέλληνας συγγραφέας εἶπε: «Ἄν
ἦταν δυνατόν οἱ συνεδριάσεις τῶν Ἡνωμένων Ἐθνῶν νά
γίνωνται στήν Ὀλυμπία, θά μπορούσαμε νά ἐλπίζωμε ὅτι
οἱ σημερινές ἀντιθέσεις θά λιγόστευαν, τά αἰσθήματα θά
μαλάκωναν καί ἡ ἁρμονία θά βασίλευε ἀνάμεσα στά ἄ-
τομα καί στούς λαούς.»

---

is a small plain of Elis where the Olympic games took place every four years
in honor of Olympian Zeus from 776 B.C. to the end of 4th century A.D.
35. *Bloodless.*   36. *Institutions.*   37. See footnote 6 of Lesson 16.

ΚΥΡΙΑ ΠΕΤΡΙΔΗ: Συμφωνῶ ἀπολύτως.

ΠΕΤΡΙΔΗΣ: ᾿Αλλά, ἀγαπητοί μου φίλοι, ὅπως σᾶς εἶπα καὶ προηγουμένως, ἡ Ἑλλάδα δὲν εἶναι μόνον τὰ μνημεῖα καὶ οἱ τάφοι τῶν προγόνων μας. ῍Αν θέλετε νὰ ἔχετε μιὰ ζωντανὴ εἰκόνα τῆς Ἑλλάδος, τῆς ἀθάνατης Ἑλλάδος πρέπει νὰ ἐπισκεφθῆτε καὶ τὴν ῍Ηπειρο καὶ τὴ Μακεδονία καὶ τὴ Θράκη καὶ τὴ Θεσσαλία καὶ τὴ Δυτικὴ Στερεὰ Ἑλλάδα[19]. Πρέπει νὰ ἰδῆτε τὸν ῍Ελληνα ἐπάνω στὴ δουλειά του, νὰ γνωρίσετε τοὺς θεσμούς του[36], νὰ ἐξοικειωθῆτε μὲ τὰ πνευματικά, τὰ ἐθνικὰ καὶ τὰ οἰκονομικά του προβλήματα. Πρέπει νὰ γνωρίσετε τὶς ἐκδηλώσεις τῆς ζωῆς τῆς νέας Ἑλλάδος στὸν τομέα τῆς τέχνης, τῶν γραμμάτων...

ΚΩΣΤΑΣ: Συμφωνῶ μαζί σας. Αὐτὸ εἶναι ποὺ ζητοῦμε.

ΕΛΕΝΗ: Χαίρομαι πολύ. ῍Ετσι ἡ παραμονή μας στὴν ὡραία αὐτὴ χώρα θὰ παραταθῆ.

ΚΩΣΤΑΣ: Πολὺ καλά. Πρέπει ὅμως νὰ εἰδοποιήσωμε τὸ πρακτορεῖο νὰ μᾶς κρατήσουν θέσεις ὄχι γιὰ τὸ ἑπόμενο ἀλλὰ γιὰ τὸ μεθεπόμενο ταξίδι τοῦ «᾿Ολύμπια» ἢ τοῦ «Βασίλισσα Φρειδερίκη»[37].

ΣΜΙΘ: ῍Αν δὲν εἶναι δυνατὸ νὰ ἐξασφαλίσετε θέσεις σὲ ἕνα ἀπὸ τὰ δύο αὐτὰ μεγάλα ἑλληνικὰ ὑπερωκεάνεια, μπορεῖτε νὰ ταξιδέψετε ἀεροπορικῶς μὲ τὴν T. W. A. ἢ τὴν "Olympic Airways".

REFERENCE GRAMMAR

In the following pages we have attempted to present the essentials of modern Greek grammar very concisely and to point out the basic grammatical differences between Demotic (Δημοτική) and Puristic (Καθαρεύουσα).

The development and existence of Demotic, the standard spoken and literary language, and of Puristic, the language of the official documents and news reports, can be best understood if we present a cursory view of the history of the Greek language since Christ's time.

In the first century B.C. the *Koine* (Common Greek) was the language spoken in the Hellenized regions of the Near and Middle East and used in the New Testament. However, some scholars condemned the Koine as vulgar and incorrect and advocated the return to the use of Attic Greek in writing. From that time on to the fall of Constantinople (1453), with the exception of a few manifestations of the spoken language in written documents, Atticistic Greek had been used as written Greek. During the four centuries of the occupation of Greece by the Turks, both Atticistic and modern Greek had been used.

At the beginning of the nineteenth century a Greek scholar, Adamantios Korais, who lived in Paris, suggested a compromise between the nearly unintelligible Atticistic Greek and the vernacular by recommending the use of a purified vernacular which would gradually come closer to Attic Greek.

This puristic Greek, which was adopted as the official language after the liberation of Greece, became more and more archaic during the period of 1830-1880 and was used almost exclusively as the literary language on the mainland of Greece.

After 1880 the Demotic started replacing the Puristic in poetry. In 1892 the last collection of poems written in Puristic appeared. In 1888 the first important prose work in Demotic (John Psycharis' *To Taxidi*) was published. Since then the Demotic, incorporating most of the abstract lexicon of the Puristic and accepting some inflectional irregularities, has become the standard spoken and literary language. Nevertheless, the Puristic is still used in all official documents, most news reports, editorials, scientific treatises, university lectures and sermons.

1. THE ARTICLE

1.0. The Definite Article in Greek is inflected for number, gender and case. In modern Greek there are two numbers (singular and plural), three grammatical genders (masculine, feminine and neuter) and actually[1] three cases (nominative [the case of the subject], genitive [primarily the case of possession], accusative [the object case]).

1.1. The article agrees in number, gender, and case with the noun it modifies.

1.2. Declension of the Definite Article.

| | *Singular* | | |
	Masculine	*Feminine*	*Neuter*
Nominative	ὁ	ἡ	τό
Genitive	τοῦ	τῆς	τοῦ
Accusative	τόν[2]	τήν[2]	τό

	Plural		
Nominative	οἱ	οἱ (αἱ)	τά
Genitive	τῶν	τῶν	τῶν
Accusative	τούς	τίς (τάς)	τά

The forms in parentheses are those of the Puristic. They are given only when they differ from those of the Demotic.

1.3. The definite article is used much more often in Greek than in English. The most important of its special uses are:

1. Before nouns used in an abstract or a general sense:
   Μοῦ ἀρέσει παρὰ πολὺ ἡ εἰλικρίνεια.
   I like sincerity very much.

   Τὸ φιλότιμο εἶναι τὸ κυριώτερο χαρακτηριστικὸ τοῦ Ἕλληνα.
   Self-pride is the Greek's foremost characteristic.

   Τοὺς ἀρέσει ὁ καφές.
   They like coffee.

2. Before proper names:
   Ὁ Γιάννης θὰ ἔλθη αὔριο.
   John will come tomorrow.

---

1 In classical Greek there were five cases, but today the dative (the case of the indirect object) is almost never used. It has been replaced by the accusative preceded by a preposition or by the genitive (as in the case of personal pronouns).
2 The ν of the accusative is dropped in spoken Greek before nouns beginning with a continuant consonant (φ, θ, χ, σ, ζ, ρ, λ, μ, ν) and assimilated to π, τ, κ into mb, nd, ng respectively.

'Ο κύριος Καρύδης δὲν εἶναι ἐδῶ.
Mr. Carydis is not here.

3. Before the names of places and geographical divisions:

'Η 'Αθήνα εἶναι ἡ πρωτεύουσα τῆς 'Ελλάδος.
Athens is the capital of Greece.

4. Before the names of avenues, streets and squares:

'Η κυρία Παπαδοπούλου μένει στὴν ὁδὸν 'Ερμοῦ.
Mrs. Papadopoulos lives on Mercury Street.

5. Before titles or names of professions followed by a person's name:

'Ο καθηγητὴς κ. Μπουφίδης δὲν ἦλθε νὰ μᾶς ἰδῆ.
Professor Boufidis did not come to see us.

6. In a series of nouns, before each of these nouns:

Στεῖλτε μου τὰ βιβλία, τὰ περιοδικὰ καὶ τοὺς δίσκους ποὺ ἀγόρασα προχθές.
Send me the books, magazines and records I bought the day before yesterday.

7. Before designations of time such as the year, the week, and the hour, as well as before the names of the seasons and the days of the week, except when they follow some form of the verb εἶμαι and are unmodified:

Τὸ τραῖνο φεύγει στὶς δέκα.
The train leaves at ten o'clock.

'Ο Πέτρος θὰ φύγη τὴ Δευτέρα.
Peter will leave on Monday.

8. Before expressions of measure and weight, instead of the indefinite article used in English:

Πόσο ἔχει τὸ τυρὶ αὐτό; Δέκα (δραχμὲς) ἡ ὀκά.
How much is this cheese? Ten (drachmas) an oka*.

---

* A measure of weight about 2¾ pounds used in Greece, the Balkans and the countries of the Near and Middle East.

9. Before nouns designating parts of the body, personal articles of clothing:

Τὰ χέρια τῆς ᾿Αννούλας εἶναι πάντοτε καθαρά.
Little Ann's hands are always clean.

10. Before nouns modified by a possessive adjective which follows the noun:

῾Ο φίλος μου ὁ Παῦλος δὲ(ν) θὰ ἔλθη ἀπόψε.
My friend Paul will not come tonight.

11. Before nouns modified by a demonstrative adjective. In this case the definite article is placed between the demonstrative adjective and the noun:

Αὐτὸ τὸ κορίτσι εἶναι πολὺ καλό.
This girl is very good.

12. Before a noun indicating a class of objects or persons:

Τὰ κάρβουνα εἶναι ἀκριβὰ ἐφέτος.
Coal is expensive this year.

Οἱ στρατιῶτες εἶναι πειθαρχικοί.
Soldiers are obedient.

1.4. The indefinite article in Greek is identical with the numeral for one ἕνας (for the masculine), μία or μιά (for the feminine), and ἕνα (for the neuter).

It is declined as follows:

Nominative	ἕνας	μία or μιά	ἕνα
Genitive	ἑνός	μίας or μιᾶς	ἑνός
Accusative	ἕνα(ν)	μία(ν) or μιά	ἕνα

The final ν of the accusative forms is used before a vowel and the consonants π, τ and κ. In the latter case it is assimilated with the following consonant and it is pronounced respectively mb, nd and ng.

1.5. The indefinite article is not used in Greek as often as in English because it expresses to a certain extent the idea of the numeral for *one*, since it has exactly the same form as the numeral. The indefinite article is omitted:

1. Before predicate nouns modified or unmodified by adjectives:

Εἶναι δικηγόρος.   Εἶναι ἔξυπνη κοπέλλα.
He is a lawyer.   She is a smart girl.

2. Very often before nouns which function as the object of a verb:

Ὁ Νῖκος εἶχε γράμμα ἀπὸ τὴ μητέρα του.
Nick has received a letter from his mother.

3. In exclamations, with nouns preceded by τί:

Τὶ ὄμορφη γυναίκα!   Τί καλὸ παιδί!
What a beautiful woman!   What a good boy!

4. Before a noun preceded by σάν "like":

Ὁ Κώστας φαίνεται σὰν γίγαντας μπροστὰ στὸν Πέτρο.
Gus looks like a giant next to Peter.

5. In proverbs:

Σκυλὶ ποὺ γαυγίζει δὲν δαγκώνει.
A dog that barks does not bite.

2. THE NOUN

2.0. The gender in Greek is grammatical; that is, it does not depend on the sex of the noun * but on its ending. There are three genders: masculine, feminine, and neuter.

2.1. Ancient Greek and Puristic (Katharevousa) has three declensions.

The first declension includes masculine nouns in -ας (as ταμί-ας cashier, teller, treasurer) and in -ης (as ναύτ-ης sailor) feminine nouns in -α (as χώρ-α land, country) and in -η (as ζών-η zone, belt).

The second declension comprises masculine nouns in -ος (as ἄνθρωπος man), feminine in -ος (as νῆσ-ος island) and neuter in -ον (as μῆλ-ον apple).

The third declension includes masculine, feminine and neuter nouns which have one more syllable in the genitive than they do in the no-

---

* Nouns designating male beings are normally masculine and female feminine. Names of winds, months, rivers are masculine and those of trees feminine.

minative (as ὁ κόραξ, τοῦ κόρακ-ος crow; ἡ ἐφημερίς, τῆς ἐφημερίδ-ος newspaper; ἡ πόλις, τῆς πόλεως city; τὸ μάθημα, τοῦ μαθήματ-ος lesson).

In the Demotic the third declension merges with the first declension as far as its masculine and feminine* nouns are concerned.

The other declensions present a number of differences in endings from those of their counterparts in the Katharevousa.

2.2. The First Declension

Nouns of the first declension are declined in Katharevousa as follows:

SINGULAR

		MASCULINE			FEMININE	
Nom.:	ὁ	ταμί-ας	ναύτ-ης	ἡ	χώρ-α	ζών-η
Gen.:	τοῦ	ταμί-ου	ναύτ-ου	τῆς	χώρ-ας	ζών-ης
(Dat.:	τῷ	ταμί-ᾳ	ναύτ-ῃ	τῇ	χώρ-ᾳ	ζών-ῃ)
Acc.:	τὸν	ταμί-αν	ναύτ-ην	τὴν	χώρ-αν	ζών-ην
Voc.:	ὦ	ταμί-α	ναῦτ-α	ὦ	χώρ-α	ζών-η

PLURAL

		MASCULINE			FEMININE	
Nom.:	οἱ	ταμί-αι	ναῦτ-αι	αἱ	χῶρ-αι	ζῶν-αι
Gen.:	τῶν	ταμι-ῶν	ναυτ-ῶν	τῶν	χωρ-ῶν	ζων-ῶν
(Dat.:	τοῖς	ταμί-αις	ναύτ-αις	ταῖς	χώρ-αις	ζών-αις)
Acc.:	τοὺς	ταμί-ας	ναύτ-ας	τὰς	χώρ-ας	ζών-ας
Voc.:	ὦ	ταμί-αι	ναῦτ-αι	ὦ	χῶρ-αι	ζῶν-αι

The dative is scarcely used even in Puristic. It has been replaced by the genitive or the accusative preceded by a preposition, usually εἰς. The same nouns in the Demotic are declined as follows:

SINGULAR

		MASCULINE			FEMININE	
Nom.:	ὁ	ταμί-ας	ναύτ-ης	ἡ	χώρ-α	ζών-η
Gen.:	τοῦ	ταμί-α	ναύτ-η	τῆς	χώρ-ας	ζών-ης
Acc.:	τὸν	ταμί-α	ναύτ-η	τὴ (ν)	χώρ-α	ζών-η
Voc.:	ὦ	ταμί-α	ναύτ-η	ὦ	χώρ-α	ζών-η

PLURAL

		MASCULINE			FEMININE	
Nom.:	οἱ	ταμί-ες	ναῦτ-ες	οἱ	χῶρ-ες	ζῶν-ες
Gen.:	τῶν	ταμι-ῶν	ναυτ-ῶν	τῶν	χωρ-ῶν	ζων-ῶν
Acc.:	τοὺς	ταμί-ες	ναῦτ-ες	τὶς	χῶρ-ες	ζῶν-ες
Voc.:	ὦ	ταμί-ες	ναῦτ-ες	ὦ	χῶρ-ες	ζῶν-ες

* The feminine nouns retain some of the third declension endings in the common Demotic used today, as ἡ πόλη, τῆς πόλης or πολεως, τὴν πόλη, οἱ πόλεις, τῶν πόλεων, τὶς πόλεις.

2.3. The Second Declension

Nouns of the second declension are declined in Katharevousa as follows:

SINGULAR

	MASCULINE		FEMININE		NEUTER	
Nom.:	ὁ	ἄνθρωπ-ος	ἡ	νῆσ-ος	τὸ	μῆλ-ον
Gen.:	τοῦ	ἀνθρώπ-ου	τῆς	νήσ-ου	τοῦ	μήλ-ου
(Dat.:	τῷ	ἀνθρώπ-ῳ	τῇ	νήσ-ῳ	τῷ	μήλ-ῳ)
Acc.:	τὸν	ἄνθρωπ-ον	τὴν	νῆσ-ον	τὸ	μῆλ-ον
Voc.:	ὦ	ἄνθρωπ-ε	ὦ	νῆσ-ε	ὦ	μῆλ-ον

PLURAL

Nom.:	οἱ	ἄνθρωπ-οι	αἱ	νῆσ-οι	τὰ	μῆλ-α
Gen.:	τῶν	ἀνθρώπ-ων	τῶν	νήσ-ων	τῶν	μήλ-ων
(Dat.:	τοῖς	ἀνθρώπ-οις	ταῖς	νήσ-οις	τοῖς	μήλ-οις)
Acc.:	τοὺς	ἀνθρώπ-ους	τὰς	νήσ-ους	τὰ	μῆλ-α
Voc.:	ὦ	ἄνθρωπ-οι	ὦ	νῆσ-οι	ὦ	μῆλ-α

The declension of the nouns of the second declension in the Demotic is almost the same as in the Puristic. The only actually used feminine noun of the second declension is ἡ ὁδός (street), as it appears on the street signs. There is another category of neuter nouns in the Demotic that belongs to the second declension, that of nouns in -ι (as νησί island, παιδί child).

SINGULAR

Nom.:	ὁ	ἄνθρωπ-ος	τὸ	νησ-ί	τὸ	μῆλ-ο
Gen.:	τοῦ	ἀνθρώπ-ου	τοῦ	νησ-ιοῦ	τοῦ	μήλ-ου
Acc.:	τὸν	ἄνθρωπ-ο	τὸ	νησ-ί	τὸ	μῆλ-ο

PLURAL

Nom.:	οἱ	ἄνθρωπ-οι	τὰ	νησ-ιά	τὰ	μῆλ-α
Gen.:	τῶν	ἀνθρώπ-ων	τῶν	νησ-ιῶν	τῶν	μήλ-ων
Acc.:	τοὺς	ἀνθρώπ-ους	τὰ	νησ-ιά	τὰ	μῆλ-α

2.4. The Third Declension

Nouns of the third declension are declined in Katharevousa as follows:

SINGULAR

	MASCULINE		FEMININE		NEUTER	
Nom.:	ὁ	κόραξ	ἡ	ἐφημερίς	τὸ	μάθημα
Gen.:	τοῦ	κόρακ-ος	τῆς	ἐφημερίδ-ος	τοῦ	μαθήματ-ος
(Dat.:	τῷ	κόρακ-ι	τῇ	ἐφημερίδ-ι	τῷ	μαθήματ-ι)
Acc.:	τὸν	κόρακ-α	τὴν	ἐφημερίδ-α	τὸ	μάθημα
Voc.:	ὦ	κόραξ	ὦ	ἐφημερίς	ὦ	μάθημα

PLURAL

Nom.:	οἱ	κόρακ-ες	αἱ	ἐφημερίδ-ες	τά	μαθήματ-α
Gen.:	τῶν	κοράκ-ων	τῶν	ἐφημερίδ-ων	τῶν	μαθημάτ-ων
(Dat.:	τοῖς	κόραξι	ταῖς	ἐφημερί-σι	τοῖς	μαθήμα-σι)
Acc.:	τούς	κόρακ-ας	τάς	ἐφημερίδ-ας	τά	μαθήματ-α
Voc.:	ὦ	κόρακ-ες	ὦ	ἐφημερίδ-ες	ὦ	μαθήματ-α

2.5. The masculine and feminine nouns of the third declension merged with the nouns of the first declension. The neuters of the third declension that are still used have retained in the Demotic the same endings that they have in the Katharevousa. They could not merge with the nouns of the first declension because the first declension does not have any neuter nouns. Other types of neuter nouns of the third declension that are used in the Demotic are: τὸ δάσος (the forest), τοῦ δάσους (which is derived from the uncontracted form τοῦ δάσεσ-ος [the σ between two vowels drops and the vowels ε and ο are contracted to ου]), τὸ κρέας (the meat) τοῦ κρέατ-ος. They are declined in both the Demotic and the Katharevousa as follows:

	SINGULAR				PLURAL		
Nom.:	τὸ	δάσος	τὸ	κρέας	τά	δάση	τά	κρέατ-α
Gen.:	τοῦ	δάσους	τοῦ	κρέατ-ος	τῶν	δασῶν	τῶν	κρεάτ-ων
Acc.:	τὸ	δάσος	τὸ	κρέας	τά	δάση	τά	κρέατ-α
Voc.:	ὦ	δάσος	ὦ	κρέας	ὦ	δάση	ὦ	κρέατ-α

2.6 Imparisyllabic Nouns

These nouns are used only in the Demotic. They are characterized by one more syllable in the plural than they have in the singular. Most of the nouns of this group are of foreign origin. Their stems are characterized by the vowel sounds of Greek with the exception of *o* which is the characteristic of the second declension.

Typical examples of masculine and feminine nouns of this group are: ὁ σαράφης (the money-exchanger), ὁ κεφτές (the meat ball), ὁ ψαράς (the fisher or the fish-monger), ἡ γιαγιά (the grandmother), ὁ παππούς (the grandfather), ἡ ἀλεπού (the fox).

Declension of the imparisyllabics

SINGULAR

Nom.:	ὁ	σαράφης	κεφτές	ψαράς
Gen.:	τοῦ	σαράφη	κεφτέ	ψαρᾶ
Acc.:	τὸν	σαράφη	κεφτέ	ψαρά

Nom.:	ὁ	παππούς	ἡ	γιαγιά	ἀλεπού
Gen.:	τοῦ	παππού	τῆς	γιαγιᾶς	ἀλεπούς
Acc.:	τὸν	παππού	τὴν	γιαγιά	ἀλεπού

PLURAL

Nom.:	οἱ	σαράφηδες	κεφτέδες	ψαράδες
Acc.:	τοὺς	σαράφηδες	κεφτέδες	ψαράδες

Nom.:	οἱ	παππούδες	οἱ	γιαγιάδες	ἀλεπούδες
Acc.:	τοὺς	παππούδες	τὶς	γιαγιάδες	ἀλεπούδες

The genitive plural in colloquial Greek is very seldom used in general. In the imparisyllabic class of nouns, it is never actually used, except in the case "of fishermen" τῶν ψαράδων.

3. THE ADJECTIVE

3.1. Adjectives, as in English, precede the noun they modify (e.g. ὁ καλὸς ἄνθρωπος, the good man; ἡ καλὴ γυναίκα, the good woman; τὸ καλὸ παιδί, the good child; καλὰ παιδιά, good children). As you see from the examples, they agree in gender, case, and number with the noun they modify.

3.2. In classical Greek and Katharevousa, the regular adjectives are declined according to three basic schemes of declension:
1. The so-called second declension, in which the masculine and neuter are declined according to the second declension and the feminine according to the first declension:

SINGULAR

Nom.:	ὁ	καλός	ἡ	καλή	τὸ	καλόν
Gen.:	τοῦ	καλοῦ	τῆς	καλῆς	τοῦ	καλοῦ
Acc.:	τὸν	καλόν	τὴν	καλήν	τὸ	καλόν
Voc.:	ὦ	καλέ	ὦ	καλή	ὦ	καλόν

PLURAL

Nom.:	οἱ	καλοί	αἱ	καλαί	τὰ	καλά
Gen.:	τῶν	καλῶν	τῶν	καλῶν	τῶν	καλῶν
Acc.:	τοὺς	καλούς	τὰς	καλάς	τὰ	καλά
Voc.:	ὦ	καλοί	ὦ	καλαί	ὦ	καλά

This declension has not been greatly changed in Demotic. The only changes in the singular are found in the accusative masculine and feminine, where the ν is usually dropped and the nominative, accusative

and vocative of the neuter, where the ν is also dropped. In the plural the changes are limited only to the feminine, where the nominative is οἱ καλές, the accusative τὶς καλές and the vocative (ὦ) καλές.

2. The so-called third declension, in which the masculine and neuter are declined according to the third declension of nouns and the feminine according to the first declension:

SINGULAR

Nom.:	ὁ	βαθύς	ἡ	βαθεῖα	τὸ	βαθύ
Gen.:	τοῦ	βαθέος	τῆς	βαθείας	τοῦ	βαθέος
Acc.:	τὸν	βαθύν	τὴν	βαθεῖαν	τὸ	βαθύ
Voc.:	ὦ	βαθύ	ὦ	βαθεῖα	ὦ	βαθύ

PLURAL

Nom.:	οἱ	βαθεῖς	αἱ	βαθεῖαι	τὰ	βαθέα
Gen.:	τῶν	βαθέων	τῶν	βαθειῶν	τῶν	βαθέων
Acc.:	τοὺς	βαθεῖς	τὰς	βαθείας	τὰ	βαθέα

The vocative in the plural is always identical with the nominative. The adjective βαθύς (deep) is declined in Demotic as follows:

SINGULAR

Nom.:	ὁ	βαθύς	ἡ	βαθιά	τὸ	βαθύ
Gen.:	τοῦ	βαθιοῦ	τῆς	βαθιᾶς	τοῦ	βαθιοῦ
Acc.:	τὸ(ν)	βαθύ	τὴ(ν)	βαθιά	τὸ	βαθύ

PLURAL

Nom.:	οἱ	βαθιοί	οἱ	βαθιές	τὰ	βαθιά
Gen.:	τῶν	βαθιῶν	τῶν	βαθιῶν	τῶν	βαθιῶν
Acc.:	τοὺς	βαθιούς	τὶς	βαθιές	τὰ	βαθιά

In spoken Greek the Puristic forms of the masculine plural are used sometimes instead of those of the Demotic.

3. An additional scheme of the third declension, in which the masculine and feminine have the same endings and all three genders are declined according to the third declension:

SINGULAR

Nom.:	ὁ	ἡ	συνήθης	τὸ	σύνηθες
Gen.:	τοῦ	τῆς	συνήθους	τοῦ	συνήθους
Acc.:	τὸν	τὴν	συνήθη	τὸ	σύνηθες
Voc.:	ὦ	ὦ	σύνηθες	ὦ	σύνηθες

PLURAL

Nom.:	οἱ	αἱ	συνήθεις	τὰ	συνήθη
Gen.:	τῶν	τῶν	συνήθων	τῶν	συνήθων
Acc:	τοὺς	τὰς	συνήθεις	τὰ	συνήθη

In Demotic, the adjectives like συνήθης (usual) change declension and become adjectives of the so-called second declension and are declined as the adjectives belonging to that declension. For example: ὁ ἡ συνήθης, τὸ σύνηθες becomes ὁ συνηθισμένος, ἡ συνηθισμένη, τὸ συνηθισμένο.

3.3. In colloquial Greek, there are some adjectives which are declined differently from the three schemes given above. A typical adjective of this group is ὁ ζηλιάρης (jealous). This adjective in all its three genders is used very often as a noun. It is declined as an imparisyllabic in the masculine, as a first declension noun in -a in the feminine and as a second-declension noun in -o in the neuter.

SINGULAR

Nom.:	ὁ	ζηλιάρης	ἡ	ζηλιάρα	τὸ	ζηλιάρικο
Gen.:	τοῦ	ζηλιάρη	τῆς	ζηλιάρας	τοῦ	ζηλιάρικου
Acc:	τὸ(ν)	ζηλιάρη	τὴ(ν)	ζηλιάρα	τὸ	ζηλιάρικο

PLURAL

Nom.:	οἱ	ζηλιάρηδες	οἱ	ζηλιάρες	τὰ	ζηλιάρικα
Gen.:	τῶν	ζηλιάρηδων	τῶν	ζηλιάρων	τῶν	ζηλιάρικων
Acc.:	τοὺς	ζηλιάρηδες	τὶς	ζηλιάρες	τὰ	ζηλιάρικα

3.4. Irregular Adjectives

There are two irregular adjectives which are used very often. Their frequent use seems to have helped them retain their irregularities. They are ὁ πολύς (much), which in the plural is οἱ πολλοί (many) which is used also in literary English as *hoi polloi* with its classical pronunciation, and ὁ μέγας (great, large) which in Demotic became a regular second-declension adjective ὁ μεγάλος, ἡ μεγάλη, τὸ μεγάλο.

SINGULAR

Nom.:	ὁ	πολύς	ἡ	πολλή	τὸ	πολύ
Gen.:	τοῦ	πολλοῦ	τῆς	πολλῆς	τοῦ	πολλοῦ
Acc.:	τὸν	πολύ(ν)	τὴν	πολλή(ν)	τὸ	πολύ
Voc.:	ὦ	πολύ	ὦ	πολλή	ὦ	πολύ

Nom.:	ὁ	μέγας	τὸ	μέγα
Gen.:	τοῦ	μεγάλου	τοῦ	μεγάλου
Acc.:	τὸν	μέγαν	τὸ	μέγα
Voc.:	ὦ	μέγα	ὦ	μέγα

The plural of both adjectives is regular and is declined as the rest of the so-called second declension adjectives: οἱ πολλοί, αἱ πολλαί or οἱ πολλές, τὰ πολλά; οἱ μεγάλοι, αἱ μεγάλαι or οἱ μεγάλες, τὰ μεγάλα. The singular of the feminine of μέγας, ἡ μεγάλη is also declined regularly according to the first declension.

3.5. Comparison of Adjectives

The comparative and superlative are formed by the suffixes -τερος and -τατος respectively; e.g., βαθύς (deep), βαθύτερος (deeper), βαθύτατος (deepest).

In Demotic the comparative is usually formed by placing the particle πιό in front of the positive form of the adjective; e.g., πιὸ βαθύς, πιὸ βαθιά, πιὸ βαθύ. The superlative is formed by placing the definite article in front of the comparative: ὁ πιὸ βαθύς or ὁ βαθύτερος, ἡ πιὸ βαθιά or ἡ βαθύτερη, τὸ πιὸ βαθύ or τὸ βαθύτερο.

The forms in -τέρος are also used in Demotic. But there are some adjectives which form their comparative only by means of the particle πιό. They are: unchangeable adjectives as γκρί (gray) and μπλέ (blue); adjectives that are primarily used as nouns as ὁ ζηλιάρης (jealous), ὁ κατεργάρης (sly), ὁ τεμπέλης (lazy); certain of the longer adjectives as ὁ περίεργος (curious), ὁ ἀσυγύριστος (untidy); a few of the shorter adjectives as ὁ κρύος (cold); most of the adjectives denoting color as ὁ ἄσπρος (white), ὁ μαῦρος (black), ὁ πράσινος (green).

Four adjectives have irregular comparative forms:

καλός (good)	καλύτερος or καλλίτερος (better)
κακός (bad)	χειρότερος (worse)
μεγάλος (big or large)	μεγαλύτερος (large or bigger)
πολύς (much)	περισσότερος (more)

3.51. The comparison of superiority is expressed by the comparative of the adjective followed either by ἀπό with the accusative or by παρά with the nominative. The latter is used less frequently.

Ἡ Κατίνα εἶναι πιὸ ψηλὴ ἀπὸ τὴν Ἑλένη.
Kate is taller than Helen.

Ή Μαρία εἶναι πιὸ ἔξυπνη ἀπὸ τὴν Ἀγνή.
Mary is smarter than Agnes.

Αὐτὴ εἶναι ψηλότερη παρὰ ἡ ἄλλη.
She is taller than the other.

3.52. The comparison of inferiority is expressed by (ὁ)λιγώτε-
ρο(ν) (less) plus the adjective plus ἀπό with accusative or very seldom plus παρά with nominative.

Ὁ Κώστας εἶναι λιγώτερο ἐπιμελὴς ἀπὸ τὸν Γιῶργο.
Gus is less diligent than George.

In Katharevousa the comparative is followed by the genitive.

Ὁ Χρῆστος εἶναι μεγαλύτερος τοῦ Γεωργίου.
Chris is older than George.

3.53. The comparison of equality is expressed by:

1.) τόσο ... ὅσο:

Εἶναι τόσο καλὸ ὅσο καὶ τὸ ἄλλο.
It is as good as the other.

2.) σὰν (καὶ):

Εἶναι (τόσο) καλὸ σὰν (καὶ) τὸ ἄλλο.
It is as good as the other.

The latter is preferred in negative sentences.

4. THE NUMERAL

4.1. The ordinal numbers from 1 to 199 are not declined with
the exception of ἕνα, τρία and τέσσερα which are declined both
alone and in compounds. The declension of ἕνας, μία, ἕνα is given
in the indefinite article. The forms of τρία and τέσσερα are:

Nom. Acc.: τρεῖς τρεῖς τρία τέσσερε(ι)ς τέσσερε(ι)ς τέσσερα
Gen.:   τριῶν τριῶν τριῶν τεσσάρων τεσσάρων τεσσάρων

4.2. The numbers above two hundred are declinable as plural
adjectives: διακόσιοι, διακόσιες, διακόσια. From two thousand
upwards the noun χιλιάδες (fem. plur.) is used for thousands.

4.3. The ordinal adjectives are declined like adjectives of the so-
called second declension: πρῶτος, πρώτη, πρῶτο(ν) (first).

4.4. Table of Cardinal and Ordinal Numbers.

ARABIC NUMBERS	GREEK	CARDINAL NUMERALS	ORDINAL NUMERALS
1	α΄	ἕνας, μία - μιά, ἕνα	πρῶτος
2	β΄	δύο - δυό	δεύτερος
3	γ΄	τρεῖς, τρία	τρίτος
4	δ΄	τέσσερε(ι)ς, τέσσερα	τέταρτος
5	ε΄	πέντε	πέμπτος
6	ς΄	ἕξι	ἕκτος
7	ζ΄	ἑπτά - ἑφτά	ἕβδομος
8	η΄	ὀκτώ - ὀχτώ	ὄγδοος
9	θ΄	ἐννέα - ἐννιά	ἔνατος
10	ι΄	δέκα	δέκατος
11	ια΄	ἕνδεκα - ἕντεκα	ἐνδέκατος
12	ιβ΄	δώδεκα	δωδέκατος
13	ιγ΄	δεκατρεῖς, δεκατρία	δέκατος τρίτος
14	ιδ΄	δεκατέσσερε(ι)ς, δεκατέσσερα	δέκατος τέταρτος
15	ιε΄	δεκαπέντε	δέκατος πέμπτος
16	ις΄	δεκαέξι - δεκάξι	δέκατος ἕκτος
17	ιζ΄	δεκαεπτά	δέκατος ἕβδομος
18	ιη΄	δεκαοκτώ	δέκατος ὄγδοος
19	ιθ΄	δεκαεννέα	δέκατος ἔνατος
20	κ΄	εἴκοσι	εἰκοστός
21	κα΄	εἴκοσι ἕνας (μία, ἕνα)	εἰκοστὸς πρῶτος
22	κβ΄	εἴκοσι δύο	εἰκοστὸς δεύτερος
30	λ΄	τριάντα	τριακοστός
40	μ΄	σαράντα	τεσσαρακοστός
50	ν΄	πενήντα	πεντηκοστός
60	ξ΄	ἑξήντα	ἑξηκοστός
70	ο΄	ἑβδομήντα	ἑβδομηκοστός
80	π΄	ὀγδόντα	ὀγδοηκοστός
90	η΄	ἐνενήντα	ἐνενηκοστός
100	ρ΄	ἑκατό(ν)	ἑκατοστός
101	ρα΄	ἑκατὸν ἕνας (μία, ἕνα)	ἑκατοστὸς πρῶτος
102	ρβ΄	ἑκατὸ δύο	ἑκατοστὸς δεύτερος
200	σ΄	διακόσιοι, -ες, -α	διακοσιοστός
300	τ΄	τριακόσιοι, -ες, -α	τριακοσιοστός
400	υ΄	τετρακόσιοι, -ες, -α	τετρακοσιοστός
500	φ΄	πεντακόσιοι, -ες, -α	πεντακοσιοστός
600	χ΄	ἑξακόσιοι, -ες, -α	ἑξακοσιοστός

700	ψ΄	ἑπτακόσιοι, -ες, -α	ἑπτακοσιοστός
800	ω΄	ὀκτακόσιοι, -ες, -α	ὀκτακοσιοστός
900	λ΄	ἐννιακόσιοι, -ες, -α	ἐννιακοσιοστός
1000	΄α	χίλι-οι, -ες, -α	χιλιοστός
2000	΄β	δύο χιλιάδες	δισχιλιοστός
10,000*	΄ι	δέκα χιλιάδες	δεκακισχιλιοστός
100,000	΄ρ	ἑκατὸ χιλιάδες	ἑκατοντάκισχιλιοστός
1,000,000		ἕνα ἑκατομμύριο	ἑκατομμυριοστός
1,000,000,000		ἕνα δισεκατομμύριο	δισεκατομμυριοστός

A hint about the spelling of the numbers from one to ten: If they start with a vowel in Greek, they take the rough breathing when their counterpart in English begins with s; e.g. ἕξι six, ἑπτά seven; otherwise they take the smooth breathing. The only exception to this rule is ἕνας, ἕνα.

5. THE PRONOUN

5.1. Subject Pronouns

1. The personal pronouns used as subjects of verbs are:

SINGULAR		PLURAL	
ἐγώ	I	ἐμεῖς (ἡμεῖς)	we
ἐσύ (σύ)	you	ἐσεῖς (σεῖς)	you
αὐτός	he	αὐτοί	they (masc.)
αὐτή	she	αὐτές (αὐταί)	they (fem.)
αὐτό	it	αὐτά	they (neut.)

The forms in parenthesis are the ones used in Puristic. They are given only when they differ from those of the Demotic.

2. Σύ (the pronoun of the second person singular) is used only in addressing a single preson with whom the speaker is on intimate terms, for example, between members of a family, children, close friends, peasants, workers, and adults speaking to children, or addressing animals. Σύ is also used in prayers, in addressing God and saints, and in exalted, poetic language.

* In Greek the comma is used (instead of a period as in English) as a decimal point; the period is used (instead of the comma as in English) to separate the thousands. For example, the number 12,345.67 will be written in Greek as 12.345,67.

Σεῖς (the pronoun of the second person plural) is used by mere acquaintances, in polite conversation, by children in addressing adults, by subordinates in addressing their superiors.

3. The personal subject pronouns are generally omitted, except in case of ambiguity or emphasis:

Αὐτὴ δὲν (ἐ)πῆγε νὰ ἰδῇ τὴ μητέρα της.
She did not go to see her mother.

'Ενῶ αὐτὸς γράφει, αὐτὴ διαβάζει.
While he writes, she reads.

'Εγὼ γράφω καὶ σεῖς μιλᾶτε.
I write and you talk.

5.2. The object pronouns are:

Simple forms:

	1st person	2nd person	3rd person		
			SINGULAR		
			m.	f.	n.
Gen.:	μοῦ	σοῦ	τοῦ	τῆς	τοῦ
Acc.:	μέ	σέ	τόν	τήν	τό
			PLURAL		
Gen.:	μᾶς	σᾶς	τούς or τῶν		
Acc.:	μᾶς	σᾶς	τούς	τίς	τά

Emphatic forms:

	1st person	2nd person	3rd person		
			SINGULAR		
Gen.:			αὐτου(νοῦ)	αὐτη(νῆ)ς	αὐτου(νοῦ)
Acc.:	(ἐ)μένα	(ἐ)σένα	αὐτόν	αὐτήν	αὐτό
			PLURAL		
Gen.:			αὐτῶν or αὐτονῶν		
Acc.:	(ἐ)μᾶς	(ἐ)σᾶς	αὐτούς	αὐτές	αὐτά

The object pronouns are placed before the verb. Only in the case of an imperative they follow the verb: Μοῦ τὸ ἔδωσε (He gave it to me); Δός μου το (Give it to me).

The indirect object must precede the direct object when a verb governs two object pronouns: Τῆς τὸ ἐπλήρωσε (He paid it to her). The negative precedes the object pronouns: Δὲν τῆς τὸ ἐπλήρωσε (He did not pay it to her).

For emphasis and to avoid ambiguity, the emphatic forms of the object pronouns, preceded by a preposition, are sometimes used. The emphatic object pronouns are placed after the verbal form: (Αὐτός) τὰ ἔδωσε τὰ χρήματα σ' αὐτούς (He gave the money to them).

Note that the direct object in the above sentence is repeated; the first time it is expressed as a pronoun (τὰ) and the second time as a noun (τὰ χρήματα). The indirect object may also be expressed twice for emphasis: (Αὐτοὶ) μοῦ τὰ ἔδωσαν σὲ μένα (They gave it to me); ('Εγώ) τοῦ τὰ ἔδωσα τοῦ Νίκου (I gave it to Nick).

5.3. Possessive Pronouns

The possessive pronouns are identical in form with the genitive of the personal pronouns. The only difference between the two is that the possessive pronouns are not accented because they are enclitic words following the nouns they modify: ὁ πατέρας μας (our father). When the noun is accented on the third from the last syllable (the antepenult) the accent of the enclitic possessive pronoun goes to the last syllable of the preceding noun: ὁ προϊστάμενός μας (our manager).

The forms of the possessives are:

μου	my	μας	our
σου	your (familiar)	σας	your
του	his	τους	their
της	her	or	
του	its	των	

These forms are actually pronominal adjectives. They cannot be used by themselves without modifying a noun. When they are used as pronouns equivalent to the English *mine, yours*, etc., they are preceded by the substantivized adjective (ὶ)δικός (for the masculine), (ὶ)δική (for the feminine), (ὶ)δικό (for the neuter). This adjective is declined as a regular adjective of the so-called second declension.

Its forms are used as follows:

(ὁ) δικός μου   (ἡ) δική μου   (τό) δικό μου
mine (my own)

(ὁ) δικός σου   (ἡ) δική σου   (τὸ) δικό σου
yours (fam.) (your own)

(ὁ) δικός του   (ἡ) δική του   (τὸ) δικό του
his or its (his own)

(ὁ) δικός της   (ἡ) δική της   (τὸ) δικό της
hers (her own)

(ὁ) δικός μας   (ἡ) δική μας   (τὸ) δικό μας
ours (our own)

(ὁ) δικός σας   (ἡ) δική σας   (τὸ) δικό σας
yours (your own)

(ὁ) δικός τους   (ἡ) δική τους   (τὸ) δικό τους
theirs (their own)

5.4. Interrogative Pronouns

The interrogative pronouns are:

1. Ποιός, ποιά, ποιό (who, which, which one) which is declined as a regular adjective of the so-called second declension. Its Puristic forms are: ποῖος, ποία, ποῖον.

2. Τί (what) which is indeclinable. In Puristic, however, it is declined; its masculine and feminine form is τίς (who), which is declined as follows:

	SINGULAR		PLURAL	
Nom.:	τίς	τί	τινές	τινά
Gen.:	τινός	τινός	τινῶν	τινῶν
(Dat.:	τινί	τινί	τισί	τισί
Acc.:	τινά	τί	τινάς	τινά

3. Πόσος, πόση, πόσο (how much), πόσοι, πόσες, πόσα (how many) which is also declined as a regular second declension adjective. Its Puristic forms are: πόσος, πόση, πόσον, πόσοι, πόσαι, πόσα. Both ποῖος and πόσος can also be used as pronominal adjectives.

5.5. Demonstrative Pronouns

The demonstrative pronouns are:

1. Αὐτός, αὐτή, αὐτό (this or that) which is also used as a third person personal pronoun.

2. Τοῦτος, τούτη, τοῦτο   (this right here).

3. Ἐκεῖνος, ἐκείνη, ἐκεῖνο (that).

There are three degrees of *deixis* (that is, pointing out):
a) indicating something or someone near the speaker;
b) indicating something or someone near the listener;
c) indicating something or someone far from both the speaker and the listener.

Many languages use only two types of deixis, combining the second either with the first or with the third. The Greek αὐτός represents a) and b) and ἐκεῖνος, c). English *this* represents a) and *that* b) and c). Thus αὐτός could mean either this or that. *That* could be rendered either by αὐτός or by ἐκεῖνος depending on what it refers to.

Other demonstrative pronouns are:

4. Τέτοιος, τέτοια, τέτοιο (such).

5. Ἴδιος, ἴδια, ἴδιο (same).

There is no difference in form between the demonstrative pronouns and the demonstrative adjectives. All these pronouns are declined as regular adjectives of the so-called second declension.

In Puristic, in addition to αὐτός and ἐκεῖνος, there is οὗτος which is declined as follows:

SINGULAR

Nom.:	οὗτος	αὕτη	τοῦτο
Gen.:	τούτου	ταύτης	τούτου
(Dat.:	τούτῳ	ταύτῃ	τούτῳ)
Acc.:	τοῦτον	ταύτην	τοῦτο

PLURAL

Nom.:	οὗτοι	αὗται	ταῦτα
Gen.:	τούτων	τούτων	τούτων
(Dat.:	τούτοις	ταύταις	τούτοις)
Acc.:	τούτους	ταύτας	ταῦτα

Other pronouns in Puristic are: τοιοῦτος, τοιαύτη, τοιοῦτον (such) and τοσοῦτος, τοσαύτη, τοσοῦτον (so much). Both are declined as adjectives in -ος, -η, -ον.

The only difference between the demonstrative pronouns and the demonstrative adjectives is that the pronouns stand by themselves, but the demonstrative adjectives precede the nouns which they limit and modify. Examples: Pronoun: Αὐτὰ εἶναι τὰ βιβλία της (These are her books). Adjective: Αὐτὰ τὰ βιβλία εἶναι τῆς κυρίας Μαρίας Παπαδοπούλου (These books belong to Mrs. Mary Papadopoulos). Note that the definite article precedes the noun in Greek even when the latter is modified by a demonstrative pronoun.

5.6. Indefinite Pronouns

The indefinite pronouns are:

1. Those that are declined as the numeral for one ἕνας, μία, ἕνα:

   καθένας (or καθείς), καθεμία, καθένα (each one)
   κανένας (or κανείς), κα(μ)μία, κανένα (no one, none, nobody)

2. Those that are declined as adjectives of the second declension:

   ἄλλος, ἄλλη, ἄλλο (other, another)
   κάποιος, κάποια, κάποιο (someone)
   ὅλος, ὅλη, ὅλο (all, every)

3. Those that are declined as adjectives of the second declension in the plural:

   μερικοί, μερικές, μερικά (a few, some *pl.*)

4. Those that are invariable:

   κάθε (each)
   τίποτε or τίποτα (nothing)

5. Those that are differentiated only by the definite article that precedes them:

ὁ δεῖνα, ἡ δεῖνα, τὸ δεῖνα (one such and such)
ὁ τάδε, ἡ τάδε, τὸ τάδε (one such and such)

The indefinite adjectives have identical forms with the indefinite pronouns.

5.7. Relative Pronouns

The most common of the relative pronouns in Demotic is the invariable ποὺ (who, whom, which, that) which stands for all the forms that are expressed in Puristic by ὁ ὁποῖος, ἡ ὁποία, τὸ ὁποῖον which is declined as a regular adjective of the second declension.

Other relative pronouns which are used also as adjectives and are close to the indefinite pronouns in meaning are:

1. ὅποιος, ὅποια, ὅποιο (whoever); e.g., Ὅποιος θέλει ἄς ἔλθη. (Whoever wants to come, let him come.).

2. ὅ,τι (that which); e.g., Ὅ,τι θέλει ἄς γίνη. (That which is to take place, let it take place.); Κάμε ὅ,τι σοῦ εἶπα. (Do what I told you.); (The last sentence can also be expressed by: Κάμε ἐκεῖνο ποὺ σοῦ εἶπα.) Ὅ,τι πρᾶγμα κι' ἄν εἶναι, φέρε το. (Whatever [thing] is, bring it.)

3. ὅσος, ὅση, ὅσο (as much); ὅσοι, ὅσες, ὅσα (as many).

4. τόσος, τόση, τόσο (so much); τόσοι, τόσες, τόσα (so many).

In archaic Puristic there is also the relative pronoun ὅστις (who) which is declined as follows:

	SINGULAR		
Nom.:	ὅστις	ἥτις	ὅ,τι
Gen.:	οὗτινος	ἧστινος	οὗτινος
(Dat.:	ᾧτινι	ᾗτινι	ᾧτινι)
Acc.:	ὅντινα	ἥντινα	ὅ,τι

PLURAL

Nom.:	οἵτινες	αἵτινες	ἅτινα
Gen.:	ὧντινων	ὧντινων	ὧντινων
(Dat.:	οἷστισι	αἷστισι	οἷστισι)
Acc.:	οὕστινας	ἅστινας	ἅτινα

In Puristic there are also the compound pronouns ὁποιοσδήποτε (whoever), ὁσοσδήποτε (howsoever great), ὁστισδήποτε (whoever).

6. THE PREPOSITION

6.1. The use of the preposition is one of the most difficult things to master in learning a foreign language because prepositional usage is largely idiomatic. You should form the habit of observing and learning, through repetition and practice, the prepositional usages which differ from English, as you encounter them.

6.2. In classical Greek and to a certain extent in Puristic, the prepositions govern various cases; that is, they are followed by definite cases. They may be grouped according to the cases they require:

a. Prepositions that require the genitive: ἄνευ (without), ἀντί (instead), πρό (before) as in πρὸ μεσημβρίας (before noon) which is still used and is abbreviated as π.μ. which is the equivalent of English a.m.

b. Prepositions that require the dative: ἐν (in, into), σύν (with). They are very seldom used even in Puristic. They are mostly used in classical and biblical proverbial expressions which are used in modern Greek as quotations.

c. Prepositions that require the accusative: ἀνά (over), εἰς (to, in).

d. Prepositions that take either the genitive or the accusative: διά (with gen., through; with acc., because of), κατά (with gen., against; with acc., during), μετά (with gen., with; with acc., after), περί (with gen., over, about; with acc., around), ὑπέρ (with gen., for; with acc., above), ὑπό (with gen., by; with acc., under).

e. Prepositions that take either the genitive or the dative or the accusative: ἐπί (with gen., on; with dat., because of; with acc., against, during), παρά (with gen., from; with dat., by; with acc., beside), πρός (with gen., by; with dat. or acc., to).

6.3. In modern Greek most of those complicated uses have been eliminated and if some of them still occur, their occurrence is limited to a number of stereotyped expressions. In Demotic there are only seven simple prepositions which take the accusative:* ἀπό (from), γιά (for), μέ (with), μετά (after), χωρίς (without), ὡς (as far as), εἰς or σέ (to, in, on,at). The preposition εἰς is usually combined with the definite article and appears as στό(ν) (masc., sing.), στή(ν) (fem., s.), στό (neut. s.); στούς (masc. pl.), στίς (fem. pl.), στά (neut. pl.).

6.4. The simple prepositions are often preceded by adverbs with which they form many new compound prepositions: ἀνάμεσα or ἀναμεταξύ σέ (between), ἀπάνω σὲ (on or upon), ἀπέναντι ἀπὸ (across), κάτω ἀπό (underneath), ἀποπάνω ἀπό (over, above), γύρω σέ (around), δίπλα or πλαΐ σέ (beside), ἔξω ἀπό (out of) κοντά or σιμά σέ (near), μαζὶ μέ (together with), μακριὰ ἀπό (far from), μέσα σέ (inside), μπροστὰ σέ (in front of), πισὼ ἀπό (behind), πρωτύτερα or πρὶν ἀπό (before), ὕστερα ἀπό (after).

*There is also the preposition μεταξύ (between, among) which takes the genitive and is used in standard spoken Greek. However, with plural pronouns it takes also the accusative as μεταξύ μας (between or among us).

7. THE ADVERB

7.1. The ending of most adverbs in Puristic is -ως. Many of these adverbs are used in spoken Greek. The regular ending of the same adverb in Demotic is -α. For example: καλῶς, καλά (well), but ἀμέσως (immediately) in both Demotic and Puristic. There are a few adverbs which have different meanings in their two forms as ἀκριβῶς (exactly), ἀκριβά (expensively).

7.2. The comparative of the adverbs is formed as that of the adjectives. For example: καλά (well), καλύτερα or πιὸ καλά (better). The superlative is ἄριστα or κάλλιστα (best).

7.3. The most important adverbs are:

a. *Place*: ποῦ* (where [interrogative]), ὅπου (where), ἐδῶ (here), ἐκεῖ (there), ἐπάνω (up), κάτω (down), μέσα inside), ἔξω (outside), μπροστά (in front), πίσω (behind), παντοῦ (every-

where), πλησίον, κοντά or σιμά (near), μακριά (far), πλάϊ or δίπλα (next).

b. *Manner*: πῶς* (how), ἔξαφνα (suddenly).

c. *Time*: πότε (when), τώρα (now), τότε (then), σήμερα (today), χθές (yesterday), προχθές (day before yesterday), παραπροχθές (two days before yesterday), αὔριο(ν) tomorrow, μεθαύριο(ν) (day after tomorrow), ἀμέσως (immediately), ὄχι ἀκόμη (not yet), πόσον καιρό (how long), πόσην ὥρα (how long), πόσες φορές (how many times), πολλές φορές (many times), συχνά (often), σπανίως (seldom), πάλι(ν) (again).

d. *Others*: ναί (yes), μάλιστα (yes [emphatic or formal]), ὄχι (no), καθόλου (not at all).

8. THE CONJUNCTION

8.1. Coordinating conjunctions join sentences, clauses, phrases, and words of equal rank. The most common ones are: καί (and), ἀλλά (but), μά (but [emphatic colloquial]), ἤ (or), ἤ...ἤ (either...or), μήτε...μήτε *or* οὔτε...οὔτε (neither...nor).

8.2. Subordinating conjunctions introduce dependent clauses. The most common ones are: ὅταν (when), ἀφοῦ (when, since), ἐνῶ (while), πώς *or* ὅτι (that), ἐπειδή, γιατί *or* διότι (because), ἐάν, ἄν, σάν *or* ἅμα (if), πρὶν (νά) *or* προτοῦ (νά) (before), ὕστερα πού (after), μόλις (just), καθὼς *or* ὅπως (as), ὥστε (so that), γιὰ νά *or* νά (in order to).

9. THE INTERJECTION

9.1. Some of the most common interjections in Greek are:

ἄ! ah! oh!	εἴθε! God grant!	οὔφ! oh!
ἄϊ! ah!	εὖγε! bravo!	ὄχ! oh! ow!
ἀλ(λο)ίμονο! alas!	μακάρι! God grant!	πούφ! pf!
ἄλτ! stop!	μάρς! march!	σούτ! *or* στ! (hu)sh!
ἄου! ouch!	μπράβο! bravo!	φτού! ugh!
ἄχ! ah! oh!	μπά! pshaw! so what!	ὤ! say!
ἔ! say! hey!	ὄ! oh!	ὤχ! ow!

*Ποῦ and πῶς are differentiated by a different accent from πού (who, which, that), the relative pronoun, and πώς (that), the conjunction.

9.2.Exclamative phrases are used as interjections:

(Τί) Κρίμα!   What a pity!   Θεέ μου!   My God!
Χριστὸς καὶ Παναγιά!   Christ and Virgin (may help us)!
Κακομοίρη (μου)   (My) poor man!
Τὸν καημένο!   The poor man!   "Ελα (δά)!   Come (now)!
'Ορίστε!   Here is!   Ζήτω!   Long live! Hurrah!
'Εμπρός!   Forward! Come in!   'Εν τάξει!   O. K.!
"Εξω!   Out!   Περαστικά!   Speedy recovery!
Τί ὄμορφη!   How beautiful!   Σὲ καλό σου!   How could you!
Μάτια μου!   My dearest! (Lit., my eyes!)
Δὲν πειράζει!   Never mind!   Λοιπόν!   Then! So!
Γρήγορα!   Hurry up!   Σιγά-σιγά!   Take it easy!
Προσοχή!   Attention! Look out!   Καρδιά!   Courage!

10. THE VERB

10.1. In English the form of the verb changes according to the subject. We say: *I am, you are, he is*, etc. In most cases, however, the English verb changes only in the third person singular in the present. For example, we say: *I think, you think, we think, they think*, but *he thinks* or *she thinks*. Since five of the six possible forms are identical, we are not especially conscious of the problem of verb endings. On the other hand, the Greek verb has a large number of endings which differ according to subject, tense, and mood. The best way to learn the verb forms properly is in the context in which they are used.

Memorizing the endings without learning the sentence patterns of speech in which they occur may help you recognize them but not actually use them.

10.12. In the verbal system of modern Greek both the tense and the aspect are important. The concept of the aspect is expressed by two different stems: the stem of the present and the stem of the aorist; from these two stems are formed all the tenses and moods.

10.13. Modern Greek has eight tenses:

1. The *present* (ὁ ἐνεστώς) which expresses something that is going on, or a state of existence. Examples: παίζω (I play, I do

play, I am playing); πεινῶ (I am hungry); προοδεύω (I make progress).

2. The *imperfect* (ὁ παρατατικός) that expresses an action which went on for sometime in the past or has been repeated or was customary. Example: ἔπαιζα (I was playing, I used to play); (ἐ)πεινοῦσα (I was hungry [during an indefinite period of time]); (ἐ)προόδευα (I kept making progress).

3. The *durative future* (ὁ ἐξακολουθητικὸς μέλλων) which expresses an action that will be going on. Example: θὰ παίζω (I will be playing); θὰ πεινῶ (I will be hungry [for an indefinite time]); θὰ προοδεύω (I will be or keep progressing).

4. The *punctual future* (ὁ στιγμιαῖος μέλλων) that expresses an action that will take place in the future and will be completed. Example: θὰ παίξω (I will play); θὰ πεινάσω (I will be hungry [during a certain period of time]); θὰ προοδεύσω (I will make certain progress).

5. The *aorist or simple past* (ὁ ἀοριστός) which expresses a completed action or a single act in past time. Example: ἔπαιξα (I played); (ἐ)πείνασα (I was hungry [during a certain period]); (ἐ)προόδευσα (I made progress).

6. The *perfect or present perfect* (ὁ παρακείμενος) that represents an action as having taken place and having been completed. Example: ἔχω παίξει (I have played); ἔχω πεινάσει (I have been hungry); ἔχω προοδεύσει (I have made progress).

7. The *pluperfect or past perfect* (ὁ ὑπερσυντέλικος) which expresses an action that had taken place. Example: εἶχα παίξει (I had played): εἶχα πεινάσει (I had been hungry); εἶχα προοδεύσει (I had made progress).

8. The *future perfect* (ὁ τετελεσμένος μέλλων) that expresses an action that will have taken place. Example: θὰ ἔχω παίξει (I will have played); θὰ ἔχω πεινάσει (I will have been hungry): θὰ ἔχω προοδεύσει (I will have made progress). This tense is very seldom used.

10.131. The indicative of the simple past tenses (imperfect and aorist) take a prefix called augment (αὔξηση).

There are two kinds of augment, the syllabic (ή συλλαβική) and the temporal (ή χρονική).

The syllabic augment is an ε- prefixed to verbs which begin with a consonant. Example: παίζω (I play), ἔπαιζα (I was playing), ἔπαιξα (I played).

The initial ρ is usually doubled after the augment, especially in Puristic. Example: ρέει (it flows), ἔρρεε (it flowed).

The temporal augment is a lengthening or change of the initial vowel (as α changes to η, ε to η, ο to ω, οι to ῳ, αι to ῃ, αυ to ηυ, and ευ to ηυ).

In Demotic the temporal augment is not used and the syllabic is dropped when it is not accented, as μάθαμε (we learned) instead of ἐμάθαμε.

10.14. Modern Greek has only three moods: the *indicative* (ὁριστική), the *subjunctive* (ὑποτακτική) which is used in addition to its other uses in cases in which the infinitive is used in English because modern Greek has no infinitive, and the *imperative* (προστακτική). Modern Greek also has two *conditionals* (the simple and the perfect) *. From the stem of the present are formed three tenses: The present, the imperfect, and the durative future; and from the stem of the aorist are formed the aorist and the punctual future. The perfect tenses are formed by the present, imperfect and future of the auxiliary verb ἔχω (have) and a stereotyped form derived from the aoristic stem.

10.15. The semantic difference between the *present* (or *imperfective*) and *aorist* (or *perfective*) aspects can be briefly stated thus: in the forms formed from the present stem the interest is generally in the duration of the action described by the verb, and in those formed from the aorist stem, in the completion of the action described by the verb.

10.2. A few of the most frequently used verbs have only three tenses: present, imperfect and future. Two of these verbs are the auxiliaries ἔχω (to have) and εἶμαι (to be):

PRESENT

Indicative		Subjunctive	
ἔχ-ω	εἶμαι	νὰ ἔχ-ω	νὰ εἶμαι
ἔχ-εις	εἶσαι	νὰ ἔχ-ης	etc.
ἔχ-ει	εἶναι	νὰ ἔχ-η	

---

* The *simple conditional* is formed by the particle θὰ plus the imperfect and the *perfect conditional* by θὰ plus the pluperfect.

ἔχ-ομε	εἴμαστε (εἴμεθα)	νὰ ἔχ-ωμε	or ἔχουμε
ἔχ-ετε	εἶστε (εἶσθε)	νὰ ἔχ-ετε	
ἔχ-ουν	εἶναι	νὰ ἔχ-ουν	

The forms in parenthesis indicate the Puristic forms when they differ from those of the Demotic.

Note that the pronouns ἐγώ for *I*, αὐτός for *he*, etc. do not have to be expressed, because the endings themselves indicate the subject. Thus, by means of the ending -ω we know that ἔχω means *I have* and ἔχουν the ending of which is -ουν means *they have*.

Note also that there are two forms which express the so-called second person: a singular form in -εις and a plural form in -ετε. Concerning the use of these two forms, see 5.1.2.

The real present imperative of ἔχω (ἔχε *sing.*, ἔχετε *plur.*) is very seldom used. Instead of it, the subjunctive of both verbs may be used with the sense of the imperative: Νὰ εἶσθε ἕτοιμοι! Be ready!

IMPERFECT

εἶχ-α (εἶχ-ον)	I had	ἤμουν (ἤμην)	I was
εἶχ-ες		ἤσουν (ἦσο)
εἶχ-ε		ἦταν (ἦτο)
εἴχ-αμε (εἴχ-ομεν)		ἤμαστε (ἤμεθα)
εἴχ-ατε		ἤσαστε (ἦσθε)
εἶχ-αν (εἶχ-ον)		ἦταν (ἦσαν)

The forms in parenthesis indicate the puristic forms when they differ from those of the Demotic. However, some of the forms of the Puristic, especially the form ἦσαν, are used more frequently than others. There are in Demotic some additional forms for the imperfect of *to be*: ἤμουνα, ἤσουνα, ἤτανε, ἤμασταν or ἤμασθε, ἤσασταν or ἤσασθε, ἤτανε or ἤσανε. All those forms which are spelled by some writers with ει (εἴμουνα) are given only for the purpose of being recognized when encountered. Their use, nevertheless, is not recommended.

FUTURE

θὰ ἔχω I shall have	θὰ εἶμαι I shall be
θὰ ἔχης	θὰ εἶσαι
θὰ ἔχη	θὰ εἶναι
θὰ ἔχωμε or ἔχουμε	θὰ εἴμαστε
θὰ ἔχετε	θὰ εἶστε
θὰ ἔχουν	θὰ εἶναι

10.3. The best presentation of the verb can be done in a tabular form. The endings are separated from the stem of the tense by a hyphen.

There are two main categories of regular verbs in Greek: The un-contracted which are accented on the next to the last syllable and the contracted which are accented on the last syllable and take a circumflex (because of that, they are called περισπώμενα in Greek).

Concerning the formation of the aorist of a number of verbs — the stem of which ends in a certain way, here are a few rules:

1. Verbs ending in -αινω form the aorist in -ανα or in -ηνα (πεθαίνω [I die], πέθανα [I died]).

2. Verbs ending in -ωνω form the aorist in -ωσα (σκοτώνω [I kill], σκότωσα) and the passive aorist in -θηκα (σκοτώθηκα).

3. Verbs ending in -ιζω form the aorist in -ισα (φωτίζω [I light], φώτισα) and the passive aorist in -σθηκα (φωτίσθηκα).

4. Verbs ending in -αζω form the aorist in -αξα (φωνάζω [I shout], φώναξα).

5. Verbs the stem of which end in π, μπ, φ, β and ευ form the aorist in -ψα (in the Demotic) (κόβω [I cut], ἔκοψα; μαζεύω [I gather], μάζεψα*).

6. Verbs the stem of which end in θ, δ, σ form the aorist in -σα (πλάθω [I mold], ἔπλασα).

7. Verbs in the stem of which end in κ, γγ (γκ), χ, γ for the aorist in -ξα (τρέχω [I run], ἔτρεξα).

*In Puristic the aorist of this verb is ἐμάζευσα.

Present - stem　**λυν-**　　Aorist - stem　**λυσ-**

ACTIVE VOICE

	Indicative Imperfect	Durative Future	Subjunctive Present	Imperative Present
Present				
λύν-ω	ἔλυν-α	θὰ λύνω	νὰ λύν-ω	
λύν-εις	ἔλυν-ες	θὰ λύνῃς	νὰ λύν-ῃς	λύν-ε
λύν-ει	ἔλυν-ε	θὰ λύνῃ	νὰ λύν-ῃ	
λύν-ομε	(ἐ) λύν-αμε	θὰ λύνομε	νὰ λύν-ωμε	
λύν-ετε	(ἐ) λύν-ατε	θὰ λύνετε	νὰ λύν-ετε	λύν-ετε
λύν-ουν	ἔλυν-αν	θὰ λύνουν	νὰ λύν-ουν	
	Aorist	**Punctual Future**	**Aorist**	**Aorist**
	ἔλυσ-α	θὰ λύσω	νὰ λύσ-ω	
	ἔλυσ-ες	θὰ λύσῃς	νὰ λύσ-ῃς	λῦσ-ε
	ἔλυσ-ε	θὰ λύσῃ	νὰ λύσ-ῃ	
	(ἐ) λύσ-αμε	θὰ λύσωμε	νὰ λύσ-ωμε	
	(ἐ) λύσ-ατε	θὰ λύσετε	νὰ λύσ-ετε	λῦσ-(ε) τε
	ἔλυσ-αν	θὰ λύσουν	νὰ λύσ-ουν	
Perfect	**Pluperfect**	**Future Perfect**	**Perfect**	**Perfect**
ἔχω λύσει	εἶχα λύσει	θὰ ἔχω λύσει	νὰ ἔχω λύσει	

Present - stem **λυν-**   Aorist - stem **λυ-θ-**

PASSIVE VOICE

Present System

Present	Indicative Imperfect	Durative Future	Subjunctive Present	Imperative Present
λύν-ομαι	λυν-όμουν	θὰ λύνωμαι	νὰ λύνωμαι	
λύν-εσαι	λυν-όσουν	θὰ λύνεσαι	νὰ λύνεσαι	
λύν-εται	λυν-όταν	θὰ λύνεται	νὰ λύνεται	
λυν-όμαστε	λυν-όμαστε	θὰ λυνόμαστε	νὰ λυνόμαστε	
λύν-εστε	λυν-όσαστε	θὰ λύνεστε	νὰ λύνεστε	
λύν-ονται	λύν-ονταν	θὰ λύνωνται	νὰ λύνωνται	

Aorist System

Aorist	Punctual Future	Aorist Subjunctive	Aorist Imperative
λύθηκα	θὰ λυθῶ	νὰ λυθῶ	
λύθηκες	θὰ λυθῇς	νὰ λυθῇς	λύσου
λύθηκε	θὰ λυθῇ	νὰ λυθῇ	
λυθήκαμε	θὰ λυθοῦμε	νὰ λυθοῦμε	
λυθήκατε	θὰ λυθῆτε	νὰ λυθῆτε	λυθῆτε
λύθηκαν	θὰ λυθοῦν	νὰ λυθοῦν	

Perfect System

Perfect	Pluperfect	Future Perfect	Perfect Subjunctive	Perfect Imperative
ἔχω λυθῆ	εἶχα λυθῆ	θὰ ἔχω λυθῆ	νὰ ἔχω λυθῆ	

ACTIVE VOICE

Present - stem **αγαπ-**   Aorist - stem **αγαπησ-**

	Indicative		Durative Future	Subjunctive Present	Imperative Present
Present	**Imperfect**				
αγαπ-ῶ	αγαπ-οῦσα		θα αγαπῶ	νά αγαπῶ	
αγαπ-ᾶς	αγαπ-οῦσες		θα αγαπᾶς	νά αγαπᾶς	αγάπα
αγαπ-ᾶ	αγαπ-οῦσε		θα αγαπᾶ	νά αγαπᾶ	
αγαπ-οῦμε	αγαπ-οῦσαμε		θα αγαποῦμε	νά αγαποῦμε	
αγαπ-ᾶτε	αγαπ-οῦσατε		θα αγαπᾶτε	νά αγαπᾶτε	αγαπᾶτε
αγαπ-οῦν	αγαπ-οῦσαν		θα αγαποῦν	νά αγαποῦν	

Aorist	Punctual Future	Aorist	Aorist
αγάπησ-α	θα αγαπήσω	νά αγαπήσω	
αγάπησ-ες	θα αγαπήσης	νά αγαπήσης	αγάπησε
αγάπησ-ε	θα αγαπήση	νά αγαπήση	
αγαπήσ-αμε	θα αγαπήσωμε	νά αγαπήσωμε	
αγαπήσ-ατε	θα αγαπήσετε	νά αγαπήσετε	αγαπῆστε
αγάπησ-αν	θα αγαπήσουν	νά αγαπήσουν	

Perfect	**Pluperfect**	**Future Perfect**	**Perfect**
Ἔχω αγαπήσει	εἶχα αγαπήσει	θά Ἔχω αγαπήσει	νά Ἔχω αγαπήσει

Present - stem **αγαπ-**   Aorist - stem **αγαπηθ-**

PASSIVE VOICE

	Indicative			
Present	Imperfect	Durative Future	Subjunctive Present	Imperative
αγαπιέμαι	αγαπιόμουν	θα αγαπιέμαι	νά αγαπιέμαι	
αγαπιέσαι	αγαπιόσουν	θα αγαπιέσαι	νά αγαπιέσαι	
αγαπιέται	αγαπιόταν	θα αγαπιέται	νά αγαπιέται	
αγαπιούμαστε	αγαπιόμαστε	θα αγαπιούμαστε	νά αγαπιούμαστε	
αγαπιέστε	αγαπιόσαστε	θα αγαπιέστε	νά αγαπιέστε	
αγαπιούνται	αγαπιόνταν	θα αγαπιούνται	νά αγαπιούνται	
	Aorist	Punctual Future	Aorist	Aorist
	αγαπήθηκα	θα αγαπηθώ	νά αγαπηθώ	
	αγαπήθηκες	θα αγαπηθής	νά αγαπηθής	
	αγαπήθηκε	θα αγαπηθή	νά αγαπηθή	
	αγαπηθήκαμε	θα αγαπηθούμε	νά αγαπηθούμε	
	αγαπηθήκατε	θα αγαπηθήτε	νά αγαπηθήτε	
	αγαπήθηκαν	θα αγαπηθούν	νά αγαπηθούν	
Perfect	Pluperfect	Future Perfect	Perfect	Perfect
έχω αγαπηθή	είχα αγαπηθή	θα έχω αγαπηθή	νά έχω αγαπηθή	

Present · stem **λυ-**   Aorist · stem **λυσ-**

ACTIVE VOICE (KATHAREVOUSA)

Present	Indicative Imperfect	Durative Future	Subjunctive Present	Imperative Present
λύ-ω	ἔλυ-ον	θὰ λύ-ω	νὰ λύ-ω	
λύ-εις	ἔλυ-ες	θὰ λύ-ῃς	νὰ λύ-ῃς	λῦ-ε
λύ-ει	ἔλυ-ε	θὰ λύ-ῃ	νὰ λύ-ῃ	
λύ-ομεν	ἐλύ-ομεν	θὰ λύ-ωμεν	νὰ λύ-ωμεν	
λύ-ετε	ἐλύ-ετε	θὰ λύ-ητε	νὰ λύ-ητε	λύ-ετε
λύ-ουν	ἔλυ-ον	θὰ λύ-ουν	νὰ λύ-ουν	

Aorist	Punctual Future	Aorist	Aorist
ἔλυ-σ-α	θὰ λύ-σ-ω	νὰ λύ-σ-ω	
ἔλυ-σ-ας	θὰ λύ-σ-ῃς	νὰ λύ-σ-ῃς	λῦ-σ-ον
ἔλυ-σ-ε	θὰ λύ-σ-ῃ	νὰ λύ-σ-ῃ	
ἐλύ-σ-αμεν	θὰ λύ-σ-ωμεν	νὰ λύ-σ-ωμεν	
ἐλύ-σ-ατε	θὰ λύ-σ-ητε	νὰ λύ-σ-ητε	λύ-σ-ατε
ἔλυ-σ-αν	θὰ λύ-σ-ουν	νὰ λύ-σ-ουν	

Perfect	Pluperfect	Future Perfect	Perfect
ἔχω λύσει	εἶχον λύσει	θὰ ἔχω λύσει	νὰ ἔχω λύσει

Present - stem **λυ-**   Aorist - stem **λυ-θ-**

PASSIVE VOICE (KATHAREVOUSA)

Present	Indicative Imperfect	Durative Future	Subjunctive Present	Imperative Present
λύ-ομαι	ἐλυ-όμην	θὰ λύ-ωμαι	νὰ λύ-ωμαι	λύ-ου
λύ-εσαι	ἐλύ-εσο	θὰ λύ-ησαι	νὰ λύ-ησαι	
λύ-εται	ἐλύ-ετο	θὰ λύ-ηται	νὰ λύ-ηται	
λυ-όμεθα	ἐλυ-όμεθα	θὰ λυ-ώμεθα	νὰ λυ-ώμεθα	
λύ-εσθε	ἐλύ-εσθε	θὰ λύ-ησθε	νὰ λύ-ησθε	λύ-εσθε
λύ-ονται	ἐλύ-οντο	θὰ λύ-ωνται	νὰ λύ-ωνται	

	Aorist	Punctual Future	Aorist (Subjunctive)	Aorist (Imperative)
	ἐλύ-θην	θὰ λυ-θῶ	νὰ λυ-θῶ	λύ-θητι
	ἐλύ-θης	θὰ λυ-θῇς	νὰ λυ-θῇς	
	ἐλύ-θη	θὰ λυ-θῇ	νὰ λυ-θῇ	
	ἐλύ-θημεν	θὰ λυ-θῶμεν	νὰ λυ-θῶμεν	λυ-θῆτε
	ἐλύ-θητε	θὰ λυ-θῆτε	νὰ λυ-θῆτε	
	ἐλύ-θησαν	θὰ λυ-θοῦν	νὰ λυ-θοῦν	

Perfect	Pluperfect	Future Perfect	Perfect
ἔχω λυθῆ	εἶχον λυθῆ	θὰ ἔχω λυθῆ	νὰ ἔχω λυθῆ

LIST OF IRREGULAR VERBS
This list includes the most common verbs of spoken Demotic.

PRESENT	AORIST	PASSIVE AORIST	PAST PASSIVE PARTICIPLE
ἀνεβαίνω (I go up; climb)	ἀνέβηκα		ἀνεβασμένος
ἀρέσω (I am liked)	ἄρεσα		
αὐξάνω (I increase)	αὔξησα	αὐξήθηκα	αὐξημένος
ἀφήνω (I leave; let)	ἄφησα		ἀφημένος
βάζω (I put)	ἔβαλα	βάλθηκα	βαλμένος
βγάζω (I take out)	ἔβγαλα	(βγάλθηκα)	βγαλμένος
βγαίνω (I come out, I go out)	βγῆκα		βγαλμένος
βλέπω (I see)	εἶδα		
βρέχω (I wet)	ἔβρεξα	βράχηκα	βρε(γ)μένος
βρίσκω (I find)	βρῆκα	βρέθηκα	
γίνομαι (I become)	ἔγινα	γίνηκα	γινωμένος
γδέρνω (I flay, I skin)	ἔγδαρα	γδάρθηκα	γδαρμένος
γέρνω (I lean)	ἔγειρα		γερμένος
δέρνω (I beat)	ἔδειρα	δάρθηκα	δαρμένος
διαβαίνω (I pass [through])	διάβηκα		
διαμαρτύρομαι (I protest)		διαμαρτυρήθηκα	διαμαρτυρημένος
διδάσκω (I teach)	δίδαξα	διδάχθηκα	διδαγμένος
δίνω or δίδω (I give)	ἔδωσα	δόθηκα	δο(σ)μένος
ἐγκατασταίνω (or ἐγκαθιστῶ) (I establish)	ἐγκατέστησα	ἐγκαταστάθηκα	ἐγκαταστημένος
ἔρχομαι (I come)	ἦλθα		

εὐρίσκω (I find)	ηῦρα	εὑρέθην	
εὔχομαι (I wish)		εὑχήθηκα	
θέλω (I want)	θέλησα		
θέτω (I set)	ἔθεσα	ἐτέθην	-θεμένος.
κάθομαι (I sit down)	κάθισα (or κάθησα)		καθισμένος
καίω (I burn)	ἔκαυσα (or ἔκαψα)	κάηκα	καμένος
κάνω (I do; make)	ἔκανα (or ἔκαμα)		καμωμένος
καταλαβαίνω (I understand)	κατάλαβα		
κατεβαίνω (I go down)	κατέβηκα		κατεβασμένος
κλαίω (I weep; cry)	ἔκλαυσα (or ἔκλαψα)	κλαύθηκα	κλαμένος
λαβαίνω (or λαμβάνω) (I take; receive)	ἔλαβα		
λέ(γ)ω (I say)	εἶπα		εἰπωμένος
μαθαίνω (or μανθάνω) (I learn)	ἔμαθα	(μαθεύτηκε)	μαθημένος
μένω (I stay)	ἔμεινα		
μπαίνω (I go in; get in)	μπῆκα		
ντρέπομαι (I am ashamed)		ντράπηκα	
παθαίνω (I suffer)	ἔπαθα		
πεθαίνω (I die)	πέθανα		πεθαμένος
πετυχαίνω (I succeed)	πέτυχα		πετυχημένος
πέφτω (I fall) (or πίπτω)	ἔπεσα		πεσμένος

πηγαίνω (I go) (or πάω)	(ἐ)πῆγα		
πίνω (I drink)	ἤπια		πιωμένος
πλένω (I wash)	ἔπλυνα	πλύθηκα	πλυμένος
σέβομαι (I respect)		σεβάσθηκα	
σέρνω (or σύρω) (I drag)	ἔσυρα	σύρθηκα	συρμένος
σπέρνω (I sow) (or σπείρω)	ἔσπειρα	σπάρθηκα	σπαρμένος
στέκομαι (I stand [up])		στάθηκα	
στέλνω (or στέλλω) (I send)	ἔστειλα	στάλθηκα	σταλμένος
στρέφω (I turn)	ἔστρεψα	στράφηκα	στραμμένος
σωπαίνω (or σιωπῶ) (I keep silence)	σώπασα (or σιώπησα)		
τρώ(γ)ω (I eat)	ἔφαγα	φαγώθηκα	φαγωμένος
τυχαίνω (or τυγχάνω) (I chance)	ἔτυχα		(ἀπο-τυχημένος)
ὑπόσχομαι (I promise)		ὑποσχέθηκα	ὑποσχεμένος
φαίνομαι (I seem)		φάνηκα	
φεύγω (I flee, I run away)	ἔφυγα		
χαίρομαι (I am glad)		χάρηκα	
χορταίνω (I am satiated)	χόρτασα		χορτασμένος
ψέλνω (or ψάλλω) (I chant)	ἔψαλα	ψάλθηκα	ψαλμένος

GREEK-ENGLISH
DICTIONARY

A

ἀγάπη f. love
ἀγαπημένος, -η, -ο beloved, favorite
ἀγαπητός, -ή, -ό dear
ἀγαπῶ to love, to like, to be fond of
ἀγγελία f. announcement
ἄγγελος m. angel
ἀγγίζω to touch
ἀγελάδα f. cow
ἅγιος, -α, -ο holy, saint
ἀγκαλιάζω to embrace
ἀγκώνας m. elbow
ἄγνοια f. ignorance
ἀγνός, -ή, -ό pure
ἀγορά f. market, purchase
ἀγοράζω to buy, to purchase
ἀγόρι n. boy
ἀγώνας m. fight, struggle, contest
ἀδιάβροχο raincoat
ἄδεια f. permission, vacation
ἄδειος, -α, -ο empty

ἀδελφός m. brother
ἀδελφή f. sister
ἀδιάσπαστος, -η, -ο unbroken, unbreakable
ἄδικος, -η, -ο unjust, unfair
ἄδικο, ἔχω to be wrong
ἀδυναμία f. weakness
ἀδύνατος, -η, -ο weak, thin
ἀδύνατο, εἶναι it is impossible
ἀέρας m. air
ἀεροδρόμιο n. airfield, airport
ἀεροπλάνο n. airplane
ἀεροπόρος m. airman, pilot
ἀεροπορικῶς by air, via airmail
ἀηδία f. disgust
ἀθλητής m. sportsman, athlete
ἀθλητισμός m. sport
αἷμα n. blood
αἰσθάνομαι to feel
αἴσθημα n. feeling, emotion
αἴτηση* f. application, request
αἰτία f. cause, reason
αἰώνας m. century
αἰώνιος, -α, -ο eternal

In the Greek-English dictionary the following points should be noted: In the case of nouns, gender is always indicated by m. (masculine), f. (feminine) or n. (neuter). Nouns of the third declension in -ις, -εως, as πρᾶξις (act), πράξεως are given only in their Demotic form, as πράξη* (marked by an asterisk), unless the Puristic is the only one used. Adjectives, pronouns and participles are given in all three genders: καλός m., καλή f., καλό n. (good) as καλός,-ή,-ό. In the case of verbs, the first person singular of the present indicative is given in Greek. This is the basic verbal form since there is no infinitive as such in modern Greek. The corresponding English translation is given in the infinitive. In case of doublets, the first is either the Demotic form or the most frequently used spelling variant in contemporary books.

225

ἀκάθαρτος, -η, -ο dirty
ἀκούω to hear, to listen
ἀκολουθῶ to follow
ἀκόμη still
ἀκριβός, -ή, -ό expensive
ἀκριβῶς exactly
ἀκρογιαλιά f. beach, seaside
ἀλάτι (ἅλας) n. salt
ἀλατίζω to season
ἀλήθεια f. truth
ἀληθινός, -ή, -ό real, true
ἀλλά but
ἀλλαγή f. change
ἀλλάζω, ἀλλάσσω to change
ἀλληλογραφία
   f. correspondence
ἀλλιῶς otherwise
ἄλλος, -η, -ο other
ἀλμυρός, -ή, -ό salty
ἄλογο n. horse
ἀλοιφή f. ointment
Ἀμερικανίδα f. American
Ἀμερική f. America
Ἀμερικανός m. American
ἄμεσος, -η, -ο immediate,
   direct
ἀμέσως immediately,
   at once, right away
ἄμμος m. sand
ἀμπέλι n. vineyard
ἄμυνα f. defense
ἀμφιβάλλω to doubt
ἀμφιβολία f. doubt
ἄν if
ἀναβάλλω to postpone
ἀναβολή f. postponement
ἀναγγέλλω to announce
ἀναγκαῖος, -α, -ο necessary
ἀνάγκη f. need

ἀναγνωρίζω to recognize
ἀνακαλύπτω to discover,
   to find out
ἀνακάλυψη* f. discovery
ἀνακατεύω to mix, to stir
ἀναλαμβάνω to assume
ἀνάμεσα between, among
ἀνάμνηση* f. remembrance,
   recollection
ἀναμφιβόλως undoubtedly
ἀναπαύομαι to rest
ἀνάπαυση* f. rest
ἀναπνέω to breathe
ἀναπτήρας m. lighter
ἀνάπτυξη* f. development,
   growth
ἀναπτύσσω, ἀναπτύσομαι
   to develop, to grow
ἀναστατώνω to upset
ἀνατολή f. east, sunrise
ἀναχώρηση* f. departure
ἀναχωρῶ to depart, to leave
ἀναψυκτικά n. pl. refreshments
ἄνδρας m. man, husband
ἀνεβαίνω to go up, to ascend
ἄνεμος m. wind
ἀνεξαρτησία f. independence
ἄνεση* f. comfort
ἄνετος, -η, -ο comfortable
ἀνησυχία f. worry, anxiety
ἀνησυχῶ to worry, to disturb
ἀνθίζω to bloom
ἀνθισμένος, -η, -ο blooming
ἄνθος n. flower
ἀνθρώπινος, -η, -ο human
ἄνθρωπος m. man
ἀνθρωπότης f. humanity
ἀνθυγεινός, -ή, -ό unhealthy
ἀνίσχυρος, -η, -ο powerless

ἀνεψιός m. nephew
ἀνεψιά f. niece
ἀνοίγω to open
ἀνοικτός, -ή, -ό open
ἄνοιξη* spring
ἀνταμώνω to meet, to join
ἀντίγραφο n. copy
ἀντιγράφω to copy
ἀντίδραση* f. reaction
ἀντιδρῶ to react
ἀντίθεση* f. contrast,
  opposition
ἀντίθετος, -η, -ο contrary,
  opposed
ἀντικαθιστῶ to replace
ἀντικατάσταση* f. replacement
ἀντικείμενο n. object
ἀντιλαμβάνομαι to understand,
  to perceive
ἀντίληψη* f. conception,
  perception
ἀντιπρόσωπος m. representative
ἀνώτερος, -η, -ο superior
ἀξία f. value
ἀξίζω to deserve,
  to be worthy
ἄξιος,-α, -ο worthy
ἀπαίτηση* f. demand
ἀπαιτῶ to demand
ἀπαλός, -ή, -ό soft, smooth
ἀπάντηση* f. answer
ἀπαντῶ to answer, to meet
ἀπαραίτητος, -η, -ο
  indispensable, necessary
ἀπασχολημένος, -η, -ο busy
ἀπάτη f. deceit
ἀπατῶ to deceive
ἀπεικονίζω to represent,
  to portray

ἀπειλή f. threat
ἀπειλῶ to threaten
ἀπελευθερώνω to liberate
ἀπελευθέρωση* f. liberation
ἀπέναντι opposite to
ἁπλός, -ή, -ό simple
ἁπλότης f. simplicity
ἁπλώνω to spread, to lay
ἀπό from
ἀπόγευμα n. afternoon
ἀποδεικνύω to prove
ἀπόδειξη* f. proof, receipt
ἀποθηκεύω to store
ἀποθήκη f. store-room
ἀποκατάσταση* recovery
  f. reestablishment,
ἀποκοιμοῦμαι to fall asleep
ἀπολαμβάνω to enjoy
ἀπόλαυση* f. enjoyment
ἀπόλυτα or ἀπολύτως
  absolutely
ἀποσκευές f. pl. baggage
ἀπόσταση* f. distance
ἀποτελοῦμαι to consist
ἀποτελῶ to constitute
ἀπουσία f. absence
ἀπουσιάζω to be absent
ἀπόφαση* f. decision, resolution
ἀποφασίζω to decide,
  to resolve
ἀπόψε tonight
ἄποψη* view
Ἀπρίλιος m. April
ἀργά late, slowly
ἀργός, -ή, -ό slow
ἀργότερα later
ἄρθρο n. article
ἀριθμός m. number
ἀριστερά to the left

αριστερός, -ή, -ό left
άριστος, -η, -ο excellent
αρκετά enough, sufficiently
αρκετός, -ή, -ό sufficient
άρνηση* f. refusal
αρνί n. sheep, lamb
αρνούμαι to refuse, to deny
αρπάζω to grab, to catch
άρρωστος, -η, -ο sick
αρρώστια f. sickness, disease
αρχαίος, -α, -ο ancient
αρχή f. beginning
αρχηγός m. leader, chief
αρχίζω to begin, to start
αρχικός, -ή, -ό initial, original
άρωμα n. perfume, fragrance
ασήμι n. silver
ασημικά n. pl. silverware
ασθένεια f. illness, disease
ασθενής ill, weak
άσκηση* f. exercise, practice
ασπρόρουχα n. pl. linen,
αστακός m. lobster
αστειεύομαι to joke
αστείο n. joke
αστείος, -α, -ο funny
αστέρι (άστρο) n. star
αστραπή f. lightning
αστυνομία f. police
αστυνόμος m. police officer,
   sheriff
αστυνομικό τμήμα n. police
   station
ασφάλεια f. security, insurance
ασφαλής, -ής, -ές secure
ασφαλισμένος, -η, -ο insured
ασφαλώς surely
άσχημος, -η, -ο ugly, bad

ατμός m. steam
άτομο n. individual
αυγή f. dawn
αυγό n. egg
Αύγουστος m. August
αυξάνω to increase, to grow
αύξηση* f. increase, growth
αύριο tomorrow
αυτί n. ear
αυτός, -ή, -ό this
αυτοκίνητο n. automobile, car
αυτόματος, -η, -ο automatic
αφήνω to leave, to let
άφθονος, -η, -ο abundant,
   copious
αχθοφόρος m. porter
αχλάδι n. pear
άχρηστος, -η, -ο useless
άψητος, -η, -ο raw, uncooked
B
βαγόνι n. railroad car, wagon
βάζω to put, to put on
βάθος n. depth
βαθύς, -ιά, -ύ deep
βαθμός m. degree, grade
βαλίτσα f. suitcase
βαμπάκι n. cotton
βάρκα f. boat
βάρος n. weight
βαρύς, -ιά, -ύ heavy
βασίλειο n. kingdom
βασιλεύω to reign
βασιλεύς, βασιλιάς m. king
βασίλισσα f. queen
βαφή f. dye
βάφω to paint, to dye
βάψιμο n. painting, dyeing
βγάζω to take off

βέβαια, βεβαίως certainly, surely, of course
βέβαιος, -α, -ο certain, sure
βεβαιώνω to assure
βελόνα f. needle
βελόνι n. needle
βελοῦδο n. velvet
βελτιώνω to improve
βενζίνη f. gasoline
βήχας m. cough
βήχω to cough
βιάζομαι to hurry, to be in a hurry
βιάζω to force
βιαστικός, -ή, -ό in a hurry
βιβλίο n. book
βιβλιοθήκη f. book case, library
βιομηχανία f. industry
βλέπω to see
βόδι, βῶδι n. ox
βοήθεια f. help, assistance
βοηθός m. helper, assistant
βοηθητικός, -ή, -ό auxiliary
βορρᾶς (βοριάς) m. north (wind)
βοσκός m. shepherd
βουνό n. mountain
βούρτσα f. brush
βουρτσίζω to brush
βούτυρο n. butter
βραβεῖο n. prize, award
βράδυ n. evening
βραδυνός, -ή, -ό evening (adj.)
βράζω to boil
βραστός, -ή, -ό boiled
βράχος m. rock
βρεγμένος, -η, -ο wet
βρέχω to wet, to soak

βρέχει it rains
βρίσκομαι to be, to be located
βρίσκω to find
βροντή f. thunder
βροχή f. rain

Γ

γάϊδαρος m. donkey, ass
γάλα n. milk
γαλανός, -ή, -ό blue, blond
γάμος m. marriage
γαμπρός m. bridegroom, son-in-law, brother-in-law
γάντι n. glove
γαρίφαλο, γαρύφαλλο n. carnation
γάτα f. cat
γεγονός n. event
γείτονας m. neighbor
γειτονιά f. neighborhood
γέλιο n. laughter
γελῶ to laugh
γεμάτος, -η, -ο full, filled
γεμίζω to fill
γενικά, γενικῶς generally
γενικός, -ή, -ό general
γενέθλια n. pl. birthday
γέννηση* f. birth
γεῦμα n. meal, midday meal
γεύομαι to taste
γεύση* f. taste
γέφυρα f. bridge
γεωργός m. farmer
γῆ f. earth
γιά for
γιαγιά f. grandmother
γιακάς m. collar
γιαλί n. glass
γιατί why, because, for

γιατρός m. physician, doctor
γίνομαι to become
γιός, γυιός m. son
γκαράζ n. garage
γκρεμίζω to demolish,
   to throw down
γκρί(ζος), (-α), (-ο) gray
γλιστρῶ to slip
γλύκισμα n. pastry, cake
γλυκό n. jam
γλυκός, -ιά, -ό sweet
γλῶσσα f. tongue
γνώμη f. opinion
γνωρίζω to know, to inform
γνώρισμα n. trait
γνώση* f. knowledge
γνώσεις f. pl. knowledge
γνωστός m. acquaintance
γνωστή f. acquaintance
γνωστός, -ή, -ό known
γόνατο n. knee
γονιός m. parent
γονεῖς m. pl. parents
γούνα f. fur
γραβάτα f. necktie
γραμματεύς m. secretary
γραμματόσημο n. stamp
γραμμή f. line
γραφεῖο n. desk, office
γράφω to write
γρήγορα quickly
γυμνάσιο n. high school
γυμναστήριο n. gymnasium
γυναίκα f. woman
γυρεύω to look for, to seek
γυρίζω to turn
γύρος, γῦρος m. tour, round,
   turn

γύρω round, around
γωνία, γωνιά f. corner, angle

Δ

δάγκαμα, δάγκωμα n. bite
δαγκάνω, δαγκώνω to bite
δάκρυ n. tear
δακυλογράφος m. f. typist
δακτυλογραφῶ to type
δάκτυλος m. finger
δανείζομαι to borrow
δανείζω to lend
δασκάλα f. teacher
δάσκαλος m. teacher
δαχτυλίδι n. ring
δάχτυλο n. finger, toe
δείκτης m. pointer, hand
   (watch)
δεῖπνο n. supper, dinner
δείχνω to show
δέκα ten
δέκατος, -η, -ο tenth
Δεκέμβριος m. December
δέμα n. package
δέντρο n. tree
δεξιός, -ά, -ό right
δένω to bind, to tie
δέρμα n. skin, leather
δεσποινίς f. miss, young lady
Δεσπότης m. Bishop
Δευτέρα f. Monday
δευτερόλεπτο n. second (time)
δεύτερος, -η, -ο second
δέχομαι to accept
δηλώνω to declare, to state
δήλωση* f. declaration,
   statement
δήμαρχος m. mayor
δημιούργημα n. creation

δημιουργός m. creator
δημιουργῶ to create
δημοκρατία f. democracy, republic
διαβάζω to read
διαβαίνω to pass
διαβατήριο n. passport
διαβεβαίωνω to assure
διαίρεση* f. division, separation
διαιρῶ to divide, to separate
διακοπές f. pl. vacation
διακοπή f. interruption
διακόπτω to interrupt
διακόσια two hundred
διακρίνω to distinguish
διάκριση* f. distinction, discrimination
διαλέγω to choose, to select
διάλεξη* f. lecture, talk
διαλύω to dissolve
διαμάντι n. diamond
διαμαρτυρία f. protest
διαμαρτύρομαι to protest
διαμέρισμα n. apartment
διαμονή f. residence, stay
διαμορφώνω to form, to mold
διάρκεια f. duration
διαρκῶ to last
διαρκῶς continually
διασκεδάζω to amuse (oneself), to have a good time
διασκέδαση* f. amusement, entertainment
διασκεδαστικός, -ή, -ό amusing, entertaining
διασχίζω to cut through, to tear
διαταγή f. order
διατάζω to order

διατηρῶ to maintain, to preserve
διαφέρω to differ
διαφορά f. difference
διαφορετικός, -ή, -ό different
διαλέγω to pick up, to select
διδάσκω to teach
διαλέγομαι to converse
δίδυμος, -η, -ο twin
διεθνής, -ής, -ές international
διεύθυνση* f. address, management
διευθυντής, -τρια director, manager, principal
διευθύνω to direct, to manage
διήγημα n. short story
δικαιολογία f. excuse, justification
δικαιολογημένος, -η, -ο justified, excused
δικαιολογῶ to justify, to excuse
δίκαιος, -η, -ο just, fair
δικαιοσύνη f. justice
δικαστής m. judge
δίκη f. trial, lawsuit
δίκαιο, ἔχω to be right
δίνω to give
διοίκηση* f. administration
διότι because
δίπλα beside, near by
διπλός, -ή, -ό double
δίπλωμα n. diploma
διπλώνω to fold
δίσκος m. tray, record, disk
διστάζω to hesitate
δισταγμός m. hesitation
διστακτικός, -ή, -ό hesitating

δοκιμάζω to try, to test
δοκιμή f. trial, test
δολλάριο n. dollar
δόντι n. tooth
δόξα f. glory
δοξάζω to glorify
δουλεύω to work
δοῦλος m. slave
δρᾶμα n. drama, play
δραματικός, -ή, -ό dramatic
δραστήριος, -α, -ο active, efficient
δρομολόγιο n. itinerary
δρόμος m. street, road
δροσερός, -ή, -ό cool
δροσιά f. coolness
δροσιστικός, -ή, -ό refreshing
δύναμη* f. strength, power, might
δυναμικός, -ή, -ό dynamic
δυνατό, εἶναι it is possible
δυνατός, -ή, -ό strong, mighty
δύο two
δυσάρεστος, -η, -ο unpleasant
δύση* f. west, sunset
δυσκολία f difficulty, hardship
δύσκολος, -η, -ο difficult, hard
δυστύχημα n. accident
δυστυχής, -ής, -ές unfortunate
δυστυχία f. misfortune
δυστυχῶς unfortunately
δώδεκα twelve
δωδέκατος, -η, -ο twelfth
δωμάτιο n. room
δωρίζω to offer a present
δῶρο n. present, gift

E

ἑβδομάδα f. week

ἑβδομήντα seventy
ἕβδομος, -η, -ο seventh
'Εβραῖος, -α Jew, Hebrew
ἐγγονός m. grandson
ἐγγονή f. granddaughter
ἐγγράφω to register, to enroll
ἐγκατάσταση* f. establishment, installation
ἐγκρίνω to approve
ἔγκριση* f. approval
ἐγώ I
ἐδῶ here
ἐθνικός, -ή, -ό national
ἐθνικότης f. nationality
ἔθνος n. nation
εἰδικός, -ή, -ό special, specific
εἰδοποίηση* f. notice, advice
εἰδοποιῶ to notify, to inform
εἶδος n. kind, soft
εἰλικρινά sincerely
εἰλικρίνεια f. sincerity
εἰλικρινής, -ής, -ές sincere
εἰκόνα f. picture, icon
εἴκοσι twenty
εἰκοστός, -ή, -ό twentieth
εἰρήνη f. peace
εἰρωνεύομαι to speak ironically
εἰρωνία f. irony
εἰσάγω to import, to introduce
εἰσαγωγή f. import, introduction
εἰσιτήριο n. ticket
εἰσόδημα n. revenue, income
εἴσοδος f. entrance, entry
ἑκατό one hundred
ἑκατό, τοῖς per cent
ἑκατοστός, -ή, -ό hundredth
ἑκατομύριο n. million

ἐκδήλωση* f. manifestation, expression

ἔκδοση* publication, edition, issue

ἐκδρομή picnic, excursion

ἐκεῖ there

ἐκεῖνος, -η, -ο that

ἔκθεση* f. exhibition, display composition

ἐκκλησία f. church

ἐκλέγω to elect, to choose

ἐκλογή f. election

ἔκπληξη* f. surprise

ἐκπλήττω to surprise

ἔκταση* area

ἐκτίμηση* f appreciation, esteem

ἐκτιμῶ to appreciate, to estimate

ἕκτος, -η, -ο sixth

ἐκφράζω to express

ἔκφραση* f. expression

ἐλατήριο n. spring, motive

ἐλαφρός, -ή, -ό light

Ἐλβετία f. Switzerland

ἐλέγχω to control, to check up

ἐλιά f. olive

ἐλκυστικός, -ή, -ό attractive

ἐλκύω to attract

Ἑλλάδα, Ἑλλάς f. Greece

Ἕλληνας m. Greek

Ἑλληνίδα f. Greek

ἑλληνικός, -ή, -ό Greek

ἑλληνολάτρης admirer (lit., worshiper) of Greece

ἐλπίδα f. hope

ἐλπίζω to hope

ἐμεῖς we

ἔμμεσος, -η, -ο indirect

ἐμπειρία f. experience

ἐμπιστεύομαι to trust

ἐμπνέω to inspire

ἐμποδίζω to prevent, to hinder

ἐμπόδιο n. obstacle

ἐμπόρευμα n. merchandise

ἐμπορικός, -ή, -ό commercial

ἐμπόριο n. commerce, trade

ἔμπορος n. merchant, trader

ἐμφανίζομαι to appear

ἐμφανίζω to present

ἐμφάνιση* f. appearance

ἕνας m. one   μία f. one

ἕνα n. one

ἕνδεκα eleven

ἐνδιαφέρον n. interest

ἐνδιαφέρων, -ουσα, -ον interesting

ἐνενήντα ninety

ἐνέργεια f. action, energy

ἐνεργητικός, -ή, -ό active

ἐνεργῶ to act

ἐνθαρρύνω to encourage

ἐνθουσιάζομαι to become enthusiastic

ἐνθουσιάζω to inspire enthusiasm

ἐνθουσιασμός n. enthusiasm

ἐνθουσιώδης, -ης, -ες enthusiastic

ἐνθύμιο n. souvenir

ἔννατος, -η, -ο ninth

ἐννέα nine

ἔννοια f. meaning

ἐννοῶ ·to mean, to understand

ἐνοικιάζω to rent

ἐνοίκιο n. rent

ἑνότης f. unity

ἐνόχληση* f. annoyance,
nuisance
ἐνοχλητικός, -ή, -ό annoying,
troublesome
ἐνοχλῶ to annoy, to bother
ἔνοχος m. f. guilty
ἔνστικτο n. instinct
ἐν τάξει all right, O.K.
ἔνταση* f. intensity, tension
ἔντομο n. insect
ἐντύπωση* f. impression
ἐνῶ while, whereas
ἐνωμένος, -η, -ο united
ἐνώνω to unite, to join
ἔνωση* f. union, junction
ἐξάγω to export, to extract
ἐξαγωγή f. export, exportation
extraction
ἐξάδελφος, -η m., f. cousin
ἐξαίρεση* f. exception
ἐξαιρετικός, -ή, -ό exceptional,
excellent
ἐξαιρῶ to except, to exempt
ἐξακολουθῶ to continue
ἐξακόσια six hundred
ἐξαπατῶ to cheat, to deceive
ἐξαργυρώνω to cash
ἐξαρτῶμαι to depend on
ἐξασφαλίζω to secure
ἐξαφανίζομαι to disappear,
to vanish
ἐξαφάνιση* f. disappearence
ἐξέλιξη* f. evolution,
development
ἐξετάζω to examine
ἐξέταση* f. examination
ἐξήγηση* f. explanation
ἐξηγῶ to explain

ἐξήντα sixty
ἔξι six
ἔξοδα n. pl. expenses
ἔξοδος f. exit
ἐξοικειώνομαι to become
familiar
ἐξομολόγηση* f. confession
ἐξουσία f. authority, power
ἐξοχή country
ἐξοχικός, -ή, -ό rural, country
ἐξυπνάδα f. cleverness
ἔξυπνος, -η, -ο clever, intelligent,
smart
ἔξω out
ἐξωτερικό, στό abroad
ἐξωτερικός, -ή, -ό external
ἐορτάζω to celebrate
ἐορτασμός m. celebration
ἐορτή f. holiday, feast, festival
ἐπάγγελμα n. profession
ἐπαγγελματικός, -ή, -ό
professional
ἐπαναλαμβάνω to repeat
ἐπανάληψη* f. repetition
ἐπάνω up
ἔπειτα then, afterwards
ἐπηρεασμένος, -η, -ο influenced
ἐπιβιβάζομαι to embark
ἐπιγραφή f. inscription, sign
ἐπιδιορθώνω to repair, to mend
ἐπιδιόρθωση* f. repair
ἐπιδόρπιο n. dessert
ἐπίδραση* f. wish, desire
ἐπιζῶ to survive
ἐπιθυμία f. wish, desire
ἐπιθυμῶ to wish, to desire
ἐπικίνδυνος, -η, -ο dangerous
ἐπιμένω to insist, to persist

ἐπιμονή f. persistence, perseverence

ἔπιπλο n. piece of furniture

ἐπιπλωμένος, -η, -ο furnished

ἐπιπλώνω to furnish

ἐπίπλωση* f. furniture

ἐπίσημος, -η, -ο official

ἐπίσης too, also

ἐπισκέπτης, -τρια m., f. visitor

ἐπισκέπτομαι to visit

ἐπίσκεψη* f. visit, call

Ἐπίσκοπος m. Bishop

ἐπιστήμη f. science

ἐπιστημονικός, -ή, -ό scientific

ἐπιστήμων m. scientist

ἐπιστρέφω to return, to come back

ἐπιστροφή f. return

ἐπιταγή f. check, money order

ἐπιτρέπω to allow, to permit, to let

ἐπιτροπή f committee

ἐπιτυγχάνω to succeed

ἐπιτυχία f. success

ἐπιφύλαξη* f. reservation

ἐπιχείρημα n. argument

ἐπιχείρηση* f. business, enterprise

ἐπιχειρηματίας m. businessman

ἐπιχειρῶ to attempt

ἐπιχρυσώνω to gild

ἐπόμενος, -η, -ο next

ἐπομένως therefore

ἐποχή f. season, epoch

ἐπτά seven

ἐργάζομαι to work

ἐργαλεῖο n. tool

ἐργασία f. work, job

ἐργαστήριο n. laboratory, workshop

ἐργάτης, -τρια m.f. worker

ἔργο n. work

ἔργο, θεατρικό n. play

ἐργοστάσιο n. factory

ἐρείπιο n. ruin

ἔρχομαι to come

ἐρώτηση* f. question

ἐρωτῶ to ask

ἐσεῖς you, ἐσύ you sg., thou

ἐστιατόριο n. restaurant

ἐσώρρουχα n. pl. underwear

ἐσωτερικός, -ή, -ό interior, internal, inner

ἐταιρία, ἐταιρεία f. company, association, society

ἐτοιμάζομαι to prepare

ἔτοιμος, -η, -ο ready

ἔτσι so, thus

Εὐαγγέλιο n. Gospel

εὐγένεια f. politeness, courtesy

εὐγενής, -ής, -ές polite, noble

εὐγενικός, -ή, -ό polite, courteous

εὐγνωμοσύνη f. gratitude

εὐγνώμων m. f. grateful

εὐεξήγητος, -η, -ο easily explainable

εὔθυμος, -η, -ο gay

εὐθύνη f. responsibility

εὐθύς, -εῖα, -ύ straight

εὐκαιρία f. opportunity

εὐκολία f. facility, ease

εὔκολος, -η, -ο easy

εὐτυχής, -ής, -ές happy

εὐτυχία f. happiness

εὐτυχῶς fortunately

εὐχαριστημένος, -η, -ο pleased, satisfied
εὐχαρίστηση* f. pleasure
εὐχάριστος pleasant
εὐχαριστῶ to thank, thank you
εὐχαρίστως with pleasure
εὐωδιάζω to be fragrant
ἐφημερίδα f. newspaper
ἐφ' ὅσον since
ἐχθρικός, -ή, -ό hostile
ἐχθρός m. enemy
ἔχω to have
ἕως till, as far as

Z
ζάλη f. dizziness
ζαλίζομαι to be dizzy
ζαλισμένος, -η, -ο dizzy
ζάχαρη f. sugar
ζαχαροπλαστεῖο n. pastry shop, confectionery
ζεσταίνω to warm, to heat
ζέστη f. heat
ζεστός, -ή, -ό warm, hot
ζευγάρι n. pair
ζεῦγος n. couple
ζηλεύω to be jealous of
ζήλια f. jealousy
ζηλιάρης, -α jealous
ζημία f. damage, loss
ζητῶ to ask for, to demand, to beg
ζυγαριά f. pair of scales
ζυγίζω to weigh
ζύμη f. dough
ζυμώνω to knead
ζῶ to live
ζωγραφική f. painting
ζωγράφος m. painter

ζωή f. life
ζωηρός, -ή, -ό lively
ζωηρότης f. liveliness
ζώνη f. belt
ζωντανός, -ή, -ό alive
ζῶο n. animal
ζωολογικός κῆπος m. zoo

H
ἤ or
ἠθικός, -ή, -ό moral
ἠλεκτρικός, -ή, -ό electric
ἠλεκτρισμός m. electricity
ἠλίθιος, -α, -ο stupid
ἡλικία f. age
ἡλικιωμένος, -η, -ο aged, old
ἥλιος m. sun
ἡμέρα f. day
ἡμερολόγιο n. calendar
ἡμερομηνία f. date
ἡμερομίσθιο n. day's wages
ἥμερος, -η, -ο tame
ἡμισφαίριο n. hemisphere
Ἡνωμέναι Πολιτεῖαι United States
ἤπειρος f. continent
ἠρεμία f. quiet
ἤρεμος, -η, -ο quiet
ἡρωϊκός, -ή, -ό heroic
ἡρωΐδα, ἡρωῖς f. heroine
ἡρωισμός m. heroism
ἥρωας, ἥρως m. hero
ἡσυχάζω to rest
ἡσυχία f. quietness, tranquillity
ἥσυχος, -η, -ο quiet, tranquil
ἧττα f. defeat
ἡφαίστειο n. volcano
ἦχος m. sound

Θ

θαλαμηγός f. yacht
θάλασσα f. sea
θάνατος m. death
θάρρος n. courage
θαῦμα n. miracle, wonder
θαυμάζω to admire
θαυμάσιος, -α, -ο wonderful,
  marvelous
θαυμασμός m. admiration
θαυμαστής, -τρια m. f. admirer,
  fan
θεατής m. spectator
θεατρικός, -ή, -ό theatrical
θέατρο n. theater
θεῖος m. uncle
θεία f. aunt
θέλγητρο n. charm
θέλημα n. will, errand
θέληση* f. will
θέλω to want
θέμα n. subject, topic
Θεός m. God
θεραπεία f. cure, treatment
θεραπεύω to cure, to treat
θεριεύω to infuriate
θερίζω to reap
θερμόμετρο n. thermometer
θέση* f. place, position
θεσμός m. institution
θετικός, -ή, -ό positive
θέτω to place, to set
θεωρία f. theory
θεωρῶ to consider
θηλυκός, -ή, -ό feminine, female
θηρίο n. wild animal, beast
θησαυρός m. treasure
θλίψη* f. grief

θολός, -ή, -ό muddy, dim
θόρυβος m. noise
θρανίο n. school desk
θράσος n. insolence, audacity
θρεπτικός, -ή, -ό nourishing
θρησκεία f. religion
θρησκευτικός, -ή, -ό religious
θριαμβευτικός, -ή, -ό triumphant
θρίαμβος m. triumph
θύελλα f. storm
θυμίζω to remind
θυμοῦμαι to remember
θυμός m. anger
θυμώνω to be angry
θυρίδα f. ticket window
θυσία f. sacrifice
θυσιάζω to sacrifice

Ι

'Ιανουάριος m. January
ἰατρεῖο n. clinic
ἰατρός m. physician, doctor
ἰδανικό n. ideal
ἰδέα f. idea
ἰδεολογία f. ideology
ἰδεώδης, -ης, -ες ideal
ἰδιαίτερος, -η, -ο private, special
ἰδιαιτέρως privately, especially
ἰδιοκτησία f. property
ἰδιοκτήτης, -τρια owner
ἴδιος, -α, -ο same
ἰδιοσυγκρασία f. temperament
ἰδιότροπος, -η, -ο capricious, odd
ἰδιωτικός, -ή, -ό private
ἴδρυμα n. institution,
  establishment
ἱεραπόστολος m. missionary
ἱερέας (-εύς) m. priest
ἱέρεια f. priestess

ἱερός, -ή, -ό sacred, holy
ἱκανοποιημένος, -ή, -ό satisfied
ἱκανοποιῶ to satisfy
'Ιούλιος m. July
'Ιούνιος m. June
'Ιρλανδία f. Ireland
'Ιρλανδός, -ίδα Irish
ἴσιος, -α, -ο straight
ἴσκιος m. shadow
ἴσος, -η, -ο equal
ἱστορία f. history
ἱστορικός, -ή, -ό historical
ἰσχυρός, -ή, -ό powerful
ἴσως perhaps
ἴχνος n. trace, track, footprint

Κ

καθαρίζω to clean
καθαριότης f. cleanliness
καθαρός, -ή, -ό clean
κάθε every, each
καθένας, καθεμία, καθένα
   everyone
καθεδρικὸς ναός m. cathedral
καθεστώς n. regime
καθηγητής, -τρια professor
καθῆκον n. duty, task
καθημερινός, -ή -ό daily
κάθισμα n. seat
κάθομαι to sit
καθορίζω to define, to determine
καθρέπτης, καθρέφτης
   m. mirror
καθυστέρηση* f. delay
καθώς as
καί and
καινούργιος, -α, -ο new
καίω to burn
κακός, -ή, -ό bad, mean
καλά well

καλάθι n. basket
καλλιεργῶ to cultivate
καλλιτέχνης m. artist
καλλιτεχνικός, -ή, -ό artistic
καλόγηρος m. monk
καλόγρια f. nun
καλοκαίρι summer
καλός, -ή, -ό good, kind
κάλτσα f. sock, stocking
καλύπτω to cover
καλῶ to call
καλωσύνη f. kindness
καμαρώνω to be proud of,
   to take pride in
καμήλα f. camel
καμπάνα f. bell
κάμπος m. plain
Καναδάς m. Canada
καναπές m. sofa
κανείς (κανένας), καμ(μ)ία,
   κανένα nobody, nothing
κανόνας m. rule
κανονίζω to settle, to regulate
κάνω to make, to do
καπέλ(λ)ο m. hat
καπετάνιος m. captain
καπνίζω to smoke
καπνός m. smoke
κάποιος, -α, -ο someone
κάπου somewhere
κάπως somewhat
καράβι n. boat, sailboat
κάρβουνο n. coal
καρδιά f. heart
καρέκλα f. chair
καρπός m. fruit, wrist
κάρτα f. card
καρύδι n. walnut
καρφί n. nail

καρφώνω to nail
χάστανο n. chestnut
καστανός, -ή, -ό brown
καταγγέλω to sue, to denounce
κατάγομαι to be from
καταγωγή f. origin, descent
καταδικάζω to condemn
καταδίκη f. condemnation
καταθέτω to deposit
κατακρίνω to criticize, to condemn
καταλαβαίνω to undertsand
καταλαμβάνω to conquer, to occupy
κατάλληλος, -η, -ο proper, fit
κατάλογος m. list
κατανόηση* f. understanding
κατάσταση* f. situation
κατάστημα n. store, shop
καταφύγιο n. shelter
κατεβαίνω to go down, to descend
κατεύθυνση* f. direction
κατέχω to possess
κατηγορῶ to accuse
κατήχηση* f. catechism
κάτι something
κατοχή f. occupation
κάτοικος m. inhabitant, resident
κατόρθωμα n. achievement
κατορθώνω to achieve
κατσίκα f. goat
κάτω down
καφές m. coffee
καφενεῖο n. coffee house
κάψιμο n. burning
καψούλι n. capsule
κέντημα n. embroidery

κεντρικός, -ή, -ό central
κέντρο n. center
κεραμίδι n. roof tile
κεράσι n. cherry
κεραυνός m. thunderbolt
κερδίζω to win, to earn
κέρδος n. profit, benefit
κερί n. candle, wax
κεφάλαιο n. capital
κεφάλι n. head
κῆπος m. garden
κηπουρός m. gardener
κιλό n. kilogram
κινδυνεύω to be in danger
κίνδυνος m. danger
κινηματογράφος m. movies, movie theater
κίνηση* f. movement, motion
κινῶ to move
κιόλας already
κίτρινος, -η, -ο yellow
κλαδί n. branch
κλαίω to cry, to weep
κλάμμα n. crying, weeping
κλασσικός, -ή, -ό classical
κλέβω to steal
κλειδαριά f. lock
κλειδί n. key
κλειδώνω to lock
κλείνω to close, to shut
κλειστός, -ή, -ό closed, shut
κλέφτης m. thief
κληρικός m. clergyman
κληρονομιά f. inheritance, heritage
κληρονόμος m. heir
κλῆρος m. clergy
κλίμα n. climate

κλουβί n. cage
κλωστή f. thread
κόβω to cut
κοιλάδα f. valley
κοιμοῦμαι to sleep
κοινός, -ή, -ό common
κοινόν, τὸ the public
κοινότης f. community
κοινωνία f. society
κοινωνικός, -ή, -ό social
κοιτάζω to look at
κόκκαλο n. bone
κόκκινος, -η, -ο red
κολακεύω to flatter
κόλλα f. glue; sheet of paper;
   starch
κολλῶ to stick, to attach
κολοκύθι n. pumpkin, squash
κόλπος m. gulf, bay
κολύμπι n. swimming
κολυμπῶ to swim
κόμμα n. party (political);
   comma
κομμάτι n. piece
κομψός, -ή, -ό elegant
κοντά near
κοντός, -ή, -ό short
κόπος m. pain, fatigue
κορδέλ(λ)α f. ribbon
κορδόνι n. shoelace
κόρη f. daughter; pupil (eye)
κορίτσι n. girl
κορμός m. trunk
κορυφή f. top, summit, peak
κόσμημα n. jewel
κόσμος m. world
κοστίζω to cost
κοστούμι n. suit

κοτόπουλο n. chicken
κουβάρι n. ball (of thread)
κουβέρτα f. blanket
κουδούνι n. bell, doorbell
κουζίνα f. kitchen
κουμπί n. button
κουμπώνω to button
κουνέλι n. rabbit
κουνιάδος, -α m. brother-in-law
   f. sister-in-law
κουνούπι n. mosquito
κουνῶ to shake, to rock, to move
κούπα f. cup
κουπί n. oar
κουράζω to tire
κουρασμένος, -η, -ο tired
κουρδίζω to wind, to tune
κουρέας m. barber, hairdresser
κουτάλι n. spoon
κουτί n. box
κουφός, -ή, -ό deaf
κρασί n. wine
κράτος n. state
κρατῶ to hold, to keep
κρέας n. meat
κρεβάτι n. bed
κρεβατοκάμαρα f. bedroom
κρέμα f. cream
κρεμῶ to hang
κρεμ(μ)ύδι n. onion
κρεοπώλης m. butcher
κριθάρι n. barley
κρίνω to judge
κρίση* f. judgment, crisis
κρίσιμος, -η, -ο critical
κριτήριο n. criterion
κριτικός m. critic
κρύβω to hide

κρύο n. cold
κρύος, -α, -ο cold
κρυφός, -ή, -ό secret
κρυφά secretly
κρύωμα n. cold (sickness)
κρυώνω to feel cold
κτῆμα f. property
κτίζω to build
κτίριο n. building
κτυπῶ to hit, to beat, to strike
κυβέρνηση* f. government
κυβερνητικός, -ή, -ό governmental
κυβερνήτης m. governor
κυβερνῶ to govern, to rule
κύκλος m. circle
κυκλοφορία . f. circulation
κυλῶ to roll
κύμα, κῦμα n. wave
κυματίζω to wave
κυνήγι n. hunting
κυνηγός m. hunter
κυνηγῶ to hunt
κυρία f. lady, Mrs., madam
Κυριακή f. Sunday
κύριος m. gentleman, Mr.
κυρίως mainly, especially
κωμικός, -ή, -ό funny, comic
κωμωδία f. comedy

Λ (

λάδι n. oil
λάθος n. mistake, error
λαίμαργος, -η, -ο greedy
λαιμός m. throat, neck
λαμβάνω to receive, to take
λαμπάδα f. torch, big candle
λαμπρός, -ή -ό bright, brilliant
λαμπτήρας m. bulb, lamp
λάμπω to shine

λαός m. people
λάσπη f. mud
λάστιχο n. rubber, tire (car)
λατρεία f. worship
λατρεύω to worship
λαχανικά n. pl. vegetables
λέγω to say, to tell
λειτουργία f. function, liturgy
λεκάνη f. bowl, basin
λεμόνι n. lemon
λέξη* f. word
λεξικό n. dictionary
λεξιλόγιο n. vocabulary
λεοντάρι n. lion
λέπι n. scale
λεπίδα f. blade
λεπτό n. minute
λεπτός, -ή, -ό fine, thin, slender
λεπτομέρεια f. detail
λεπτότης f. delicacy, thinness,
  refinement
λερώνω to dirty, to soil
λέσχη f. club
λευκός, -ή, -ό white
λεωφορεῖο n. bus
λεωφόρος f. avenue, boulevard
ληστής m. robber, highwayman
λιανικῶς at retail
λιβάδι n. meadow
λίγος, -η, -ο little
λιγώτερος, -η, -ο less
λιμάνι n. harbor, port
λίμνη f. lake
λινό n. linen
λίπασμα n. fertilizer
λιποθυμῶ to faint
λίπος n. fat, grease
λογαριασμός m. account, bill

λογική f. logic, reason
λογικός, -ή, -ό reasonable, sensible, logical
λόγος m. speech, word
λογοτέχνης m. writer
λογοτεχνία f. literature
λοιπόν therefore, then, well
λουλούδι n. flower
λού(ζ)ομαι to bathe
λουτρό n. bath
λόφος m. hill
λυγίζω to bend
λύκος m. wolf
λύ(ν)ω to solve, to untie
λύπη f. sorrow, grief
λυπημένος, -η, -ο sad, grieved
λυποῦμαι to be sorry
λύση* f. solution

M

μά but
μαγαζί n. shop
μαγειρεύω to cook
μαγευτικός, -ή, -ό enchanting
μαγικός, -ή, -ό magic
μαγνήτης m. magnet
μαζεύω to gather, to pick
μαζί together, with
μαθαίνω to learn
μάθημα n. lesson
μαθηματικά n. pl. mathematics
μαθητής, -τρια pupil, student
Μάϊος :m. May
μακαρίτης deceased, late
μακρινός, -ή, -ό distant
μάκρος n. length
μακρυά far
μακρύς, -ιά, -ύ long
μαλακός, -ή, -ό soft

μαλακώνω to soften, to get milder
μάλιστα yes, especially, even
μαλλί n. wool
μαλλιά n. pl. hair
μᾶλλον rather
μαμά f. mama
μανία f. mania
μανικέτι n. cuff
μανίκι n. sleeve
μαντεύω to guess
μαντήλι n. handkerchief
μαξιλάρι n. pillow
μαραίνομαι to fade, to wither
μαργαρίτα f. daisy
μάρμαρο n. marble
μαρούλι n. lettuce
Μάρτιος m. March
μας our
μᾶς us
μασῶ to chew
μάταια vainly, in vain
μάτι n. eye
ματιά f. glance, look
ματογιάλια n. pl. eyeglasses
μαῦρος, -η, -ο black
μαχαίρι n. knife
μάχη f. battle
μέ with; με me
μεγαλεῖο n. grandeur
μεγαλοπρέπεια f. magnificence
μεγάλος, -η, -ο great, big, large
μεγαλύτερος, -η, -ο greater, bigger
μεγαλώνω to grow, to grow up
μέγεθος n. size
μεθαύριο n. day after tomorrow

μέθοδος f. method
μελάνη f. ink
μελέτη f. study
μελετῶ to study
μέλι n. honey
μέλισσα f. bee
μέλλον n. future
μελλοντικός, -ή, -ό future
μέλος n. member
μελωδία f. melody
μένω to stay
μερικοί, -ές some
μέρος n. part, place, side
μέσα inside
μεσαῖος, -α, -ο middle
μεσαιωνικός, -ή, -ό medieval
μεσάνυχτα n. pl. midnight
μέση f. middle, waist
μεσημέρι n. noon
μέσο n. means
μετά after, with
μεταβάλλω to change,
  to transform
μεταβολή change, transformation
μετακομίζω to move
μέταλλο n. metal
μετανάστης m. emigrate,
  immigrate
μετανοῶ to repent, to change
  one's mind
μετάξι n. silk
μεταξύ between, among
μεταξωτός, -ή, -ό silk
μεταφέρω to transport
μεταφράζω to translate
μετάφραση* f. translation
μεταχειρίζομαι to use, to treat
μετοχή f. share, participle

μέτοχος m. stockholder,
  participant
μέτρημα n. measuring
μετρητοῖς, τοῖς cash
μέτριος, -α, -ο medium,
  moderate, average
μετριοφροσύνη f. modesty
μέτρο n. meter, measure
μετρῶ to measure, to count
μή don't
μηδέν n. zero
μῆλο n. apple
μῆκος n. length
μήνας m. month
μήπως lest, perhaps, if
μητέρα f. mother
μητρόπολη* f. metropolis,
  cathedral
μηχανή f. engine, machine
μηχάνημα n. machine
μηχανικός m. engineer, mechanic
μῖγμα n. mixture
μικρόβιο n. germ, microbe
μικρός, -ή, -ό small, little
μικρότερος, -η, -ο smaller, younger
μικροσκόπιο n. microscope
μικτός, -ή, -ό mixed
μίλι n. mile
μιλῶ to speak, to talk
μιμοῦμαι to imitate, to mimic
μισός, -ή, -ό half
μῖσος n. hatred
μισῶ to hate
μνῆμα n. grave, monument
μνημεῖο n. monument
μόδα f. fashion
μοιάζω to resemble, to look like
μοιράζομαι to share

μοιράζω to distribute, to divide
μόλις just, as soon as, scarcely, hardly
μολύβι n. pencil
μοναδικός, -ή, -ό unique
μοναχός, -ή, -ό alone
μόνο only
μόνος, -η, -ο alone, single
μορφή f. form, face, figure
μορφώνω to educate, to form
μόρφωση* f. education
μοσχάρι n. calf, veal
μου my, μοῦ me
μουσεῖο n. museum
μουσική f. music
μουσικός m. musician
μουστάκι n. mustache
μπαίνω to enter, to go in
μπαλκόνι n. balcony
μπάνιο n. bath, swimming
μπαοῦλο n. trunk
μπιφτέκι n. steak
μπουκάλι n. bottle
μπλούζα f. blouse
μπορῶ can, may, to be able
μπράτσο n. arm
μπροστά before, in front of
μυαλό n. brain
μυθιστόρημα n. novel
μύθος, μῦθος m. legend, fable
μύγα, μυῖγα f. fly
μύλος m. mill
μυρίζω to smell
μυρμήγκι n. ant
μυρωδιά f. smell
μῦς m. muscle; mouse
μυστήριο n. mystery; sacrament
μυστηριώδης, -ης, -ες mysterious

μυστικός, -ή, -ό secret
μυτερός, -ή, -ό pointed, sharp
μωρό n. baby
μωσαϊκό n. mosaic

N

ναί yes
ναός m. temple, church
ναῦλο n. freight, fare
ναύτης m. sailor
ναυτικό n. navy
ναυτικός m. seaman
νέα n. pl. news
νεκρός, -ή, -ό dead
νεολαία f. youth, young people
νέος m. young man
νέα f. young woman
νέος, -α, -ο new, young
νεότης f. youth
νερό n. water
νεῦρο n. nerve
νεώτερος, -η, -ο younger, modern
νησί n. island
νηστεία f. fast, lent
νηστεύω to fast
νίκη f. victory
νικῶ to win, to defeat, to beat
Νοέμβριος m. November
νόημα n. meaning
νοιώθω to feel
νομίζω to think
νομικός, -ή, -ό legal
νόμισμα n. coin
νόμος m. law
νομός m. prefect
νοσοκομεῖο n. hospital
νοσοκόμος, -α m. f. nurse
νοσταλγία f. nostalgia

νόστιμος, -η, -ο tasty, delicious, pretty
νότος m. south
νοῦς m. mind
ντομάτα f. tomato
ντουλάπι n. cupboard
ντύνομαι to dress
νυστάζω to be sleepy
νύφη f. bride, sister-in-law, daughter-in-law
νύχι n. nail
νύκτα, νύχτα f. night
νωρίς early

Ξ

ξακουστός, -ή, -ό famous
ξανά again
ξανθομαλλούσα f. blond
ξανθός, -ή, -ό blond, fair
ξαφνικά suddenly
ξεκινῶ to start, to set out
ξεκουράζομαι to rest
ξεναγός m. guide
ξενοδοχεῖο n. hotel
ξένος, -η, -ο strange, foreign, alien
ξένος, -η stranger, foreigner
ξεντύνομαι to undress
ξερός, -η, -ο dry
ξεσηκώνω to arouse
ξεχνῶ to forget
ξοδεύω to spend (money)
ξύδι, ξίδι n. vinegar
ξύλο n. wood
ξυλουργός m. carpenter
ξυλώνω to undo
ξυνός, -ή, -ό sour, acid
ξύνω to scratch, to scrape
ξυπνῶ to awake, to get up

ξυράφι n. razor
ξυρίζω to shave
ξωκκλήσι n. country chapel

Ο

ὀγδόντα eighty
ὄγδοος, -η, -ο eighth
ὄγκος n. volume, bulk, mass
ὁδηγία f. instruction, direction
ὁδηγός m. guide, driver, conductor
ὁδηγῶ to guide, to drive
ὀδοντογιατρός m. dentist
ὀδοντόπαστα f. toothpaste
ὁδός f. street
οἰκογένεια f. family
οἰκονομία f. economy, finances, saving
οἰκονομικός, -ή, -ό economic, financial
οἰκονομῶ to save, to economize
οἶκος m. house
οἰνόπνευμα n. alcohol
ὀκτώ eight
Ὀκτώβριος m. October
ὁλόκληρος, -η, -ο entire, whole
ὅλος, -η, -ο all
ὁμάδα f. group
ὁμαλός, -ή, -ό regular, even
ὁμιλητής m. speaker
ὁμιλητικός, -ή, -ό talkative
ὁμιλία f. talk, conversation
ὁμίχλη f. fog
ὁμογενής m. of the same ethnic group
ὅμοιος, -α, -ο same, alike, similar
ὁμοιότης f. resemblance, similarity

ὁμολογία f. confession,
admission
ὁμολογῶ to confess, to admit
ὀμπρέλ(λ)α f. umbrella
ὅμως but, yet, however, though
ὀνειρεύομαι to dream
ὄνειρο n. dream
ὄνομα n. name
ὀνομάζομαι to be named, to be
called
ὀνομάζω to name
ὀξύ acid
ὀξύς, -εῖα, -ύ sharp
ὅπλο n. weapon, arm
ὁποῖος, -α, -ο who, which, that
ὅπου where
ὁπουδήποτε wherever
ὅπως as, like
ὅραση* f. sight
ὄργανο n. instrument
ὀργανώνω to organize
ὀργάνωση* f. organization
ὀρεκτικός, -ή, -ό appetizing
ὄρεξη* f. appetite
ὄρθιος, -α, -ο standing
ὀρθόδοξος, -η, -ο orthodox
ὀρθός, -ή, -ό right, correct
ὁρίζοντας m. horizon
ὁριζόντιος, -α, -ο horizontal
ὁρίζω to define, to fix
ὅριο n. limit
ὁρκίζομαι to swear, to take an
oath
ὅρκος m. oath, vow
ὁρμή f. impetus, impulse
ὁρμητικός, -ή, -ό impetuous
ὁρμῶ to rush, to dash
ὅρος m. condition, term

ὄρος n. mountain
ὀρυχεῖο n. mine
ὀρφανός, -ή, -ό orphan
ὄσπριο n. dry vegetable
ὄστρακο n. shell
ὄσφρηση* f. smelling
ὅταν when
ὅτι that, what
ὁτιδήποτε whatever
οὐδέτερος, -η, -ο neuter
οὐρά f. tail
οὐρανός m. sky
οὐσία f. substance, essence
οὔτε not even
οὔτε...οὔτε neither...nor
ὀφείλω to owe, must
ὄχθη f. bank (river)
ὄχι no
ὄψη* f. face, appearance
Π
πάγος m. ice
παγωνιά f. frost
παγώνω to freeze
παγωτό n. ice cream
παθαίνω to suffer
πάθος n. passion
παιγνίδι n. game, toy
παιδεύω to torture
παιδί n. child
παιδικός, -ή, -ό children's,
childish
παίζω to play
παίκτης -τρια player
παίρνω to take
παλάμη f. palm (hand)
παλάτι n. palace
πάλη f. fight, wrestling,
struggle

παλιός, -ά, -ό old
παλληκάρι n. brave young man
παλτό n. overcoat
πανεπιστήμιο n. university
πανηγύρι n. fair
πανί n. cloth
παντελόνι n. trousers
παντοπωλείο n. grocery store
πάντοτε always
παντού everywhere
παντρεύομαι to marry, to get married
παπάς, παππάς m. priest
πάπια f. duck
παπ(π)ούς, παππούς grandfather
παπούτσι n. shoe
παραγγελία f. order
παραγγέλω to order
παράγραφος f. paragraph
παράγω to produce
παραγωγή f. production
παράδειγμα n. example, illustration
παράδεισος m. paradise, heaven
παραδίδομαι to surrender, to give up
παράδοση* f. tradition, lecture lesson
παράθυρο n. window
παρακολουθώ to watch, to attend
παρακούω to disobey, to hear wrongly
παραλείπω to omit
παράλειψη* f. omission
παραλία f. sea shore
παράλληλος, -η, -ο parallel

παράλυτος, -η, -ο paralytic
παραμονή f. stay
παραμύθι n. story, fable
παράνομος, -η, -ο illegal
παράξενος, -η, -ο strange
παράπονο n. complaint
παραπονούμαι to complain
παράσημο n. medal, decoration
Παρασκευή f. Friday
παράσταση* f. show, performance
παρατήρηση* f. observation, remark
παρατηρώ to observe
παρέλαση* parade
παρελθόν n. past
παρεξήγηση* f. misunderstanding
πάρκο n. park
παρόμοιος, -α, -ο similar
παρόν n. present
παρουσία f. presence
παρουσιάζομαι to appear
παρουσιάζω to present
Πάσχα n. Easter
πατάτα f. potato
πατέρας m. father
πάτημα n. step
Πατριάρχης m. Patriarch
πατρίδα f. homeland
πατρικός, -ή, -ό fatherly, of the father
πατριώτης m. patriot
πατριωτικός, -ή, -ό patriotic
πατριωτισμός m. patriotism
πατώ to step, to press
πάτωμα n. floor, story
παύω to stop, to end

παύση* f. stop, pause
πάχος n. fat, thickness
παχύς, -ιά, -ύ fat, thick
πεδιάδα f. plain
πεζογράφος m. prose writer
πεζοδρόμιο n. sidewalk
πεζός m. pedestrian
πεθαίνω to die
πεθαμένος, -η, -ο dead
πεθερός, -ά m. father-in-law
   f. mother-in-law
πείθω to convince; to persuade
πεινώ to be hungry
πείρα, πεῖρα f. experience
πειράζω to annoy, to tease,
   to vex
πείραμα n. experiment
πέλαγος n. sea
πελώριος, -α, -ο enormous, huge
Πέμπτη f. Thursday
πέμπτος, -η, -ο fifth
πένθος n. mourning
πενήντα fifty
πέν(ν)α f. pen
πέντε five
πέπλο n. veil
πέπλος m. veil
περασμένος, -η, -ο past, bygone
περιγραφή f. description
περιγράφω to describe
περιεχόμενο n. the content(s)
περιέχω to contain, to
   include
περιηγητής, -τρια m., f. tourist
περιλαμβάνω to comprise
περιμένω to wait, to wait for
περίοδος f. period, session
περιορίζω to limit, to restict
περιορισμός m. restriction

περιουσία f. fortune, property
περιοχή f. district, area
περίπατος m. walk, ride·
περ(ι)πατῶ to walk
περιπέτεια f. adventure
περιπλανῶμαι to wander about
περίπου about, nearly
περίπτερο pavilion, news-stand,
   tobacco-stand
περισσότερος, -η, -ο more
πέρισυ last year
περιττός, -ή, -ό superfluous,
   unnecessary
περίφημος, -η, -ο famous
περιωρισμένος, -η, -ο limited
περνῶ to pass, to cross
πέτρα f. stone
πετρέλαιο n. kerosene,
   petroleum
πετσέτα f. napkin, towel
πεῦκο n. pine tree
πέφτω to fall, to drop
πηγάδι n. well
πηγαίνω to go
πήδημα n. jump, leap
πηδῶ to jump
πιά any more
πιάνω to catch, to seize
πιατάκι n. saucer
πιᾶτο n. plate, dish
πιέζω to press, to squeeze
πίεση* f. pressure
πιθανόν probably
πίθηκος m. monkey, ape
πικρός, -ή, -ό bitter
πίνακας m. blackboard, table,
   index
πίνω to drink
πιπέρι n. pepper

πιστεύω   to believe
πίστη*   f. faith
πιστοποιητικό   n. certificate
πιστός, -ή, -ό   faithful, loyal
πίστωση*   f. credit
πίσω   back, behind
πίτα, πήττα   f. pie
πλάθω   to form, to knead
   (bread)
πλατεῖα   f. square
πλάτος   n. width
πλατύς, -ιά, -ύ   wide, broad
πλέκω   to knit
πλέον   more, any more
πλεονέκτημα   n. advantage
πλένω   wash
πλευρά   f. side
πλέω   to float, to sail
πληγή   f. wound
πληγώνω   to wound, to hurt
πλῆθος   n. multitude, crowd
πληθυσμός   m. population
πλήρης, -ης, -ες   full, complete
πληροφορία   f. information
πληροφορῶ   to inform
πληρωμή   f. payment
πληρώνω   to pay
πλησιάζω   to approach,
   to come near
πλοίαρχος   m. captain (of a
   ship)
πλοῖο   n. ship, boat, vessel
πλοκή   f. plot
πλούσιος, -α, -ο   rich, wealthy
πλουτίζω   to enrich
πλοῦτος   m. wealth, riches
πλυντήριο   n. laundry
πνεῦμα   n. spirit, mind
   intellect, wit

πνευματικός, -ή, -ό   intellectual,
   spiritual
πνευματώδης   witty
πνεύμονας (πνεύμων)   m. lung
πνίγομαι   to drown, to choke
πνίγω   to strangle, to drown
ποδήλατο   n. bicycle
πόδι   n. foot, leg, paw
πόθος   m. desire, longing
ποίημα   n. poem
ποίηση*   f. poetry
ποιητής   m. poet; maker
ποιητικός, -ή, -ό   poetic
ποικιλία   f. variety
ποινή   f. sentence, punishment
ποιός, -ά, -ό   who, which, what
ποιότης   f. quality
πόλεμος   m. war
πολεμῶ   to fight
πόλη*   f. city, town
πολιτεία   f. state, big city
πολίτης   m. citizen
πολιτική   f. politics
πολιτικός, -ή, -ό   political
πολιτισμός   m. civilization,
   culture
πολιτιστικός, -ή, -ό   cultural
πολλοί, -ές, -ά   many
πόλος   m. pole
πολύ   very, much, a great deal of
πολυθρόνα   f. armchair
πολύς, πολλή, πολύ   much
πολυτέλεια   f. luxury
πολυτελής, -ής, -ές   luxurious
πολύτιμος, -η, -ο   precious
πολυύμνητος, -η, -ο   famous
   (lit., much sung)
πονηρός, -ή, -ό   sly, cunning
πονόδοντος   m. toothache

πονοκέφαλος m. headache
πόνος m. pain
ποντίκι (ποντικός) n. (m.) mouse
πονῶ to ache, to feel pain
πόρτα f. door, gate
πορτοκάλι n. orange
ποσό n. amount, sum
πόσος, -η, -ο how much
πόσοι, -ες, -α how many
ποσοστό n. percentage
ποσότης f. quantity
ποτάμι (ποταμός) n. (m.) river
πότε when (interrogative)
ποτήρι n. drinking glass
ποτίζω to water
ποτό n. drink
πού that, who, which
ποῦ where (interrogative)
πούδρα f. powder
πουλί n. bird
πουλῶ to sell
ποῦρο n. cigar
πρᾶγμα n. thing
πράγματι indeed
πραγματικά really, in fact
πραγματικός, -ή, -ό real, actual
πραγματικότης f. reality
πρακτικός, -ή, -ό practical
πράκτορας (πράκτωρ) m. agent
πρακτορεῖο n. agency
πράξη* f. act, action, deed
πράσινος, -η, -ο green
πρέπει must
πρεσβευτής m. ambassador
πρίν before, previously
προάστειο n. suburb

προβάλλω to appear, to show oneself
πρόβατο n. sheep
προβιβάζω to promote
προβλέπω to foresee
πρόβλημα n. problem
πρόγευμα n. breakfast
πρόγονος m. ancestor
πρόγραμμα m. program, time-table
πρόεδρος m. president, chairman
προειδοποίηση* f. warning, notice
προειδοποιῶ to warn
προετοιμάζω to prepare
προετοιμασία f. preparation
προηγούμενος, -η, -ο previous
προηγουμένως previously
προθήκη f. shop-window
προθυμία f. willingness, eagerness, promptness
πρόθυμος, -η, -ο willing, eager prompt
προϊόν n. product
προκαταβολή f. down payment
προκατάληψη* f. prejudice
πρόκληση* f. challenge, provocation
πρόληψη* f. superstition, prevention
προμηθεύω to provide, to supply
προνόμιο n. privilege
προξενεῖο n. consulate
πρόξενος m. consul
προοδευτικός, -ή, -ό progressive
προοδεύω to progress

πρόοδος f. progress

προορισμός m. destiny, destination

πρός to, toward, towards

προσαρμόζω to adjust, to adapt

προσβάλλω to offend, to attack

προσβολή f. offense, affront, insult, attack

προσευχή prayer

προσεύχομαι to pray

προσέχω to be careful, to pay attention, to look out

πρόσθεση* f. addition

προσθέτω to add

προσκαλώ to invite

πρόσκληση* f. invitation

πρόσκοπος m. scout

προσκύνημα n. pilgrimage; shrine

προσκυνητής, -τρια pilgrim

προσοχή f. attention

προσπάθεια f. effort, endeavor

προσπαθώ to try, to endeavor

προστασία f. protection

προστατεύω to protect

προστάτης m. protector, patron

πρόστιμο n. fine

προσφέρω to offer, to present, to contribute

προσφορά f. offer, contribution

προσωπικός, -ή, -ό personal

πρόσωπο n. person, face

πρόταση* f. proposition, suggestion

προτείνω to propose, to suggest

προτεραιότης f. priority

προτέρημα n. merit, advantage

προτίμηση* f. preference

προτιμότερος, -η, -ο preferable

προτιμώ to prefer

προτού before

πρόφαση* f. excuse

προφέρω to pronounce

προφήτης m. prophet

προφορά f. pronunciation

προφορικός, -ή, -ό oral

προφυλάγω to protect, to guard

προφύλαξη* f. precaution

πρόχειρος, -η, -ο handy, improvised

προχθές the day before yesterday

προχωρώ to advance, to go on

πρωί n. morning

πρωταγωνιστής, -τρια leading man, woman

πρώτος, -η, -ο first

πρωτότυπος, -η, -ο original

πτώση* f. fall; case (gramm.)

πυκνός, -ή, -ό thick, dense

πύλη f. gate, door

πύργος m. tower, castle

πυρετός m. fever

πυροβολισμός m. shot, gunshot

πυροτέχνημα n. firework

πωλώ to sell

πώς that

πῶς how

P

ράβω to sew

ραδιόφωνο n. radio, radio set

ραντεβού n. date

ράφτης m. tailor

ράχη* f. back

ράψιμο n. sewing

ρεῦμα n. current, stream, draught

ρῆμα n. verb
ρητό n. saying
ρίζα f. root
ρίχνω to throw
ρόδα f. wheel
ροδάκινο n. peach
ρουφῶ to guzzle
ροῦχα n. pl. clothes
ρύζι n. rice
ρυθμός m. rhythm, style
ρυτίδα f. wrinkle
Ρωσ(σ)ία f. Russia
Ρῶσ(σ)ος, Ρωσ(σ)ίδα Russian

Σ

Σάββατο n. Saturday
σαγόνι n. chin
σακκί n. bag, sack
σαλάτα f. salad
σάλτσα f. gravy, sauce
σάν like, as
σαπούνι n. soap
σαράντα forty
σας your σᾶς you (accus.)
σάτιρα f. satire
σβήνω to erase, to put out, to
quench, to extinguish
σέ you (accus.) ; to, at, in, on
σεβασμός m. respect, reverence
σέβομαι to respect, to revere
σειρά f. row, file, line
σελήνη f. moon
σελίδα f. page
Σεπτέμβριος m. September
σηκώνομαι to rise, to get up
σηκώνω to raise, to lift, to carry
σῆμα n. sign, signal, mark, badge
σημάδι n. sign, signal, badge
σημαία f. flag, banner

σημαίνω to mean, to signify;
to ring (bell)
σημαντικός, -ή, -ό significant,
considerable
σημασία f. meaning,
significance, sense
σημεῖο n. sign, spot, point
σημειώνω to mark, to note
σημείωμα n. note,
memorandum
σημείωση* f. note
σήμερα today
σημερινός, -ή, -ό of today
σιγά slowly, gently, quietly
σιγαρέττο n. cigarette
σίδερο n. iron
σιδερώνω to iron
σιδηρόδρομος m. railroad, train
σιντόνι n. bed sheet
σιρόπι n. sirup
σιτάρι n. wheat
σιχαίνομαι to loathe, to be
disgusted
σιωπή f. silence
σιωπηλός, -ή, -ό silent
σιωπῶ to be silent
σκάβω to dig
σκάζω to burst, to crack
σκάλα f. staircase, ladder
σκάλες f. pl. stairs
σκαλίζω to hoe, to dig
σκαμνί n. stool
σκελετός m. skeleton, framework
σκεπάζω to cover
σκεπτικός, -ή, -ό thoughtful
σκέπτομαι to think
σκέψη* f. thought
σκηνή f. stage, scene, tent

σκιά   f. shade, shadow
σκληρός, -ή, -ό   hard, tough,
   cruel
σκόνη   f. dust, powder
σκοπός   m. aim, purpose,
   objective; tune
σκοπού, από   on purpose
σκορπίζω   to scatter, to spread
σκοτάδι   n. darkness
σκοτεινός, -ή, -ό   dark
σκοτώνω   to kill
σκουλήκι   n. worm
σκύβω   to stoop
σκυλί (σκύλος)   n. (m.) dog
σοβαρά   seriously
σοβαρός, -ή, -ό   serious, grave
σοκολάτα   f. chocolate
σούπα   f. soup
σοφία   f, wisdom
σοφός, -ή, -ό   wise, learned
σπάγγος   m. string
σπάζω   to break
σπαθί   n. sword
σπάνια   rarely, seldom
σπάνιος, -α, -ο   rare
σπατάλη   f. waste
σπαταλώ   to waste
σπέρνω   to sow
σπεύδω   to hurry, to hasten
σπηλιά   f. cave, cavern
σπίρτο   n. match
σπίτι   n. home, house
σπόρος   m. seed
σπουδάζω   to study
σπουδαίος, -α, -ο   important
σπουδαιότης   f. importance
σπουδαστής, -τρια   student
σπουδή   f. study

σπρώχνω   to push
σταγόνα   f. drop
στάδιο   n. stadium, stage, career
σταδιοδρομία   f. career
στάζω   to drip, to drop
σταθερός, -ή, -ό   stable, firm,
   steady, constant
σταθερότης   f. firmness, stability
σταθμός   m. station, stop
στάλα   f. drop
σταματώ   to stop
στάση*   f. stop
σταύλος   m. stable
σταυρός   m. cross
σταφίδα   f. raisin, currant
σταφύλι   n. grape
στάχτη   f. ash
στάχυ   n. ear of wheat
στέγη   f. roof, shelter
στεγνός, -ή, -ό   dry
στεγνώνω   to dry
στέκομαι   to stand
στέλλω   to send
στέμμα   n. crown
στεναγμός   m. sigh
στενάζω   to sigh
στενογραφία   f. shorthand
στενοκέφαλος, -η, -ο   narrow-
   minded
στενός, -ή, -ό   narrow, tight
στενοχώρια   f. distress, trouble,
   inconvenience
στενοχωρώ   to embarrass,
   to oppress
στερεός, -ή, -ό   solid, fast
στέρηση*   f. privation
στεφάνι   n. wreath

στέψη* f. coronation, wedding, ceremony
στῆθος n. chest, breast
στήλη f. column, pillar
στήριγμα n. support
στηρίζω to support, to base
στιγμή f. moment, instant
στίχος m. verse, line
στοιχεῖο n. element, rudiment
στοιχειώδης, -ης, -ες elementary
στοίχημα n. bet
στοιχηματίζω to bet
στολή f. uniform
στολίζω to decorate, to trim
στολισμός m. decoration, ornament
στόλος m. fleet
στόμα n. mouth
στομάχι n. stomach
στοργή f. affection, fondness
στόχος m. target
στραβός, -ή, -ό crooked
στραγγίζω to strain, to drain
στρατιώτης m. soldier
στρατιωτικός, -ή, -ό military
στρατόπεδο n. camp
στρατός m. army
στρείδι n. oyster
στρέμμα n. acre
στρέφομαι to turn, to revolve
στρέφω to turn
στρογγυλός, -ή, -ό round
στροφή f. turn, turning, stanza
στρυφνός, -ή, -ό harsh
στρῶμα n. mattress, layer
στυλογράφος n. fountain pen
στῦλος m. pillar, column, post
στυλώνω to support

σύ you (singular)
συγγενής m. f. relative
συγγνώμη f. pardon, forgiveness
συγγραφέας (συγγραφεύς) m. author, writer
συγκεκριμένος, -η, -ο concrete
συγκέντρωση* f. gathering, concentration
συγκίνηση* f. emotion
συγκινητικός, -ή, -ό moving, touching
συγκοινωνία f. communication
συγκοινωνῶ to communicate
συγκρατῶ to restrain, to keep
συγκρίνω to compare
σύγκριση* f. comparison
συγκριτικός, -ή, -ό comparative
σύγκρουση* f. collision, conflict
συγχαίρω to congratulate
συγχαρητήρια n. pl. congratulations
συγχέω to confuse
σύγχρονος, -η, -ο contemporary, modern
σύγχυση* f. confusion
συγχώρηση* f. pardon, forgiveness
συγχωρῶ to forgive, to excuse
συγχωρεῖτε, μέ excuse me, pardon me
συζήτηση* f. discussion, debate, conversation
συζητῶ to discuss, to debate
σύζυγος m. husband, f. wife
σύκο, σῦκο n. fig
συλλαβή f. syllable
συλλαμβάνω to catch, to arrest, to conceive

συλλογή f. collection
συλλογίζομαι to think, to meditate
σύλλογος m. association, club
συλλυπητήρια n. pl. condolence, sympathy
συλλυποῦμαι to condole with, to express sympathy
συμβαίνω to happen
συμβιβάζομαι to compromise, to settle
συμβιβάζω to reconcile
συμβιβασμός m. settlement, compromise
συμβολαιογράφος m. notary, notary public
συμβόλαιο n. contract
συμβολικός, -ή, -ό symbolic(al)
σύμβολο n. symbol
συμβουλεύω to advise
συμβουλή f. advice
συμμαθητής, -τρια school-mate, class-mate
συμμαχία f. alliance
σύμμαχος m. ally
συμπάθεια f. sympathy, compassion, liking
συμπαθητικός, -ή, -ό nice; sympathetic
συμπατριώτης m. fellow country-man, compatriot
συμπεραίνω to conclude
συμπέρασμα n. conclusion
συμπεριφορά f. behavior
συμπληρώνω to supplement
συμπλοκή f. conflict, fight
συμπονῶ to sympathize, to feel compassion

σύμπτωμα n. symptom
σύμπτωση* f. coincidence
συμφέρει it is to one's interest
συμφέρον n. interest
συμφοιτητής, -τρια f. fellow student
σύμφωνα μέ according to, in accordance with
συμφωνία f. agreement
σύμφωνος, -η, -ο agreeing, συμφωνῶ to agree
συμφώνως in accordance with
συναγωνισμός m. competition
συνάδελφος m. colleague
συναίσθημα n. feeling, sensation
συναλλαγή f. exchange, transaction
συνάλλαγμα n. exchange, bill
συναναστροφή f. company
συνάντηση* f. meeting, encounter
συναντῶ to meet
συναρπαστικός, -ή, -ό exciting
συναυλία f. concert
σύνδεσμος m. bond, tie, connection
συνδέω to connect, to join
συνδρομή f. subscription, assistance
συνδρομητής, -τρια subscriber
συνδυάζω to combine
συνδυασμός m. combination
συνεδρίαση* f. meeting, session
συνέδριο n. convention, congress
συνείδηση* f. conscience
συνεννόηση* f. understanding

συνεννοοῦμαι to come to an understanding
συνέντευξη* f. interview, appointment
συνέπεια f. consequence
συνεργάζομαι to cooperate, to collaborate
συνεργασία f. cooperation, collaboration
συνεργάτης m. coworker, fellow worker, collaborator
συνέταιρος m. partner, associate
συνέχεια f. continuation
συνεχής, -ής, -ές continuous
συνεχίζω to continue, to go on
συνήθεια f. habit, usage
συνήθης, -ης, -ες usual, habitual
συνηθίζω to have the habit of, to get used to, to accustom
συνηθισμένος, -η, -ο used to
σύνθεση* f. composition, formation
συνθέτης m. composer
σύνθετος, -η, -ο compound, complex
συνθέτω to compose
συνθήκη f. treaty, condition
σύνθημα n. signal
συνιστῶ to recommend
συννεφιασμένος, -η, -ο cloudy
σύννεφο n. cloud
συνοδεύω to accompany
συνοικία f. quarter
συνοικισμός m. settlement
συνομιλία f. conversation
συνομιλῶ to talk
σύνορο n. border, frontier
συνταγή f. recipe, formula, prescription

σύνταγμα n. constitution; regiment
συνταγματικός, -ή, -ό constitutional
συντάκτης m. editor
σύνταξη* f. pension, editing
συντήρηση* f. maintenance, support
συντηρητικός, -ή, -ό conservative
συντηρῶ to maintain
συντομεύω to abbreviate, to shorten
σύντομος, -η ,-ο short, brief
συντόμως in short, briefly
συντροφεύω to keep company
συντροφιά f. company
σύντροφος m. companion
σύρμα n. wire
συρτάρι n. drawer
σύρω to draw
σύσταση* f. recommendation
σύστημα n. system
συστηματικός, -ή, -ό systematic
συστήνω to introduce, to recommend
συχνά often, frequently
συχνός, -ή, -ό frequent
σφάζω to slay
σφαίρα, σφαῖρα f. bullet, sphere, globe, ball
σφάλλω to be wrong
σφάλμα n. mistake, error
σφουγγάρι n. sponge
σφραγίδα f. seal, stamp
σφραγίζω to seal
σφυγμός m. pulse
σφυρί n. hammer
σφύριγμα n. whistle
σφυρίζω to whistle

σφυρίχτρα f. whistle
σχεδιάζω to plan, to design, to draw
σχέδιο n. plan, sketch
σχεδόν almost, nearly
σχέση* f. relation, connection
σχῆμα n. form, shape, figure
σχηματίζω to form
σχηματισμός m. formation
σχίζω to tear
σχοινί n. rope, string
σχολαστικός, -ή, -ό pedantic
σχολείο n. school
σχολή f. school, faculty
σχολιάζω to comment
σχολιαστής m. commentator
σχολικός, -ή, -ό of school, scholastic
σχόλιο n. comment
σώζω to save
σωληνάρι(ο) n. tube
σωλήνας m. pipe
σῶμα m. body
σωματείο n. organization, association
σωματικός, -ή, -ό bodily
σωρός m. pile, heap
σωστά correctly
σωστός, -ή, -ό correct
σωτήρας m. savior
σωτηρία f. salvation

T

ταβέρνα f. tavern shop
ταινία f. ribbon, tape, film
ταιριάζω to fit, to match
τακούνι n. heel
τακτικός, -ή, -ό regular

τακτοποίηση* f. putting in order, arrangement
τακτοποιῶ to arrange
ταλαιπωρία f. suffering, hardship
ταλαιπωροῦμαι to suffer hardships
ταλαιπωρῶ to harass
ταλέντο n. talent
ταμείο n. treasury
ταμίας m. treasurer, cashier
ταμιευτήριο n. savings bank
τάξη* f. class, order
ταξιδεύω to travel
ταξίδι n. travel, trip
ταξιδιώτης m. traveler
ταπεινός, -ή, -ό humble
ταράζω to disturb
ταραχή f. agitation, disturbance
τάση* f. tendency, trend
ταυτότης f. identity
ταφή f. burial
τάφος m. grave, tomb
ταχυδρομείο n. mail, post office
ταχυδρόμος m. mailman
ταχυδρομῶ to mail, to post
ταχύς, -εῖα, -ύ fast, quick
ταχύτης f. speed, rapidity
τέλειος, -α, -ο perfect
τελειόφοιτος, -η graduate
τελειώνω to finish
τελετή f. ceremony
τελευταῖος, -α, -ο last
τελικός, -ή, -ό final
τέλος n. end
τελωνείο n. custom house
τεμπέλης -α lazy

τεμπελιά f. laziness
τέρας n. monster
τέσσερα four
Τετάρτη f. Wednesday
τέταρτος, -η, -ο fourth
τέτοιος, -α, -ο such
τετράγωνο n. square, block
τετράδιο n. note-book
τετρακόσια four hundred
τέχνασμα n. trick
τέχνη f. art
τεχνητός, -ή, -ό artificial
τεχνικός, -ή, -ό technical
τεχνίτης m. technician
τζάμι n. window-pane, glass
τηγάνι n. frying pan
τηγανίζω to fry
τηλεγράφημα n. telegram
τηλεγραφῶ to telegraph, to wire
τηλεόραση* f. television
τηλεφώνημα n. telephone call
τηλεφωνητής, -τρια operator
τηλέφωνο n. telephone
τηλεφωνῶ to telephone, to call
τί what
τιμή f. price, honor
τίμιος, -α, -ο honest
τιμιότης f. honesty
τιμολόγιο n. price-list
τιμόνι n. steering wheel; rudder
τιμῶ to honor
τιμωρία f. punishment
τιμωρῶ to punish
τινάζω to shake
τίποτα nothing
τίτλος m. title
τμῆμα n. section, department
τοῖχος m. wall

τόκος m. interest
τολμηρός, -ή, -ό bold, daring
τολμῶ to dare
τομέας m. sector
τόμος n. volume
τονίζω to accent, to stress
τόνος m. accent, tone
τόξο n. bow, arch
τοπεῖο n. landscape
τοπικός, -ή, -ό local
τοποθεσία f. location
τόπος m. place, site, spot
τόσος, -η, -ο so, so much
τόσο ... ὅσο as ... as, so. ... as
τότε then, at that time
τουλάχιστο at least
Τουρκία f. Turkey
τούτοις, ἐν nevertheless
τουφέκι n. gun, rifle
τραβῶ to pull
τραγικός, -ή, -ό tragic
τραγούδι n. song
τραγουδιστής, -τρια singer
τραγουδῶ to sing
τραγωδία f. tragedy
τραῖνο n. train
τράπεζα f. bank
τραπεζαρία f. dining room
τραπέζι n. table
τραπεζομάνδηλο n. tablecloth
τραῦμα n. wound
τραχύς, -εῖα, -ύ rough
τρέλλα f. madness, insanity
τρελλός, -ή, -ό insane, mad, crazy
τρέμω to tremble, to shiver, to shake
τρέφω to feed

τρέχω to run
τρία three
τριακόσια three hundred
τριάντα thirty
τριαντάφυλλο n. rose
τρίβω to rub
τριγύρω around
τρίγωνο n. triangle
τρικυμία f. storm
Τρίτη f. Tuesday
τρίτος, -η, -ο third
τρίχα f. hair
τρομάζω to terrify;
to be terrified
τρομακτικός, -ή, -ό terrible,
frightful
τρομερά terribly
τρομερός, -ή, -ό terrible
τρόμος n. terror
τρόπος m. way, manner
τροφή f. food
τρύπα f. hole
τρυπώ to make a hole
τρυφερός, -ή, -ό tender
τρώγω to eat
τσαϊ n. tea
τσάντα f. purse, handbag
τσέπη f. pocket
τσιγάρο n. cigarette
τυλίγω to wrap
τύμπανο n. drum
τυπικός, -ή, -ό typical
τυπογραφείο n. printing shop
τυπογράφος m. printer
τύπος m. press, type
τυπώνω to print
τυραννία f. tyranny
τυραννώ to torture

τυρί n. cheese
τυφλός -ή, -ό blind
τυχερός, -ή, -ό lucky, fortunate
τύχη f. luck, fortune
τυχόν by chance
τύψη* f. remorse
τώρα now, at present

Υ

υγεία f. health
υγιεινός, -ή, -ό healthy
υγρασία f. humidity
υγρός, -ή, -ό wet, liquid, humid
υλικός, -ή, -ό material
υλικό n. material
ύμνος m. hymn
ύπαιθρο n. outdoor(s), open
air
υπακούω to obey
υπάλληλος m. employee
ύπαρξη* f. existence
υπάρχω to exist
υπερασπίζω to defend
υπεράσπιση* f. defense
υπερβολή f. exaggeration
υπερβολικός, -ή, -ό excessive
υπερηφάνεια f. pride
υπερήφανος, -η, -ο proud
υπεύθυνος, -η, -ο responsible
υπηρεσία f. service
υπηρέτης, -τρια servant, maid
υπηρετώ to serve
ύπνος m. sleep
υποβρύχιο n. submarine
υπόγειο n. cellar, basement
υπογραμμίζω to underline
υπογραφή f. signature
υπογράφω to sign

υποδέχομαι to welcome, to receive
υποδοχή f. reception, welcome
υπόθεση* f. supposition; matter, affair; business
υποθέτω to suppose
υποκάμισο n. shirt
υποκρισία f. hypocrisy
υποκριτής, -τρια hypocrite
υπολογισμός m. estimate
υπόλοιπο n. rest, remainder
υπομονή f. patience
υπομονητικός, -ή, -ό patient
υποπτεύομαι to suspect
ύποπτος, -η, -ο suspected
υποστηρίζω to support
υποστήριξη* f. support
υπόσχεση* f. promise
υπόσχομαι to promise
υποτροφία f. scholarship
υπουργείο n. ministry, cabinet
υπουργός m. minister
υποφέρω to suffer
υποχρεώνω to oblige, to compel
υποχρέωση* f. obligation
υποχρεωτικός, -ή, -ό compulsory
υποχώρηση* f. retreat
υποχωρώ to retire, to give in
υποψήφιος, -α, -ο candidate
υποψία f. suspicion
ύστερα after, afterwards
υφαίνω to weave
ύφασμα n. cloth, fabric
ύφος n. style
υψηλός, -ή, -ό high, tall
ύψος n. height
ύψωμα n. hill

Φ

φαγητό n. meal, food

φαίνομαι to seem, to look
φαινομενικός, -ή, -ό apparent
φάκελος m. envelope; file; folder
φακός m. lens; flashlight
φαλακρός bald
φανατικός, -ή, -ό fanatic(al)
φανερός, -ή, -ό evident, obvious
φανερώνω to reveal, to disclose
φαντάζομαι to imagine
φαντασία f. imagination
φάντασμα n. ghost
φανταστικός, -ή, -ό imaginary
φαρμακείο n. drugstore, pharmacy
φάρμακο n. medicine, drug
φαρμακοποιός n. pharmacist
φάρος m. lighthouse
φασόλι n. bean
φάτνη f. manger
Φεβρουάριος m. February
φεγγάρι n. moon
φέγγω to shine, to gleam
φελλός m. cork
φέρ(ν)ω to bring, to bear
φέρσιμο n. behavior, conduct
φέτα f. slice
φεύγω to leave, to go away
φήμη f. fame
φθάνω to arrive, to reach
φθηνός, -ή, -ό cheap, inexpensive
φθινόπωρο n. autumn, fall
φθόνος m. envy
φθορά f. ruin, damage, destruction
φίδι n. snake
φιλάργυρος, -η, -ο stingy
φιλελεύθερος, -η, -ο liberal
φιλί n. kiss
φιλόδοξος, -η, -ο ambitious

φιλολογικός, -ή, -ό literary
φιλοξενία f. hospitality
φιλόξενος, -η, -ο hospitable
φιλοξενῶ to entertain,
   to extend hospitality
φίλος m. friend
φίλη f. friend
φιλοσοφία f. philosophy
φιλόσοφος m. philosopher
φιλότιμο n. self-respect, self-pride
φιλότιμος, -η, -ο conscientious
φιλῶ to kiss
φλέβα f. vein
φλόγα f. flame
φλυαρία f. chatter
φλύαρος, -η, -ο chatterer,
   talkative
φλυαρῶ to talk, to chatter
φλυτζάνι n. small cup
φοβερός, -ή, -ό dreadful
φοβίζω to frighten
φοβισμένος, -η, -ο frightened
φόβος m. fear
φοβοῦμαι to fear, to be afraid
φοιτητής, -τρια student
φοιτητικός, -ή, -ό student (adj.)
φοιτῶ to attend
φορά f. time, course
φόρεμα n. dress, garment
φορολογία f. taxation
φόρος m. tax
φορτίο n. load, burden
φορτώνω to load
φορῶ to wear
φούντα f. tassel, pompon
φουντώνω to spread, to grow
φουρνάρης m. baker
φουρνίζω to bake

φοῦρνος m. oven
φούσκα f. bubble, blister
φουσκώνω to swell
φούστα f. skirt
φράζω to block up, to obstruct
φράουλα f. strawberry
φράση* f. phrase, sentence
φράχτης m. fence
φρέσκος, -η, -ο fresh
φρικτός, -ή, -ό horrible
φρόνιμος, -η, -ο quiet, wise,
   prudent
φροντίδα f. care, concern
φροντίζω to take care, to look
   after
φρούριο n. fort
φροῦτο n. fruit
φρύδι n. eyebrow
φταρνίζομαι to sneeze
φτέρνα, πτέρνα f. heel (of the
   foot)
φτώχεια f. poverty
φτωχός, -ή, -ό poor
φυλάγω, φυλάσσω to keep,
   to guard
φύλακας m. guard, keeper
φυλακή f. prison, jail
φυλακίζω to imprison
φυλή f. race; tribe
φύλλο n. leaf, sheet
φύλο n. sex
φύση* f. nature
φυσικά naturally
φυσική f. physics
φυσικός, -ή, -ό natural, physical
φυσῶ to blow
φυτεύω to plant
φυτό n. plant

φυτρώνω to sprout
φωλιά f. nest
φωνάζω to cry, to shout
φωνή f. voice, cry
φῶς n. light
φωταέριο n. gas
φωτιά f. fire
φωτίζω to light, to enlighten
φωτογραφία f. photograph,
   photo
φωτογραφίζω to photograph
φωτογραφικὴ μηχανή f. camera

X

χαίρετε good-bye
χαιρετισμός m. greeting;
   regards
χαιρετῶ to greet, to salute
χαίρομαι to be glad
χαλάζι n. hail
χαλασμένος, -η, -ο out of order
χαλκός m. copper
χαλ(ν)ῶ to spoil
χαμένος, -η, -ο lost
χαμηλός, -ή, -ό low
χαμηλώνω to lower
χαμόγελο n. smile
χαμογελῶ to smile
χάνομαι to get lost
χάνω to lose
χάος n. chaos
χάπι n. pill
χαρά f. joy
χαρακτήρας m. character
χαρακτηριστικός, -ή, -ό
   characteristic
χάρη* f. favor
χάρις εις thanks to
χαρίζω to present, to make a
   present

χάρισμα n. gift, talent
χαριτωμένος, -η, -ο charming
χάρτης m. map, charter
χαρτί n. paper
χαρτοπωλεῖο n. stationery
χασμουριέμαι to yawn
χείλι n. lip
χειμώνας m. winter
χελιδόνι n. swallow
χέρι n. hand
χημεία f. chemistry
χημικός m. chemist
χήνα f. goose
χήρα f. widow
χῆρος m. widower
χθές yesterday
χθεσινός, -ή, -ό of yesterday
χίλια one thousand
χιλιόμετρο n. kilometer
χιόνι n. snow
χιονίζω to snow
χλιαρός, -ή, -ό tepid, lukewarm
χλωμός, -ή -ό pale
χοῖρος m. swine, hog, pig
χολή f. bile, gall
χονδρικῶς wholesale
χοντρός, -ή, -ό fat, thick
χορδή f. string, cord
χορευτής, -τρια dancer
χορεύω to dance
χορός m. dance, dancing
χορταίνω to be satisfied
χορτάρι, χόρτο n. grass, herb
χορταρικά n. pl. vegetables
χρειάζομαι to need
χρέος n. debt, obligation
χρ(ε)ωστῶ to owe
χρῆμα n. money

χρηματιστήριο n. stock exchange
χρήση* f. use
χρησιμεύω to be of use, to be used for
χρησιμοποιῶ to use
χρήσιμος, -η, -ο useful
χριστιανικός -ή, -ό Christian
χριστιανισμός m. Christianity
χριστιανός -ή Christian
Χριστός m. Christ
Χριστούγεννα n. pl. Christmas
χρονολογία f. date
χρόνος m. time, year
χρυσάνθεμο n. chrysanthemum
χρυσάφι n. gold
χρυσός m. gold
χρυσός, -ή, -ό gold, golden
χρῶμα n. color
χτένι n. comb
χτενίζω to comb
χτυπῶ to beat, to hit, to strike
χυδαῖος, -α, -ο vulgar, rude
χυμός m. juice
χῶμα n. earth, soil
χωνεύω to digest
χώρα f. country, land
χωράφι n. field
χωριάτης, -τισσα peasant
χωρίζω to separate, to divide
χωρικός, -ή peasant, villager
χωριό n. village
χωρίς without
χωρισμός m. separation
χωριστός, -ή, -ό separate

Ψ

ψαλίδι n. scissors
ψάλλω to sing, to chant

ψαλμός m. psalm, chant
ψάλτης m. chanter
ψαρεύω to fish
ψάρι n. fish
ψάχνω to look for, to search
ψέμμα n. lie
ψεύτης, -τρα liar
ψεύτικος, -η, ο false
ψηλός, -ή, -ό high, tall
ψήνω to roast, to bake
ψητός, -ή, -ό roast, roasted
ψηφίζω to vote
ψῆφος f. vote
ψιθυρίζω to whisper
ψυγεῖο n. refrigerator
ψύξη* f. refrigeration
ψυχαγωγία f. recreation
ψυχή f. soul
ψυχολογία f. psychology
ψύχρα f. chill
ψυχραιμία f. coolness, composure
ψύχραιμος, -η, -ο cold-blooded

Ω

ὠκεανός m. ocean
ὦμος m. shoulder
ὠμός, -ή, -ό raw
ὥρα f. hour, time
ὡραῖος, -α, -ο beautiful, handsome
ὡραιότης .f. beauty
ὡριμάζω to mature, to ripen
ὥριμος, -η, -ο ripe, mature
ὥς until, as far as
ὥστε so that
ὠφέλεια f. profit, benefit
ὠφέλιμος, -η -ο useful
ὠφελῶ to benefit, to be of use
ὠχρός, -ή, -ό pale

ENGLISH-GREEK
DICTIONARY

A

able ἱκανός, -ή, -ό
able, to be μπορῶ
abroad στὸ ἐξωτερικό
absolutely ἀπολύτως
accept, to δέχομαι
accident (τὸ) δυστύχημα
accompany, to συνοδεύω
ache (ὁ) πόνος
across ἀπέναντι
act (ἡ) πράξη*
act, to ἐνεργῶ
action (ἡ) ἐνέργεια, (ἡ) δράση
add, to προσθέτω
addition (ἡ) πρόσθεση*
address (ἡ) διεύθυνση*
admire, to θαυμάζω
advice (ἡ) συμβουλή
advise, to συμβουλεύω

afraid, to be φοβοῦμαι
afternoon (τὸ) ἀπόγευμα
afterwards ἔπειτα
again ξανά
age (ἡ) ἡλικία
agency (τὸ) πρακτορεῖο
agreeable εὐχάριστος, -η, -ο
ahead μπροστά
air (ὁ) ἀέρας
airplane (τὸ) ἀεροπλάνο
airport (τὸ) ἀεροδρόμιο
alcohol (τὸ) οἰνόπνευμα
alive ζωντανός, -ή, -ό
all ὅλος, -η, -ο
allow, to ἐπιτρέπω
almost σχεδόν
alone μόνος, -η, -ο
already ἤδη, κιόλας
also ἐπίσης

In the English-Greek dictionary the following points should be noted: In the case of nouns, gender is indicated by the definite article placed in parentheses before the noun it refers to; (ὁ) stands for masculine, (ἡ) for feminine, (τὸ) for neuter. Adjectives and participles are given in all three genders: χρήσιμος m., χρήσιμη f., χρήσιμο n. (useful), χρήσιμος, -η, -ο. In the case of verbs, the infinitive form is given in English as be able, to or play, to. The corresponding Greek translation is given in the first person singular of the present indicative which is the basic verbal form in Greek, as μπορῶ or παίζω. Numerals, pronouns, prepositions, and conjunctions are not included in the English-Greek part of this two-way dictionary because their forms, meaning, and function can be better explained in a Reference Grammar. Therefore, look for them in the respective chapters of the Reference Grammar.

* The feminine nouns marked with an asterisk have, in addition to the form given, another form in Puristic in -ις (gen. -εως), as πρόσθεσις (addition), προσθέσεως.

always πάντοτε, πάντα
America (ἡ) 'Αμερική
American (ὁ) 'Αμερικανός
   (ἡ) 'Αμερικανίδα
amount (τὸ) ποσό
amusing διασκεδαστικός, -ή, -ό
ancient ἀρχαῖος, -α, -ο
angry θυμωμένος, -η, -ο
angry, to be θυμώνω
animal (τὸ) ζῶο
answer (ἡ) ἀπάντηση*
anywhere ὁπουδήποτε
apartment (τὸ) διαμέρισμα
appear, to ἐμφανίζομαι
appearance (ἡ) ἐμφάνιση*
appetite (ἡ) ὄρεξη*
apple (τὸ) μῆλο
appointment (ἡ) συνάντηση*,
   (τὸ) ραντεβού
appreciate, to ἐκτιμῶ
approach, to πλησιάζω
approve, to ἐγκρίνω
approximately περίπου
April (ὁ) 'Απρίλιος
arm (τὸ) μπράτσο
armchair (ἡ) πολυθρόνα
army (ὁ) στρατός
arrive, to φθάνω
art (ἡ) τέχνη
article (τὸ) ἄρθρο,
   (τὸ) ἀντικείμενο
artificial τεχνητός, -ή, -ό
artist (ὁ) καλλιτέχνης,
   (ἡ) καλλιτέχνιδα or καλλιτέχ-
   νις**
ask, to (ἐ)ρωτῶ, ζητῶ

assure, to βεβαιώνω
at once ἀμέσως
attend, to παρακολουθῶ
attractive ἑλκυστικός,-ή, -ό
August (ὁ) Αὔγουστος
aunt (ἡ) θεία
authentic αὐθεντικός, -ή, -ό
author (ὁ) συγγραφέας
authorities οἱ ἀρχές or αἱ ἀρχαί
automatic αὐτόματος, -η, -ο
automobile (τὸ) αὐτοκίνητο
autumn (τὸ) φθινόπωρο
avenue (ἡ) λεωφόρος
avoid, to ἀποφεύγω
awaken, to ξυπνῶ

B

bad κακός, -ή, -ό
baggage (οἱ) ἀποσκευές
bank (ἡ) τράπεζα, (ἡ) ὄχθη
basket (τὸ) καλάθι
bath (τὸ) μπάνιο, (τὸ) λουτρό
bathe, to λού(ζ)ομαι
bathroom (τὸ) λουτρό, (τὸ)
   μπάνιο
battle (ἡ) μάχη
beach (ἡ) ἀκρογιαλιά
beautiful ὡραῖος, -α, -ο
beauty (ἡ) ὀμορφιά, (ἡ) ὡ-
   ραιότης, (ἡ) καλλονή, (τὸ)
   κάλλος
become γίνομαι
bed (τὸ) κρεβάτι
bedroom (ἡ) κρεβατοκάμαρα
beef (τὸ) βωδινό (κρέας)
begin, to ἀρχίζω
Belgium (τὸ) Βέλγιο

** Regarding doublets given in this dictionary, the first is either the Demotic or the most frequently used spelling variant in contemporary books.

believe, to πιστεύω
bell (ἡ) καμπάνα,
    (τὸ) κουδούνι
belt (ἡ) ζώνη
bet, to στοιχηματίζω
better καλύτερος or καλλίτε-
    ρος, -η, -ο
bicycle (τὸ) ποδήλατο
big μεγάλος, -η, -ο
bill (ὁ) λογαριασμός,
    (τὸ) χαρτονόμισμα
bird (τὸ) πουλί
birth (ἡ) γέννηση*
birthday (τὰ) γενέθλια
bite, to δαγκάνω or δαγκώνω
bitter πικρός, -ή, -ό
black μαῦρος, -η, -ο
blade (ἡ) λεπίδα
blanket (ἡ) κουβέρτα
blond ξανθός, -ή, -ό
blood (τὸ) αἷμα
blouse (ἡ) μπλούζα
blow φυσῶ
blue γαλάζιος, -α, -ο, μπλέ
boat (τὸ) πλοῖο, (τὸ) καράβι,
    (ἡ) βάρκα
body (τὸ) σῶμα
boil, to βράζω
bottle (τὸ) μπουκάλι
box (τὸ) κουτί
boy (τὸ) ἀγόρι
branch (τὸ) κλαδί
bread (τὸ) ψωμί
break, to σπάζω
breakfast (τὸ) πρόγευμα
breath (ἡ) ἀναπνοή, (ἡ) ἀνάσα
breathe, to ἀναπνέω
bride (ἡ) νύφη
bridge (ἡ) γέφυρα

brief σύντομος, -η, -ο,
    βραχύς, -εῖα, -ύ
bright or brilliant
    λαμπρός, -ή, -ό
bring, to φέρ(ν)ω
broad πλατύς, -εῖα, -ύ
brother (ὁ) ἀδελφός
brown καφέ, καστανός, -ή, -ό
brush (ἡ) βούρτσα
brush, to βουρτσίζω
build, to κτίζω
building (τὸ) κτίριο
burn, to καίω
bus (τὸ) λεωφορεῖο
business (ἡ) ἐπιχείρηση*
busy ἀπασχολημένος, -η, -ο
butcher (ὁ) κρεοπώλης,
    (ὁ) χασάπης
butter (τὸ) βούτυρο
button (τὸ) κουμπί
buy, to ἀγοράζω

C

cabin (ἡ) καμπίνα
calendar (τὸ) ἡμερολόγιο
call, to καλῶ, φωνάζω
camera (ἡ) φωτογραφική
    μηχανή
Canada (ὁ) Καναδάς
captain (ὁ) πλοίαρχος,
car (τὸ) αὐτοκίνητο
car (railroad) (τὸ) βαγόνι
card (ἡ) κάρτα
career (ἡ) σταδιοδρομία
carry,to μεταφέρω
cash τοῖς μετρητοῖς
cash, to ἐξαργυρώνω
cashier (ὁ) ταμίας
cat (ὁ) γάτος, (ἡ) γάτα
catch, to πιάνω, ἀρπάζω

cathedral (ὁ) καθεδρικὸς
  ναός, (ἡ) μητρόπολη*
cause (ἡ) αἰτία
celebrate, to ἑορτάζω
cemetery (τὸ) νεκροταφεῖο
center (τὸ) κέντρο
central κεντρικός, -ή, -ό
century (ὁ) αἰών(ας)
certain βέβαιος, -α, -ο
certainly βεβαίως, ἀσφαλῶς
chair (ἡ) καρέκλα
change (ἡ) ἀλλαγή,
  (τὰ) ψιλά
change, to ἀλλάζω
character (ὁ) χαρακτήρ(ας)
cheap φθηνός, -ή, -ό
check (ἡ) ἐπιταγή
check, to ἐλέγχω
cheese (τὸ) τυρί
chestnut (τὸ) κάστανο
chicken (ἡ) κότα
chief (ὁ) ἀρχηγος
child (τὸ) παιδί
chin (τὸ) σαγόνι
chocolate (ἡ) σοκολάτα
choose, to διαλέγω, ἐκλέγω
Christmas (τὰ) Χριστούγεννα
church (ἡ) ἐκκλησία
cigar (τὸ) ποῦρο
cigarette (τὸ) τσιγάρο,
  (τὸ) σιγαρέττο
city (ἡ) πόλη*
civilization (ὁ) πολιτισμός
class (ἡ) τάξη*
clean καθαρός, -ή, -ό
clean, to καθαρίζω
climate (τὸ) κλίμα or κλῖμα
close, to κλείνω

closet (τὸ) ντουλάπι
cloth (τὸ) πανί
clothes (τὰ) ροῦχα
cloud (τὸ) σύννεφο
coal (τὸ) κάρβουνο
coat (τὸ) (ἐ)πανωφόρι,
  (τὸ) παλτό
coffee (ὁ) καφές
cold κρύος, -α, -ο
collar (ὁ) γιακάς
collection (ἡ) συλλογή
color (τὸ) χρῶμα
comb (τὸ) χτένι, (ἡ) τσατσάρα
comb, to χτενίζω
come, to ἔρχομαι
come in, to μπαίνω
comfortable ἄνετος, -η,- ο
commerce (τὸ) ἐμπόριο
commercial ἐμπορικός, -ή, -ό,
company (ἡ) συντροφιά,
  (ἡ) ἑταιρεία or ἑταιρία
compare, to συγκρίνω
comparison (ἡ) σύγκριση*
complain, to παραπονοῦμαι
complete πλήρης, -ης, -ες
completely πλήρως
concert (ἡ) συναυλία
confession (ἡ) ἐξομολόγηση*
continue, to συνεχίζω
cook, to μαγειρεύω
cool δροσερός, -ή, -ό
copy (τὸ) ἀντίγραφο
corner (ἡ) γωνία
correct σωστός, -ή, -ό, ὀρθός, -ή, -ό
correspondence
  (ἡ) ἀλληλογραφία
cost, to στοιχίζω, κοστίζω
cotton (τὸ) βαμβάκι

cough, to βήχω
count, to μετρῶ
country (ἡ) χώρα, (ἡ) ἐξοχή
couple (τὸ) ζεῦγος
courage (τὸ) θάρρος
course, of βεβαίως
cousin (ὁ) ἐξάδελφος,
(ἡ) ἐξαδέλφη
cover, to σκεπάζω
cow (ἡ) ἀγελάδα
cream (ἡ) κρέμα
credit (ἡ) πίστωση*
crisis (ἡ) κρίση*
cry, to κλαίω
cuff (τὸ) μανικέτι
cup (ἡ) κούπα, (τὸ) φλιτζάνι
or φλυτζάνι
curtain (ἡ) κουρτίνα,
(τὸ) παραπέτασμα
custom (τὸ) ἔθιμο
customs (τὸ) τελωνεῖο
cut, to κόβω
cutlet (ἡ) κοτολέτα

D

daily καθημερινός, -ή, -ό
damage (ἡ) ζημία
damp ὑγρός, -ή, -ό,
βρεγμένος, -η, -ο
dance (ὁ) χορός
dance, to χορεύω
danger (ὁ) κίνδυνος
dangerous ἐπικίνδυνος, -η, -ο
dare, to τολμῶ
dark σκοτεινός, -ή, -ό,
σκοῦρος, -η, -ο
darkness (τὸ) σκοτάδι
darling ἀγαπημένος, -η, -ο
date (ἡ) ἡμερομηνία,

(ἡ) χρονολογία,
(τὸ) ραντεβού
daughter (ἡ) κόρη,
(ἡ) θυγατέρα
dawn (ἡ) αὐγή
day (ἡ) ἡμέρα or μέρα
dead νεκρός, -ή, -ό,
πεθαμένος, -η, -ο
deaf κουφός, -ή, -ό
dear ἀγαπητός, -ή, -ό,
ἀκριβός, -ή, -ό
death (ὁ) θάνατος
debt (τὸ) χρέος
deceive ἀπατῶ, ἐξαπατῶ, γελῶ
December (ὁ) Δεκέμβριος
decide, to ἀποφασίζω
decision (ἡ) ἀπόφαση*
declare, to δηλώνω
deed (ἡ) πράξη*
deep βαθύς, -εῖα, -ύ
defend, to ὑπερασπίζω
degree (ὁ) βαθμός,
(τὸ) πτυχίο
delay (ἡ) καθυστέρηση*
delay, to καθυστερῶ
delicious νόστιμος, -η, -ο
deliver, to διανέμω, παραδίδω
demand, to ἀπαιτῶ
dentist (ὁ) ὀδοντογιατρός
deny, to ἀρνοῦμαι
depart, to ἀναχωρῶ
departure (ἡ) ἀναχώρηση*
depend, to ἐξαρτῶμαι
deposit, to καταθέτω
descend, to κατεβαίνω
describe, to περιγράφω
description (ἡ) περιγραφή
deserve, to ἀξίζω

desire, to ἐπιθυμῶ, ποθῶ
desk (τὸ) γραφεῖο
dessert (τὸ) ἐπιδόρπιο
detail (ἡ) λεπτομέρεια
develop, to ἀναπτύσσω,
    ἀναπτύσσομαι
diamond (τὸ) διαμάντι,
    (ὁ) ἀδάμας
dictionary (τὸ) λεξικό
die, to πεθαίνω
difference (ἡ) διαφορά
different διαφορετικός, -ή, -ό
difficult δύσκολος, -η, -ο
difficulty (ἡ) δυσκολία
dinner (τὸ) γεῦμα
dining-room (ἡ) τραπεζαρία
diploma (τὸ) δίπλωμα
direction (ἡ) διεύθυνση*,
    (ἡ) κατεύθυνση*
directly ἀπ' εὐθείας, ἄμεσα
dirty ἀκάθαρτος, -η, -ο,
    βρώμικος, -η, -ο
disappear, to ἐξαφανίζομαι
discover, to ἀνακαλύπτω
discuss, to συζητῶ, μελετῶ
disgust (ἡ) ἀηδία
dish (τὸ) πιάτο
distance (ἡ) ἀπόσταση*
distant μακρινός, -ή, -ό
distinguish, to διακρίνω,
    ξεχωρίζω
disturb, to ἀνησυχῶ, ἐνοχλῶ
divide, to διαιρῶ
dizziness (ἡ) ζάλη
do, to κάνω
doctor (ὁ) γιατρός or ἰατρός
dog (τὸ) σκυλί, (ὁ) σκύλος
dollar (τὸ) δολλάριο

donkey (τὸ) γαϊδούρι,
    (ὁ) ὄνος
door (ἡ) πόρτα
double διπλός, -ή, -ό
doubt (ἡ) ἀμφιβολία
doubt, to ἀμφιβάλλω
down κάτω
dozen (ἡ) δωδεκάδα,
    (ἡ) ντουζίνα
draft (τὸ) ρεῦμα
drama (τὸ) δρᾶμα
dream (τὸ) ὄνειρο
dress (τὸ) φόρεμα
dress, to ντύνομαι
dressmaker (ὁ) ράφτης,
    (ἡ) ράφτρια, (ἡ) μοδίστ(ρ)α
drink (τὸ) ποτό
drink, to πίνω
drive, to ὁδηγῶ
driver (ὁ) ὁδηγός
drugstore (τὸ) φαρμακεῖο
dry στεγνός, -ή. -ό,
    ξηρός or ξερός, -ή. -ό
duck (ἡ) πάπια
dye, to βάφω

E

each κάθε
eager πρόθυμος, -η, -ο
ear (τὸ) αὐτί
early (ἐ)νωρίς
earn, to κερδίζω
earth (ἡ) γῆ
Easter (τὸ) Πάσχα
easy εὔκολος, -η, -ο
eat, to τρώγω
egg (τὸ) αὐγό
elbow (ὁ) ἀγκών(ας)
electric ἠλεκτρικός, -ή, -ό

electricity (ὁ) ἠλεκτρισμός
elegant κομψός, -ή, -ό
elevator (τὸ) ἀσανσέρ,
  (ὁ) ἀνελκυστήρ(ας)
embrace, to ἀγκαλιάζω
employe (ὁ) (ἡ) ὑπάλληλος
empty ἄδειος, -α, -ο
enchanting μαγευτικός, -ή, -ό
end (τὸ) τέλος
enemy (ὁ) ἐχθρός
engineer (ὁ) μηχανικός
England (ἡ) Ἀγγλία
English (ὁ) Ἄγγλος,
  (ἡ) Ἀγγλίδα· (τὰ) ἀγγλικά
enjoy, to ἀπολαμβάνω,
  χαίρομαι
enough ἀρκετά, ἀρκετός, -ή, -ό
enter, to μπαίνω, εἰσέρχομαι
enthusiasm (ὁ) ἐνθουσιασμός
enthusiastic ἐνθουσιώδης,
  -ης, -ες
entire ὁλόκληρος, -η, -ο
entrance (ἡ) εἴσοδος
envelope (ὁ) φάκελος
equal ἴσος, -η, -ο
error (τὸ) λάθος
escape, to ἀποδρῶ
especially ἰδίως
evening (τὸ) βράδυ
event (τὸ) γεγονός
everywhere παντοῦ
exactly ἀκριβῶς
exaggerate, to ὑπερβάλλω
examine, to ἐξετάζω
examination (ἡ) ἐξέταση*
example (τὸ) παράδειγμα
excellent ἄριστος, -η, -ο
exchange (ἡ) συναλλαγή

exciting συναρπαστικός, -ή, -ό
excuse, to δικαιολογῶ,
  συγχωρῶ
excuse me μὲ συγχωρεῖτε,
  συγγνώμη
exist, to ὑπάρχω
exit (ἡ) ἔξοδος
expensive ἀκριβός, -ή, -ό
experience (ἡ) πείρα or πεῖρα
explain, to ἐξηγῶ
explanation (ἡ) ἐξήγηση*
export, to ἐξάγω
express, to ἐκφράζω
expression (ἡ) ἔκφραση*
extinguish, to σβήνω or σβύνω
eye (τὸ) μάτι
eyeglasses (τὰ) ματογιάλια
eyesight (ἡ) ὅραση*

F
fabric (τὸ) ὕφασμα
face (τὸ) πρόσωπο
factory (τὸ) ἐργοστάσιο
faint, to λιποθυμῶ
faith (ἡ) πίστη*
fall, to πέφτω, πίπτω
false ψεύτικος, -η, -ο
family (ἡ) οἰκογένεια
famous περίφημος, -η, -ο
far μακρυά
farmer (ὁ) γεωργός,
  (ὁ) ἀγρότης
fashion (ἡ) μόδα
fast γρήγορα, γοργά
fat παχύς, -ιά, -ύ, λιπαρός, -ή, -ό
father (ὁ) πατέρας
favor (ἡ) χάρη*, (ἡ) εὔνοια
favorable εὐνοϊκός, -ή, -ό
favorite εὐνοούμενος, -η, -ο

fear (ὁ) φόβος
February (ὁ) Φεβρουάριος
feel, to αἰσθάνομαι
festival (ἡ) ἑορτή or γιορτή
fever (ὁ) πυρετός
field (τὸ) χωράφι, (ὁ) ἀγρός
fill, to γεμίζω
film (ἡ) ταινία, (τὸ) φίλμ
find, to βρίσκω or εὑρίσκω
find out, to ἀνακαλύπτω,
    πληροφοροῦμαι
finger (τὸ) δάκτυλο
finish, to τελειώνω
fire (ἡ) φωτιά
fish (τὸ) ψάρι
flame (ἡ) φλόγα
floor (τὸ) πάτωμα
flower (τὸ) λουλούδι,
    (τὸ) ἄνθος
fly (ἡ) μύγα or μυῖγα
fly, to πετῶ
fog (ἡ) ὁμίχλη, (ἡ) καταχνιά
follow, to ἀκολουθῶ
food (τὸ) φαγητό, (ἡ) τροφή
foot (τὸ) πόδι
force (ἡ) δύναμη*·
force, to βιάζω*
foreign ξένος, -η, -ο
foreigner (ὁ) ξένος
forget, to ξεχνῶ
forgive, to συγχωρῶ
form (τὸ) σχῆμα, (ἡ) μορφή
fortunately εὐτυχῶς
forward μπροστά, ἐμπρός
France (ἡ) Γαλλία
free ἐλεύθερος, -η, -ο
freedom (ἡ) ἐλευθερία
freeze, to παγώνω

French (ὁ) Γάλλος,
    (ἡ) Γαλλίδα· (τὰ) γαλλικά
frequently συχνά
fresh φρέσκος, -η, -ο,
    νωπός, -ή, -ό
Friday (ἡ) Παρασκευή
friend (ὁ) φίλος, (ἡ) φίλη
friendship (ἡ) φιλία
frightened φοβισμένος, -η, -ο
frost (ἡ) παγωνιά
fruit (τὸ) φροῦτο
fry, to τηγανίζω
funny ἀστεῖος, -α, -ο
fur (ἡ) γούνα
furnished ἐπιπλωμένος, -η, -ο
furniture (ἡ) ἐπίπλωση*

G

game (τὸ) παιγνίδι
garage (τὸ) γκαράζ
garden (ὁ) κῆπος
gas (τὸ) φωταέριο
gasoline (ἡ) βενζίνη
gather μαζεύω
gay εὔθυμος, -η, -ο
general γενικός, -ή, -ό
general (ὁ) στρατηγός
generally γενικά or γενικῶς
Germany (ἡ) Γερμανία
German (ὁ) Γερμανός,
    (ἡ) Γερμανίδα· (τὰ) γερμα-
    νικά
get up, to σηκώνομαι
gift (τὸ) δῶρο
give, to δίνω
glad χαρούμενος, -η, -ο,
    εὐχαριστημένος, -η, -ο
glass (τὸ) ποτήρι,
    (τὸ) τζάμι, (τὸ) γιαλί

glory (ἡ) δόξα
glove (τὸ) γάντι
go, to πηγαίνω
go up, to ἀνεβαίνω
goat (ἡ) κατσίκα, (ἡ) γίδα
gold (ὁ) χρυσός, (τὸ) χρυσάφι
good καλός, -ή, -ό
good-bye χαίρετε, ἀντίο
government (ἡ) κυβέρνηση*
granddaughter (ἡ) ἐγγονή
grandfather (ὁ) παππούς
or παππούς
grandmother (ἡ) γιαγιά
grandson (ὁ) ἐγγονός
grape (τὸ) σταφύλι
grapefruit (ἡ) φράπα
grateful εὐγνώμων, -ων, -ον
grass (τὸ) χορτάρι,
(τὸ) χόρτο, (τὸ) γρασίδι
grave (ὁ) τάφος, (τὸ) μνῆμα
gravy (ἡ) σάλτσα
gray γκρί, γκρίζος, -α, -ο
great μεγάλος, -η, -ο
Greece (ἡ) Ἑλλάδα or Ἑλλάς
Greek (ὁ) Ἕλλην(ας),
(ἡ) Ἑλληνίδα· (τὰ) ἑλληνικά
green πράσινος, -η, -ο
greet, to χαιρετῶ
greeting (ὁ) χαιρετισμός
grocery (τὸ) παντοπωλεῖο,
(τὸ) μπακάλικο
grow, to μεγαλώνω, αὐξάνω
guess, to μαντεύω
guest προσκεκλημένος, -η
guide, to ὁδηγῶ

H

hair (τὰ) μαλλιά
hairdresser (ὁ) κουρέας,

(ἡ) κομμώτρια
half μισός, -ή. -ό
ham (τὸ) ζαμπόν,
(τὸ) χοιρομέρι
hammer (τὸ) σφυρί
hand (τὸ) χέρι
(ὁ) δείκτης
handkerchief (τὸ) μαντήλι
or μαντίλι
hang, to κρεμῶ
happiness (ἡ) εὐτυχία
happy εὐτυχής, -ής, -ές,
εὐτυχισμένος, -η, -ο
hard σκληρός, -ή, -ό,
δύσκολος, -η, -ο
hat (τὸ) καπέλο or καπέλλο
hate, to μισῶ
have, to ἔχω
head (τὸ) κεφάλι
headache (ὁ) πονοκέφαλος
health (ἡ) ὑγεία
healthy ὑγιής, -ής, -ές
hear, to ἀκούω
heart (ἡ) καρδιά
heat (ἡ) ζέστη
heat, to ζεσταίνω
heavy βαρύς, -ιά, -ύ
heel (τὸ) τακούνι,
(ἡ) φτέρνα
height (τὸ) ὕψος
help (ἡ) βοήθεια
help, to βοηθῶ
here ἐδῶ
hesitate, to διστάζω
hide, to κρύβω
high (ὑ)ψηλός, -ή, -ό
high school (τὸ) γυμνάσιο

hill (ὁ) λόφος,
 (τὸ) ὕψωμα
historical ἱστορικός, -ή, -ό
history (ἡ) ἱστορία
hit, to κτυπῶ
hold, to κρατῶ
holiday (ἡ) γιορτή or ἑορτή
holy ἅγιος, -α, -ο
home (τὸ) σπίτι
honest τίμιος, -α, -ο
honesty (ἡ) τιμιότης
honey (τὸ) μέλι
honor (ἡ) τιμή
honor, to τιμῶ
hope (ἡ) ἐλπίδα
hope, to ἐλπίζω
horn (car) (τὸ) κλάξον
horse (τὸ) ἄλογο
hospital (τὸ) νοσοκομεῖο
hospitality (ἡ) φιλοξενία
hot ζεστός, -ή, -ό
hotel (τὸ) ξενοδοχεῖο
hour (ἡ) ὥρα
house (τὸ) σπίτι, (ἡ) οἰκία
how πῶς
how much πόσο
human ἀνθρώπινος, -η, -ο
humanity (ἡ) ἀνθρωπότης
humidity (ἡ) ὑγρασία
hunger (ἡ) πείνα or πεῖνα
hungry, to be πεινῶ
hunt, to κυνηγῶ
hunting (τὸ) κυνήγι
hurry, to βιάζομαι
hurt, to πληγώνω, προσβάλλω
husband (ὁ) σύζυγος,
 (ὁ) ἄντρας

I

ice (ὁ) πάγος
ice cream (τὸ) παγωτό
idea (ἡ) ἰδέα
ill, to be εἶμαι ἄρρωστος,
 ἀσθενῶ
imagine, to φαντάζομαι
immediately ἀμέσως
import, to εἰσάγω
important σπουδαῖος, -α, -ο
impression (ἡ) ἐντύπωση*
impossible ἀδύνατο (ν)
improve, to βελτιώνω
include, to περιλαμβάνω
income (τὸ) εἰσόδημα
indeed πράγματι
industry (ἡ) βιομηχανία
inform, to πληροφορῶ
information πληροφορία,
 (οἱ) πληροφορίες
ink (ἡ) μελάνη
insect (τὸ) ἔντομο
insecticide (τὸ) ἐντομοκτόνο
insist, to ἐπιμένω
insurance (ἡ) ἀσφάλεια
intelligent ἔξυπνος, -η, -ο,
 εὐφυής, -ής, -ές
interest (τὸ) ἐνδιαφέρον
interesting ἐνδιαφέρων,
 -ουσα, -ον
interrupt, to διακόπτω
introduce, to συστήνω, συνιστῶ
introduction (ἡ) εἰσαγωγή,
 (ἡ) σύσταση*
invitation (ἡ) πρόσκληση*
invite, to προσκαλῶ
iron (τὸ) σίδερο
irony (ἡ) εἰρωνία

island (τὸ) νησί, (ἡ) νῆσος
Italian (ὁ) 'Ιταλός,
(ἡ) 'Ιταλίδα· (τὰ) ἰταλικά
Italy (ἡ) 'Ιταλία

J

jacket (ἡ) ζακέτα
jam (τὸ) γλυκό
January (ὁ) 'Ιανουάριος
jealous (ὁ) ζηλιάρης
Jew (ὁ) 'Εβραῖος,
(ἡ) 'Εβραία
join, to ἑνώνω
joke (τὸ) ἀστεῖο
joke, to ἀστειεύομαι
joy (ἡ) χαρά
July (ὁ) 'Ιούλιος
jump, to πηδῶ
June (ὁ) 'Ιούνιος
justice (ἡ) δικαιοσύνη

K

keep, to κρατῶ, φυλάγω
key (τὸ) κλειδί
kilogram (τὸ) κιλό,
(τὸ) χιλιόγραμμο
kilometer (τὸ) χιλιόμετρο
kind καλός, -ή. -ό
kind (τὸ) εἶδος
kindness (ἡ) καλωσύνη
king (ὁ) βασιλιάς
or βασιλεύς
kiss, to φιλῶ
kitchen (ἡ) κουζίνα
knee (τὸ) γόνατο
knife (τὸ) μαχαίρι
knock, to κτυπῶ
know, to γνωρίζω, ξέρω
knowledge (ἡ) γνώση*,
(οἱ) γνώσεις

L

labor (ἡ) ἐργασία
lace, shoe (τὸ) κορδόνι
lady (ἡ) κυρία
lake (ἡ) λίμνη
lamb (τὸ) ἀρνί
lamp (ἡ) λάμπα
lamp bulb (ὁ) λαμπτήρ(ας)
land, to προσγειώνομαι
language (ἡ) γλώσσα
or γλῶσσα
large μεγάλος, -η, -ο
last τελευταῖος, -α, -ο
last, to διαρκῶ
late ἀργά
later ἀργότερα
laugh, to γελῶ
laughter (τὸ) γέλιο
laundry (τὸ) πλυντήριο
law (ὁ) νόμος
lazy (ὁ) τεμπέλης,
(ἡ) τεμπέλα
leaf (τὸ) φύλλο
learn, to μαθαίνω
least, at τουλάχιστο
leather (τὸ) δέρμα
leave, to ἀφήνω, φεύγω ἀπό
lecture (ἡ) διάλεξη*
left ἀριστερός, -ή, -ό,
ἀριστερά
leg (ἡ) κνήμη, (τὸ) μπούτι
lemon (τὸ) λεμόνι
lend, to δανείζω
less λιγώτερο
lesson (τὸ) μάθημα
let, to ἀφήνω, ἐπιτρέπω
letter (τὸ) γράμμα
lettuce (τὸ) μαρούλι

library (ἡ) βιβλιοθήκη
lie (τὸ) ψέμα or ψέμμα
lie, to ψεύδομαι, λέγω ψέματα
life (ἡ) ζωή
lift, to σηκώνω
light (τὸ) φῶς
light ἐλαφρός, -ή, -ό
light, to ἀνάβω (τὸ φῶς)
lighter (ὁ) ἀναπτήρας,
lightning (ἡ) ἀστραπή
like, to μcῦ ἀρέσει
  or μ' ἀρέσει, ἀγαπῶ
line (ἡ) γραμμή
linen (τὸ) λινό,
  (τὰ) ἀσπρόρουχα
lion (τὸ) λιοντάρι, (ὁ) λέων
lip (τὸ) χείλι, (τὸ) χεῖλος
list (ὁ) κατάλογος
listen, to ἀκούω
literature (ἡ) λογοτεχνία
little μικρός, -ή, -ό, λίγο
live, to ζῶ, κατοικῶ, μένω
load, to φορτώνω
lobster (ὁ) ἀστακός
located, to be βρίσκομαι
  or εὑρίσκομαι
lock (ἡ) κλειδωνιά
logical λογικός, -ή, -ό
long μακρύς, -ιά, -ύ
look at, to κοιτάζω or κυττάζω
look for, to ψάχνω, γυρεύω
look like, to μοιάζω
lose, to χάνω
lost χαμένος, -η, -ο
loud δυνατός, -ή, -ό
love (ἡ) ἀγάπη
love, to ἀγαπῶ
low χαμηλός, -ή, -ό

luck (ἡ) τύχη
lucky τυχερός, -ή, -ό
lunch (τὸ) γεῦμα
lung (τὸ) πλεμόνι, (ὁ) πνεύμονας or πνεύμων
luxury (ἡ) πολυτέλεια

M

machine (ἡ) μηχανή,
  (τὸ) μηχάνημα
magic μαγικός, -ή, -ό
maid (ἡ) ὑπηρέτρια
mail (τὸ) ταχυδρομεῖο
main κύριος, -α, -ο
make, to κάνω
man (ὁ) ἄνθρωπος,
  (ὁ) ἄνδρας
manage, to διευθύνω, κατορθώνω
manager (ὁ) διευθυντής
manner (ὁ) τρόπος
many πολλοί, -ές, -ά
map (ὁ) χάρτης
marble (τὸ) μάρμαρο
March (ὁ) Μάρτιος
mark (τὸ) σημεῖο,
  (τὸ) σημάδι
market (ἡ) ἀγορά
marriage (ὁ) γάμος
marry, to παντρεύομαι
marvelous θαυμάσιος, -α, -ο
match (τὸ) σπίρτο
match, to ταιριάζω
mathematics (τὰ) μαθηματικά
material (τὸ) ὑλικό
mattress (τὸ) στρῶμα
May (ὁ) Μάϊος
may μπορῶ
mayor (ὁ) δήμαρχος

mean, to σημαίνω, ἐννοῶ
meaning (ἡ) σημασία,
  (ἡ) ἔννοια
means (τὸ) μέσο
measure (τὸ) μέτρο
meat (τὸ) κρέας
medicine (τὸ) φάρμακο,
  (ἡ) ἰατρική
meet, to συναντῶ
meeting (ἡ) συνάντηση*,
  (ἡ) συνεδρίαση*
melody (ἡ) μελωδία
mend, to μπαλώνω,
  ἐπιδιορθώνω
menu (τὸ) μενού,
  (ὁ) κατάλογος φαγητῶν
merchandise (τὸ) ἐμπόρευμα
merchant (ὁ) ἔμπορος
metal (τὸ) μέταλλο
meter (τὸ) μέτρο
midnight (τὰ) μεσάνυχτα
milk (τὸ) γάλα
mind (τὸ) μυαλό,
  (τὸ) πνεῦμα
mine (τὸ) ὀρυχεῖο
minute (τὸ) λεπτό
mirror (ὁ) καθρέπτης
Miss (ἡ) Δεσποινίς
miss, to χάνω, μοῦ λείπει
mistaken, to be κάνω λάθος
mister (ὁ) κύριος; (voc.) κύριε
misunderstand, to παρεξηγῶ
misunderstanding
  (ἡ) παρεξήγηση*
mix, to ἀνακατεύω
moderate μέτριος, -α, -ο
modern σύγχρονος, -η, -ο,
  μοντέρνος, -α, -ο

moment (ἡ) στιγμή
Monday (ἡ) Δευτέρα
money (τὸ) χρῆμα,
  (τὰ) χρήματα
month (ὁ) μήνας
monthly μηνιαῖος, -α, -ο
monument (τὸ) μνημεῖο
moon (τὸ) φεγγάρι,
  (ἡ) σελήνη
more περισσότερο
morning (τὸ) πρωί
mosquito (τὸ) κουνούπι
most πιὸ πολύ
mother (ἡ) μητέρα
motion picture (ἡ) ταινία,
  (τὸ) φίλμ
motor (ἡ) μηχανή
motorcycle (ἡ) μοτοσυκλέτα
mountain (τὸ) βουνό
mouth (τὸ) στόμα
move, to μετακινῶ, κινοῦμαι
movement (ἡ) κίνηση*
movie theater
  (ὁ) κινηματογράφος
much πολύ
mud (ἡ) λάσπη
museum (τὸ) μουσεῖο
music (ἡ) μουσική
musician (ὁ) μουσικός
must πρέπει
mustache (τὸ) μουστάκι
mysterious μυστηριώδης,
  -ης, -ες

N

nail (τὸ) νύχι, (τὸ) καρφί
name (τὸ) ὄνομα
napkin (ἡ) πετσέτα
narrow στενός, -ή, -ό

nation (τό) ἔθνος
national ἐθνικός, -ή, -ό
nationality (ἡ) ἐθνικότης,
 (ἡ) ὑπηκοότης
natural φυσικός, -ή, -ό
naturally φυσικά
nature (ἡ) φύση*
navy (τό) ναυτικό
near κοντά, πλησίον
nearly σχεδόν
necessary ἀναγκαῖος, -α, -ο
neck (ὁ) λαιμός
necktie (ἡ) γραβάτα
need (ἡ) ἀνάγκη
need, to χρειάζομαι
needle (ἡ) βελόνα,
 (τό) βελόνι
neighbor (ὁ) γείτονας,
 (ἡ) γειτόνισσα
neighborhood (ἡ) γειτονιά
nephew (ὁ) ἀνεψιός
 or ἀνιψιός
never ποτέ
new νέος, -α, -ο,
 καινούργιος, -α, -ο
newlyweds (οἱ) νεόνυμφοι
news (τά) νέα
newspaper (ἡ) ἐφημερίδα
next ἐπόμενος, -η, -ο
night (ἡ) νύκτα
no ὄχι
noise (ὁ) θόρυβος
noon (τό) μεσημέρι
north (ὁ) βορρᾶς or βοριάς
not δέν, μή
notebook (τό) σημειωματάριο,
 (τό) τετράδιο
nothing τίποτε or τίποτα

notice (ἡ) εἰδοποίηση*
 (ἡ) σημείωση*
November (ὁ) Νοέμβριος
now τώρα
number (ὁ) ἀριθμός
nurse (ἡ) νοσοκόμα
nut (τό) καρύδι

O

object (τό) ἀντικείμενο
obligation (ἡ) ὑποχρέωση*
occupation (τό) ἐπάγγελμα,
 (ἡ) ἀπασχόληση*, (ἡ) κα-
 τοχή
occupy, to κατέχω
ocean (ὁ) ὠκεανός
October (ὁ) Ὀκτώβριος
offer, to προσφέρω
office (τό) γραφεῖο
officer (ὁ) ἀξιωματικός
official ἐπίσημος, -η, -ο
often συχνά
oil (τό) λάδι
ointment (ἡ) ἀλοιφή
O.K. ἐν τάξει
old παλιός or παληός
 or παλαιός, -α, -ο
olive (ἡ) ἐλιά or ἐληά
once μιά φορά, ἄπαξ
onion (τό) κρεμύδι
only μόνο(ν)
open ἀνοικτός, -ή, -ό
open, to ἀνοίγω
opinion (ἡ) γνώμη
opportunity (ἡ) εὐκαιρία
oppose, to εἶμαι ἐναντίον,
 ἀντιτίθεμαι
orange (τό) πορτοκάλι

order (ἡ) διαταγή,
 (ἡ) παραγγελία
order, to διατάζω, παραγγέλλω
organization (ἡ) ὀργάνωση*
other ἄλλος, -η, -ο
otherwise ἀλλιῶς
out or outside ἔξω
out of order χαλασμένος, -η, -ο
overcoat (τὸ) παλτό,
 (ἐ)πανωφόρι
owe, to ὀφείλω
owner (ὁ) ἰδιοκτήτης
ox (τὸ) βόδι
oyster (τὸ) στρείδι

P

package (τὸ) δέμα
page (ἡ) σελίδα
pain (ὁ) πόνος
paint (ἡ) βαφή, (τὸ) χρῶμα
paint, to βάφω, ζωγραφίζω
painter (ὁ) ζωγράφος
pair (τὸ) ζευγάρι
palace (τὸ) παλάτι
pale χλωμός, -ή, -ό
palm (ἡ) παλάμη
pan (τὸ) τηγάνι
paper (τὸ) χαρτί
parents (οἱ) γονεῖς
park (τὸ) ·πάρκο
part (τὸ) μέρος
pass, to περνῶ
passport (τὸ) διαβατήριο
past (τὸ) παρελθόν
pastry (τὸ) γλύκισμα
patriarch (ὁ) Πατριάρχης
patriotism (ὁ) πατριωτισμός
pattern (τὸ) σχέδιο
pay, to πληρώνω

payment (ἡ) πληρωμή
peace (ἡ) εἰρήνη
peach (τὸ) ροδάκινο
pear (τὸ) ἀχλάδι, (ἡ) ἀχλάδα
peasant (ὁ) χωρικός
pen (ἡ) πένα
pen, fountain στυλο(γράφος)
pencil (τὸ) μολύβι or μολίβι
people (ὁ) κόσμος, (ὁ) λαός
pepper (τὸ) πιπέρι
per cent τοῖς ἑκατό
perfect τέλειος, -α, -ο
performance (ἡ) παράσταση*
perfume (τὸ) ἄρωμα,
 (ἡ) μυρωδιά
perhaps ἴσως
period (ἡ) περίοδος
perish, to χάνομαι
permit, to ἐπιτρέπω
person (τὸ) πρόσωπο
personal προσωπικός, -ή, -ό
perspire, to ἱδρώνω
perspiration (ὁ) ἵδρωτας
persuade, to πείθω
petroleum (τὸ) πετρέλαιο
photograph (ἡ) φωτογραφία
photograph, to φωτογραφίζω
picture (ἡ) εἰκόνα
pie (ἡ) πίτα or πήττα
piece (τὸ) κομμάτι
pier (ἡ) ἀποβάθρα
pile (ὁ) σωρός
pill (τὸ) χάπι
pillow (τὸ) μαξιλάρι
 (ἡ) καρφίτσα
pipe (ὁ) σωλήν(ας),
 (ἡ) πίπα

pitcher (τό) κανάτι,
(ἡ) κανάτα
place (ὁ) τόπος, (τό) μέρος
plan (τό) σχέδιο
plane, by ἀεροπορικῶς
plant (τό) φυτό
plant, to φυτεύω
play (τό) παιγνίδι,
(τό) (θεατρικὸ) ἔργο
play, to παίζω
pleasant εὐχάριστος, -η, -ο
please παρακαλῶ
please, to εὐχαριστῶ
pleasure (ἡ) εὐχαρίστηση*
pocket (ἡ) τσέπη
poem (τό) ποίημα
poet (ὁ) ποιητής
poetry (ἡ) ποίηση*
point (τό) σημεῖο
point out, to δείχνω
Poland (ἡ) Πολωνία
police (ἡ) ἀστυνομία
policeman (ὁ) ἀστυφύλακας,
χωροφύλακας
police officer (ὁ) ἀστυνόμος
police station
(τό) ἀστυνομικὸ τμῆμα
polite εὐγενής
political πολιτικός, -ή, -ό
politics (ἡ) πολιτική
poor πτωχός, -ή, -ό
popular δημοφιλής, -ής, -ές
pork (τό) χοιρινό
port (τό) λιμάνι,
(ὁ) λιμένας or λιμήν
porter (ὁ) ἀχθοφόρος, χαμάλης
position (ἡ) θέση*
possible δυνατό(ν)

postman (ὁ) ταχυδρόμος
post office (τό) ταχυδρομεῖο
postpone, to ἀναβάλλω
potato (ἡ) πατάτα
pound (ἡ) λίτρα
poverty (ἡ) φτώχια,
(ἡ) ἔνδεια
powder (ἡ) πούδρα
power (ἡ) δύναμη*, (ἡ) ἰσχύς
powerful ἰσχυρός, -ή, -ό
practical πρακτικός, -ή, -ό
practice (ἡ) ἄσκηση*
praise, to ἐπαινῶ
pray, to προσεύχομαι
prayer (ἡ) προσευχή
precious πολύτιμος, -η, -ο
precisely ἀκριβῶς
prefer, to προτιμῶ
prejudice (ἡ) προκατάληψη*
prepare, to προετοιμάζω
prescription (ἡ) συνταγή
present (τό) παρόν
present, to παρουσιάζω
press (ὁ) τύπος
press, to πιέζω
pretend, to ὑποκρίνομαι
pretty ὄμορφος, -η, -ο
prevent, to ἐμποδίζω
previous προηγούμενος, -η, -ο
previously προηγουμένως
price (ἡ) τιμή
prince (ὁ) πρίγκηπας
princess (ἡ) πριγκήπισσα
print, to τυπώνω
printed matter (τό) ἔντυπο
private ἰδιωτικός, -ή, -ό
prize (τό) βραβεῖο
probably πιθανῶς

proceed, to προχωρῶ
produce, to παράγω
product (τὸ) προϊόν
profit (τὸ) κέρδος
program (τὸ) πρόγραμμα
promise, to ὑπόσχομαι
pronounce, to προφέρω
pronunciation (ἡ) προφορά
propose, to προτείνω
protest (ἡ) διαμαρτυρία
protest, to διαμαρτύρομαι
prove, to ἀποδεικνύω
pull, to τραβῶ
pure ἁγνός, -ή, -ό
purpose (ὁ) σκοπός
purpose, on ἐπίτηδες,
   ἀπὸ σκοποῦ
push, to σπρώχνω
put, to βάζω, θέτω
put on, to βάζω, φορῶ

Q
quality (ἡ) ποιότης
quantity (ἡ) ποσότης
quarter (τὸ) τέταρτο
queen (ἡ) βασίλισσα
question (ἡ) ἐρώτηση*
quick ταχύς, -εῖα, -ύ
   or γρήγορος, -η, -ο
quickly γρήγορα
quit, to παραιτοῦμαι

R
rabbit (τὸ) κουνέλι
race (ἡ) φυλή
radio (τὸ) ραδιό(φωνο)
railroad (ὁ) σιδηρόδρομος
rain (ἡ) βροχή
rain, to βρέχει
raincoat (τὸ) ἀδιάβροχο

raise, to σηκώνω
rare σπάνιος, -α, -ο
rather μᾶλλον
raw ὠμός, -ή, -ό
razor (τὸ) ξυράφι
razor blade (ἡ) λεπίδα
   ξυραφιοῦ, (τὸ) ξυραφάκι
reach, to φθάνω
react, to ἀντιδρῶ
read, to διαβάζω
ready ἕτοιμος, -η, -ο
real πραγματικός, -ή, -ό
really πραγματικά,
   ἀλήθεια, πράγματι
reason (ἡ) αἰτία
reasonable λογικός, -ή, -ό
receipt (ἡ) ἀπόδειξη*
receive, to λαμβάνω, δέχομαι
recently προσφάτως,
   τελευταίως
reception (ἡ) δεξίωση*
recognize, to ἀναγνωρίζω
recommend, to συστήνω,
   συνιστῶ
recover, to γίνομαι καλά,
   ἀνακτῶ
red κόκκινος, -η, -ο,
   ἐρυθρός, -ά, -ό
refreshment (τὸ) ἀναψυκτικό
refrigerator (ἡ) παγωνιέρα
   (τὸ) ψυγεῖο
refuse, to ἀρνοῦμαι
register, to ἐγγράφω
registered letter
   (ἡ) συστημένη ἐπιστολή
regret, to λυποῦμαι
relation (ἡ) σχέση*
relative (ὁ) (ἡ) συγγενής

religion (ἡ) θρησκεία
religious θρησκευτικός, -ή, -ό
remain, to (παρα)μένω
remainder (τὸ) ὑπόλοιπο
remember, to θυμοῦμαι
or θυμᾶμαι
remind, to θυμίζω
rent (τὸ) ἐνοίκιο
rent, to ἐνοικιάζω
repair, to ἐπιδιορθώνω
repeat, to ἐπαναλαμβάνω
replace, to ἀντικαθιστῶ
represent, to ἀντιπροσωπεύω
representative
(ὁ) ἀντιπρόσωπος
republic (ἡ) δημοκρατία
resemblance (ἡ) ὁμοιότης
resemble, to ὁμοιάζω
reservation (ἡ) ρεζερβασιόν,
(ἡ) ἐπιφύλαξη*
respect (ὁ) σεβασμός
respect, to σέβομαι
responsible ὑπεύθυνος, -η, -ο
rest (τὸ) ὑπόλοιπο,
(ἡ) ἀνάπαυση*
rest, to ἀναπαύομαι,
ξεκουράζομαι
restaurant (τὸ) ἐστιατόριο
restriction (ὁ) περιορισμός
return, to ἐπιστρέφω
ribbon (ἡ) κορδέλα
or κορδέλλα
rice (τὸ) ρύζι
rich πλούσιος, -α, -ο
right σωστός, -ή, -ό,
δεξιός, -ά, -ό
right, to the δεξιά
right away ἀμέσως

ring (τὸ) δαχτυλίδι
ring, to χτυπῶ (τὸ κουδούνι)
rise, to σηκώνομαι
river (ὁ) ποταμός,
(τὸ) ποτάμι
road (ὁ) δρόμος
roast (τὸ) ψητό
rock (ὁ) βράχος
roll, to τυλίγω, κυλῶ
roof (ἡ) στέγη
room (τὸ) δωμάτιο
rose (τὸ) τριαντάφυλλο,
(τὸ) ρόδο
rough τραχύς, -εῖα, -ύ
round στρογγυλός, -ή, -ό
ruin (τὸ) ἐρείπιο
rule, to κυβερνῶ
Rumania (ἡ) Ρουμανία
run, to τρέχω
Russia (ἡ) Ρωσ(σ)ία
Russian (ὁ) Ρῶσ(σ)ος,
(ἡ) Ρωσ(σ)ίδα
S
sad λυπημένος, -η, -ο,
λυπητερός, -ή, -ό
sadness (ἡ) λύπη
safe ἀσφαλής, -ής, -ές
safety (ἡ) ἀσφάλεια
sail, to πλέω
salad (ἡ) σαλάτα
salt (τὸ) ἁλάτι
salty ἁλμυρός, -ή, -ό
same ἴδιος, -α, -ο
sand (ὁ) ἄμμος
satisfy, to ἱκανοποιῶ
Saturday (τὸ) Σάββατο
saucer (τὸ) πιατάκι
save, to σώζω

say, to λέγω
scene (ή) σκηνή
school (τό) σχολείο
science (ή) ἐπιστήμη
scientist (ό) (ή) ἐπιστήμων
scissors (τό) ψαλίδι
sea (ή) θάλασσα
seal (ή) σφραγίδα
seashore (ή) ἀκρογιαλιά
season (ή) ἐποχή
seat (τό) κάθισμα
second (τό) δευτερόλεπτο
see, to βλέπω
seek, to γυρεύω, ψάχνω
seem, to φαίνομαι
sell, to πουλῶ or πωλῶ
send, to στέλλω
sentence (ή) πρόταση*,
    (ή) ποινή
September (ό) Σεπτέμβριος
serious σοβαρός, -ή, -ό
seriously σοβαρά
servant (ό) ὑπηρέτης
serve, to ὑπηρετῶ
sew, to ράβω
shade (ή) σκιά
shadow (ό) ἴσκιος
shake, to κουνῶ, τρέμω,
    τινάζω
share (τό) μερίδιο
share, to μοιράζομαι
sharp ὀξύς, -εῖα, -ύ,
    μυτερός, -ή, -ό
shave, to ξυρίζω, ξυρίζομαι
sheep (τό) πρόβατο
sheet (τό) σιντόνι
sheet of paper φύλλο χαρτιοῦ
shell (τό) ὄστρακο

shine, to λάμπω
ship (τό) πλοῖο
shirt (τό) ὑποκάμισο
    or πουκάμισο
shoe (τό) παπούτσι
shop (τό) μαγαζί
short κοντός, -ή, -ό
shoulder (ό) ὦμος
shout, to φωνάζω
show (τό) θέαμα
show, to δείχνω
shower (τό) ντούς
shut, to κλείνω
sick ἄρρωστος, -η, -ο
sick, to get ἀρρωσταίνω
side (ή) πλευρά
sidewalk (τό) πεζοδρόμιο
sign (τό) σημεῖο,
    (ή) ἐπιγραφή
sign, to ὑπογράφω
signature (ή) ὑπογραφή
silence (ή) σιωπή
silent σιωπηλός, -ή, -ό
silk (τό) μετάξι
silver (τό) ἀσήμι,
    (ό) ἄργυρος
silverware (τά) ἀσημικά
similar παρόμοιος, -α, -ο
simple ἁπλός, -ή, -ό
simplicity (ή) ἁπλότης
sincere εἰλικρινής, -ής, -ές
sincerity (ή) εἰλικρίνεια
sing, to τραγουδῶ
single μόνος, -η, -ο
sister (ή) ἀδελφή
sister-in-law (ή) νύφη,
    (ή) κουνιάδα
sit (down), to κάθομαι

size (τό) μέγεθος, νούμερο
skin (τό) δέρμα
skirt (ή) φούστα
sky (ό) ούρανός
skyscraper (ό) ούρανοξύστης
sleep, to κοιμοῦμαι
sleeve (τό) μανίκι
slice (ή) φέτα
slip (τό) κομπινεζόν,
  (τό) μεσοφόρι
slip, to γλιστρῶ
slow άργός, -ή, -ό
slowly σιγά
small μικρός, -ή, -ό
smell, to μυρίζω
smile, to χαμογελῶ
smoke (ό) καπνός
smoke, to καπνίζω
sneeze, to φταρνίζομαι
snow (τό) χιόνι
snow, to χιονίζει
so ἔτσι, τοιουτοτρόπως
soak μουσκεύω
soap (τό) σαπούνι
sock (ή) κάλτσα
sofa (ό) καναπές
soft μαλακός, -ή, -ό,
  άπαλός, -ή, -ό
soldier (ό) στρατιώτης
sole (ή) σόλα
sometimes κάποτε,
  μερικές φορές
something κάτι
somewhere κάπου
son (ό) γιός or γυιός
song (τό) τραγούδι
soon σὲ λίγο, σύντομα
sorrow (ή) λύπη

sorry, to be λυποῦμαι
soul (ή) ψυχή
sound (ό) ἦχος
soup (ή) σούπα
south (ό) νότος
souvenir (τό) ένθύμιο
Spain (ή) Ἰσπανία
Spanish (ό) Ἰσπανός,
  (ή) Ἰσπανίδα
speak, to (ό)μιλῶ
special είδικός, -ή, -ό
specify, to καθορίζω
speed (ή) ταχύτης
spend, to (έ)ξοδεύω
  περνῶ
spoil, to χαλνῶ
sponge (τό) σφουγγάρι
spoon (τό) κουτάλι
sports (ό) άθλητισμός
spread, to άπλώνω
spring (ή) ἄνοιξη*
spring (τό) έλατήριο
square (τό) τετράγωνο
square (ή) πλατεία
  or πλατεῖα
stage (ή) σκηνή
stairs (οί) σκάλες
stairway (ή) σκάλα
stamp (τό) γραμματόσημο
stand, to στέκομαι
star (τό) άστέρι, (τό) ἄστρο
start, to άρχίζω, ξεκινῶ
state (ή) πολιτεία,
  (τό) κράτος, (ή) κατάσταση*
statement (ή) δήλωση*
station (ό) σταθμός
stay, to μένω
steak (τό) μπιφτέκ(ι)

steal, to κλέβω
steam heat (τò) καλοριφέρ
steering wheel (τò) τιμόνι
still ἀκόμη, ὅμως
stocking (ἡ) κάλτσα
stomach (τò) στομάχι
stone (ἡ) πέτρα
stop, to σταματῶ
stop (ἡ) στάση*
store (τò) κατάστημα
store, to ἀποθηκεύω
storm (ἡ) θύελλα
story (ἡ) ἱστορία
story (floor) (τò) πάτωμα
straight ἴσιος, -α, -ο
strange παράξενος, -η, -ο
strawberry (ἡ) φράουλα
street (ὁ) δρόμος, (ἡ) ὁδός
strike, to κτυπῶ
string (ὁ) σπάγγος,
    (ἡ) χορδή
strong δυνατός, -ή, -ό
student (ὁ) μαθητής,
    (ἡ) μαθήτρια, (ὁ) φοιτητής,
    (ἡ) φοιτήτρια
study (ἡ) μελέτη
study, to μελετῶ
stupid ἠλίθιος, -α, -ο, βλάκας
subject (τò) θέμα,
    (τò) ὑποκείμενο
suburb (τò) προάστειο
subway (ὁ) ὑπόγειος
    (σιδηρόδρομος)
succeed πετυχαίνω
    or ἐπιτυγχάνω
success (ἡ) ἐπιτυχία
such τέτοιος, -α, -ο
sudden ξαφνικός, -ή, -ό

suddenly ξαφνικά, ἔξαφνσ
suffer, to ὑποφέρω
sugar (ἡ) ζάχαρη
suit (τò) κοστούμι
suitcase (ἡ) βαλίτσα
sum (τò) ποσό
summer (τò) καλοκαίρι
sun (ὁ) ἥλιος
Sunday (ἡ) Κυριακή
sunrise (ἡ) ἀνατολή
    (τοῦ ἡλίου)
sunset (ἡ) δύση* (τοῦ ἡλίου)
superior ἀνώτερος, -η, -ο
supper (τò) δεῖπνο, (τò) σουπέ
supply, to προμηθεύω
support, to ὑποστηρίζω
suppose, to ὑποθέτω
sure βέβαιος, -α, -ο
surprise (ἡ) ἔκπληξη*
surprise, to ἐκπλήττω
surround, to τριγυρίζω
suspect, to ὑποπτεύομαι
sweep, to σκουπίζω
sweet γλυκός, -ιά, -ό
swim, to κολυμπῶ
swimming (τò) κολύμπι
Swiss (ὁ) Ἐλβετός,
    (ἡ) Ἐλβετίδα
Switzerland (ἡ) Ἐλβετία
sympathy (ἡ) συμπάθεια,
    (ἡ) συμπόνια
symptom (τò) σύμπτωμα
system (τò) σύστημα

T

table (τò) τραπέζι
tablecloth
    (τò) τραπεζομάνδηλο
tailor (ὁ) ράφτης

take, to παίρνω
take off, to βγάζω
tall (ύ)ψηλός, -ή, -ό
taste (ή) γεύση*, (τό) γοῦστο
taste, to γεύομαι
tax (ό) φόρος
taxi (τό) ταξί
tea (τό) τσάϊ
teach, to διδάσκω
teacher (ό) δάσκαλος,
   (ή) δασκάλα
tear (τό) δάκρυ
tear, to σχίζω
telegram (τό) τηλεγράφημα
telegraph, to τηλεγραφῶ
telephone (τό) τηλέφωνο
telephone, to τηλεφωνῶ
telephone call (τό) τηλεφώνημα
telephone operator
   (ή) τηλεφωνήτρια
television (ή) τηλεόραση*
tell, to λέγω
temperature (ή) θερμοκρασία
tender τρυφερός,-ή, -ό
terrible τρομερός, -ή, -ό
thank, to εὐχαριστῶ
theater (τό) θέατρο
then τότε, ἔπειτα
there ἐκεῖ
there is, are ὑπάρχει,
   ὑπάρχουν, ἔχει
thermometer (τό) θερμόμετρο
thin ἀδύνατος, -η, -ο,
   λεπτός, -ή, -ό
thing (τό) πρᾶγμα
   or πρᾶγμα
think, to σκέπτομαι
thirst (ή) δίψα

thirsty, to be διψῶ
thought (ή) σκέψη*
thread (ή) κλωστή
threaten, to ἀπειλῶ
throat (ό) λαιμός
throw, to ρίχνω
thunder (ή) βροντή
Thursday (ή) Πέμπτη
ticket (τό) εἰσιτήριο
ticket window (ή) θυρίδα
tight στενός, -ή, -ό
time (ό) χρόνος, (ό) καιρός
time table (τό) δρομολόγιο
tip (τό) πουρμπουάρ,
   (τό) φιλοδώρημα
tire λάστιχο αὐτοκινήτου
tired κουρασμένος, -η, -ο
tobacco (ό) καπνός
today σήμερα
together μαζί
toilet (τό) μέρος,
   (ή) τουαλέτα
tomato (ή) ντομάτα
tomb (ό) τάφος
tomorrow αὔριο(ν)
tongue (ή) γλώσσα
   or γλῶσσα
tonight ἀπόψε
too ἐπίσης
too much παρά πολύ
tooth (τό) δόντι
toothbush (ή) ὀδοντόβουρτσα
toothpaste (ή) ὀδοντόπαστα
top (ή) κορυφή
touch, to ἀγγίζω or ἐγγίζω
tough σκληρός, -ή, -ό
tourist (ό) περιηγητής,
   (ή) περιηγήτρια

towel (ή) πετσέτα
tower (ὁ) πύργος
town (ή) πόλη*
toy (τὸ) παιγνίδι
trade (τὸ) ἐμπόριο
tragedy (ή) τραγωδία
train (τὸ) τραῖνο
translate, to μεταφράζω
travel, to ταξιδεύω
traveler (ὁ) ταξιδιώτης
tray (ὁ) δίσκος
tree (τὸ) δέντρο
trial (ή) δίκη
trip (τὸ) ταξίδι
trouble (ή) φασαρία,
    (ή) ἐνόχληση*, (ή) δυσκολία
trousers (τὸ) παντελόνι
truck (τὸ) φορτηγό
    (αὐτοκίνητο)
true ἀληθής, -ής, -ές
trunk (τὸ) μπαοῦλο,
    (ὁ) κορμός
truth (ή) ἀλήθεια
try, to δοκιμάζω,
    προσπαθῶ, δικάζω
Tuesday (ή) Τρίτη
Turkey (ή) Τουρκία
turn, to γυρίζω,
    στρέφω, στρέφομαι
turn on the light, to
    ἀνάβω τὸ φῶς
turn off the light, to
    σβήνω τὸ φῶς
twice δύο φορές
twin δίδυμος, -η, -ο
typewrite, to δακτυλογραφῶ
typewriter (ή) δακτυλογραφικὴ
    μηχανή

U

ugly ἄσχημος, -η, -ο
umbrella (ή) ὀμπρέλα
    or ὀμπρέλλα
uncle (ὁ) θεῖος
understand, to καταλαβαίνω
underwear (τὰ) ἐσώρρουχα
undoubtedly ἀναμφιβόλως
undress, to ξεντύνομαι
unfortunately δυστυχῶς
unhealthy ἀνθυγιεινός, -ή, -ό
uniform (ή) στολή
union (ή) ἕνωση*
united ἐνωμένος, -η, -ο
United States (αἱ) Ἡνωμέναι
    Πολιτεῖαι
university (τὸ) πανεπιστήμιο
unpleasant δυσάρεστος, -η, -ο
up ἐπάνω
upset, to ἀναστατώνω
upstairs στὸ ἐπάνω πάτωμα
urgent ἐπείγων, -ουσα, -ον
use (ή) χρήση*
use, to χρησιμοποιῶ
useful χρήσιμος, -η, -ο
useless ἄχρηστος, -η, -ο
usually συνήθως

V

vacation (οἱ) διακοπές
vain, in ματαίως, μάταια
valley (ή) κοιλάδα
value (ή) ἀξία
variety (ή) ποικιλία
veal (τὸ) μοσχάρι
vegetables (τὰ) χορταρικά
velvet (τὸ) βελοῦδο
very πολύ
vest (τὸ) γελέκο or γιλέκο

victory (ή) νίκη
view (ή) ἄποψη*, (ή) θέα
vinegar (τὸ) ξύδι or ξίδι
visit (ή) ἐπίσκεψη*
visit, to ἐπισκέπτομαι
visitor (ὁ) ἐπισκέπτης,
 (ή) ἐπισκέπτρια
voice (ή) φωνή

W

waist (ή) μέση
wait, to περιμένω
waiter (τὸ) γκαρσόν(ι)
waiting room (ή) αἴθουσα
 ἀναμονῆς
wake up, to ξυπνῶ
walk (ὁ) περίπατος
walk, to περιπατῶ
wall (ὁ) τοῖχος
want, to θέλω
war (ὁ) πόλεμος
wardrobe (ή) ντουλάπα
warm ζεστός, -ή, -ό
warm, to ζεσταίνω
warn, to προειδοποιῶ
wash, to πλένω or πλύνω
wash oneself, to πλένομαι
 or πλύνομαι
wash basin (ή) λεκάνη
waste, to σπαταλῶ
watch (τὸ) ρολό(γ)ι
watch, to παρακολουθῶ,
 φυλάγω, προσέχω
watchmaker (ὁ) ὡρολογοποιός,
 (ὁ) ρολογάς
watch out προσέξτε
water (τὸ) νερό
wave (τὸ) κύμα or κῦμα
way (ὁ) δρόμος, (ὁ) τρόπος

wealth (τὰ) πλούτη
weather (ὁ) καιρός
Wednesday (ή) Τετάρτη
week (ή) ἑβδομάδα
weigh, to ζυγίζω
weight (τὸ) βάρος
welcome καλῶς ὡρίσατε
well καλά
west (ή) δύση*
wet ὑγρός, -ή, -ό,
 βρεμμένος, -η, -ο
wheat (τὸ) σιτάρι
wheel (ή) ρόδα, (ὁ) τροχός
when ὅταν, πότε
where ὅπου, ποῦ
white ἄσπρος, -η, -ο,
 λευκός, -ή, -ό
wholesale χονδρικῶς
why γιατί
wide πλατύς, -ιά, -ύ
 φαρδύς, -ιά, -ύ
wife (ή) σύζυγος,
 (ή) γυναίκα
will (ή) θέληση*,
 (ή) διαθήκη
win, to κερδίζω, νικῶ
wind (ὁ) ἄνεμος
wind, to κουρδίζω
window (τὸ) παράθυρο
wine (τὸ) κρασί, (ὁ) οἶνος
wing (ή) πτέρυγα,
 (ή) φτερούγα
winter (ὁ) χειμώνας
wish (ή) ἐπιθυμία,
 (ή) εὐχή
wish, to ἐπιθυμῶ, εὔχομαι
witty πνευματώδης, -ης, -ες
wolf (ὁ) λύκος

woman (ἡ) γυναίκα
wonderful θαυμάσιος, -α, -ο
wood (τό) ξύλο
wool (τό) μαλλί
word (ἡ) λέξη*
work (ἡ) ἐργασία,
  (ἡ) δουλειά
work, to ἐργάζομαι,
  δουλεύω
work (of art) ἔργο (τέχνης)
world (ὁ) κόσμος
worry (ἡ) φροντίδα,
  (ἡ) στενοχώρια, (ἡ) ἔγνοια
worse χειρότερος,-η, -ο
worth (ἡ) ἀξία
worthy ἄξιος, -α, -ο
wrap, to τυλίγω
wrinkle (ἡ) ρυτίδα
wrinkle, to τσαλακώνω

wrist (ὁ) καρπός
wrist watch ρολόγι τοῦ χεριοῦ
write, to γράφω
writer (ὁ) συγγραφέας
wrong, to be δὲν ἔχω δίκαιο,
  ἔχω ἄδικο, κάνω λάθος

Y

year (ὁ) χρόνος,
  (ἡ) χρονιά, (τό) ἔτος
yellow κίτρινος, -η, -ο
yes ναί, μάλιστα
yesterday χθές
yet ἀκόμη, καὶ ὅμως
young νέος, -α, -ο
youth (ἡ) νεότης, (ἡ) νεολαία

Z

zero μηδέν
zone (ἡ) ζώνη

One of the best ways to continue your study of Greek is by listening to Greek radio programs and by reading Greek newspapers like «Ἀτλαντίς» and «Ἐθνικὸς Κῆρυξ» and Greek magazines like the monthly "Atlantis", the Athenian «Εἰκόνες», «Ταχυδρόμος», «Θησαυρός», «Ρομάντζο», «Θεατής», the literary «Νέα Ἑστία», «Κρῖκος», «Ἀκτῖνες», and the organ of the Greek Archdiocese «Ὀρθόδοξος Παρατηρητής». In order to read newspapers and magazines you would probably need a larger dictionary than this. Anyone of the following may be recommended:

English-Modern Greek and Modern Greek-English Dictionary published by *Atlantis*. Thumb indexed. Pocket size, 389 pp. $3.00.

English - Greek and Greek - English Dictionary of the *National Herald* ('Εθνικὸς Κῆρυξ), compiled by Carroll N. Brown. Thumb indexed, 935 pp., $6.00.

Divry's English - Greek and Greek - English Dictionary. 469 pp. Cloth with indexes, $4.00. Leather, with indexes and maps, $5.00

English - Greek and Greek-English Dictionary by I. Kykkotis. Regular Edition, 644 pp., $3.95. Available through the R. D. Cortina Co., Inc., 136 West 52nd Street, New York 19, N. Y.